Ocean Speed

Ocean Speed

A True-life Journey to Rescue and Revelation

by

Captain Bob Krieg

SEAWORTHY PUBLICATIONS, INC. • MELBOURNE, FLORIDA

Ocean Speed
A True-life Journey to Rescue and Revelation
Copyright ©2024 by Captain Bob Krieg
ISBN 978-1-948494-92-2
Published in the USA by:
Seaworthy Publications, Inc.
6300 N Wickham Rd.
Unit #130-416
Melbourne, FL 32940
Phone 321-389-2506
e-mail orders@seaworthy.com - www.seaworthy.com

All rights reserved. No part of this book may be reproduced, stored in a retrieval system, or transmitted in any form, or by any means, electronic, mechanical, photocopying, recording, or by any storage and retrieval system, without permission in writing from the publisher.

Whether indicated on the chart or not, all charts in this book are for informational use only and not to be used for navigational purposes.

Library of Congress Cataloging-in-Publication Data

Names: Krieg, Bob, 1945- author.
Title: Ocean speed : a true-life journey to rescue and revelation / by Bob Krieg.
Description: Melbourne, Florida : Seaworthy Publications, Inc., 2024. | Summary: "Four hundred nautical miles remained on Captain Bob's singlehanded passage from Mauritius to South Africa when maritime duty called making those the most difficult sea miles ever sailed over the prior twenty-six years. He delayed the pleasures of safe harbour and risked his yacht and life to save a mariner from peril at sea. This autobiographic nautical adventure recounts the foundation for the events of those days south of Madagascar by reviewing sailing skills gained and confidence acquired while sailing to the Channel Islands off the California coast, yacht club racing earning boat of the year honors, Great Lakes Singlehanded Society competition, redesigning a custom steel sloop, attending a demanding maritime school to earn a coveted international professional mariners license, skippering charter boats and instructing sailing classes in St. Petersburg, Florida. He presents ocean cruising preparation by making upgrades to steering, navigation safety, refrigeration, water making, radio communications and the addition of wind and solar power to ensure reliable performance under demanding sailing conditions far at sea. Other takeaways for those considering singlehanded ocean sailing are watchkeeping procedures while sleeping, daily life under sail, the requirements to legally enter nation states, and respecting rules, regulations and customs of societies far different from the homeland. Side stories illuminate those who attempt to leverage power over others and single women wandering the planet crewing, some wanting to be entertained by a single skipper aboard a substantial sailing yacht. Feel the knockdowns, the recoveries, the losses and redemptions and live the event that led him to reluctantly allow the long-lived sailing adventure slip into memory"-- Provided by publisher.
Identifiers: LCCN 2024009173 (print) | LCCN 2024009174 (ebook) | ISBN 9781948494922 (paperback) | ISBN 9781948494939 (epub)
Subjects: LCSH: Search and rescue operations--Indian Ocean. | Survival at sea--Indian Ocean. | Sailors--United States--Biography.
Classification: LCC GV810.92.K75 A3 2024 (print) | LCC GV810.92.K75 (ebook) | DDC 363.12/381091652--dc23/eng/20240402
LC record available at https://lccn.loc.gov/2024009173
LC ebook record available at https://lccn.loc.gov/2024009174

Table of Contents

Dedication vi
Author's Note vii
Life Course 1
Dazzled 8
Waypoints to Sea 16
Recovery 23
Choices 38
Enchantment 49
The Big Blue 62
Restart 72
Ocean Solo 79
The Long White Cloud 87
Homeward Bound 95
Indian Ocean 108
Mauritius Commitment 116
Duty 125
South Africa 134
Atlantic Islands 146
Revelation 156
Appendix 162
About the Author 183

Dedication

This true sea story is dedicated to my great-great-grandmother Margarethe Halmes, born on October 4, 1838, in Rhineland-Palatinate, Germany, who lived her own sea story when shipboard in 1854 sailing to America with parents, sister, and brother. She contracted cholera at sea and soon was pronounced dead. By permission of the captain the body remained in the hold for three days before burial. She was conscious of all that passed around her but could make no sign. Just before the time for the burial, her mother, Mary Noel, felt her hands, noticed they were warm, summoned the surgeon, and steps were taken to revive her. While living in a Chicago town, she married Morz Krieg in 1855, remaining there until 1870 when they moved to Nebraska, relocating to Plattsmouth, then Crete, and then DeWitt in 1873. Morz died in 1883 and she married Frederick Slough in 1887. Her scribbled census signatures appeared to read Margetta Holmes, the name that headed her obituary, parts of which were extracted for the above, recounting her life until her death on September 27, 1903. In total she had ten children, seven of whom survived to carry her spirit and legacy forward. Every holiday season as I grew up, my father retold the story of the family fleeing wars and religious persecution, of that ocean voyage incident cited in her obituary, and of their farming and creative contributions to a new homeland throughout the generations until I came along.

Author's Note

When acquaintances learn that I sail, many times they ask what and where. When I mention I sailed around the world, they want to hear about the adventure. Some said I ought to write a book. With little to do while hiding from Covid, I began to write. Fortunately, during the circumnavigation I snapped photos, shot videos, and saved emails and bank statements that I had since forgotten about. Examining the archives prompted me to retrieve the old logbooks, one in particular containing entries made at about 0600, 1200, 1800, and 2400 daily since transiting the Panama Canal. Each image and note stimulated recall, some lifting me to understand the reasons why events occurred as they did that I had not realized at the time. With those resources, the manuscript grew to over 180,000 words. Three years of writing, author zoom meetings, writers' groups, editing services, and rewrites reduced the memoir to what it is today, my best recollection of the true course of a life's sailing events.

During this sail I met many people who influenced my sailing life journey and could recognize them all, however out of respect for the privacy of those I could not reach and those who wish to remain anonymous, I changed some names, keeping their involvement in my journey alive. Also, I have not included the names of sailors befriended at anchorages and marinas around the world (or the names of their sailing vessels) if I could not contact them. The dialogue flowing throughout the memoir is a reasonable representation of the interactions that would have occurred at the time.

I want to thank editors Christopher Noel and Robert Kenney for guiding me from an elementary writer to a graduate author. Recognition by Seaworthy Publications, Inc. would not have been possible without my deep immersion with the Pitch to Published writers' group found online at GetaBookDeal101.

Textbook references relating to International Yachtmaster licensing and the foundation for the VHF Radio Protocol aboard *Scooter* are supplied courtesy of International Yacht Training Worldwide. Permission to use the chart window prints from the Nobeltec software aboard was granted by the marketing director at MaxSea/Nobeltec. Reproduction of small marked-up extracts for charts AUS 607 Cocos (Keeling) Island, South Keeling and AUS 608 Christmas Island was granted under license by the Australian Hydrographic Office. Permission to use a section of *Atlas of Pilot Charts* as an illustration was granted by ProStar Publications, Inc. All chart illustrations in this memoir are not to be used for navigation purposes.

When sailing from Florida I sailed into a metric world and have described measurements in this memoir using that system. For readers unfamiliar with that scheme, basic conversions I used while sailing the planet are available in the Appendix.

To assist visual understanding of courses sailed, current, and wind directions please refer to the compass card on the following page.

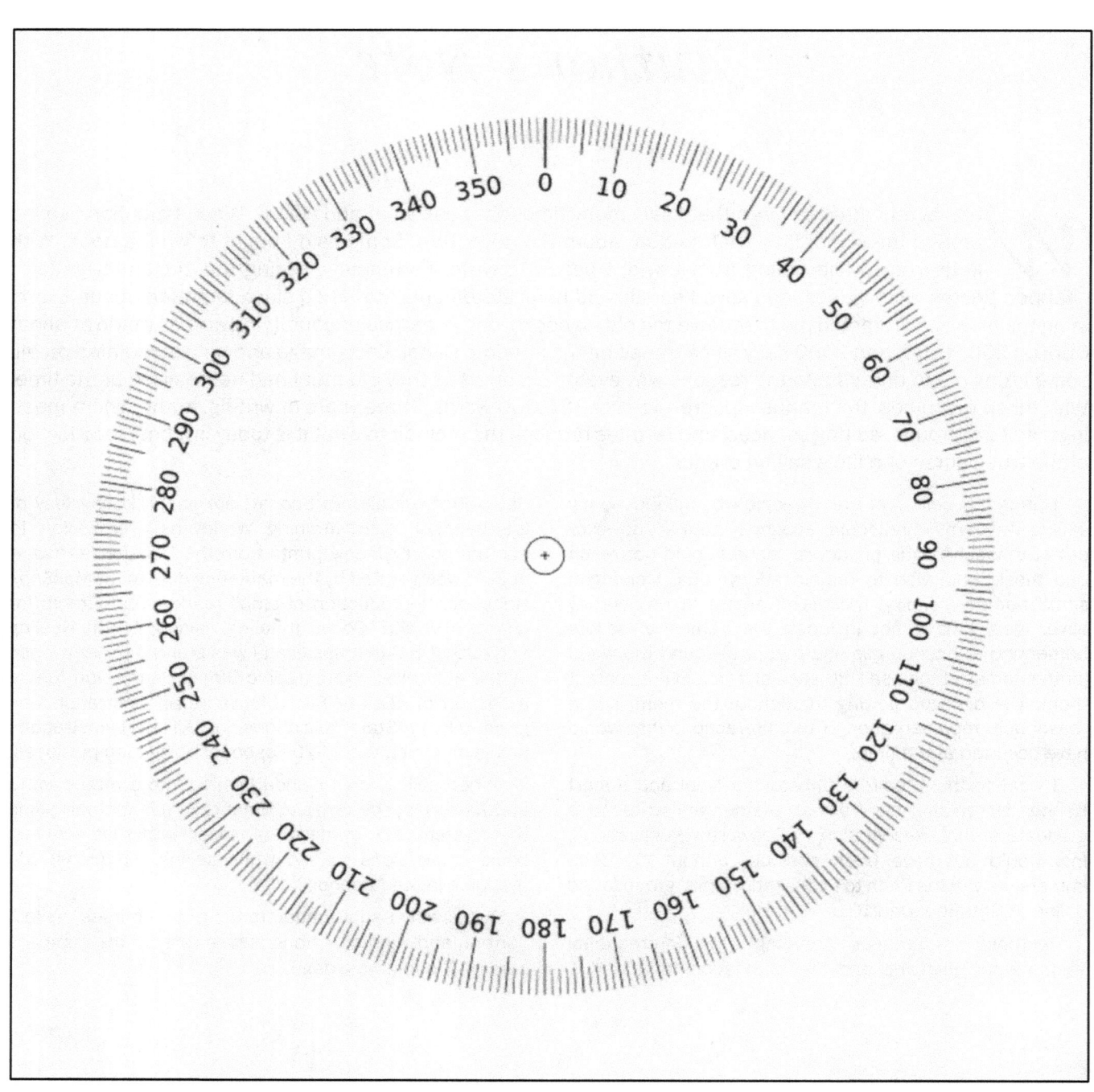

Life Course

Sunset shadows played on my window curtain, moved by a warm Kansas breeze, as I leaned on bed pillows propped against the headboard at the age of five, denying the need for sleep. While the curtains swayed, I turned the pages of a picture book making my first journey to the ocean. The boy in the book launched a toy sailboat in the stream that babbled through the farmland behind the barn. To his surprise, rapid water swept the sailboat downstream out of sight, but for the sailboat it was the beginning of a thrilling adventure. The stream joined other streams and flowed on into white-water rapids smashing against huge rocks, which the tiny sailboat dashed around. Overcoming obstacles by its strength of resolve, its accumulated learnings, and craftiness, it arrived at a lazy river flowing into a wide, calm bay. Relaxing from the treacherous ride, it floated on tidal currents into the limitless ocean, where it sailed on fair winds to experience unbounded horizons and eternal adventure. Years later, images of the picture book and those moments reading it remain crystal clear, as though the story may have been a foretelling of life events to come.

Motion pictures Dad shot throughout the year with the camera he bought from a war photographer and then screened them on Christmas Day fixed my memories of Mom, Dad, and sister Marilyn in the Kansas house. Like many postwar moms and those before her, Mom kept the home, mothering, housekeeping, and preparing meals. Dad made our lifestyle possible by working in the auto industry, beginning his career in the inspection department at the Lansing, Michigan, Oldsmobile assembly plant in 1935. The changeover to weapons manufacturing during the war qualified him for draft deferment, and at war's end he accepted a position as the chief inspector at the Kansas City, Kansas, plant to help shepherd its transition from aircraft to auto production. Years later, his auto manufacturing career led the family to New Jersey, where I first tasted the tang of the ocean. I wore long pants and long-sleeved shirts to prevent sunburn while playing in the surf that slithered frothy white bubbles up the beach. It was unlike swimming off the rickety wood dock at Granddad's cottage on Houghton Lake, Michigan during vacation weeks. We followed Dad's career to Delaware, only a few hours' drive from Cape May, New Jersey, our new weekend playground. From there, the drive home led us past the MayCraft cabin cruiser assembly plant that Dad had to stop at to assess its quality control methods. The plant tour stirred him to order a twenty-five-foot MayCraft cabin cruiser at the Philadelphia boat show that winter.

Mom and Dad named the boat *Marilyn Mae* after my adopted sister, who arrived one year before me, the daughter of Dad's cousin who could not afford to raise a fourth daughter during the war years. The boat had a galley and a head. Sis and I slept in the bow "V" bunks, while Mom and Dad slept on a bunk formed by lowering the saloon table and shifting the seat cushion backs to the tabletop, making a full-length mattress. Sometimes, Dad and I trolled lures off the Jersey shore on sunny Saturday afternoons while Mom and Sis shopped in Cape May or Wildwood. They had issues with the motion of the ocean.

The next spring, Dad and I motored *Marilyn Mae* up Delaware Bay, through the Chesapeake and Delaware Canal, and down the Elk River to a slip at the Bridgeview Marina on the Bohemian River to join the fleet of powerboats Dad's work buddies operated on the bay. During summer weekends, children from the little flotilla played on bay beaches while moms and dads sipped adult beverages and whiffed the sea-like aroma of crabs steaming in the pot after they were lured up to the boat from the murky water with chicken bones tied to hand lines. At the season's end, Dad and I delivered *Marilyn Mae* back to Cape May for the winter. In July of the following year, he proudly announced that we would spend the rest of the season aboard *Marilyn Mae II*, the new Trojan 31 as seen on the *Sea Hunt* TV show. To Dad's glee, they were made in Lancaster, Pennsylvania, a lazy drive from home through Amish countryside.

Our family enjoyed long weekends aboard *Marilyn Mae II* somewhere on the Chesapeake Bay from spring launch to fall haul out regardless of the weather. On winter weekends after heavy snowfall, Dad drove the family across the countryside to the marina to brush the snow off the canvas cover with tender broom strokes. Before spring launch, I helped caulk and paint the bottom, tidy up inside, and service engines in preparation for another season.

The summer before high school senior year, my reading of Michener's *Hawaii* opened me to adult pleasures in the face of Dad's relentless warnings to keep my fly zipped up on dates at drive-in movies in Mom's long white tail-finned Buick sedan. His Victorian standards toward women shaped my behavior around girls and focused my responsibilities as a future husband, breadwinner, and father by the time I arrived on campus to major in premed, suggested by Dad because distant relatives were doctors.

I earned my way to academic probation, regained admission after summer school, then got dropped from undergraduate studies at the end of the third semester, falling victim to a combination of attention deficit and poor choices made without parental supervision. Instead of waiting to be drafted into the army and ordered to Vietnam, I joined the navy and chose to specialize in nuclear electronics after scoring high on qualification tests, thinking it would open a career in that industry following the four-year enlistment. However, the boot camp graduation medical exam revealed that I had a red-green visual deficiency, excluding me from all rates except boatswain's mate, dental technician, and hospital corpsman, according to the examiners. I selected hospital corpsman, having no idea that corpsmen provided medical care with marine field units in Vietnam. After graduation from the Hospital Corps School at Great Lakes Naval Training Station, I was ordered to the Field Medical Service School at Camp Lejeune, North Carolina, to transition into serving with marines. My first duty station orders directed me to report to the naval hospital in Key West, Florida. When not practicing corpsman duties in the emergency room or in the sick officer's ward, I snorkeled island shallows, fished offshore with a recreational services boat, and walked beaches during that six-month stint in paradise. Orders to the Ninth Marine Amphibious Brigade, Fleet Marine Force arrived, taking me to Okinawa for assignment, hopefully somewhere in the Pacific other than Vietnam. Wartime reality arrived on December 1, 1967. Strapped into a seat next to the open door of a roaring Sikorsky helicopter, gazing down to defoliated jungle before the ride ended in a dry rice patty only paces south of the DMZ, I arrived to become the doc for the First Platoon, Alpha Company, First Battalion, Fourth Marines. That day lives with me in vivid color and sound, as do many fixed during the following six months of slogging through partially defoliated jungles from the DMZ to south of Dong Ha and sprinting into sandbagged bunkers at Con Thien, receiving artillery and rocket incoming. I enjoyed R and R, a one-week vacation in Penang, Malaysia, and intentionally partook in adult pleasures for the first time, knowing I had another six months in Vietnam to face and not wanting to leave this life without experiencing that.

Returning stateside for my next duty station, I endured the gauntlet of stones and eggs thrown by protesters on the long walk from the airplane to the hangar at the Marine Corps Air Station, El Toro, California. The next day at the Philadelphia airport, I searched for Dad, who was supposed to be waiting in the crowd at the top of the escalator. His brown hair had turned silver, telling me much about what he and Mom had lived through as they watched the news and read my brutally honest accounts of combat actions in my twice-weekly letters home. I sent some to his work office address for him to cull the more dreadful events that could upset Mom, but he numbered and saved them all.

After a thirty-day leave, I began serving as the base medical representative and instructor at a navy reserve training center in Utica, New York. The instructing challenge stimulated me to deliver subject matter more creatively than presented in the navy course materials. Short hair in a college town during those turbulent, rebellious antiwar years announced that I was in the military, but I stood tall and enrolled in night school at Utica College and aced a mathematics course. With an eye on advancement, I scored high on the exam for hospital corpsman first class but needed to reenlist to make that E6 rate. I called the navy detailer somewhere in Washington, who pulled my records and counseled me that upon my reenlistment my next duty station would be aboard a destroyer in the North Atlantic Fleet for eighteen months as an independent duty corpsman. With nearly four years in the navy, I had not stepped on the deck of a ship and would have to commit four more years in order to experience life at sea.

That phone chat prompted me to reevaluate my life's course. A month later, the director of admissions at the University of Delaware responded to my reapplication, advising that I was readmitted under a special academic probation, requiring that, during the first semester and during each succeeding semester thereafter, I would have to reduce my quality point deficiency at a rate acceptable to the dean of my college and that failure to do so would result in being dropped from the undergraduate division.

In a flash three years went by. I funded tuition, an off-campus apartment, a Triumph sports car, and dating expenses with the GI Bill, Vietnam savings, and working Friday nights at the Newark, Delaware, General Motors assembly plant or doing the night audit at the local Howard Johnson motel. A variety of roommates assisted with the rent expense each semester. In my senior year, Dan, an army veteran became my last roomie. He managed diversion from his studies by hopping railroad trains to experience the unspoiled countryside as seen by hobos back in the day, a hobby I thought strange until a gal answered his posting for a train-hopping partner on a student center bulletin board. Dan knew every train and route on the Baltimore and Ohio line and where they slowed enough to hop on and off. The response to his ad resulted in a plan to meet on Main Street in town, hop a train, and ride it to where they could jump off in Elkton, Maryland. I volunteered to pick them up in Elkton, not because I had nothing else to do but because I just had to meet the gal who would find joy in that kind of adventure.

Donna squeezed her long legs into the small space behind the Triumph's red leather seats. Her long brown hair flagged in the wind while I drove with the top down. Her quick, bubbly wit and flashing smiles projected a maturity exceeding anything I had experienced from the campus kids I had been dating. She interned as a physical therapist at a hospital in Wilmington and occasionally appeared at the apartment with Dan on weekends until the winter break. I seized the opportunity to see what she was all about when Dan called from his parents' home in New Jersey to say the snow-covered roads made it impossible for him to make the dinner date Donna had planned for that Saturday evening, and he wanted me to call her because her phone rang busy every time he called. I delayed relaying the message until about the time Dan was due to arrive for dinner and, after apologizing for the untimely call, offered to sit in at the last moment to savor her creation. Following that meal and hours-long conversation, I dated her occasionally when Dan was out with someone else, and I was not working the night audit at the motel.

On graduation day, with a BS in business, concentrating in finance, I had Dad glowing with pride about his son, the first in the family line to graduate college. After the ceremony, I spent weeks at the campus career center reading job postings leading to interviews that resulted in the realization that my pitches about well-earned navy leadership skills would be unconsidered in the compensation package. One guy told me I would inspect and record parts assembled on electric motors for eighteen months before I could possibly move higher in the finance department. Back at the recruiting office, I came across a posting by a local car dealer seeking college grads to enter retail auto sales. Ability-based earning appealed to me, and I began selling Pontiacs in Wilmington.

Dad and Mom sold the Trojan 31 the year of my failed attempt at college and later purchased an Airstream trailer they towed to Florida for the winter. When Dad asked me to check on the house while they were away, I suggested I move my stuff from the apartment into the finished basement and take up residence there until they returned. It would be a good deal for me, rent free, just pay the bills and he agreed. All during that time I had been casually dating Donna and others.

I sat alone on Super Bowl Sunday in the recliner in the wood paneled basement, ready to cheer my team, not having had time to arrange a date for the game, when Donna called. She wanted to cancel the custom Firebird order I had put together for her and keep her old Ford Falcon because she had just been proposed to. It was another life-changing moment. I had no idea she was dating someone that serious. I was two years out of college, twenty-eight years old, and had enjoyed the bachelor life without the responsibilities I had been prepared for by my upbringing long enough. After I steered the conversation to us and what future we could have together I switched the TV off and drove over to her apartment in the falling snow. While turning into her complex I passed a fresh set of tire tracks in the new snow leading away from her apartment door. Facing her in that moment of clarity, I realized that I wanted her in my life and proposed right then. She accepted and later I learned that the tracks in the snow were made by the other guy's MG. I moved from the folks' basement into her apartment, and following the ceremony we honeymooned in Jamaica.

Mom and Dad were overjoyed about my decision to marry and carry the traditional family values forward, but unlike Dad's generation, I recognized Donna's career aspirations demanded she be a home manager instead of a homemaker like Mom and her ancestors. At tax time we realized that a home-mortgage interest deduction would reduce our tax burden, and we bought our first house in Hockessin, Delaware with a VA mortgage. Married life with the prospect of parenthood joyously directed our lives. We furnished the house, made a basement office, and outfitted the second bedroom for our first child.

In my second year of auto sales, the dealer signed an agreement to retail Hondas and a year later became the only BMW dealer in the state. Finding it enjoyable to demonstrate why the engineering and handling of that performance car justified the sticker price, which was rarely discounted, six months later I had outsold the rest of the sales team. The dealer called me to his office and offered me a unique position as the exclusive BMW sales rep, excluding me from selling Pontiacs and Hondas. Concerned that my income could shrink until I grew the BMW sales to equal my earnings from selling all three, he suggested I call Donna to discuss that possible outcome. I asked if I would have a BMW as a demo. When he said yes, I said I did not need to call Donna. That evening, the shiny blue BMW 2002 demonstrator looked great in the driveway.

While selling BMWs, I reflected on Dad's career and how corporate-funded relocations had moved the family around the country, exposing us to different places, people, and customs. I sent letters touting my military service, education, and retail auto sales successes to the Honda, BMW, and Pontiac corporate offices. The Pontiac office in Cherry Hill, New Jersey responded, and after my employer approved my desire to interview, I became the family's third-generation General Motors employee, following Dad and his dad, who began his auto career working for Ransom E. Olds. That employment lineage meant a lot to Dad, I could tell, when he recounted his early days at the Lansing plant, rebuilding the Kansas plant after a massive flood, and the respect and promotions earned by hard work. He died of a massive heart attack a month after I started the new job, and I felt committed to reaching further heights in the corporation than he and his father. Starting at the bottom of the corporate ladder, I attended thirty-seven classes, learning all things service engineering, and applied that knowledge to improving dealer product servicing at stores in Delaware, southern New Jersey, eastern Pennsylvania, and down the Delmarva Peninsula.

Donna and I delayed parenting five years while establishing our careers then Kirsten came into our lives. My job required occasional overnight travel, so to have focused time together we purchased camping gear and spent weekends in nature's silent freedom.

Some weekends we made the nine-hour drive to see Donna's mom, Teddy, living in a custom-built log cabin her preacher son-in-law built near Pittsburgh after talking her into selling her condo and leaving her senior support group of friends in Maryland. "It will be rent free; just keep it up and it is yours for life," he said at the time of his transfer to Texas, shortly after the house was completed, wanting to keep the log cabin as a retirement home. I spent a vacation week hand-leveling the furrows around the spacious yard previously plowed by an Amish man with a horse, then raked in grass seed, visualizing the house sitting on a grassy hill by summer's end. The Saturday evening before driving home, I answered the doorbell and greeted a man claiming to be an appraiser for the real estate company the preacher hired to sell the house. An hour later, after a lengthy call with her son-in-law, Teddy learned that she had to move because he had to sell the house, but he offered no housing substitute, fundamentally putting her on the street that day. With no place for her to go, my family-focused values called me to invite her to live with us. Donna and I sold our first house and moved to a newly built home a few miles away with enough room for Teddy's bedroom and living room furniture, even her piano, giving her separate accommodations with the comfort of her lifelong possessions.

One weekend after the move, the husband of one of Donna's physical therapy colleagues invited me for a Saturday sail on Chesapeake Bay in his small sailboat. "It's a Flying Scot," he said as he pulled the cord to start the outboard motor. In open water, he hoisted the sails while I held the tiller. He explained what was going on with the sails, the centerboard, and the rudder of that nineteen-foot sailboat. Soaking up his words, I learned that by using two fluids, the wind and water, I could sail the boat wherever I wanted. I shared my enthusiasm for the experience at home, thinking one of those boats would be a great addition to our family weekend escapes.

Donna worried about it tipping over but yielded after a Saturday camping adventure with the Scot's owners at the Elk Neck campgrounds. I held the hull steady in waste deep water with the centerboard up while our friends pulled the main halyard to starboard, leaning the mast parallel to the water. The boat floated and no water spilled in, immediately dissolving her worries. A month later, after budget deliberations, we ordered a Scot and as though predestined I received a transfer to the corporate office in Pontiac, Michigan the week the boat was built.

At the Flying Scot factory in Deer Park, Maryland, I hitched the new boat trailer to the car and drove north. I parked it on the driveway extension next to our new home. After a deep freeze, I rolled it onto the back yard and began reading how-to-sail books, itching to rig the boat for the first time. Spring weather teased me to step the mast after moving the trailer onto the patio behind the garage. I attached the shrouds to the chain plates, climbed aboard, and inserted the mast foot into a pivot on what the directions called a "tabernacle." The masthead extended way past the stern deck. I lifted the mast and hand over hand, pushing it up while straddling the centerboard trunk until the mast stood straight up, making it easy for Donna to connect the forestay. We cheered our achievement and reread the directions to lower the mast. What could go wrong? As I held the mast in place, grasping it at arms-length, Donna disconnected the forestay. The mast tilted as I walked aft. Holding it at arm's length, I stepped farther aft along the side of the centerboard. Attempting to lay it on my right shoulder and pivot on my right foot in one continuous movement to place it gently onto the stern deck, I stepped past the center of gravity of the entire rig. The trailer hitch end sprang up, the boat's stern banged on the patio, and my new deck shoe stuck to the deck, as advertised, forcing my right knee to twist out of joint. I rolled out of the boat grabbing my irregular looking knee as the trailer and boat dropped back down, banging the trailer tongue wheel on the patio deck. Donna mixed a triple Manhattan that went down fast while my knee throbbed with every heartbeat. I lay on the backyard grass holding ice packs in place and waited for refills. The knee mended somewhat over time while I limped around the house and office hallways, but the underlying damage lingered.

That summer we rigged and launched the Scot at Stony Creek Lake and learned how to tack and jibe to keep the boat moving. Midsummer, we towed the boat loaded with gear to Houghton Lake for a week of camping and sailing on big water, inspired by our new-found skills. The boat was easy to get into, rig, and sail into the wind after retrieving the anchor near the campsite beach. Our son, Nathan, had joined the crew and, at the age of six months, nestled in a blanket under the bow deck while Kirsten, age seven, held her first fishing pole. We dragged Granddad's old lures while sailing along the lake's west shore weed beds and hooked walleyes and bass that thrashed around on deck, spewing fishy smells, all new experiences and fun for Kirsten. Sailing skills improved, anxiety faded, and confidence increased. One morning I climbed in after attaching the new video camera to a pivot off the stern, hoisted the main, pulled up the anchor, and sailed away to experience my first solo sail. Weekends later we launched the Scot at the Selfridge Public Boat Launch on Lake St. Clair and sailed across Anchor Bay to Strawberry Island for swim time in the cool refreshing water.

Two sailing seasons full of learnings passed while I worked first as a regional technical service manager, assisting dealer service personnel with challenging repairs over the phone. Then as the assistant national warranty manager before being transferred to the office in Westlake Village, California, to manage service operations in Southern California, southern Nevada, Arizona, and New Mexico. Donna made a few calls and landed a position with a medical center in Thousand Oaks.

Once we recovered from the frenzied pace of the relocation, we made the Scot ready to sail on the big, blue Pacific. Before leaving home, I would call the marina, and when we arrived we'd find the boat tied to a dock ready for us to rig sails, attach the small outboard, load the cooler, and be off to manage the inbound wave set at the Channel Islands harbor entrance. Thundering surf beyond the jetties warned us to attend to sailing needs instead of sightseeing. We improved our sailing skills while day sailing up the coast past the Ventura Marina inlet and south to Point Mugu. Later, more experienced and full of confidence, we sailed over the slow-rolling blue swells under clear blue sky twenty-some miles out to Anacapa Island with no VHF radio and no compass, navigating within sight of land the way it had been done for thousands of years.

Eighteen months of sailing almost every weekend ended when I was transferred to Kansas City as the zone marketing manager, a new corporate concept to address local opportunities invisible to the national marketing team back in Michigan. Donna found a place to practice physical therapy on the first phone call. We stored the Scot on the trailer with mast up in the yard at Perry Lake and resumed the family weekend fun until it was too cold to sail. Sixteen months into that assignment, whispers about another transfer arrived, either to the West or East Coast. We had mastered sailing basics with the Scot. Visions of sailing with a growing family led us to trade the Scot on a thirty-foot Hunter sloop with a dealer at Stockton Lake, Missouri. We named her *Margetta* to pay homage to the family matriarch, who came to America from Germany aboard a sailing ship back in the 1850s. The week after we signed the papers, my boss handed me a slip of paper and told me to call my next boss in the new General Motors Thousand Oaks, California office. Back in familiar territory, I became the network planning manager, overseeing the location and construction of Pontiac retail stores to improve market share. Donna called her prior physical therapy department and resumed patient care. By then we had become pros at buying and selling homes, packing and moving, and unpacking and adjusting to new environments.

After *Margetta* arrived by truck at the Ventura Marina, we spent a month of weekends living aboard and learning how to maneuver under power around the harbor and in and out of the slip in light morning air. Mid-afternoon sea breezes lifted kites I flew for the kids a short walk from the dock. When our confidence had grown, we motored out past the jetties to sea in the early morning and hoisted the sails for our first ocean sail.

Friday evening meals aboard began our weekend fun before long hours under sail on Saturday. Over time, we became more comfortable aboard and less worried about being far from the coast. The Channel Islands summoned us to experience overnight anchoring in coves and bays, and our children's laughter echoed off the rocky hills. Kirsten, tall at ten, looking more like a twelve-year old, became my certified scuba buddy after weeks of instruction at a local dive school. We anchored off Santa Cruz Island at Pelican Bay, Prisoners' Harbor, Potato Bay, or Coches Priestos to explore the sea floor, walk beaches,

Margetta at Pelican Bay

and lay on deck stargazing, and our tans broadcast our time in nature.

In darkness one Sunday morning in late October, while anchored in Pelican Bay close to the cliffs, Santa Ana winds drove large waves into the bay, and they rebounded from the vertical cliff face smashed against the oncoming seas. *Margetta* rode over the sloppy wash while swinging around the anchor line for hours. At dawn, I prepped the main sail for hoist, started the engine, and hand over hand, raised the anchor loaded with slimy kelp while Donna steered. The seas lifted the bow one moment and dropped it into a deep trough the next. At wide open throttle, we crept into the heavy wind and bashing seas, throwing white foam across the deck. The engine alarm screamed. The oil pressure light flashed. I shut off the engine and shouted, "Take the wheel." The kids were wide-eyed while holding on down below. With a do-it-now response, I sprang up to the rolling cabin top slippery with wind driven foam as *Margetta* slid to portside toward the cliffs. The wind shrilled in the rigging while I hoisted the violently flogging main sail to a reef and returned to the cockpit to sheet it into shape. *Margetta* got under way, steered by Donna's capable hands on a starboard beam reach, heading north with enough speed to clear the rocky cliff booming with the thunder of crashing waves.

The engine started hours later and ran without failure. The alarm had most likely been triggered by an oil pressure drop when the oil sloshed away from the pump pickup as the boat violently pitched up and down. I managed that entire fast sail hoist and getting underway by applying Scot learnings, without which a nightmare catastrophe would have occurred. It was the aha moment that drove me to grow more sailing experience and competence before attempting risky times at sea.

Nine months after that unforgettable event, Pontiac transferred me back to corporate headquarters in Michigan, tasked to implement a program to bring about a unique exterior design theme for Pontiac stores nationwide they called the Advanced Retail Environment or ARE. It would be my job to sell the program to dealers and wholesale managers along with coaching architecture firms nationwide to apply specific design standards. The transfer came a few months after Donna's employer offered her a department head position that she declined because she knew we could be moving at any time. As the family prepared to move to house number seven, Donna called the hospital where she had worked eight years before and resumed the same position.

At home the day I announced the relocation, Teddy threw her hands in the air and covered her ears saying, "I have had enough. I will not live through more months of box packing and unpacking again." She called an old friend in Pittsburgh and made arrangements to move in with her straightaway. She had been our savior for nine years, cooking, cleaning, laundry washing and ironing, and picking up after the kids, relieving them of that responsibility. While Teddy managed the household, we had been living on easy street, working our jobs and sailing on weekends. The good corporate wife requirement to handle the home environment and keep the house proper for Realtors to present while the bread winner selected the next house and worked the new job fell squarely on Donna for the first time. She worked her job and managed the kids and Realtors while I worked, searched for the next

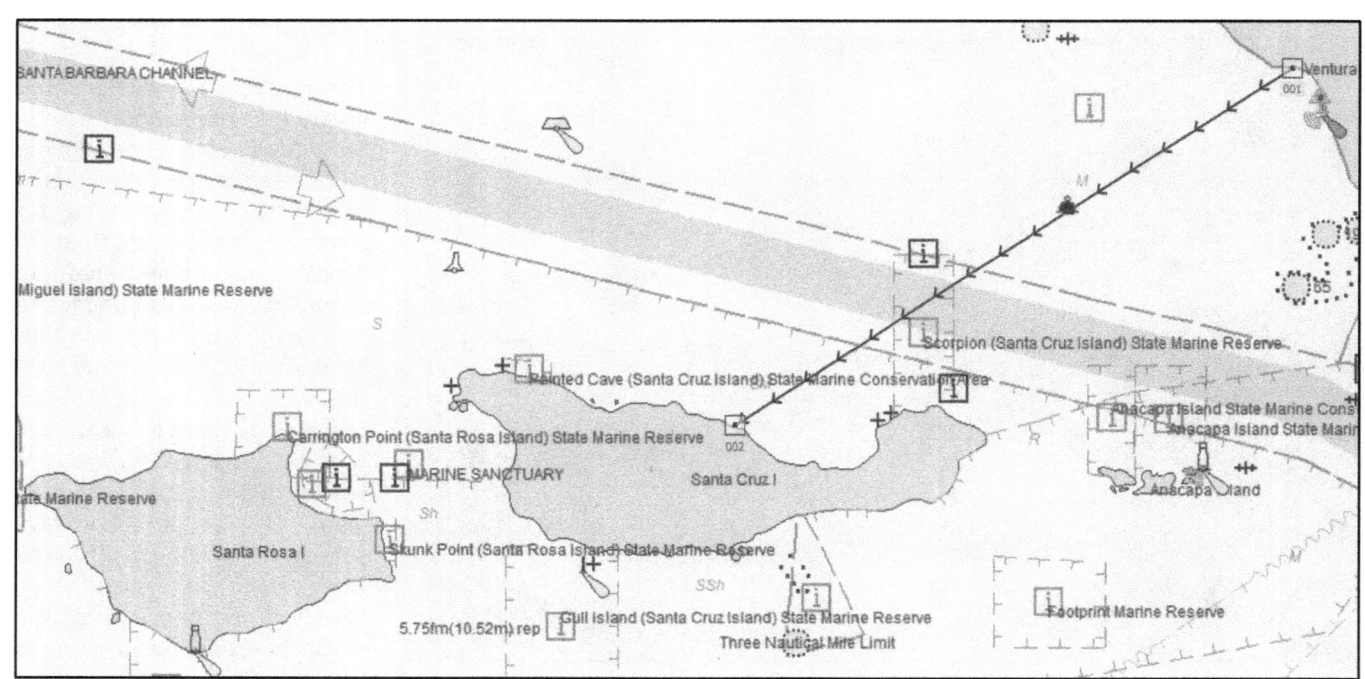

Pelican Bay with Margetta

home, and managed *Margetta*'s launch on the gray water of the Clinton River that flowed to Lake St. Clair.

A model home, perfect in every way for all our stuff, came on the market. I signed the purchase agreement, obtained a bridge loan, and moved the relocation forward. While I traveled coast to coast for my new assignment, box unpacking and school introductions had to be managed by Donna before she started her new physical therapy position.

Once settled in our new home, we renewed sailing on the sweet waters of Lake St. Clair. Don Trager, a past yacht club commodore we met at the marina, coaxed us to join the Horizon Sail Club. A few weekends later, we finished our first race on Lake St. Clair, a Jack and Jill event for a him and a her, after everyone else crossed the line. *Margetta*'s crew had no idea how to sail her fast. We sailed vacation weeks cruising the Great Lakes knowing that the next transfer could end that pleasure.

Evolving in the new job, I faced the difficulty of selling an architectural redesign program costing dealers thousands of dollars with no corporate financial support, but I stayed keen to meet the challenge. Traveling the country, I pitched the program to car dealers who bought into the concept and received pushback from less visionary senior field managers who were reluctant to promote the new program in their area of responsibility. I recognized that I had to bring the field team to see the benefits of consistent retail store imaging. Sailing had become my stress relief therapy program. At the helm, I focused on the totality of the experience and all the forces working around me, allowing no time to relieve job pressures. Tying the last dock line at Sunday's end, my mind had been rebooted. That helped me face the work issues until I winterized *Margetta* and hauled her to sit on a cradle covered for the six-month wait for spring launch.

Captured by the beauty of the puffy white clouds passing by the window on a long flight home from the West Coast, I fantasized about the heart-warming reception that could be waiting for me at home, with my kids yelling "Daddy's home" as they ran to give me a hug in front of my wife, eagerly waiting to be next. However, my heart sank knowing that those wonderful moments would not be lived. Instead, I would enter from the garage, through the laundry room, and into the great room to find everyone watching TV, not wanting me to interrupt their viewing joy. Returning from another week away reduced me to a weekend visitor and housekeeper. With Teddy no longer involved, our relationship was challenged by differing methods of child-rearing and home management in my absence. Donna worked at her job and mothered alone at home the best she could all week, applying the parenting style she knew. Returning home, I counseled the kids more often about being responsible for personal items and keeping their rooms neat than giving them hugs, yet I understood Donna's need to discount my rules, giving her time to get her more important mothering tasks completed, and my abdominal stress pains became more acute.

Evaluating ways to deliver my inherited parenting method, I thought about how the kids would respond to visiting Dad on weekends at his home or aboard *Margetta*. The kids could compare two expectations of personal responsibility and choose which model to follow as they mature. My time with them would be far less about being a taskmaster and much more about being a father, leader, teacher, mentor, and adventurer. I struggled with the parenting lifestyle instilled back in my youth, hurt by the thought that divorce dishonored generational family values.

Dazzled

Deciding to stay the course with the family, I launched *Margetta* after the lake ice melted to begin another season of weekends on the water. We sailed a two-week vacation along the Canadian coast of Lake Huron to Tobermory, Canada, with scuba gear aboard. I wanted to dive with Kirsten on an old wreck at Tub Harbor. While living that adventure, I required that the kids maintain their things in neat order, the established procedure since our first weekend aboard years before. Occasionally, I noticed Donna withdrawing quietly within herself. Maybe she labored with our parenting differences as much as I did or worried that with the next transfer, she would have to restart her career instead of climb to a leadership role she had earned at her current practice. Shortly after we returned to our workaday lives, we began discussing relationship issues and agreed to see a marriage counselor.

After hours of individual chats with the counselor we agreed to go our separate ways, keeping both of us as parents in front of the kids. Together, we wrote our agreement giving Donna the house, furniture, car, and sole control of the financial portfolio intended for the kid's college, with me financially supporting them far beyond state requirements at the top end of the child support scale. Fortunately, my job required driving new Pontiac product evaluation vehicles solving my transportation needs. With Donna's income and my child support assistance they could continue living in the same house while I took over *Margetta*'s ship mortgage and ownership expenses.

In December, an attorney presented our agreement to a judge who finalized the divorce. I found an apartment with a large bedroom and another room for my Universal Gym. All I needed to buy was a bed, a small divan, and a TV. I sat with the kids, one at a time, and lovingly explained that I would be living in a new place where they could go for weekends of fun in the huge pool on the apartment grounds, and that it would be a new adventure for them to look forward to during the week.

Release from that home stressor allowed me to more effectively manage work issues and focus on becoming a serious sailing competitor. I studied performance sailing books in the evenings and on work flights around the country, sailed with volunteer crew, and at times crewed for others to observe winning techniques. Applying the learnings, sometimes *Margetta* placed first. I added a spinnaker, a gennaker, a second cabin-mounted winch, and other go-fast sail handling hardware. Thinking that boat performance equipment and tactics were only part of the winning equation, I began developing crew that could be counted on to appear for every race. That crew came together and stayed together to earn boat of the year honors after Horizon Sail Club merged with North Star Sail Club.

The owner of a Nelson Merek 40 mentioned after a post-race award gathering that she noticed how I seemed to be one with the boat and suggested I consider competing with the Great Lakes Singlehanded Society in the Port Huron to Mackinac Island challenge known as the Mac Solo. Deciding to give it a go, I installed an autopilot and qualified after submitting my log to the race committee documenting a one-hundred-mile solo sail around Lake St. Clair in twenty-four hours. Three days and two nights after the Mac Solo start, I placed second in my group and went on to sail other GLSS challenges on Lake Huron and Lake St. Clair that year. Long-distance solo sailing stimulated my appetite for a large blue water boat, but with future financial responsibilities for the kids and my commitment to rehab a 1942-vintage house I bought in Birmingham, an ocean boat was out of reach.

A door to ocean sailing opened when I read an ad in the back of a sailing magazine about custom steel boat projects by Bruce Roberts, who designed steel and aluminum vessels. I could modify one of his designs and contract to have a motoring hull built leaving the interior and rigging for me to complete myself over time. I ordered his book of construction plans. The New York 46 hull design showed a skeg-hung rudder aft of a fin keel that my research said would make the boat less probable to be tripped broadside by a super large wave because seas would flow between the skeg and the keel. I contracted with Bruce and began adding my ideas onto the first of many sets of plans on my workspace, a four by eight sheet of plywood resting on sawhorses amid the clutter in the basement of my home renovation project. I penciled my ideas on his plans and returned the marked-up paper. Bruce would apply my changes to his AutoCAD file, print them out, and send me a copy. I would make additional changes for him to include on the AutoCAD. Over time, I extensively modified the steel boat plans, raced *Margetta* with crew, solo sailed GLSS events, traveled for work, played with the kids on weekends, and remodeled all the rooms in the old house.

A woman I met at a colleague's house party the summer after the divorce spoke about her passion for sailing. Seeing each other often, I invited her for a day on the water further bonding our relationship. Comforted with the consistency of committed dating, every moment with her brought joy and contentment when on the water, at her home, and while visiting her extended family. However, two years into the intense relationship, when I talked about ocean sailing in our retirement years with the steel boat, she felt we were getting overly involved and wanted freedom to experience other dating partners instead of going behind my back, a morality I honored. Living single again, I sensed again how much a devoted relationship with a woman who enjoyed sailing meant to me. I missed everything about her, but held true to her wish even though seeing her on the deck of a competitive yacht as it motored down the Clinton River to the lake for that day's regatta left me hollow.

Amid racing, renovating the old Birmingham house, work, and time with the kids, I wrote my first dating ad profile to run in a matchmaker pamphlet found next to the real estate brochures in a supermarket entranceway. Twenty-five dollars got my profile printed, and I could respond to a profile by letter at no charge. At the time, I had no idea that personal ads were the acceptable method for single adults to reach out to each other.

New to the dating game, I experienced a wealthy widow living in large home in Grosse Pointe, a doctor that said she could buy me any boat I desired who wanted a stepdad for her son, a single working mom seeking erotic escape, and a woman owner of numerous rental homes looking for her third handyman husband. Over time, I had many first dates, a few second dates, and very rarely a third date, meeting women who had lingering relationship issues or had misrepresented themselves. I suppose they were saying the same about the men they encountered as well. After a year of working the system, I quit to focus on core life objectives: the house rehab, yacht racing, managing the ARE program, and the kids. Letters with responses to my personal ad continued to arrive. I quickly read and tossed them into the lower drawer of the new kitchen cabinets that took a week of evening work to install. With the main floor and basement renovated, I began working the empty open attic space into a large room with a carpeted floor and a finished stairway, adding more living square footage to the small house. It would make the perfect office or third bedroom and be a unique selling feature.

Late one Saturday afternoon, Kirsten climbed the steps to the attic, where Nathan and I were hanging insulation, and suggested I write back to the woman who wrote the letter she held out to me that she found with the others I had tossed into the drawer. Her encouragement, repeated often that weekend, worked against my determination to quit the dating chase. I stewed about it for days then, inspired by Kirsten, called the number in the letter. After a lengthy talk we agreed to meet for dinner at a Royal Oak restaurant.

The way she looked and the way she talked captured and held my attention like no other. Her ever-present smile beamed inner happiness, personal confidence, and living contentment. Her black eyes and eyebrows contrasted fair skin tones framed by auburn hair falling to her shoulders. Her conversational positivism enhanced her stunning appearance beyond my expectation, and I did not want the dinner date to end. Over time, we shared life stories, hers at times about the way she walked, the legacy of her childhood battle with polio. Her first husband had become dependent on her income, could not hold a job, and spent weeks lounging around the house in between each job he was fired from or quit. One evening after work, she found him stroking white powder lines with a razor blade on the living room cocktail table and filed for divorce. She sold the ranch house and furnished a two-story home in Royal Oak, Michigan, over the eleven years before our first date.

We sailed weekends and anchored overnight on Lake St. Clair before winter haul out. Time together was easy, and we clicked in all ways—focus, libido, energy, goals, life expectations, background, family plan and implementation, respect for each other's accomplishments and abilities, and spirit of adventure. We amazed each other's world and transformed our lives. Dazzled best described the profound effect we had on each other; we went everywhere and did everything together. At Christmas, I presented her with a large, neatly wrapped hat box. With the lid removed, she found a densely packed layer of colorful curled ribbons and burrowed through, discovering an oyster shell layered with pearls hiding the engagement ring below. Surprise! We found a Justice of the Peace and had a private wedding in February of 1996 witnessed by her mom, my kids, and a work colleague and his wife. Because we had two houses to sell and an "Our House" to find, we wasted no time on a honeymoon.

Cindy loved the freedom and adventure of sailing. Her desire to be a knowledgeable sailing partner inspired her to devote a vacation week the month after we married to attend Womanship in Fort Myers, Florida, to learn from women the nuances of sailing yacht operation, maintenance, and living aboard. She returned full of tips we applied aboard that spring.

The concept of building a large ocean yacht we affectionately called "Our Boat" from the Bruce Roberts plans intrigued her as much as searching for Our House. That house search led us to a new development close to the boat, but it would require a long drive to work. Cindy never imposed limitations on projects. The phrase, "Cannot do," was not in her vocabulary. Pitfalls and loopholes were resolved to a successful conclusion. Later we discovered a development built by the same contractor midway between the boat and our workplaces, but all the models were different from the one we liked near the boat. Our chase to interview the development contractor resulted in him agreeing to build the favored model in the second location.

Our mix of living room furniture would not work in our new home. We relieved that concern when we learned the model house would be listed for sale, and we offered to buy the entire staged living room ensemble. The contractor accepted our offer and upon closing transferred all the furniture to our new home. We blended the contents of two households into one; furnished bedrooms for Kirsten and Nate, giving each their special place on weekends; and decorated the guest bathroom walls with black-and-white photos of our ancestors. One of Cindy's cracked and scarred old photos featured the image of her father's great-grandmother, a Native American. Back in the early 1800s, when her ancestors befriended a tribe in Indiana where they had settled after immigration from Germany, they were alerted about a pending massacre and quickly moved to Canada. Years later, they moved to a farm in Michigan. The photo confirmed the source of Cindy's high cheekbones and stunning eyes.

In the basement at Our House, I continued to make changes to the steel boat project until satisfied. Bruce produced a complete set of finished plans along with a set of large paper templates for cutting all the steel plates necessary to piece together the complete hull. She was impressive: hard dodger, skeg hung rudder, cutter rigged, freshwater tank in the keel for ballast, and a fuel tank mounted low but accessible.

A Canadian couple sailed *Margetta* home shortly after I listed her for sale, but I saved the gennaker and spinnaker, thinking they could be reshaped into sunshades over the backyard patio. With the ship mortgage paid off we set out to search for a steel boat fabricator, finding a very capable one in North Carolina. Our pitches to bankers for construction loans were unsuccessful. All viewed our proposal as just another high-risk backyard boat project that had no value until it floated, meaning that it had no recovery value should there be a loan default during construction. We planned our third visit to North Carolina around a Friday meeting at the builder's bank to discuss a loan that would be a win for us, the bank, and the builder, and drove down on Thursday after receiving positive feedback from the bank. While we waited at the motel, Cindy read an ad in a sailing magazine about an Amel. It described a blue water boat in great detail and, for the first time in all my years of sailing, I learned about a production boat designed specifically for ocean cruising. It was no wonder that I did not recognize the name. It was French built. A demonstrator waited for us in Fort Lauderdale ready for inspection. After calling to verify that the demonstrator was still available, we decided right then to head south the next morning. On our way, we called the fabricator and the bank to put a hold on the meeting.

Entering the brokers office, I said, "We're here to look at the *A*-mel." A guy stood up from behind is desk saying, "You mean the "Ah-*MELL*." The Amel Super Maramu by Chantiers Amel in La Rochelle, France turned out to be a spectacular discovery. People could sit in the cockpit below the side decks, feeling secure in the boat, as opposed to sitting up above the side decks exposed to sea splash. The helm wheel, mounted on the cockpit's port bulkhead within reach of a saddle-shaped seat, offered protection from the elements while steering. A large compass dome sat on the shelf directly in front of the wheel. An instrument panel with wind, depth, and speed readouts occupied the space forward of the compass. Beyond the instrument array a hard windshield protected cockpit occupants from wind and sea spray and rose to a hard dodger overhead. A person could stand up and work all around the engine accessed by tilting up the center cockpit deck and securing it with a short line and hook from the mizzen mast. The hatch cover between the center cockpit and the saloon steps, uniquely fashioned like a guillotine, dropped down out of sight when opened. Three ordinary steps instead of a steep ladder facilitated access to the saloon from the center cockpit. Epoxy sealing along the seam between the hull and the deck ensured no leaking as the vessel rolled in the seas. The hull had two watertight bulkheads, the first aft of a huge chain locker and the second aft of the forward cabin and a head with shower. Water from the forward head and chain locker flowed through tubes to the only wet bilge space, located under the engine, leaving all space under the saloon decking dry for food storage. A large aft owner's cabin had a head with shower that also drained through tubes into the wet bilge and also had a vanity for the lady of the yacht. A water tank in the keel was part of the ballast package and could be cleaned through access hatches located under the main saloon table. Stainless steel handrails surrounded the deck instead of coated wire lifelines. Two bow lazarettes, each large enough for three people to crouch inside with the hatch down, flanked an electric windlass. Heavy-duty hinges attached the rudder to a skeg that arched forward close to the hull to join a wide fin keel flat on the bottom making careening possible. Holes in the main and mizzen chain plates afforded reception of container crane clevis bolts, facilitating haul outs at shipping ports worldwide for bottom work or placement on a trailer. Cindy loved it, but the price exceeded our estimates to build, power, and rig the custom steel boat. We decided to suspend the steel boat project and search for a used one, or as Amel described them, "experienced," and drove back to Michigan.

Three months later, a 14.6-meter (forty-eight-foot) 1984 Amel Maramu with twelve years of ocean experience appeared in a January sailing magazine ad. I called the broker and arranged to see the boat that Saturday in Florida. We drove Friday, stayed at a hotel in Okeechobee, and met the broker and owner at the Indiantown Marina on the St. Lucie Canal. The ketch, named *Meg*, had been on the market for a year after a seven-year circumnavigation. The broker said it was time for the owner to be relieved from sailing. Our first look told us why.

Thickly rolled-on white hull paint above the waterline gave a shoddy orange peel appearance. A very heavy layer of fresh bottom paint suggested an obvious attempt to hide large blisters. Under the nav instrument panel, wires hung with connections made by twisting bare wire ends together and wrapping the twist with electrical tape. Rust coated the water heater. A layer of what appeared to be tar coated the space under the engine, spiking my suspicion that engine waste oil had been pumped overboard at sea after being dumped onto the engine room deck where it flowed into the bilge below. During the sailing evaluation *Meg* did not take on water, the engine ran, and the sails looked acceptable, but an obvious radical bend in the main boom remained after lowering the sail. The freezer, refrigerator, and most of the navigation devices failed to operate, but both heads worked, pumping only straight overboard. *Meg* appeared to be an overused and abused toy cast aside, no longer wanted. It needed massive amounts of work to bring it back to proper yacht quality and seaworthiness, but we could see that the internal hull structure looked sound. It was an Amel, built for ocean sailing, and I had much to negotiate over. I could clean it up, truck it home, make upgrades, and sail it in GLSS events to learn how to manage a cutter-rigged ketch single-handed. It would be the perfect platform around which Cindy and I could structure global sailing adventures in our retirement years. The steel boat project had been an enormous, deep dive into sailing yacht systems, hull design, and rigging. The learnings would be directly applied to *Meg*'s rehabilitation.

Meg first seen

The seller accepted our offer, comprehending the needed work to bring the yacht back to life, and we secured an affordable ship's mortgage. Cindy and I signed as the new owners seven days after we walked the decks for the first time. Two British sailors recommended by the broker delivered *Meg* to the New River Marina in Fort Lauderdale, where the work began. A yacht refitting professional, also recommended by the broker, faxed work completion summaries to me and I returned payments. Major project items included: replacing the water heater, adding a holding tank for the aft head, replacing anchor chain and main boom, cleaning the engine compartment deck and underlying bilge, stripping and replacing bottom paint, and refinishing the hull above the waterline. When the transom nameplates with the words "Meg" and "Hamburg" fell to the ground, the sailing yacht *Meg* ceased to exist. The backside of the plates revealed the Amel's first name, *Mandarine* out of Berlin.

With nearly a two-meter draft, the boat would be difficult to maneuver in the shallow Clinton River, where I had berthed *Margetta*. Our search for a deep-water marina took us to the Bridgeview Marina in Sarnia, Canada, just over the Bluewater Bridge from Port Huron, Michigan, only a fifty-minute drive from home. During another exploratory drive we discovered Brands' Marina in Port Clinton, Ohio, on Lake Erie. There the boat could be prepared for a spring launch and the motor trip up the rivers to Sarnia.

Late in April, we arrived in Florida to see the boat secured on a truck and settle up with all involved, then drove overnight to wait at Brands' Marina for Our Boat to arrive. The tractor trailer rig, with the boat perched on top, turned into the marina entrance and stopped inside the gate. I got out of the car and walked along the starboard side to discover damage along the hull and the rub rail. The driver, deeply apologetic, said the drive went well until the night before, when he rested at a truck stop. A rig pulled in next to him and, when it departed, the trailer's rear corner dragged along the starboard side of the boat. Fortunately, the marina housed a boat repair shop. Amel shipped a new rub rail, and the starboard side looked new when the repairs were finished. Brownell Boat Transport graciously stepped up to the full cost of the work. After the repair, Our boat occupied a corner inside a covered building, making it possible for me to work on the boat regardless of the weather using my newly purchased, extensive metric tool kit.

Like all boat owners, Cindy and I toiled over boat names for weeks. Morning drive radio personalities, two women, comically reflected one Monday about their weekend adventures. I listened to their story about a freckle-faced kid seen that weekend, reminding her of a kid she knew in her youth. The boy wore a beanie with a propeller on top. Everyone called him *Scooter*. Wham! *Scooter* froze in my mind. At home, *Scooter* also struck Cindy's fancy. The weekend after receiving the documentation certificate we applied the vinyl lettering *Scooter* onto the transom, Cindy drizzled champagne over the bow, and we made final preparations for launch day.

Navigation station at the time of purchase

We sailed *Scooter* for the first time on the passage from Port Clinton, north across Lake Erie, to anchor overnight near Lakewood Beach on the Canadian shore. At daybreak the next morning, we motored into the Detroit River current, crossed Lake St. Clair, and fought the St. Clair River current to Bridgeview Marina, arriving after dark.

The following weekend we started projects intentionally delayed until *Scooter* floated. I removed

Deck-to-hull seam damage

Applying Womanship training

the original refrigerator and separate freezer box, both chilled by an engine-mounted compressor that required now-banned Freon, and replaced the refrigerator with one that operated with 12 volt DC boat power or 120 volt AC shore power. The cavity that held the freezer became a dry storage area. I gutted and replaced all nav station wiring, removed inoperative instruments, and sent the Magnavox global positioning system (GPS) unit out for repair. After all the cushions were returned from a custom shop in Sarnia recovered with fire retardant material, we sailed on Lake Huron, learning how to fly three, four, and at times five sails.

Before hauling for the winter, I removed the masts with the marina gin pole and stored them on a designated mast stand. A full-length boat cover came together by shaping steel tubes into a framework that arched from side to side. To hold the tubes in place and prevent damage, I stepped them on wood blocks where the deck met the toe rail. The tubes did a good job of supporting ten-ounce canvas tarps to keep the snow from piling on the cabin tops. I flooded the engine's sea-water coolant system with an antifreeze mix to protect from freezing to forty degrees below zero, added diesel stabilizer to the fuel tank, drained both heads, pumped the fresh water tank as dry as I could, added vodka to the puddle at the bottom of the water tank, and blew out the water lines with a shop vac. During *Scooter's* first ever winter experience, I replaced the mismatched bridge instruments with ones that would talk to each other and could be monitored by a repeater at the nav station, had the main sail reshaped to like new, and overhauled the winches.

At the annual GLSS conference that winter, a guest speaker knowledgeable about sleeping, spoke about sleep cycles, how long we sleep and what woke us up. He recommended we learn our sleep cycle by keeping a tablet and pen next to a clock on a nightstand and recording every time we rolled over and woke during the night. To my surprise, my sleep cycle averaged ninety minutes.

The weekend after launch I calibrated the wind instrument while sailing in circles and pushed myself to learn how to single-handedly trim and shift sails to get the most boat speed on various points of sail. Cindy paid close attention to each maneuver and sail change. Original and backup autopilots performed adequately on the placid lake while I trained for the GLSS Mackinac Solo, however, a comment by the prior owner that he had to hand steer for two days and a night during a storm while crossing the Gulf of Mexico because the auto pilot failed to keep the boat on course haunted my solo preparations.

A soft breeze drifted over the cool, glassy Lake Huron water the morning of the GLSS Mackinac Solo in the summer of 1998. I slowly tacked and jibed *Scooter* near the start line while flying only the main then hoisted a sleeve containing the spinnaker, known in Amel jargon as a "ballooner," forward of the main mast. At the gun, I quickly pulled the sleeve up revealing the original, heavily stained, and discolored ballooner. Committee boat photos captured me playing with the ballooner while Mark Gutteridge easily sailed *Gutsy* through *Scooter's* wind shadow.

Sometime after the start, the air filled enough for me to hoist the mizzen. With that trimmed, I launched *Margetta's* gennaker from the mizzen mast revealing the watermelon and blue sail as it began to take shape.

Rounding the first mark off the port of Goderich, Canada at 2100, I headed *Scooter* north into the night. The only blips on the radar showed that the cluster of northbound sailors had spread far apart on the lake all moving faster than *Scooter*. I switched the radar to standby and prepared to work my sleep cycle for the first time aboard. I moved the starboard divan's seat back from its daytime position over to the divan's edge, converting it into a kind of leeboard, thereby turning the divan into a pilot's bunk where I would sleep safe from sliding off as the boat rolled. After winding an alarm clock and setting it to ring in ninety minutes, I placed it next to the fiddle of the saloon table in easy reach from the pilot's bunk and rolled over to hug a pillow. I listened to the lake tinkle the hull until realizing I was not tired enough to slip into dreamland. Two hours later I tried it again and my body went limp in the calm. When the buzzer woke me, I switched the radar to scan, stepped up to the cockpit, looked forward then all around, and returned to the radar screen to see the same bogies moving farther away. Trusting the radar, I repeated the sleep cycle.

Controlling boat functions from under the hard dodger on the rainy morning of the last day, I stayed dry unlike others sitting behind their helm wheel in the open, shivering in the cold and the wet under foul weather gear. Later that afternoon, I tacked *Scooter* directly into a stiff breeze right out of the west in the narrow passage between Bois Blanc and Mackinac Islands. The first few tacks were easy. I rotated the autopilot course controller dial one hundred degrees. The autopilot made the turn. I followed the turn, eased a sheet, scampered across the cockpit to the other winch, flipped the genoa past the mast, wrapped the sheet around the winch, jammed in the winch handle, and wound until the genoa took shape. A few minutes later I had to tack again. Tiring after a dozen tacks, I mustered the will to continue not wanting to finish last.

Moments after crossing the finish line, I lowered the sails and motored toward the outer dock at the Mackinac Yacht Club, where skippers who had finished before me shared their stories with media folks while helping others dock. I backed *Scooter* into a slip, flipped bow lines around pilings, and tossed stern lines to the dock help.

While standing on top of the aft cabin chatting with other skippers on the dock, a young reporter held her mic out at me and asked how I did while the camera man at her side focused in. I told her I finished last in my division but not last overall. She looked at me with wider eyes and asked me what happened. Loaded with fatigue and not ready to entertain a lengthy interview, I swung my right arm back saying, "Does that look like a race boat? I had four sails flying off two masts to keep up with those race boats with two sails and one mast. It's an ocean boat that had been at sea for twelve years unlike the others. I sailed to improve my sailing skills. Finishing meant more to me than how I placed." Months later my comments appeared in a sailing magazine.

Cindy, Nathan, and his buddy joined me for the two week's return cruise down the Canadian coast. Summer on the water brought enjoyment every weekend until haul out and freeze preparation. While *Scooter* sat on the hard that winter, I overhauled boat parts and refinished the main saloon table in the basement.

At One Pontiac Plaza, talk flowed around the coffee and donut stand about the coming merger of Pontiac Division with GMC Truck Division and the relocation of offices to the Renaissance Center in Detroit. Rumor had it that there would be retirements, transfers, and terminations. At my

Light air start

Gutsy passing

desk, I looked over to the photo on the wall of *Margetta* anchored in Pelican Cove on Santa Cruz Island and smiled, knowing I had been on the right life course all along, and I said a silent thank you to GM for transferring me to where I could be stimulated by Mother Ocean. The next year, as the divisions merged, I elected the attractive retirement package and funded *Scooter* upgrades through various employment opportunities found in the auto capital of the world.

Whispers about a merger of Detroit Edison with Con Edison began to drift around Cindy's human resources department along with speculations about restructuring the new entity with half the available personnel. With that, Cindy anticipated breaking through the glass ceiling she had been battling her entire career, and my imaginings about cruising the world's oceans intensified. We had completed most of the desired upgrades to make *Scooter* pleasing to live on away from the dock, and weekends were all about sailing. That spring, word came to Cindy's office that the merger would happen after both companies signed at a meeting to be held in June, and that an attractive early retirement package for which she qualified would be offered. Considering our Caribbean sailing plans, she arranged interviews in Annapolis, Maryland and in Orlando, Tampa, and Miami, Florida. Her phone conversation with Sykes Enterprises, Inc., an inbound telemarketing company, resulted in an interview in Tampa, where she was offered a human resources directorship to develop an online product knowledge university. They wanted her to start immediately. Days later she accepted the Detroit Edison retirement package. The directorship position fulfilled her working life's aspiration. We placed a deposit on a newly built house in Sun City Center, Florida, and rented a small furnished apartment for her to stay in during the transition. Back in Michigan, we listed our house for sale, and after accepting an offer, Cindy flew to Florida to begin her new career.

We set a closing date on the Michigan house for late September and closed on the Florida house with a bridge loan. Cindy moved into the empty home and slept nights on an air mattress while I readied *Scooter* for the trip south through the Erie Canal that had to be transited by the end of October when it would close for the winter. Stopping at the Bluewater Bridge US Customs office to buy a customs decal I needed before bringing *Scooter* into the States from Canada, I watched a TV monitor behind the counter showing smoke streaming from the World Trade Center towers. When the border reopened, I purchased the customs decal and applied it to the port side saloon window. Days later, I followed the moving van to Florida, driving our minivan with the ten-foot Caribe reinforced inflatable boat (RIB) that came with *Meg* strapped onto the roof. Back in Michigan, I tidied up the house for the new owner and drove over the bridge to begin living full-time aboard *Scooter*.

Wanting to get eyes on where to prepare *Scooter* for transiting the Erie Canal, I drove to Buffalo, New York. The Erie Canal guidebook noted that the Black Rock Channel and Lock at the end of the long canal next to the Niagara River had to be transited during daylight. Should I arrive late in the day, I would need to have a place to stay overnight. The fuel dock at the Erie Basin Marina closed at 1700, but the manager said that it was ok to tie up until 0800 the next day. With that understanding, I drove to see Cindy and flew back to Detroit, where old sailing buddy Don Trager waited to take me to *Scooter* to begin my Florida delivery journey.

Waypoints to Sea

I motored *Scooter* south to Lake St. Clair, spent the night at anchor off Grosse Point Yacht Club, motored down the Detroit River past the Renaissance Center, and overnighted on a mooring at Put-in-Bay on Lake Erie. In good air, I sailed downwind to the Erie Basin, transited the lock, and tied to a wall across from Wardell Boat Yard in Tonawanda, New York. The next day at Wardell's, I removed the booms and unstepped and secured the masts over the dodger on previously cut wood supports. A couple from the sail club joined me with their young son for the Erie Canal transit. At the end of each motoring day, we found a place to spend the night tied to a wall at a town, stopping last at Waterford, where the family boarded a bus and returned to their car in Tonawanda. I changed the engine oil and filter, negotiated the Troy Lock, and motored down the Hudson River to Hop-O-Nose Marina. I wanted to step the masts there but found their gin pole would not reach the mizzen. Folks said that the next best place to stop would be the Peterson Marina in Upper Nyack near the Tappan Zee Bridge. After *Scooter* became a sailing yacht again at Peterson's, I motored down the river, picked up a mooring in the Great Kills Harbor, and waited for an offshore breeze to sail south along the Jersey shore. Sailing all night and most of the next day brought me to anchor in Cape May Bay, New Jersey, for a six-hour rest. That night I motored around Cape May, up the Delaware Bay with the flood tide, transited the Chesapeake and Delaware Canal, motored down the Elk River, and spent the night at Worton Creek, Maryland, familiar to me from the *Marilyn Mae II* days. The next evening, I tied *Scooter* to a dock on Spa Creek in Annapolis, where I waited for Reg Brown and Bob Van Eck, two longtime sailing friends who volunteered to crew on the passage to Florida. We sailed *Scooter* down the bay to enter the Intracoastal Waterway (ICW) at Norfolk just south of the naval base. *Scooter* flushed out of the ICW at Beaufort, North Carolina, and we sailed offshore to Charleston, South Carolina. We rested at the marina where Reg kept his yacht then entered the ICW for days of motoring to Fort Lauderdale.

Even though I had accumulated eighteen years of sailing experience, I wanted to satisfy an inner drive for professional maritime knowledge that would take me to a higher level of achievement and enhance safety during our future ocean adventures. My earlier application to attend an International Yacht Training Worldwide (IYT) program that delivered commercial captaining certifications recognized and respected worldwide was accepted. I docked *Scooter* at a marina on the New River, bused to see Cindy for a week, and drove the minivan back to the boat to prepare for the intensive training program.

I arrived early at IYT on South Miami Road in Fort Lauderdale and followed directions to a classroom with two dozen seats at eight tables. As the room filled, the growing chatter revealed sailing backgrounds. Deck hands (deckies) in their twenties working aboard superyachts wanted to earn the maritime license that would propel their career up the command ladder. Some shared temporary rooms at the local crew quarters. A few others wanted to legally skipper their dad's commercial fishing boat, and one had crewing experience on a large racing yacht. Hearing the many conversations among the men—there were no women in the shore-based course—I realized I alone owned and operated a sailing yacht.

From a cluster of white uniforms at the door, a man with four gold stripes on shoulder boards walked in, introduced himself to the class as the instructor, and welcomed us to our first day of shore-based training. Beginning with the nearest student to his right, he asked each man to introduce himself and the vessel he served. When the last student finished his introduction, the captain asked all to stand and greet the students at our table. As the chatter dwindled, the captain directed us to take our seats then announced that only one of the three of us would pass the shore-based course. Chair movements stopped. All sat straight up, looking forward. With the students' full

attention, the captain summarized the course material to be mastered while passing out a hardbound book titled, *The Shore-Based Course*. It's table of contents read:
- Chartwork Instruments
- Charts, Latitude, and Longitude
- Distance, Speed, Time, and Direction
- The Magnetic Compass, Variation and Deviation
- Position Lines and Position Fixes
- Dead Reckoning and Estimated Positions
- Tides, Currents, Course to Steer to Counteract a Current
- Meteorology
- Pilotage and Passage Planning
- Electronic Navigation Aids
- International Regulations for Preventing Collisions at Sea.

He went on to review the required additional off-site courses at remote locations after the shore-based course for those new to professional crewing: first time deckies and stewardesses - the ladies who serve meals and beverages and impeccably maintain the yacht's interior who were not taking the shore-based course - and of course me. The five off-site courses required by the International Convention on Standards of Training Certification and Watchkeeping for Seafarers (STCW) to work on vessels larger than twenty-four meters, ships, ferries, cruise ships, and megayachts were titled:
- Basic Firefighting (at Resolve Fire and Hazard Response, Inc.)
- Personal Safety and Social Responsibility
- Elementary First Aid
- Personal Survival Techniques
- Radio Communications

Each shore-based course module ended with an exam, some requiring written answers, which eliminated the possibility of guessing the best multiple-choice answer. Each exam had to be passed in order to continue on to the next module. The class population thinned the morning after each exam.

After completing the shore-based course, I attended the off-site modules. Firefighting must have been physically challenging for the new hire stewardesses. Over fire-retardant coveralls, we fitted a self-contained breathing apparatus (SCBA) on our back, adjusted the face mask, hefted a large fire extinguisher can, sat it on the cement deck and sprayed the base of a roaring fire inside a simulated ship compartment. Then we dragged a hundred-fifty-pound dummy along the deck of a smoke-filled room and moved on to other live firefighting situations and strenuous activities.

The personal safety and social responsibility course covered emergency procedures, safe working practices, preventing marine pollution, effective shipboard communications, human relations, shipboard workplace environment, safety procedures, accident prevention, health, hygiene, shipboard management structure, drugs, alcohol, and watchkeeping responsibilities.

The elementary first aid course proved to be an excellent CPR refresher.

The first day of the personal survival techniques class covered shipboard emergencies, principles of survival, survival equipment, and abandon ship methods to increase the odds of surviving at sea. The next day, everyone had to demonstrate classroom learnings in a large hotel pool. We inverted a round life raft, the position it could actually be deployed, and righted it and climbed up the mini rope ladder to experience the difficulty of entry in calm pool water. I visualized boarding the raft in a real-world situation. Then everyone donned neoprene survival immersion suits poolside, entered the pool, floated in the face up position, and learned how to move about.

The radio communications course gave me knowledge I soon put into action: radio theory, terms, licensing requirements, radio procedure, proper very high frequency (VHF) and single sideband (SSB) radio installation, weather information, emergency communications, the purpose and use of an emergency position-indicating radio beacon (EPIRB), and the need for a distress procedural card visible at all times on the nav desk.

Three additional steps remained for those seeking the professional ticket: application of shore-based learnings during a three-day, two-night on the water exercise proctored by an instructor, passing an onboard practical exam while sailing, and sitting for an hour-long oral exam probing our understanding of subject matter.

I joined three classmates aboard a forty-foot sailboat at the Las Olas Marina the day before the sea trial. One from the Republic of South Africa graduated university with a biology degree and wanted to buy a farm back home. Learning from a friend that he could earn and save money crewing, because superyacht crew had all meals and uniforms provided, and income could be paid at international banks with forgiving taxation terms, he found his way to be a deckie. A Norwegian sailor crewing on a superyacht as a lifestyle seized the training opportunity to climb the maritime ladder. Another had crewed weekends on a San Francisco Bay racing yacht while away from his Internet coding responsibilities. Later in the day, a man who single-handedly delivered a Leopard catamaran for its Cape Town builder to a Fort Lauderdale broker came aboard. Having to depart with the yacht before the on the water evaluations and final exam in Cape Town, IYT allowed him to finalize the process with us.

Offshore, we rotated through skippering, sail trimming, and navigating positions, mentored by an IYT officer as we set courses to steer, tacked, gybed, reefed, navigated across a current, and practiced man overboard recovery under sail. At the end of that long day, we navigated Fisherman's Channel, Government Cut, and Biscayne Channel into Biscayne Bay and anchored for the night close in, west of Key Biscayne. On day two, we demonstrated making running fixes while sailing north along the coast and then south to where we again negotiated the narrow Biscayne Channel before anchoring in the same cove as the night before.

At dusk on the final day, we returned to the marina slip and the officer departed after advising that the evaluator would arrive at 0800 expecting to see our pilotage notes from the marina to the Bar Cut and the fair water marker at the entrance to Port Everglades. Pilotage notes, we learned, begin at the bottom of a page and flow up the page describing aids to navigation (ATON) and the course and distance between them along the passage.

The South African said that his yacht captain knew the evaluator who would be aboard the next day, a South African Navy captain, strong on crew teamwork and verbal communication. We prepared dinner aboard and cleaned up before moving to a covered picnic table near the marina gate to review our course material. After dark, the laundromat across the street became our study room, where bright florescent lights illuminated our notes and charts spread on top of the washers and dryers. We worked on our piloting notes and reviewed course material until staying up much later would harm the next day's performance on the water.

Up at 0630, showered and shaved, we waited for the evaluator. At 0730 he knocked on the cabin top, came aboard, summoned us to the deck near the helm, and introduced himself. He read a name from his clipboard, looked up when he heard a loud, "Here," paused to study the face, and called out the next name. Following the roll call, the evaluator reviewed his mission saying in a firm command voice, "You . . . have all passed the yachtmaster . . . shore-based training . . . and the off-site courses or you would not be here. Now . . . it is my job to determine . . . if you are capable . . . of sailing my wife . . . and children . . . from here to London . . . safely . . . on this vessel . . . and make it an enjoyable experience." Wide-eyed glances flashed among us. The evaluator looked at his clipboard and selected the guy who had just delivered the yacht from South Africa for the first oral exam. He said he would return in ten minutes to begin, and that all others should wait at the shaded picnic table at the dock's land end. Four of us grabbed course books and notes to review ashore.

An hour later, the delivery skipper arrived at the picnic table to say that the San Francisco racer was next. The Norwegian asked how it went, and the skipper said that when he gave what he thought the evaluator wanted, he was asked another question on the same topic drilling deeper into the subject. When the San Fran racer came back to the table to announce that the Norwegian was next to be evaluated, I asked him what he thought about the exam. He said with a snarky attitude, "This whole thing's competitive. I'm saying nothing." I was the fourth to be called, and as I descended the ladder into the saloon the evaluator asked me what time the bascule bridge that we had to pass on the way to the fair water marker would open.

Being familiar with the ICW bridge opening schemes after spending days in transit with *Scooter*, I knew that the bridge would open on the hour only if the bridge operator could see the vessel that was making a radio request on VHF channel nine. I told him that we had to make the noon opening or wait an hour. He appointed me to be the first skipper to take the yacht out to the fair water marker and directed me to round up my crew, assign positions, and make the noon bridge opening.

Moments later, at the picnic table, I alerted the crew about what had to be done and assigned positions based on the performances seen during the prior days aboard—navigator, port and starboard jib sheet trimmers, and main sheet trimmer. They understood the need for immediate action when I mentioned that we had to make the noon bridge opening. In no time, I had the engine running and the deckies had the dock lines off. As I made sternway out of the slip the crew fended off the pilings then dressed the dock lines. I maneuvered the yacht into the channel to become visible to the bridge operator when the navigator requested the opening over the radio. The navigator sat at the nav desk below as required, unable to look outside. We put our rehearsed plan to impress the evaluator with how we communicated commands, driven by the tip from the South African megayacht captain, into action. I called out compass course, boat speed, and current speed to the main sheet trimmer stationed at the top of the saloon ladder who said, "Aye, aye." The trimmer relayed that information to the navigator who repeated it, saying, "Aye, aye," adjusted the compass course to true, plotted the course on the chart, and processed the speed/time/distance equation to calculate the time to the next marker. With that done, he called out the color and number of the next marker, a compass course to steer, and the time it would be passed to the trimmer, who acknowledged, "Aye, aye," and relayed it to me. I acknowledged saying, "Aye, aye," while altering compass course. Our use of "aye, aye" confirmed our understanding and intention to comply.

At the direction of the evaluator, we rotated through each position, demonstrating our ability to maneuver the yacht under sail or process navigation. While sailing south along the coast, I sat through my orals as did one other when we sailed back north. The evaluator directed us to motor to the Dania Cut-Off Canal where he would evaluate our ability to maneuver under power. Each took a turn at the helm bringing the boat to a stop at a specific piling with the starboard side close enough for crew to step off with dock lines in hand, a maneuver I had great experience with after motoring the Erie Canal and the ICW. When the boat's transom stopped at the target piling the acting skipper smiled large and all students but one gave thumbs up. The experienced deckies and the Leopard catamaran skipper had become a supportive, competent team I enjoyed being part of.

Late in the afternoon the evaluator ordered us to secure the boat in a slip at the Nova University marina just inside the Bar Cut at Port Everglades. When the lines were dressed, he called us one at a time up to a picnic table on the grassy knoll to review his assessment. All but one returned to the boat with a huge smile to be greeted with, "Congratulations, Captain," by the others. The racer from San Francisco returned to the boat with a straight face and said he would have to retake the sailing evaluation. The next day at the training facility I received my well-earned captain's license, Master of Yachts Two-hundred Tons Offshore, recognized by the Cayman Islands Shipping Registry, the Bahamian Maritime Authority, the Republic of the Marshall Islands, and the Irish Department of Marine.

At month's end, with the help of Reg and Bob, I had *Scooter* berthed at the Regatta Point Marina on the Manatee River in Bradenton, Florida, where the keel stuck in the muddy bottom at low tide. Months later, after passing the USCG Master Mariner exam, I secured sail and tow endorsements then earned American Sailing Association Instructor certifications. With those accreditations, I began teaching sailing in St. Petersburg, my next career. Cindy's mother, Eileen, moved in with us after selling her house in Michigan at our request. I could not accept the eighty-year-old freezing alone in her home during a power outage when she could be with us in an age restricted community with much for her to do. Cindy and I were together, she with the position of her dreams and I with an internationally recognized commercial captain's license and the boat of my dreams in waters that could be sailed year-round.

Restoring the sun-weathered Caribe RIB in the garage still fresh with the heavy aroma of new cement filled the hours at home while Cindy worked and I was free from maritime endeavors. I filled and faired deep gouges along its fiberglass bottom and sanded and coated all hard surfaces with two-part epoxy. With a new Sailrite sewing machine, I created a custom Sunbrella cover to protect the sky side of the pontoons from the sun and a cover for when it was lashed inverted on the aft cabin top. The sun cover made the RIB look old and unappealing, a theft deterrent disguise. To finish the job, I painted the name *Jazz* on the transom. For me, speeding along in the RIB would be like being "on the jazz," an expression often heard in the TV series *The A-Team*. The vision became the name. On weekends, Cindy and I lived aboard *Scooter*, sailing the bay or zipping in *Jazz* when *Scooter's* keel stuck in the mud at low tide

Sometimes during fast runs far up the Manatee River, past the Interstate 75 bridge, other boats sped by, and we just had to jump their wakes while laughing and yelling, "Whoop-de-do," before zipping back to *Scooter* to prepare dinner and snuggle for the night in the owner's cabin. At home, late in the week following one wave-jumping episode, while watching TV Cindy said, "I've got a pain in my back right over here,"

"Where, here?" I said pressing the palm of my hand about where she had stroked.

"A little lower."

"How about here?" I pressed below her left shoulder blade.

"Ooo, that's the spot."

I rubbed awhile. "Did that help?"

"A little but it's still sore."

"Maybe you pulled a muscle when we jumped that wave before *Jazz* bumped the prop on the bottom."

"I could have, I'll take a Tylenol tonight before bed."

"Here, sit on the footrest and I'll rub it for a while."

An hour later, my massaging had had little effect. The Tylenol helped her sleep but did little to ease the low-grade pain. The next week she developed a chest cold. Unlike the colds one soon fights off, hers lingered for weeks. A doctor at Tampa General listened with a stethoscope, tapped this and that, asked questions, and wrote out a prescription. The medication had some effect on her cold but the back pain continued. On the second visit the doctor ordered lab work. Days later, a nurse called asking Cindy to return for the test results.

In his small office we quietly listened to the doctor say that it could be nothing at all and that sometimes the indicators are misleading. The lab report showed a slightly elevated PSA. Asked why he ordered that lab work generally performed for men, the doctor said he included it with other tests following Cindy's prolonged chest issues because prostate-specific antigen had been found in women's abnormal tissue. He said calmly that it required a closer look, putting both of us at ease with his nonchalant demeanor, and went on to say that he wanted her to see a specialist to look further and eliminate anything unusual.

At home, whatever bothered her had no effect on her tendency to grab my arm and say, "Take me to the other room and make me smile."

Swirling visits through an oncologist's practice resulted in a CAT scan that exposed a suspicious shadow above her diaphragm and below her left lung. There was no hurry or crisis projected by the doctor and his staff as we arranged for a fine needle aspiration of the small mass.

Still approaching the issue in a casual manner after saying that they had yet to make a determination, Cindy had to return to Tampa General to have the tiny mass removed.

The following week, Eileen and I waited in the lounge until a nurse entered and summoned us to follow her. The doctor met us in the hallway outside the recovery room's automatic swinging doors to say the lab found the mass to be non-small cell cancer. Eileen quickly asked how long Cindy had. The doctor said it was good to have found it early. Cindy started chemotherapy and after recovering from surgery returned to work.

We bought the house in the Sun City Center age-restricted community to have a place to live during the summer and leave unattended wintertime while exploring the Caribbean aboard *Scooter* once Cindy retired from her job. Our conversations about that dream became less frequent while Cindy received chemo treatments. The oncologist pointed to the glowing spots on the scans, commenting that they were getting smaller compared to the earlier scans. He saw progress and Cindy continued chemotherapy.

The afterthought of Eileen's moving in with us stimulated me to look for a house with specific mother-in-law space just like with Teddy years before. A home builder in the town of Ruskin, bordering Sun City Center, offered floor plans that could be somewhat modified. Designing a custom home, I thought, would give Cindy and Eileen something to look forward to other than work and chemotherapy treatments. Together, we finalized the floor plan into an arrangement defining two-bedroom suites flanking an east facing open living space with a view to a parklike backyard through near-ceiling-high windows. Cindy wanted a large open kitchen, living, and dining area where she could stand at the kitchen sink, look left into the living room to see the large rear projection TV below an arched shelf displaying a miniature city scape with her favorite figures, glance straight to view the backyard garden and sky out the tall windows, then right, past the dining area to the sliding lanai doors. We started construction on our custom dream home in October of 2002 after the oncologist reported progress.

Managing *Scooter* improvements, instructing sailing, skippering charter boats, and delivering yachts filled my days while Cindy enjoyed her director of training position at Sykes, actually employing her master's degree in education. We moved to the top of the waiting list at the Harborage Marina in St. Petersburg and lazily sailed *Scooter* up Tampa Bay to fill the first available slip. Cindy and Eileen busied themselves with shopping for decorations after we moved to the new house in May as I earned ASA Advanced Coastal Cruising and Coastal Navigation Instructor certifications. Chemotherapy continued as did the daily routine, and the backyard garden responded to Cindy's magic touch.

During an office visit late that summer the oncologist pointed out a new spot on the scan where the original mass had been removed. Cindy's oxygen level was low. That day the oncologist ordered oxygen to be available during daily activity, impossible to manage at her dream job. Every visit with the oncologist until that moment had cheered Cindy on with positive test results, pushing her conquering attitude that parlayed directly into her online university creations for Sykes. Exceeding her work objectives earned kudos from senior management and drove her to anticipate the thrill of witnessing the program roll-out. Instead of arriving home with stories of the day's achievements, when Cindy transferred her project to others, a shell of her spirit entered. My role became clear; fill the emptiness of unrealized success with meaningful activities to carry her to full remission, focus on diet and exercise, sail *Scooter* often, and take on the challenges ahead the same way she ran with the online university. The Social Security office accepted her application for disability that had been supported with a letter from the oncologist, and we adjusted finances to stay secure.

Rain-laden tropical storm Henri blew in from the Gulf of Mexico on September 6th, causing no damage around the house, but the power went out, stopping the oxygen generator. The medical supply company had suspended deliveries prior to Henri's arrival, and we had one bottle as backup. While thirty-knot winds bent the trees and blew rain sideways, I put Cindy and Eileen in the second-row seats next to the minivan's sliding doors and began driving through semiflooded streets and under dark traffic lights swinging below quivering wires. About ninety minutes later at the Brandon Regional Hospital twenty miles away people in scrubs directed Cindy to lay on a gurney. A nurse strapped an oxygen tube to her nose after I explained why we were there. Another person in scrubs moved her down a hall and returned her later to where Eileen and I had been waiting. As Cindy lay alert, breathing easy with oxygen, I wondered what the fuss was all about. Shortly, a doctor led me into a small room with a monitor and pointed to a brain tumor on the X-ray taken moments before. The contrast die used to cause the cancer cells to glow during prior CAT scans also caused the brain to glow hiding the tumor.

Radiation treatments began in concert with chemotherapy. Cindy kept a positive, gonna make it attitude even though she lost her driver's license due to the oncologist's requirement to report her brain radiation treatments to the DMV. Midsummer heat kept us mostly indoors when I was not teaching sailing classes or tending to Cindy's backyard garden while she watched through the large windows. Occasionally she summoned me to make her smile. Our routine around the house continued during the fall and winter of that year until we faced another test.

On the morning of January 14th, moments after starting the minivan outside the gym where I did an intense exercise routine twice weekly with machines followed by lapping the Olympic pool several times, a pain hit my left chest, causing me to wonder how I pulled that muscle. Rubbing my chest had no effect. The pain intensified. Not good, I thought, I need to make it home. Less than fifteen minutes later I pulled into the driveway, found the aspirin bottle, took two, and stretched out on the bed. The pain stayed the same—sharp, not changing. Knowing EMS would take longer to get to the house than it would take to drive to the nearby hospital, I told Cindy to take me to the emergency room. Though her driver's license had been suspended, she was my immediate hope.

Curled in pain, I staggered through the ER door up to the counter seeing no one. Had I arrived in an ambulance, ER staff would be waiting. A woman in scrubs came around the corner, saw my condition, directed me to a lay on a gurney in a small room, and called for help. After a helicopter ride to the same hospital where Cindy's brain tumor was discovered, I watched a stent expand to open my left anterior descending artery live on a monitor to my left, instantly stopping the pain. Discharged the next morning, the doctor noted my blood work indicated it should not have happened, that I was in excellent health, but he prescribed routine cardiac meds to be taken daily. I pushed through weeks of cardiac rehab before approval to resume maritime work.

The forecast models for Hurricane Charlie in mid-August showed the strike line right up Tampa Bay and over St. Petersburg, warning us that the storm surge could be high enough to lift the marina's floating docks to near the top of the cement pilings. After removing the sails and before doubling dock lines, I checked the yachts in the adjacent slips, finding *Scooter's* main mast in alignment with both. In heavy wind the boats could lean far enough to force the masts to snag each other. I moved *Scooter* forward in the slip avoiding that danger and secured the double dock lines. At the house, I moved furniture, TVs, and computer desks away from windows and designated the laundry room as our go-to room in the event of window breakage. Heavy wind swirled the trees in driving rain while the storm's eye rolled over Punta Gorda eighty-five miles to our south with 130 mph winds. The storm tracked northeast across the state, leaving *Scooter* and the house undamaged.

The next hurricane, Francis, came in from the Atlantic coast. I prepped the boat, and again it escaped damage while the storm tracked north of Tampa. Then Hurricane Jeanne followed on a similar path a few weeks later. By then chemotherapy and radiation sessions had left their mark on Cindy. She had lost much weight after her appetite faded, and the radiation had robbed her memory, leaving her only aware of the moment.

A Methodist minister recommended by our hospice advisor stopped by one afternoon. During our talk while seated in the living room Cindy asked what it was like to die. Eileen and I listened as the minister comforted her with words about seeing the faces of those loved ones waiting for her. Cindy and I had a strong Christian foundation, with Sunday school back in our childhood days, and always tried to practice the Golden Rule as adults. The minister's words eased Cindy's worries, leaving her behaving as though she had something to look forward to, a new beginning.

Hospice supplied a hospital bed when Cindy could no longer shift into and out of the wheelchair. I placed it in the living room near the tall windows where she could view her colorful foliage filling the inclined back yard, watch the sun rise and the clouds go by, and listen to Eileen and I talk while working kitchen chores. At night, I unfolded the convertible couch to sleep nearby, assuring her of my constant presence. The weekly visiting hospice nurse directed me to ease her pains, maybe also worries, with morphine drops onto her lips. On the nurse's fourth visitation, she said that Cindy had deteriorated significantly since seeing her last, an observation Eileen and I had not made while living close by her side.

Early morning light woke me before the sun streamed through the large windows to brighten the room. Laying in the opened convertible bed sensing that light, I heard Cindy breathe slowly and deeply. I went to her side. She breathed deeper and faster in loud rasping breaths. Minutes later, she flailed her arms and legs, fighting what was about to happen. Next to her on the window side of the bed I caressed her right arm and hand while saying I was there for her and placed a few morphine drops on her lips. From the kitchen, Eileen approached and knelt quietly at the opposite side of the bed after I called her name. Our eyes met with an understanding glance, and together we repeated our love for Cindy to comfort her, saying that it was ok for her to go and that we would be ok while caressing her arms and shoulders. It calmed her for the moment. We repeated our loving words. Cindy squirmed and flailed her legs again during a long struggling breath, lay calm for a moment after exhaling, inhaled deeply, lay still for a moment then exhaled very slowly and rested, still, forever.

The kitchen wall clock showed 0730 when I returned to saying I loved her and that I'd be ok. Eileen and I continued to stroke her arms and shoulders, feeling she could hear us. I suspected her departing spirit watched me from high in the room as I said good-bye, but it vanished when I looked up. The sense of her spirit lingered while I hugged her mom and then called the hospice nurse. Together, Eileen and I returned to Cindy's side and repeated that it was ok for her to leave, that she was not alone.

Soon an ambulance arrived without a sound. Two attendants asked Eileen and I to wait outside on the lanai where we sat in the warmth of the morning sun while they quietly took her away. The seven-year romance with a friend, a lover, and sailing soulmate, throughout which there was never a word spoken between us in anger, had come to an end. During our soft talk to fill the silence on the lanai, I felt Cindy watching us, a sense felt whenever I returned to the house to see the emptiness, one of many things in my life experiences I do not understand.

For the longest time, the oncologist's supporting comments gave us hope that she would respond to the chemotherapy. Then when the brain became involved Eileen and I eased into believing our girl would leave us. Over time, Eileen and I had prepared ourselves to let her go, and when she passed it was not traumatic, not surprising, not shocking. There was no devastating bereavement about sudden loss that had to be lived through and overcome as there would have been if she had been snatched from our world by accidental death, leaving an instant empty space that she had occupied. We prayed for remission from the first day, two years earlier. All through hospice, I accepted that she would lose her battle and that our dream adventure together at sea would be unrealized. The morning she joined her father and brother arrived earlier than I had hoped. I still wonder how those last moments would have been had she met no one to dazzle for those seven years.

Instead of the usual twenty-two-hour, fast-lane drive from Florida to Michigan made years before, Eileen and I quietly poked along for two days in the slow lane with Cindy's urn on the back seat on our way to her celebration of life at the Auburn, Michigan, United Methodist Church.

We delivered Cindy's urn to the cemetery caretaker to be interred next to her father and brother and began our homeward motor trip. It was a different ride with just the two of us in the minivan. Driving Route 75 across Ohio flatlands, our conversations drifted toward the future then back to Eileen's grief following the instant loss of her son Jack when he was eighteen and the slow loss of her husband from emphysema after smoking since his teenage years with the marines in the Pacific. Not wanting to experience that again, she repeatedly moaned why her son, her husband, and now her daughter had died before her, and that it was not supposed to be that way.

We stopped to overnight at a hotel in Chattanooga. Our dinner-table talk at a country restaurant near the hotel circled around what to do when we returned to the house. Waiting for our orders to be served, I shared the reasons Cindy and I moved into the Sun City Center area and why we requested she join us. She listened quietly. I brought her to recall times with those she had met at the local recreation center, the sewing and craft hobby groups, and the bocce ball players. Her smile told me she enjoyed her new friends. I went on to add that she had lived alone for seven years in Michigan before moving in with us and could still manage living alone in a small, easy-to-maintain place among others her age. She remarked that at eighty-four, she wanted to move the remainder of life forward as soon as possible. I suggested that we look for a place in Kings Point, a gated community in Sun City Center with small villas and a grand community center with endless things for her to do and friends to make. Eileen pressed me. "Ok, that's me. But what are you going to do?"

Not wanting to hint that I felt Cindy's presence everywhere in the house, I answered, "I cannot live in that big house alone. I could move onto the boat for a while. The main thing I want is for you to be happy and comfortable."

"Well, I have made some friends, but, Bob, I watched you and Cindy together. You need someone in your life, I can see it. Go find someone to enjoy it with."

"That is not what I had in mind, Mom."

"You will see. I have after losing all my family. I came here to be with Cindy and you. And now, I will find others. It may take you some time, but you will see."

"Well, we have more pressing things to do. Find a place for you, make it yours, and sell the house after figuring out what to do with everything."

"You don't see it yet. But you will."

We found an affordable one-bedroom condo for her in Kings Point. I painted the walls, replaced the carpets, and cleaned the lanai. Local movers placed selected furniture in the condo from the house and filled the kitchen with her pick of things from the cupboards. Kirsten and her man friend collected what they could tow north, and the St. Vincent de Paul Society collected the remainder, including our extensive corporate wardrobes. I filled a storage compartment in St. Petersburg with tools and other cherished items and moved basic needs aboard *Scooter*.

Recovery

By the time the house sold just before Christmas, I had settled into living aboard, and Eileen had found new octogenarian friends. Because the annual slip contract expired in February, I extended it for another year to give me enough time to complete an ocean preparation list that I had worked on for years.

I developed a cohesive work plan to achieve a fully integrated collection of systems and avoid the need to remove or relocate a component in order to install another component as the result of an afterthought. *Meg's* owner said he had to hand steer for two days and nights on storm seas while crossing the Gulf of Mexico because the autopilot failed to hold a course. He had a backup autopilot installed in Panama and said it needed constant maintenance during their seven-year honeymoon circumnavigation. Both autopilots functioned satisfactorily for me on the relatively flat waters of Lake Huron. So, at the time, I thought that his problems were due to lack of maintenance complicated by the numerous improper electrical connections. But on Tampa Bay, before Cindy's spirit moved on, the primary autopilot quit working, and I added replacing the autopilot to the ocean preparation list.

To me, the most important component aboard an offshore sailing yacht would be an autopilot capable of maintaining course under extreme weather conditions and the electric power to operate it. My online search revealed that Neco, the maker of the primary autopilot, was no longer making the device, and that parts were not available. Solutions to the problem bounced in my head for weeks until I remembered the *Offshore Cruising Encyclopedia* by Linda and Steve Dashew, a 1,232-page masterpiece about their design of large ocean sailing yachts I had read in Michigan. I found it buried in a locker onboard and searched through it for auto pilot systems they designed into their large boats. William Hamm, of WH Autopilots in Bainbridge Island, Washington, had supplied a custom system for the Dashews' sixty-four-foot *Sundeer*. A brief online search brought me his phone number. He listened to my description of how the Neco unit worked the steering and said the entire system could be replaced with components he engineered for large yachts. I sent photos and after more discussion I ordered the parts.

Boats with solar panels, wind generators, antennas, and fishing equipment supported by structures made of stainless-steel tubing called arches floated in marina slips near *Scooter*. The structures varied in appearance from professionally fabricated as though they were part of the boat manufacturing process to what looked like last-minute afterthoughts bolted on just to get the job done. While researching arch designs, I evaluated the machines and electronic devices I wanted on board and decided when they should be installed. Some required hauling the boat, some required having all parts on hand during the arch design, some needed to have the masts removed, and some could be added at any time. My work plan came together.

Plan completion required far more than evening and weekend hours. I suspended instructing sailing and skippering yachts for Sailing Florida at the Vinoy Marina in St. Petersburg and looked for a place to live while working in the boatyard. Fortunately, Patrick, the second-in-command at Sailing Florida, rented space in his house that included full kitchen and back porch privileges. The bedroom connected to a bathroom through a hallway at one side of the house giving me acceptable privacy. After I moved in the first week of January, I placed the contents of *Scooter's* lazarettes on the back porch along with the Mercury outboard and Magma barbeque, then unfolded a table and chair at the foot of the bed, setting up a mini office.

I hauled *Scooter* at a yard on Salt Creek in February and worked almost daily until all haul-out projects on the work plan were completed and proceeded to address the post-haul-out projects at the slip. The new steering system came together by removing the existing auto pilot and mechanical steering parts from the steering wheel shaft all the way to the rudder post tiller arms. It took three days to install the WH hydraulic pump at the helm, the electric pumps and diverter valves on a platform under the aft

OCEAN PREPARATION

- Certify life raft
- Design and fabricate Arch with solar, wind, antennas, RIB bow
- Have mast steps welded to main
- Install AIS, SSB, VHF, CARD, AM/FM/CD, GPS1&2 on new wood panel
- Install flexible pitch 3 blade prop- balance fixed prop
- Install forward scanning sonar unit with display on the bridge
- Install freezer
- Install modem from Laptop to SSB for Internet at sea
- Install water maker
- Make space for rapid deployment of life raft and abandon ship bag
- Obtain floating abandon ship bag – plan contents
- Obtain 300' of 3/8 anchor chain, 100' of 1"rode – keep existing dock lines
- Obtain and install electronic navigation charts on the laptop
- Obtain EPIRB – mount at hatch
- Obtain handheld GPS
- Obtain handheld VHF
- Obtain Marine Radio Operators Permit for SSB/VHF Ship Radio Station
- Obtain paper charts to backup laptop charts
- Obtain Sextant
- Obtain three solar panels
- Obtain two wind generators
- Obtain cruising guides
- Overhaul Perkins Injection Pump
- Paint bottom
- Paint outboard motor to look old having no theft value
- Refinish deck and cabin tops
- Replace aft head holding tank with sewage treatment plant
- Replace compass with global balance compass for both hemispheres
- Replace genoa roller furler – bearings worn
- Replace weather fax with current technology
- Replace all standing rigging – corrosion on turnbuckles
- Replace NECO autopilot
- Replace dodger LEXAN windows
- Repair leak in fuel tank
- Seal RIB pontoons – stop air leaks
- Sell hatch air conditioner
- Sell RIB trailer
- Service ESPAR diesel heater – fuel odor on startup

WORK PLAN			
TASK	UNIT / MACHINE / DEVICE	RESPONSIBLE	WHEN
FUEL TANK REPAIR		?	PRE HAULOUT
NAV DESK INSTRUMENT PANEL			PRE HAULOUT
HAULOUT		SALT CREEK MARINA	
STANDING RIGGING		SSMR	HAULOUT
DECK RE-FINISH		?	HAULOUT
BOTTON PAINT			HAULOUT
FEATHERING PROPELLER	MAX PORP		HAULOUT
GENOA ROLLER FURLER	PROFURL	SSMR	HAULOUT
FREEZER	GLACIER BAY		THRU HULL HAULOUT
WATER MAKER	SPECTRA		THRU HULL HAULOUT
SEWAGE PLANT	LECTRASAN		THRU HULL HAULOUT
HEATER OVERHAUL	ESPAR		THRU HULL HAULOUT
FORWARD SCAN SONAR	INTERPHASE		TRANSDUCER HAULOUT
ARCH		EMBREE WELDING	HAULOUT
AIS	SIMRAD A 150		ARCH ANTENNA MOUNT HAULOUT
WEATHER FAX	FURUNO		ARCH ANTENNA MOUNT HAULOUT
BACK-UP GPS	MAGNAVOX MX420		ARCH ANTENNA MOUNT HAULOUT
RADAR	FURUNO 36-MILE		MIZZEN MOUNT HAULOUT
SOLAR	KYOCERA		ARCH DESIGN MEASURE
WIND POWER	KISS		ARCH DESIGN MEASURE
C.A.R.D.	ANTENNA		ARCH DESIGN MEASURE
SSB RADIO	ICOM IC-M802	SSMR	BACK STAY INSULATORS HAULOUT
INTERNET & EMAILS	PACTOR III MODEM		POST HAULOUT
ELECTRONIC CHARTS	NOBELTEC ADMIRAL		POST HAULOUT
PAPER CHARTS	BLUE WATER BOOKS		POST HAULOUT
COMPASS	5' DANFORTH GLOBAL BALANCE		POST HAULOUT
HANDHELD GPS	STANDARD HORIZON HX280S		POST HAULOUT
HANDHELD VHF	GARMIN GPS 76		POST HAULOUT
ABANDON SHIP BAG	WEST MARINE		POST HAULOUT
REPLACE NECO	WH AUTOPILOT C-P3		POST HAULOUT
BATTERY BOX COVER			POST HAULOUT
EPIRB	WEST MARINE		POST HAULOUT
LIFE RAFT CERTIFICATION		USCG	POST HAULOUT
ANCHOR CHAIN & RODE		WEST MARING	POST HAULOUT
INJECTION REMOVE AND REPLACE		H DIESEL	POST HAULOUT
INJECTION PUMP OVERHAUL		SOUTH EAST POWER SYSTEMS	POST HAULOUT

Work plan

cabin mattress, and the hydraulic rams to the tiller arms. With those in place, I mounted the controller on a switch panel next to the steps from the saloon to the cockpit, secured the compass under the center saloon table, and bolted the master processor near the helm pump and the two motor pump processors next to the pump platform.

The completed arch held three solar panels, two wind generators, and antenna mounts for two GPS's, a collision avoidance radar detector (CARD), and a weather fax antenna, all integrated seamlessly with the arch as though the system was factory made. Side-mounted solar panels could be adjusted from a vertical stow position to face the sun. Adjustable concentric support tubes with holes to accept retaining pins held the panels in place. Instead of davits, a bow shaped apparatus would pivot over the transom from its upright stowed position behind the arch to hoist the RIB out of the water to prevent theft while at anchor.

The finished sail inventory included new number one and number two jibs and a storm sail that I called the number three, all of which would fly from the mainmast's inner stay tacked to a fitting on the foredeck aft of the anchor windlass. When I flew the larger number one jib on the inner stay it overlapped the main by 10 percent of the distance between the forestay tack and the main mast. The number two filled 100 percent of that distance. With the spinnaker pole held far out to the side while running downwind I could hold either jib firmly in place with a sheet run through the pole's end.

The main sheet ran from the boom down to a block attached to a car mounted on a track that ran across the cabin top forward of the hard dodger. From that car the sheet ran up to a single block under the boom, aft over the dodger to a block on the forward side of the mizzenmast, and down to a winch near the cockpit seat. While sailing, sheets controlling the jib, main, mizzen, and

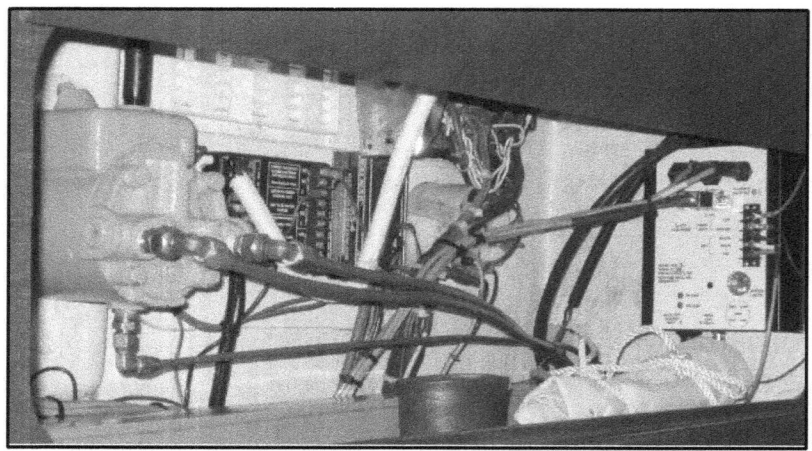
Capilano pump and WH master processor box installed

WH autopilot motors installed

WH autopilot steering cylinders and rudder position sensor installed

the preventers could be trimmed from sitting positions in the cockpit. When the sailing conditions were just right, I could fly any jib on a stay running from the mizzen top to a pad eye forward of the hard dodger, making four sails up.

By the time the new systems were installed my sights had lifted beyond island hopping in the Caribbean to exploring historic Pacific beaches that Cindy's dad had walked with the marines and visiting diverse societies I'd read about in my youth. During trials out in the Gulf of Mexico the rudder moved fast from lock to lock following commands made at the control head. The deployed solar panels and wind generators delivered twelve volt current to all systems, which functioned as designed: water pumps, desalinator, freezer, and sewage treatment plant. *Scooter* was ready to fulfill my dreams.

Back at the slip, I loaded Nobeltec Admiral electronic chart CDs for the world into the laptop, which received (GPS) data through a cable lead from the Leica GPS. I planned to order permit codes online to unlock charts for future passages as I made my way around the Pacific. The expense was worth being able to view a chart on the laptop, move the cursor toward land, and zoom in until a detailed harbor chart appeared. To maintain navigation skills, I wanted paper charts aboard onto which I could note noontime positions, course, and speed then project the next day's noon positions. Thinking about how to survive should all navigating electronics fail, I thought about buying a sextant after locating the textbook, notes, and blank charts I kept after taking a celestial navigation adult education course back in the California days with *Margetta*.

Wanting to hold the paper charts in my hands to decide which ones would work best before purchase, I drove to Bluewater Books and Charts in Fort Lauderdale. After an hour of wandering around scrutinizing my needs, I purchased *Atlas of Pilot Charts* of the North and South Pacific, North and South Atlantic, and the Indian Ocean; charts of the Panama Canal; Admiralty charts of approaches to Pacific islands; both volumes of the *Pacific Islands Pilot*, the *East African Pilot*, a sextant, and *Sight Reduction Tables for Air Navigation*.

Back aboard, I thought over the remaining time-consuming items on the list. Earlier in the year I paid off the ship's mortgage with house equity. Investment in quality vessel systems, maritime knowledge, and sailing skills replaced any need for an outrageously expensive ocean cruising insurance policy. However, I wanted to cover the possibility of passing the boat to the kids should I not survive the adventure. Cindy's name had to be removed from the document and replaced with those of the kids, making them co-owners. With that they would be able to sell the boat but would also be responsible for all owner expenses. With document

Arch with wind generators, solar panels, and antennas

Cockpit view from below

Storm jib on pole

application forms, last will and testament, and asset transfer directions in hand, I drove to have the kids sign and made sure they understood their responsibilities and the methods for seeing the boat to its next owner anywhere in the world should they choose.

The last open items got checked off the ocean preparation list. I girdled the recertified life raft with a sling and secured it on a shelf under the port cockpit seat. Should I ever want to abandon the boat, I would hook a staged block and tackle from the girdle to an eye on the hard dodger above, making the raft easy to hoist and deploy. The EPIRB registration and ship radio station authorization arrived in the marina mailroom. Voyagers Mail Forwarding in Islamorada, created by Seth Herman, a retired Caribbean cruiser, made an excellent home address for my Florida driver's license. A month later, Seth began holding all my incoming mail until I emailed where to send the package.

The age clock seemed to tick faster the closer I got to the big six zero. I wanted to enjoy living the dream while I was physically able, and the dream was not all about sailing the world's oceans solo. Eileen's words about finding companionship came back to me midway through that year as sweltering high noon heat ended the day's job early. I utilized the free time to explore the wonder of Internet dating. First dates, however, were pretentious profile disclosure encounters just like the old days before I met Cindy. With a handful of wasted hours relearning deceitful agendas, I decided to no longer be lured into cocktail hour marathons or escapeless dinner dates with women I would never see again and had an ah-ha moment.

I evaluated sincerity before the first date while seated on the Vinoy Hotel veranda where I had a clear view across the brick-paved valet parking area entrance from Fifth Avenue. To my left were the boats at the marina where I instructed sailing. Straight ahead, I looked over walkways in the grassy park. To my right, people strolled along the Beach Drive sidewalk. On late afternoons, while an overhead fan stirred warm air, I observed potential first dates following my directions to park across the street, walk across the Vinoy's brick driveway, climb the entrance steps to the veranda, and look to their left to find the guy in my profile. Two first dates who obviously lied about their physical fitness disqualified themselves as they approached the veranda and searched for me after I ducked inside and disappeared. Yet, I continued my scheme on the veranda hoping to witness sincerity.

Lynn mentioned on our first phone chat that she contracts with medical organizations, grew up in the Hamptons, never married, and enjoyed new adventures like her sail to Chaguaramas, Trinidad, with friends. From my past experience with a therapist, I enquired about what grad school she attended and when. I summarized my past, including where I grew up and graduated college. She knew as much about Wilmington and Newark, Delaware as I knew about the Hamptons and asked if my profile photo was current and other relevancies in mellow tones, vetting me. At sunset that Friday, we shared life stories while sipping wine and people-watching on the Vinoy veranda and planned to meet at 400 Beach Seafood & Tap House late Saturday afternoon. That dinner date included strolling along Beach Street to inspect menus at other restaurants while planning our Sunday lunch. I felt years younger while she held my elbow because she was years younger.

Sunday afternoon, standing next to *Scooter* propped up on jack stands at the yard, Lynn showed interest in seeing Patrick's house and how I was living. I had no inclination that she had anything else in mind while she followed me to the house. That changed when she hopped on the bed directly after entering the room. Momentarily surprised and full of respect for women lectured into me by Dad, I lingered next to the nightstand in the corner near the window not wanting her to think I would jump in bed with just anybody. She tapped next to her on the bed and said, "Come here; get comfortable; let's talk some." I was glad I habitually made the bed first thing every morning and propped up pillows, spun next to her side, and talked more about sailing the Caribbean. She followed my visions as I rolled through mental images of island cruising from Nassau down the Bahamas to the Turks and Caicos, Dominican Republic, the Virgin Islands, and the eastern Caribbean islands. I must have set the hook really good. She invited me for dinner at her apartment the next Friday and held me captive until midmorning.

Over time, boat projects got finished and we dated, doing all the things singles want to do as early as possible, and a sailing partner began to emerge. She found *Scooter's* galley workable and adapted to operating the manually pumped head and Lectrasan sewage treatment plant. Her vision of living aboard sharpened when I demonstrated how to sail *Scooter* on the bay and motor along the ICW to Boca Ciega Bay for an overnight, where she took her first cold water shower on deck. Not real cold, just in the low eighties, the temperature of the seawater surrounding the in-keel tank. We enjoyed watching the sunset from soft lounge chairs on the foredeck before retiring to listen to the wavelets crinkling against the hull. I knew it was serious when we drove to Arlington, Virginia, to introduce me to her sister and brother-in-law, both working across the river in some capacity they were very reluctant to talk about.

I introduced her to the advanced sailing modules not covered in the ASA class materials that I developed for those who wanted to learn more: anchor retrieval hand signals to be given from the bow to the helm person; VHF protocol; and, of great importance, the *Scooter* Mayday card, my guide to making a Mayday call, displayed under Lexan on the nav desktop. I walked her through frequency setting and the push-to-talk button on the side of the mic, what to say when initiating a call, and how to shift from channel sixteen to a working channel. Our lives could depend on her ability to make a call should I be disabled. She knew about the heart attack I had almost two years

Mizzen jib flying between main and mizzen

earlier, the stent that was installed in a coronary artery, and the meds I was taking. I had no lingering issues, and the cardiologist had cleared me to go, but there was always some risk. My intention was to help her avoid a situation similar to what occurred back in the *Margetta* days during Santa Ana winds off Ventura, California. I followed radio chatter revolving around a skipper who fell overboard trying to secure a dingy, leaving his novice companion frantically trying to call for help on the unfamiliar radio. Harbor patrol eventually rescued her while a helicopter searched for the guy. Lynn showed little interest in radio procedures and shied away from participating in sail set and trim at the time but easily handled the helm, following my anchor set and retrieval hand signals from the bow. I wondered about what role she actually played while sailing with friends and thought. Ok, she may have sailing skills to call on I have not seen. The thought that I could bring her to be a fully functional, independent crew persisted, and I resolved that a major part of my skippering responsibility would be to insure she had a good time while on board and during adventures ashore. It would be better than sailing alone.

Meal planning evolved from a magazine article about making a seven-day menu, defining breakfast, lunch, dinner, and snacks for each day. We thought out meals for one week, itemized individual meal components on an Excel spread sheet, and extended each item four times, giving us a planned inventory for one month's provisioning. More than an inventory sheet, it called out the full count, location on board, and items to be purchased at any time. A can of food would be subtracted from the full count when consumed, giving a number to purchase that would restore full inventory removing the need to dig through the saloon compartments to make a shopping list before going ashore. It would be a living document residing in the nav desk.

In late January of 2006, Lynn terminated her employment contract and sold her car to her sister. After overhauling the diesel injection pump, I had *Scooter* ready to sail, but my son, daughter, and her man friend wanted to drive down from Michigan for a send-off party. The kids arrived in the evening after driving all day and needed rest. We met for breakfast at the Lucky Dill Deli in downtown St. Petersburg to begin our celebration. At noon on Saturday, February 4th, after the morning dock line cutting ceremony, we waved good-bye, and the kids drove my minivan home.

Steady thirty-five-knot winds right out of the north drove *Scooter* down the bay to the mouth of the Manatee River, where I dropped sails and motored the narrow channel to anchor near Fort Desoto to begin an operating system shakedown routine. There, any needed repairs or overlooked supplies could be obtained nearby. It gave us time to adjust to not being able to jump off the boat for a shower or a snack at the marina restaurant and, for Lynn, time to continue growing her confidence.

Four days later, I hauled anchor to begin an overnight 157-mile sail to Key West. The WH autopilot held the course as I slept ninety minutes and Lynn managed her first watch rotation. The next morning, I furled sails and motored through a flock of crab pot floats on the way to the Northwest Channel to Key West. While I was focused on the floats Lynn came up the saloon steps. "This meter should be moving, adding minutes?" Between clusters of floats, I switched the autopilot on and saw that the engine hour meter's minute drum had stopped turning, noted

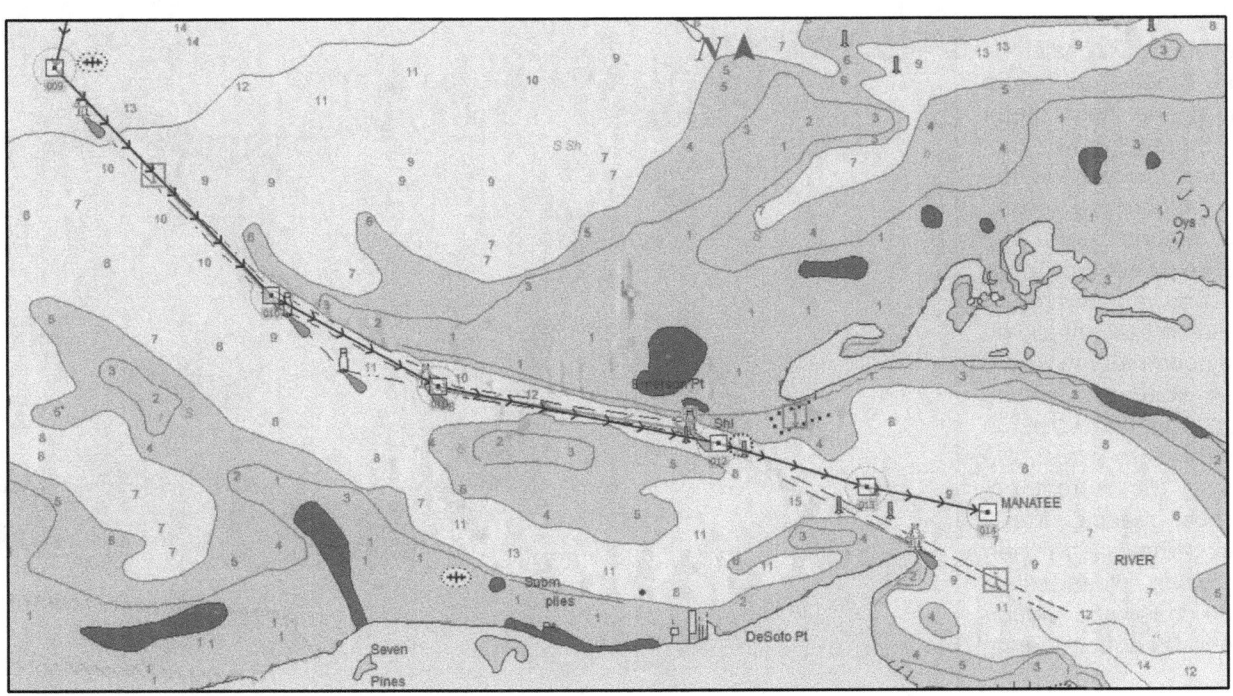

Anchored four nights on Manatee River

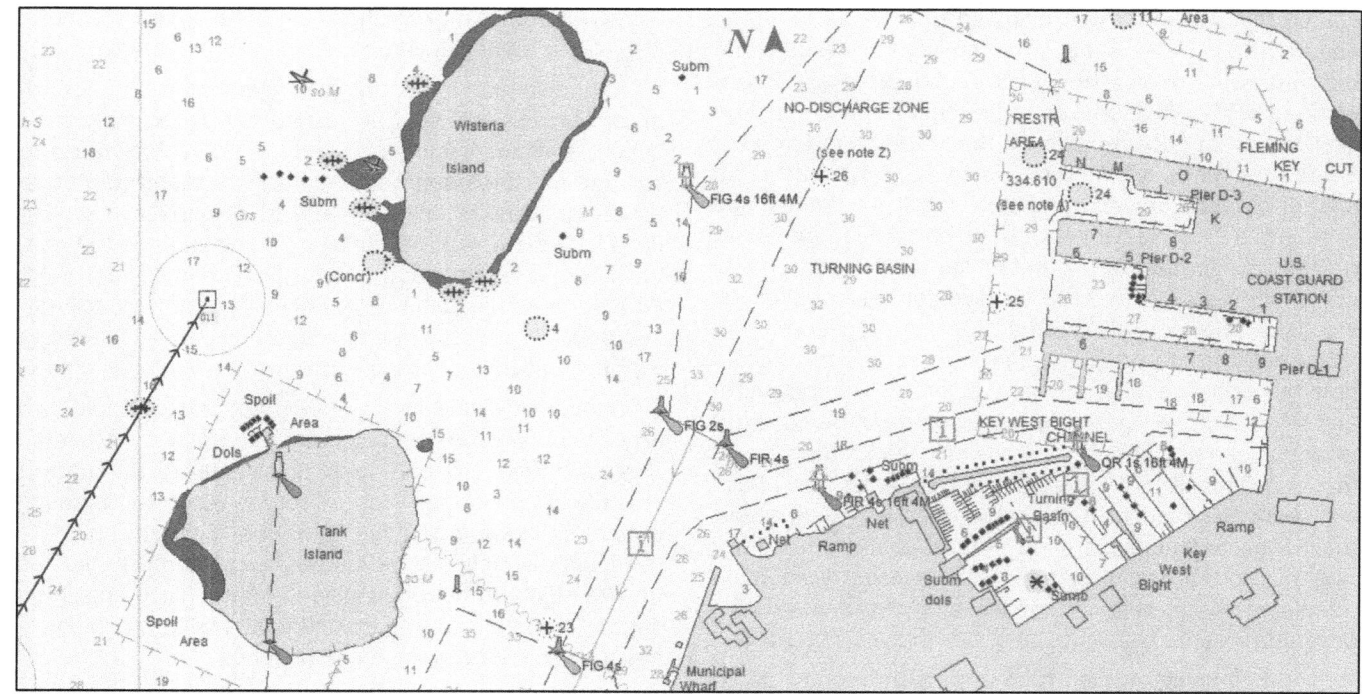

Key West Anchorage

the time and the location, on the laptop Nobeltec display, and returned to the helm. As I piloted Scooter down the channel to Key West, I was impressed with the accuracy of the new Leica GPS, placing the boat icon on the screen at the buoys and beacons as they passed.

At anchor off Wisteria Island, I measured twelve volts at the hour meter when the engine was running and condemned the meter. Ashore we looked for a marine store and some Key West fun. To my relief and amazement, I spotted an exact duplicate of the hour meter at an old marine store on Caroline Street. I made notes in the logbook to add 6,030 hours to the current engine hour reading after I replaced the failed meter. Cool days, clear skies, and no cruise ships made the four days of wandering about the island an enjoyable first stop on our sailing adventure.

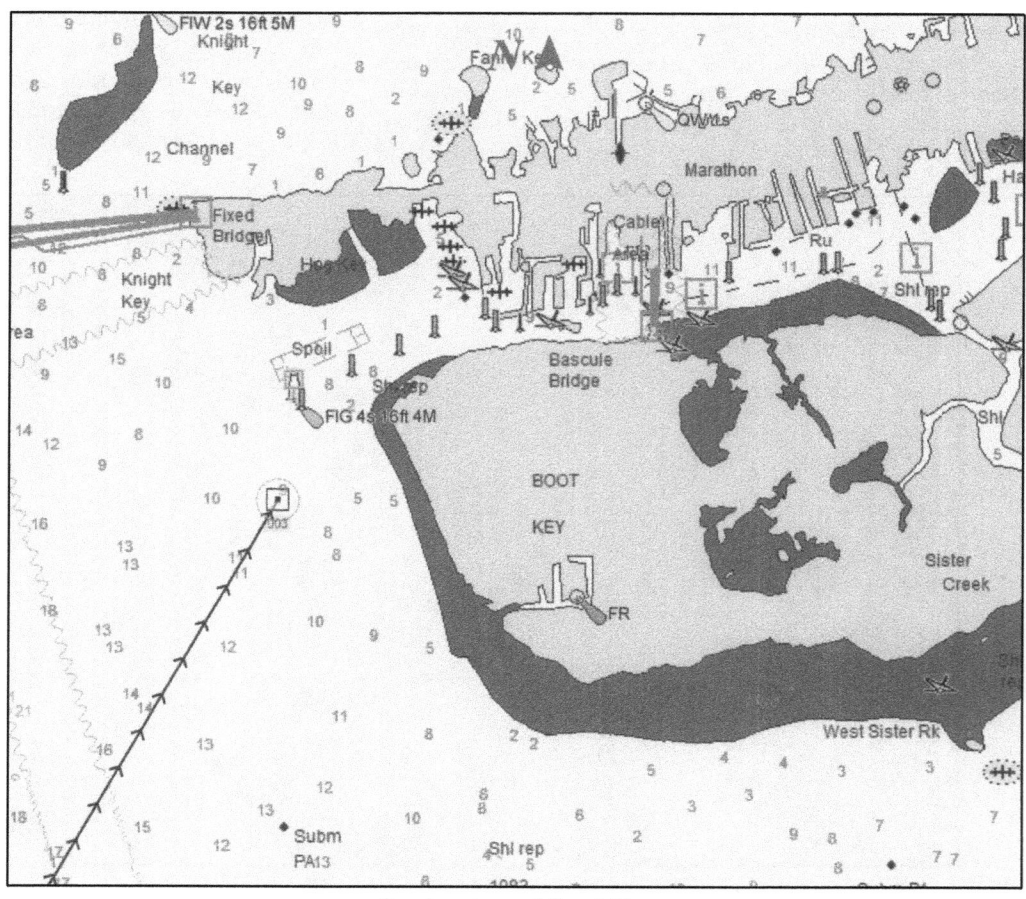

Anchorage at Boot Key

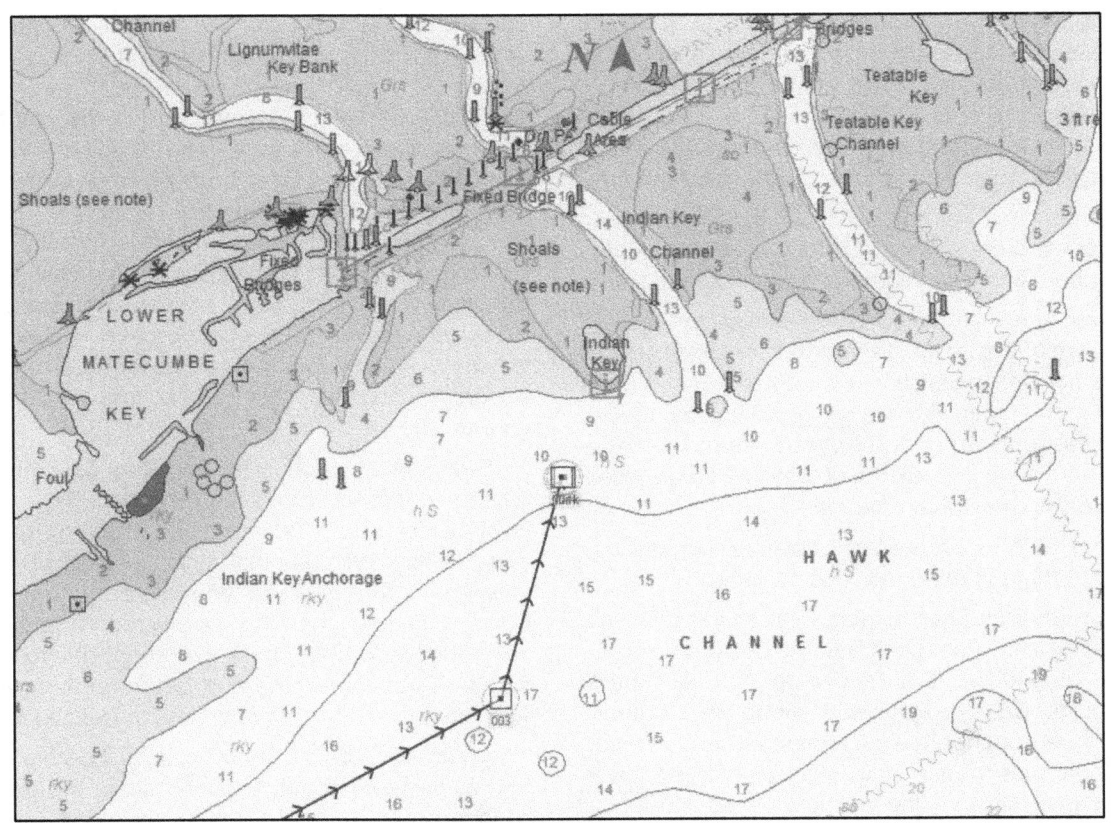
Anchorage at Indian Key

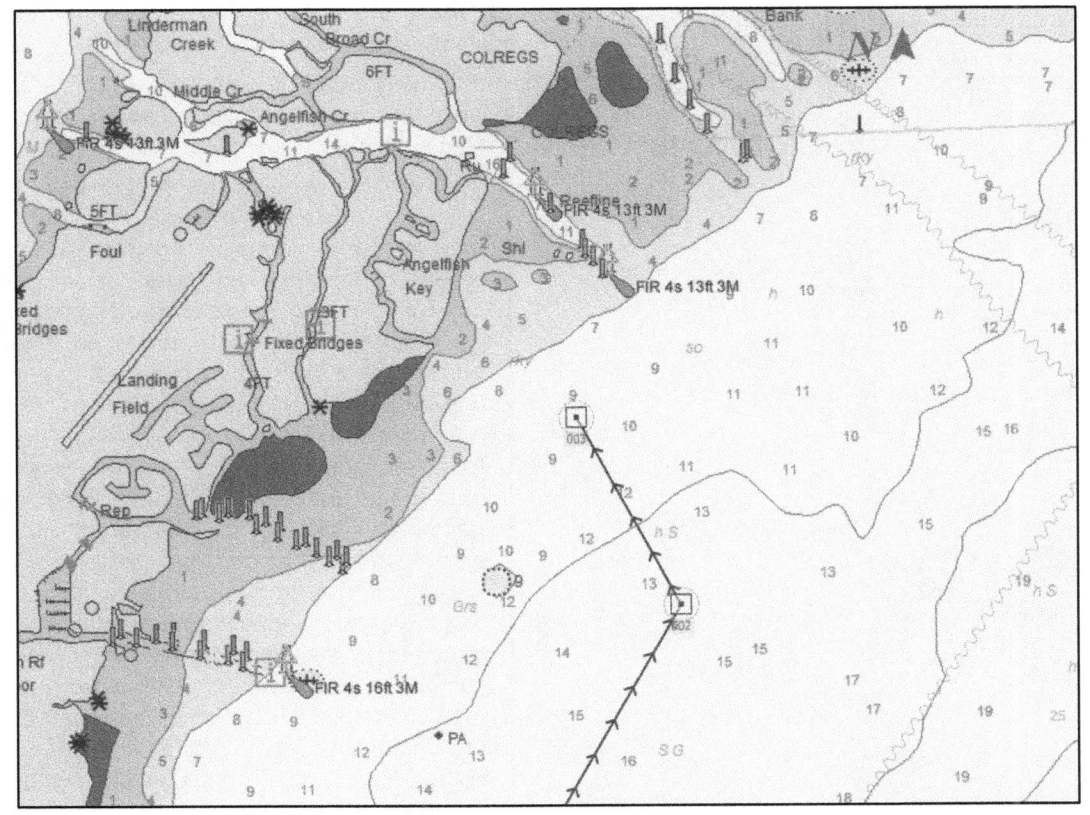
Anchorage at Angelfish Key

Recovery • 31

On the fourteenth, I motored *Scooter* away from the party town's anchorage and negotiated the shallow Hawk Channel north to Boot Key at the southern point of Marathon. I explained to Lynn the importance of monitoring the Nobeltec display for adequate water depth ahead while I watched the forward scanning sonar display at the helm.

The next morning, we motor sailed in light air to Indian Key. We spent two days riding *Jazz* to Lower Matecumbe Key to look about and wait for improved air from the south.

The air remained light. NOAA Weather Radio on the VHF called out more of the same. Six hours of motoring took us north to anchor off Angelfish Key south of a marked cut through the reef to open water. It was a perfect location to start the passage to Gun Cay, our entrance to the Bahamas. There at Angelfish Creek *Scooter* swung on the hook, positioned to sail away from America.

Two hours before sunrise Lynn asked, "Are sure you want to go out there in the dark? Over the reef?"

Pointing to the Nobeltec display, I eased her fear. "It's the same as daylight. Just can't see the bottom when we sail over the ground track." I stepped up to the cockpit to start the engine. On my way forward along the starboard deck I continued anchor-hoisting training. "You can see me at the bow with the steaming light on, so just follow my hand signals. We'll be fine." With big eyes, she stood in front of the helm seat gripping the wheel, watching me hoist the anchor. I piloted *Scooter's* icon through the reef cut on the laptop screen to open sea, the first hazardous navigating with Nobeltec Admiral in darkness. From sunup to late afternoon, we sailed *Scooter* slightly north or south of the plotted diagonal ground track across the Straits of Florida to pass between Gun Cay and North Cat Cay in the Bahamas. Sailing north of the ground track at the time of approach, we watched a cay rise from the sea, a speck on the horizon at first. As we sailed, the cay grew wider at the horizon then another speck grew from the sea to its south. With the sails down, I motored *Scooter* on the Nobeltec ground track to the plotted passage between the cays. Worried moments passed until, about two miles from the pass on the Nobeltec chart, I could see clear water flanked by sandy beaches and cautiously piloted *Scooter* forward, keeping her icon moving along the chart ground track.

Swinging at anchor behind Gun Cay that night we planned our route across the very shallow Great Bahamas Bank, which would require close attention to the laptop and the forward scanning sonar. Instead of dangerously sailing in water with only centimeters under the keel at times, I followed the safe water ground track plotted on the Nobeltec for a ten-hour motorboat ride to a spot deep enough to anchor and swing in the currents at low tide. We'd be in position for a short sail to Nassau the next day.

A stiff breeze met us at Nassau harbor. My attempt to anchor resulted in dragging it along the bottom until I hollered from the bow, "This isn't working," while Lynn at the helm seat looked in the direction we were drifting. "The guidebook must be right, the bottom is hard," I shouted

"Yeah, and if that's right, full of junk too," she said, bringing up speed to turn into the wind.

Not wanting to hook a piece of hundred-year-old history as *Scooter* slipped sideways to the wind, I said, "Let's roll it up."

We hand signaled the anchor back into the bow roller, motored past the cruise port, under two bridges, and tied at the Nassau Yacht Haven fuel dock. The yellow quarantine flag flying under the Bahamas courtesy flag below the starboard spreader announced we required clearing in, and in no time a customs official boarded. Clearing-in formalities varied among International Maritime Organization (IMO) nations. Some are stringent and some are lax. The procedure is to vet all people aboard, review the vessel's nation-of-origin documents, inspect for restricted or quarantined items, and assess the health of all aboard. The greater the restrictions the greater are the possible pitfalls for the cruiser. Some customs, immigration, and quarantine administrators manage the process in a formal, dignified manner, while others are more casual. Some use their immense power to coerce and manipulate less seasoned or unprepared cruisers and international political agendas are occasionally at play. When departing an IMO nation, clearing out formalities include passport stamping, completing a form identifying the nations that are planned to be visited

Gun Cay Anchorage

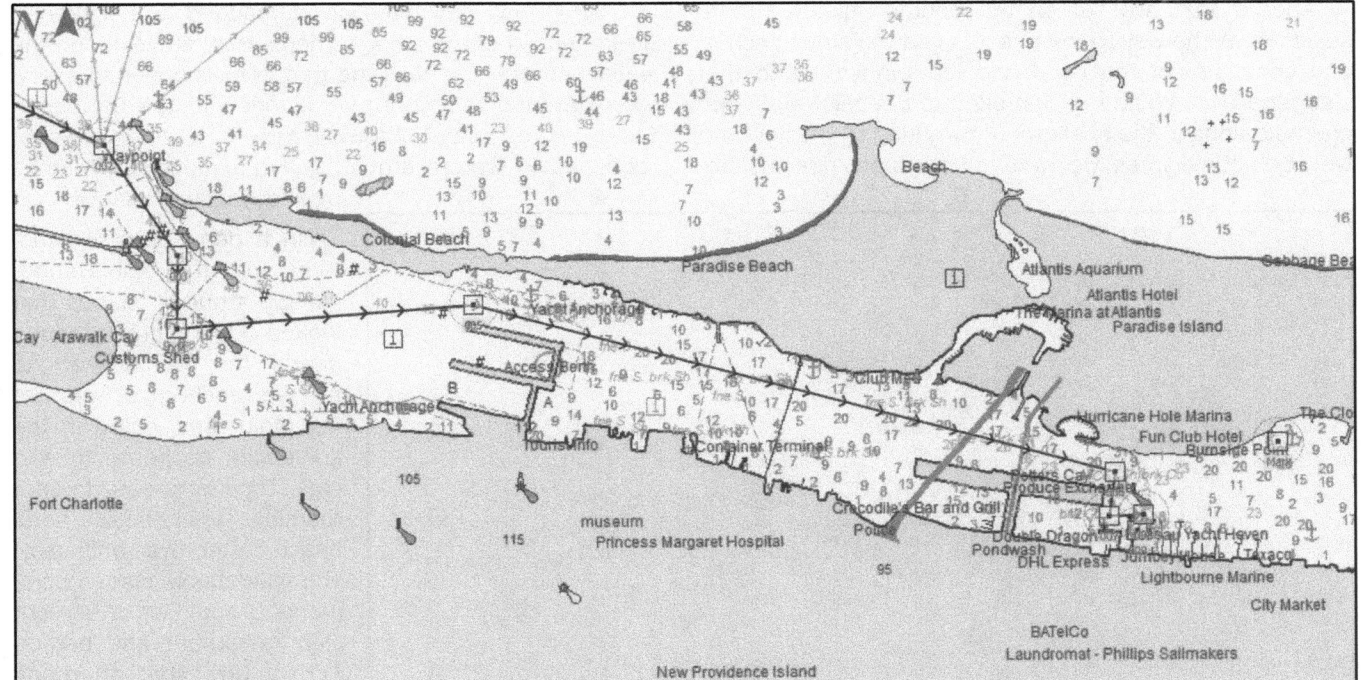

Nassau Harbor

on future legs of the voyage, and receiving a Certificate of Clearance, a document stating that the vessel is approved to leave the country. Those forms are required at the next nation as part of that nation's clearing-in process. Prior to departing the current nation, a prudent skipper would ensure that he or she understood the arrival formalities at the destination nation to avoid being held accountable in some unpleasant way along with all aboard.

At the end of the process, we had Bahamas Immigration Arrival Cards and a temporary cruising permit with a fishing license. My understanding was that I did not need to physically clear out of the Bahamas at a customs office if *Scooter* was out of the Bahamas in three months. I paid the three-hundred-dollar fee and moved *Scooter* to a slip with the stern facing the stiff breeze.

My longtime weather station of choice back in St. Pete had been the SSB broadcasts of the Marine Weather Center by Chris Parker. While walking the Nassau docks in the breeze, I met an experienced Caribbean cruiser and learned about Buoyweather.com. I could log on anywhere in the world through the PACTOR modem to the SSB radio. I grew my confidence in Buoyweather's system by comparing forecasts with Parker's.

We explored Nassau streets until the wind fell to a whisper, and I could back *Scooter* out of the slip. Seven hours of motoring brought us to Highborne Cay, forty miles south, for what I hoped to be our first playtime swimming off the boarding ladder in crystal clear water. The anchor set right away, and I walked aft to swing the ladder down saying, "Let's jump in right now."

"I'mmmm . . . not . . . sure about swimming here."

Surprised, I looked up at her while standing knee deep on the bottom step. "Really?"

"Can we go to the beach and walk?"

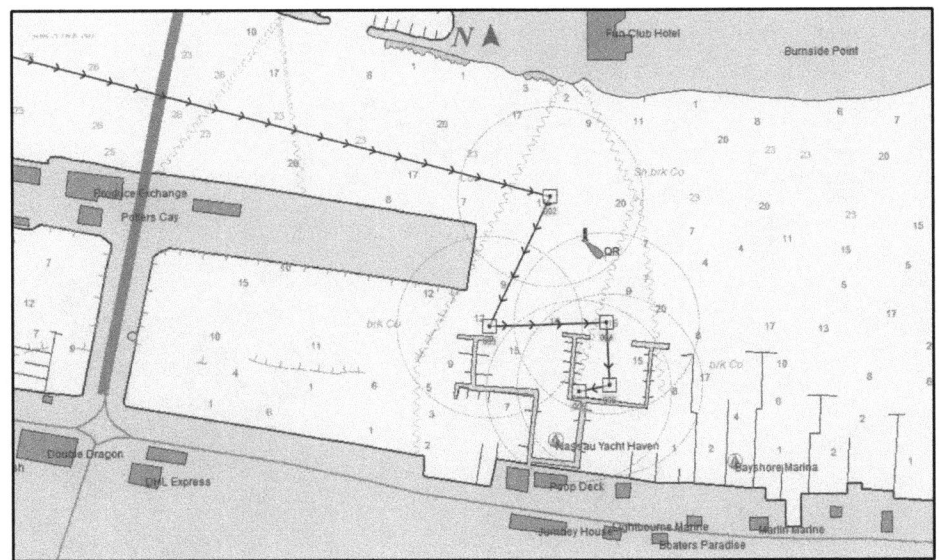

Nassau Yacht Haven

Recovery • 33

Aboard *Jazz*, we sat on the pontoon sides getting splashed all the way to the beach. I laid the small anchor and chain up on the sand and led Lynn out into the clear shallows. While I backstroked to deeper water, she crabbed along in the shallows not wanting to get her hair wet. Sometime later, we watched a couple ride fast to the beach while standing on their RIB. It looked like an excellent way to ride *Jazz* ashore without getting wet. Back aboard, I pulled a section of PVC tubing from the spare parts inventory left over from the massive refit. With little modification, I attached it to the motor's throttle control at the end of the tiller handle, and we gave it a try. Lynn stood forward of me holding the painter while I gripped the PVC tube extension with my left hand, wrapped my right arm around her waist, and asked if she was ready. When she nodded, I said, "Set . . . go," and twisted the tube. The Mercury, with a hydrofoil mounted above the prop, revved, and *Jazz* jumped on top of the water in a few heartbeats. With two days of practice standing while zipping to and from the wide white beach we were capable enough to arrive ashore in dry attire.

Living that new lifestyle demanded a heightened awareness of surroundings wherever we traveled, on the water and ashore. Realizing that crime happened everywhere around the world, we listened to the Caribbean Safety and Security Net (CSSN) daily for updates on yacht robberies in waters around island nations and crimes against yachties ashore.

In a dead calm, we motored forty-four miles south along a string of islands that looked like green-topped pearls on the horizon to a safe anchorage west of Big Major Cay, noted in the guidebook as home to wild pigs. They were easy to spot roaming the bright sand beach after we anchored. The guidebook also recommended sampling the yacht club restaurant and bar on Staniel Cay. That afternoon we stood on *Jazz* dressed in island dinner attire of shorts, golf shirt, and flip-flops as we zipped around the western tip of the island and crossed a flatwater bay to the yacht club dock. I locked *Jazz* to the dinghy dock, and we climbed the steps to the clubhouse to find the bar. I knew *Jazz* would be safe as it looked old and weathered with faded-looking Sunbrella covers not shouting that *Scooter* had been left unattended.

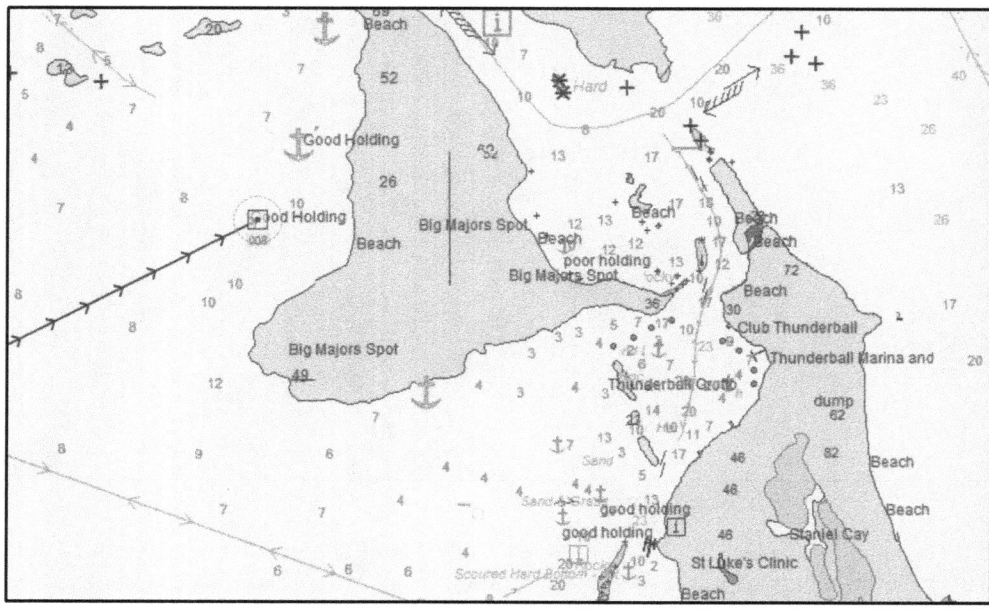
Big Major

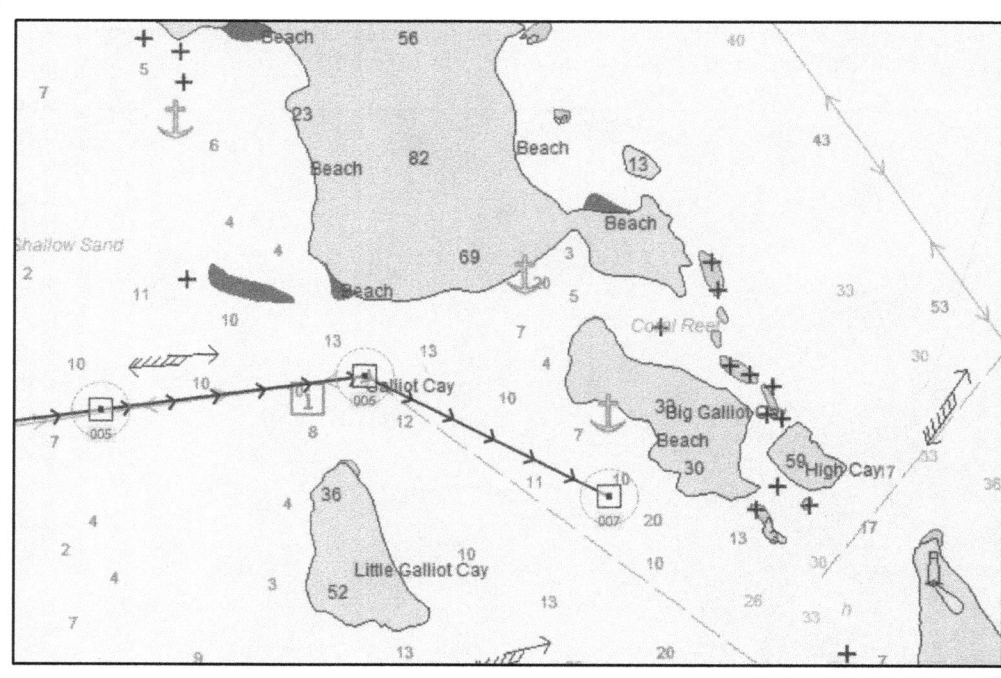
Anchorage at Big Galliot Cay

Most RIBs and dinghies seen had *Tender to Myboat* scrolled on the transom or side pontoons, clearly announcing to nefarious individuals that perhaps the yacht named *Myboat* was unoccupied. The newer the RIB and outboard appeared, the more likely it would be a theft target, not just in the Caribbean but anywhere on the planet. Earlier at Patrick's house, to dissuade theft, I removed the Mercury decals from the outboard and spray painted it light blue, making it look as though it had been in the sun for years. Wisps of red paint added a touch of rust. When mounted on *Jazz*, a special outboard motor lock inhibited removal. A clear plastic-coated six-millimeter stainless steel cable with swaged loops at each end became a security painter with one end locked to a pad eye on the inside hull at the bow and the other end locked to a dock cleat or whatever secure place that could be found. It would not be an easy RIB to steal if someone actually wanted what looked like a rusted outboard on a patched up, ratty old dingy.

When the weather cleared, I decided to head south to George Town on Great Exuma, part of the Bahamas. To break up the distance we anchored at Big Galliot Cay and sipped wine while a light breeze played with our hair as we sat on the foredeck enjoying a pink sunset.

After breakfast, I motored *Scooter* out the narrow passage between the islands, headed into the wind, and set the autopilot. I stepped up to the side deck intending to hoist the main sail and called out, "Lynn, come on up with me, and I'll show you how this is done."

"It's ok. I'll watch from here. It's a beautiful morning."

"Well, now's a good time to learn up close."

"All right. I'll do it. Watch me."

I thought that the fresh breeze was more than what Lynn had experienced before and had caused her to shy from helping. With the main up, I hoisted the mizzen, clicked the autopilot to course, rolled out the genoa, then rigged the mizzen staysail. What a sight, *Scooter* flying four sails with true wind over the starboard hip at nineteen knots. Holding a port list of only two degrees, she slashed over the waves, sometimes at over eight knots. It felt like riding a Greyhound bus doing seventy on the freeway.

Lynn continued to put off sail handling. Seven hours later we entered Great Exuma's harbor and motored around looking for a place to anchor among a fleet of sailing yachts. It happened to be race week, an annual event off Regatta Point. Lynn and I joined the crowd ashore on the large bleachers swarmed with spectators near the race committee towers, where the race officials presided over 450 entrants.

Post-race bar hopping put us in such good spirits that breakfast time came late. Midday, under heavy clouds, instant high wind and rain blew in from a surprise thunderstorm that Chris Parker called a "squall," and *Scooter* began to drift sideways to the wind, announcing

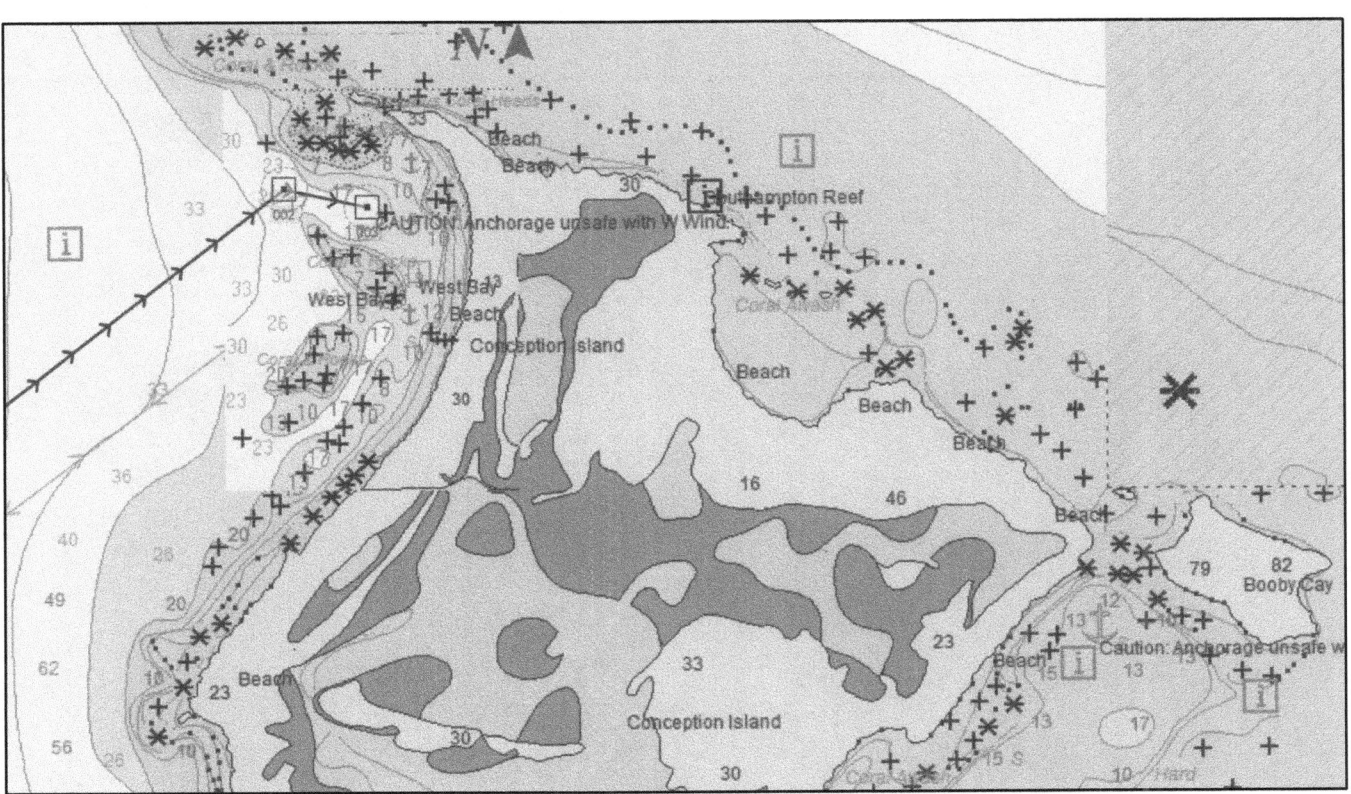

Conception Island anchorage

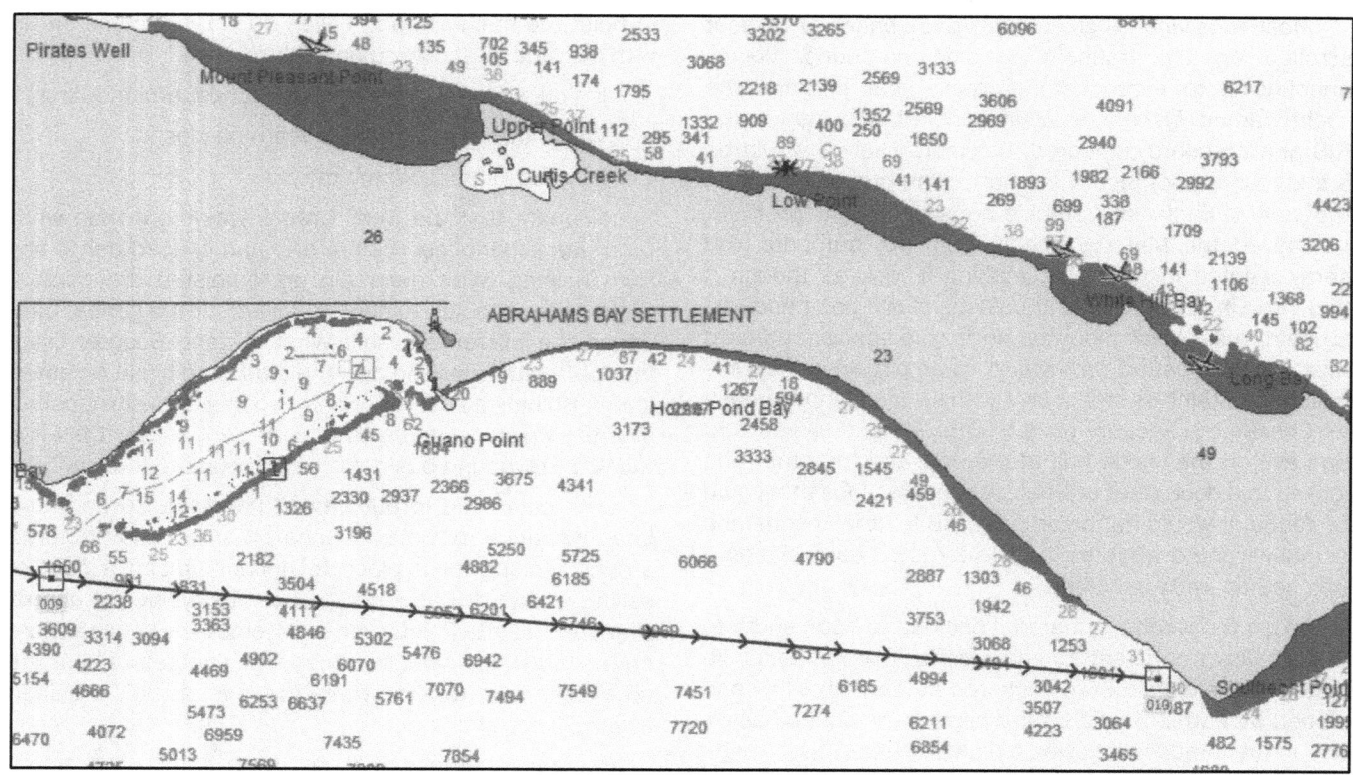

Mayaguana anchorage

the sixty-pound plow anchor had broken free of the bottom. It was dumb anchoring. Not enough scope. I turned the key, always in the ignition when aboard, to heat for a few seconds then to start. Mr. Stink, the Perkins 4-154 diesel engine that had earned that name, came to life, and I called Lynn to take the helm. She turned Scooter into the wind, holding her in place. I rushed forward, pulled the chain stopper pin to let the chain run free, opened the port

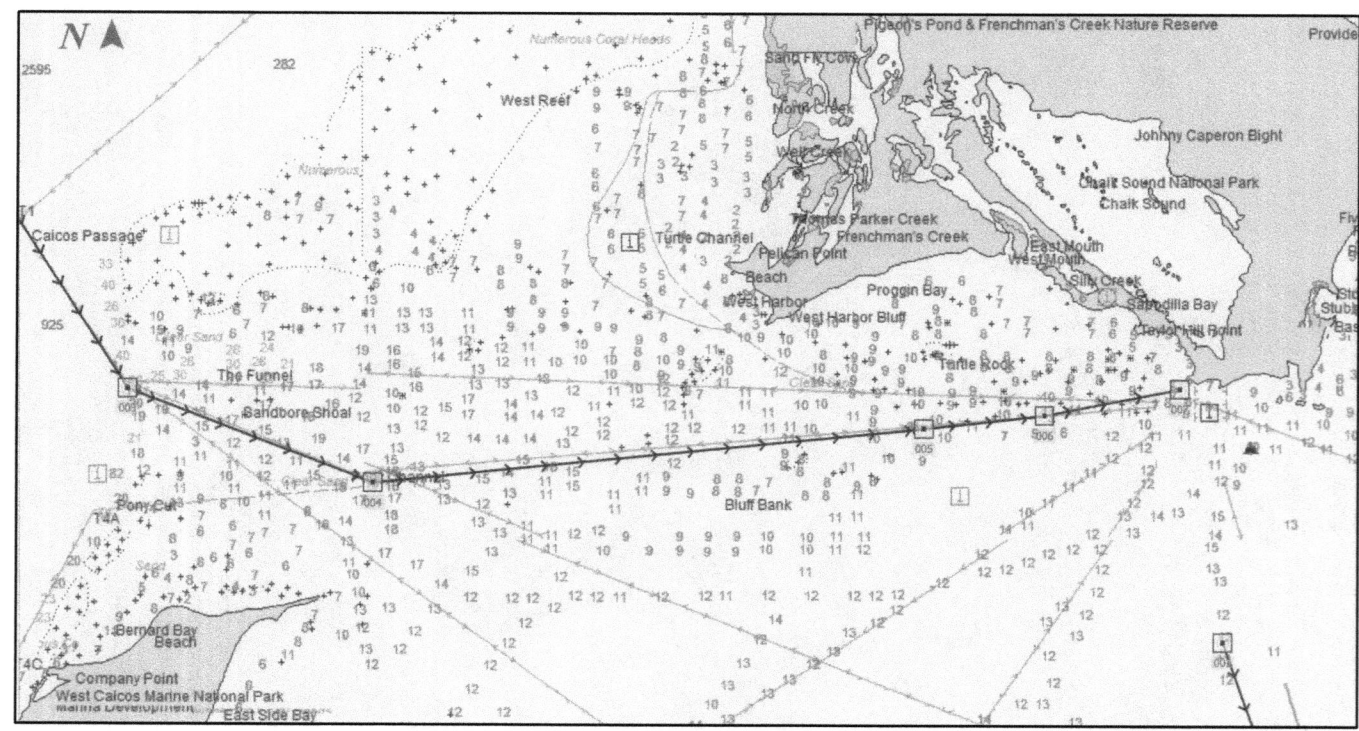

Arriving Sapodilla

36 • *Ocean Speed*

bow lazarette, grabbed the end of a staged anchor chain, attached it to the forty-five-pound plow on the port bow roller, pushed the anchor out, and paid out chain hand over hand. Lynn eased off the throttle, and *Scooter* drifted broadside until both anchors bit the bottom with a good length of chain. Five o'clock came early that afternoon.

Race week party time ranged from George Town bars to beach barbeque gatherings. One beach crowd I spotted with the long eyes, my slang for the Fujinon binoculars, raised enough curiosity for Lynn to accompany me on the adventure. After beaching *Jazz*, we blended with cruising couples meeting and greeting for the first time or reliving past encounters. RIBs and dinghies lined the beach. Smoke drifted in the breeze from a fire heating a grill in a stone-surrounded pit. I felt at ease chatting with others in the cruising life, while Lynn withdrew, saying little until a woman stepped off the bow of a large RIB being held close to the water's edge by two guys in white shirts and khaki cargo shorts, looking to be crew from the super yacht anchored in the harbor. The woman said hello to Lynn, speaking softly, selecting her words decisively. We learned during the chat that it was her yacht that sparkled lights the full length below the waterline after sunset. She and Lynn must have attended the same schools, I thought as I stood by following their conversation. We milled around watching cruisers party for an hour until Lynn wanted to return to the boat and relax before dinner. The next day I was the only solo cruiser chatting it up with the beach crowd, explaining that Lynn was resting after a morning shopping trip.

Chris Parker predicted manageable air for a day sail northeast around Cape Santa Maria at the northern end of Long Island to Conception Island, where I hoped to find more shallow water for play and explore another beach. Again, Lynn begged off helping with sail hoisting and trimming. After we set the anchor, she watched me swim around inspecting *Scooter's* bottom.

To be south of historical tropical storm waters by June, I planned to sail directly to Mayaguana, bypassing many islands that could be visited another time. Zooming into the Nobeltec chart area near shore on the southeast corner of the island, I spotted water shallow enough to anchor and marked it with an anchor icon. At noon, after the first overnight Caribbean sail of 170 miles on a moonlit sea, I slipped the plow in where the boat icon hovered over the anchor icon.

We hauled the anchor one minute after midnight to make the fifty-mile sail south to the Turks and Caicos, where I had to negotiate the coral-strewn passage through the shallows at the east end of the Caicos Bank. While the autopilot held *Scooter* on course in light air, I again asked Lynn to wake me from my ninety-minute nap if the wind picked up or fell off, knowing that she had no idea how to trim sails, having always put off training to some other day. At 1030 we negotiated the east end of the Caicos Bank and anchored in Sapodilla Bay in the south of Providenciales, one of the islands of the Turks and Caicos. Lynn softly spoke about how the sharp green of the island played against the turquoise and blue of the wide, shallow bank. The sight was worth every minute of sailing to get there. We were tired from the long night's sail but prepped anyway to go ashore to clear in with customs.

I zigged *Jazz* around hawsers strung from cement pylons up to a ship towering overhead, then with the motor tipped up to avoid prop damage, and zagged around old tires coated with green scum in shallow water. *Jazz* scraped the rocky bottom as we approached a steep hill littered with chunks of shattered cement pavement slabs. Lynn stepped out to hold *Jazz* in the shallows while I waded toward the cement pile. With the shore bag slung over my shoulder, I climbed up the hill of fractured cement and strolled around rusted I beams, wrecked boats, and damaged shipping containers. Between large tractors rumbling by I glimpsed a sign reading "Customs Office" over a door on the side of a two-story building.

Stomping most of the wet, sandy mud off my sandals, I opened the door that had the notice "Don't let the door slam" taped to its window. It took some effort to overpower the strong spring and ease the door closed once inside. No one greeted me in the office littered with files; ragged, yellow out-of-date auto appraisal guides; and manila folders labeled with ship names. A movie played on a small, flat computer screen over in the corner. I waited, called, went behind the counter, looked around a back room, saw no one, and walked out the front door that no one but me heard slam.

Around the side of the unpainted cinder block building, I found an open door leading to a stairway with slick tile steps, new handrails, and unpainted drywall. At the stair top, unpainted doors without doorknobs opened into semifinished rooms filled wall to wall with large buckets, paper scraps, and construction stuff. A woman's voice drifted through the unfinished window. I went back down the slippery tile steps and around to the truck entrance where I saw a group of men and a woman near a shiny new pickup truck. They were discussing important business by the looks on their faces and their body language. A tall guy with a glistening medallion hanging from a chain around his neck held a clipboard. Of the group, he looked to be the one in charge. I told him who I was and why I was there and followed him into the office with the door that slammed. He gave me forms to complete. It was ok if I filled out Lynn's forms and signed them for her. Twenty-eight US dollars got both of us seven days on the island, but the passports had to be stamped at an office in town. We thought it was risky to leave *Jazz* unlocked on the rocks while wandering about town and returned aboard to plan the ground track across the Caicos Bank to the east side of the island, where we could visit another office to finalize clearing in.

Choices

Crossing the shallow bank would not be dangerous if I kept *Scooter* on the dotted line displayed on the laptop identifying safe water. Otherwise, the keel could hit any one of the many large rocks littering the bottom. Ten hours of slow motoring along the track led us to open water, where we turned north past Long Cay then west to anchor at Cockburn Harbor off South Caicos Island. The laptop chart showed adequate water in the swing radius around the anchor that quickly set. The next morning, we zipped in to visit the immigration office for passport stamping and wandered around until noon.

A dive flag icon and the note, "the Admiral's Aquarium," drew my interest on the laptop chart. I called Lynn to see the chart and the shallow depth markings, but she continued to show no interest in deciphering the screen display. Looking over the aquarium with the long eyes, a constant tone of shimmering aqua water all the way to the beach came into view. I coaxed Lynn into visiting the area with me to see what it was all about. "Come on with me. I'll bring an extra mask if you want to explore the bottom or just stay on *Jazz* and watch."

In chest-deep clear water, I lowered the anchor onto sand, slid over the side, cleared my mask, and stroked forward to see an infinite number of brightly colored small fish hovering in the shadows of headstone like slabs placed upright on the brilliant sandy bottom. It looked like an aquarium all right, and it stretched as far as I could see. Reporting the discovery to Lynn, I excited her enough to slip over the side. We snorkeled over grave marker slabs and elkhorn coral patches, seeing schools of small fish darting about. Getting aboard *Jazz* was easier than I thought it would be after I found a shallow spot. Lynn stood on the bottom, jumped up onto the side pontoon, swung a leg over and rolled into the boat.

"Now, wasn't that easy?" I said.

"Oh sure," she said, squirming around to sit on the side pontoon.

Clearing out was as easy as clearing in. The officer stamped our passports and departure documents after I promised to sail for the Dominican Republic the next night from Big Sand Cay. Approaching the cay, about a mile from its white sand beach, a vertical wall rose from the dark blue sea to a sandy plateau in the crystal-clear water creating the illusion of *Scooter* flying over a tall city building. I dove to inspect the bottom after Lynn again softly stated her disinterest in swimming off the boarding ladder. For me, checking the bottom was an excuse to free dive down to grab a handful of bottom sand and fix another

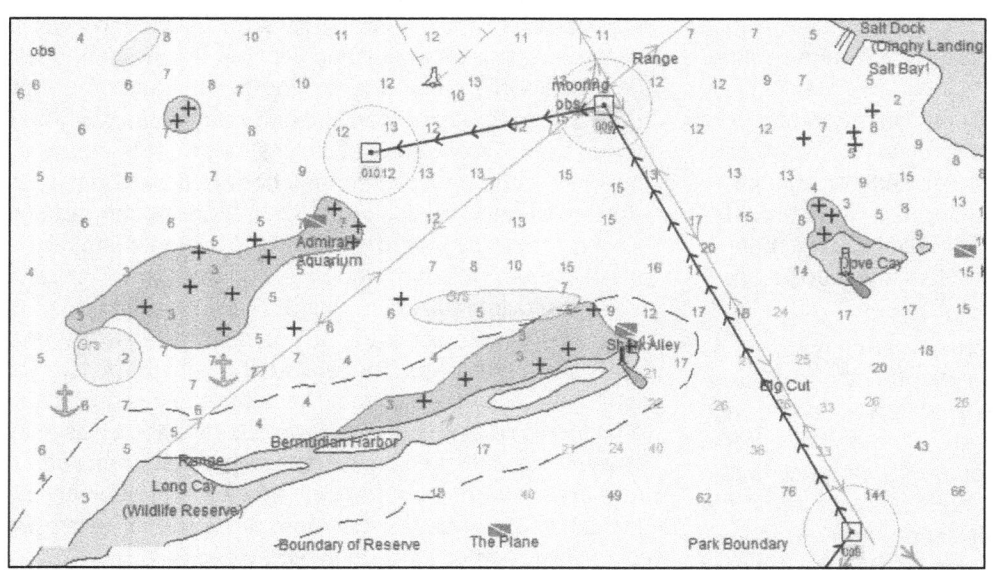

Admiral's Aquarium

memory of looking up at *Scooter's* hull suspended above in the brilliant aqua light.

Lynn whipped up another super meal in her galley paradise before sunset. That night I had *Scooter* sailing on a beam reach with full genoa, main, and mizzen in nineteen knots of air right out of the east, running down the eighty-mile ground track to the Dominican Republic. It seemed as though *Scooter* wanted to leap off wave crests while surging over eight knots at times. Cannonades of florescent sea critters fired to port and starboard in the bow spray. Sweeping past the center cockpit fast, they joined the wake in the moonlit, iridescent waters astern. With my heightened sailing confidence after night sails and weeks of skinny water passages, I yelled out, "Yeah!" in excitement as Lynn slept, not feeling well.

On the approach to the entrance of Bahía de Luperón, a voice on VHF channel sixteen advised to shift to another frequency for the harbor morning report. The net controller announced that 160 boats occupied the bay and read a brief weather and local news report. A small boat waiting outside the shallow bay entrance came alongside. Its operator offered to guide me into the bay after he told me about the fuel and watering service he could provide.

Motoring in the slightly deeper bay past a few anchored sailing yachts, a female voice boomed from the VHF speaker, "Sailing yacht *Scooter*, find a place in the group, ease your anchor into the muck, back off easy, and let the anchor sink in. If you try to set the anchor, it'll only plow a furrow in the bottom surface slime."

I responded with, "Roger. *Scooter* standing by, one six." Soon after finding space to swing, I had the anchor sinking into the bottom muck and rolled out chain as a light breeze laced with a faint sewer odor drifted *Scooter* astern. When it appeared as though the ground tackle was holding, I let out more chain and began to organize the foredeck.

No more than five minutes after locking the chain stopper, an outboard motorboat approached the port side. A uniformed officer with highly polished black shoes and shiny black belt stood on a seat in the center of the boat. He climbed over the port rail without asking permission, followed by a gaggle of civilian-clothed companions all wearing leather street shoes. They slid around the saloon table, opened notebooks, asked questions, and made entries with stern faces. A civilian-clothed man asked if I had gums.

"Gums? You want gum?"

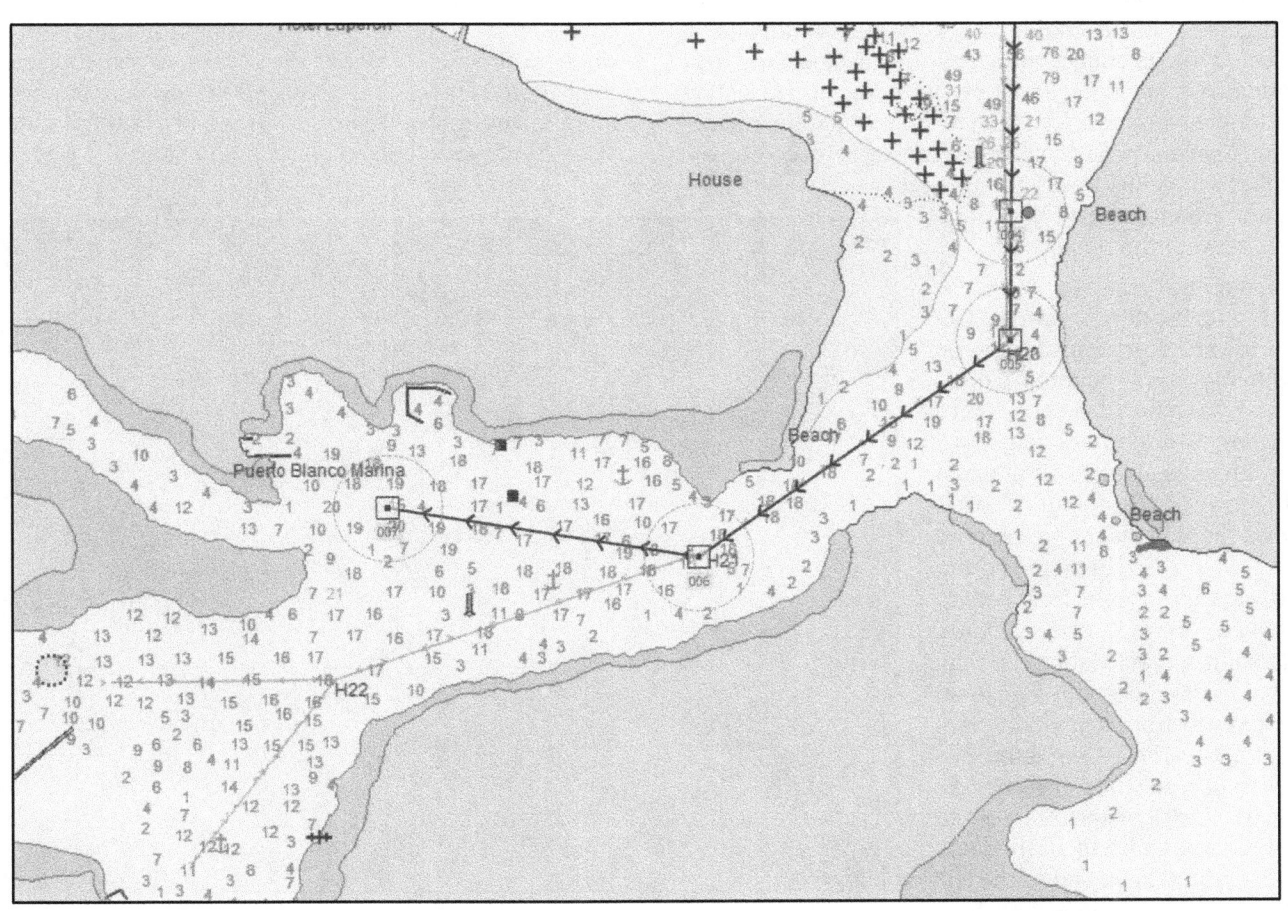

Luperón Bay

Luperón Yacht Club

He made a gesture with his finger and thumb. "Si. You have gums?"

"Oh, guns! No guns."

While that played out, one explored the aft cabin and returned to join the group around the saloon table. No one opened lockers, saloon cabinets, or drawers. They made their notes from passports and vessel documents, collected ten US dollars, and departed, leaving papers that required further processing by the port captain ashore. We launched *Jazz* and idled to a partially submerged, floating government dock, finding enough space between semirotted planks to slip the wire painter around, loop it back, and secure it with the padlock.

From the rickety dock we strolled up the narrow Avenida Duarte toward the town of Luperón and found the port captain's quarters at the end of a long, uphill walkway. Two men in camouflage army fatigues at loose parade rest with worn M-16s stared straight as we approached and entered the house. In a back room, the port captain, attired in a heavily starched and pressed uniform, spit shined black leather boots, and a highly polished wide belt, greeted us from behind a dark wood desk. The silver-plated pistol with carved white grips held in a shiny black holster attached to his belt screamed to be noticed. Rows of ribbons plastered the left side of his tunic, more than I expected to see in that small Caribbean state. Stars adorned his shoulders and tunic collars, and shiny pins glistened on his right tunic pocket. Unaware of the nation's engagement in that many military actions I wondered if the ribbons and medals were for good conduct, best dressed officer, highest boot shine, or parade participation or if they were power projection trinkets collected after the American military's involvement in 1965. He stamped the papers given to us by the boarding party, asked casual questions, collected ten dollars each, and directed me to take the forms to the office in the trailer across the Avenida down the hill.

I opened a screen door at the top of three wood steps on the side of a mobile trailer sitting on cinder blocks. Inside we faced a windowless office with a fan in a corner up near the ceiling blowing urine-laced air over a uniformed officer seated behind a small wood desk. We started the clearing in process by paying twenty-five dollars each before he stamped the papers. Business finished with him when he directed us to take the papers, to our relief, out of the odiferous office and through a narrow door to another room in the trailer. There, an assembly of three men in street clothes sat behind desks in the heat. The first desk

Luperón Yacht Club bar

Luperón harbor from the Yacht Club

worker presented us with tourist cards costing ten dollars each that we had to sign, have stamped by the uniformed officer back in the odor-laden room, and dropped into a locked wooden box marked "Tourist." Returning to the larger office, we approached the second desk, where our passports were again examined and papers restamped. That worker stroked our names at the bottom of a page full of names after collecting a ten-dollar registration fee each and then stamped our papers. At the last desk, in front of the exit door, I paid twenty dollars for vessel clearing-in approval. On the way out he said the agriculture agents would visit to check vegetables around 4:00 p.m. Happy that the cruising guide cautioned about the cash-demanding clearing-in process, I knew we would be ready, but first we had to explore the town.

We strolled past open entrances of wood and cinder block dwellings. The old buildings housed sofas and beds clearly visible from the street through open doors. Small rooms contained all the accumulated possessions of a lifetime. Interiors were neat, beds made, floors swept. Some women had infants on their laps but were not smiling in the heat. Dogs moved their emaciated bodies slowly from shade to shade. Seniors chewed the noon meal, some it seemed only with their gums. *Motoconchos*, small motorbikes, buzzed riders everywhere. Through a window under the sign "Banco" on the side of a building, I processed currency from my credit card for Dominican pesos.

Roaming about the town we came upon Captain Steve's, an open-air cement-floor market with tables and chairs on a patio overlooking the street. In the light breeze, I ordered two cheeseburgers, a Cerveza Presidente beer for me, and a can of Coke for Lynn. Captain Steve catered to the cruising crowd, proudly offering specialties like Gringo Chicken packaged just like gringos would find it at home in the states—no neck or feet, wrapped in clear plastic, and presented in a refrigerated display case. "Locals buy chicken with neck and feet. Gringos can't bring themselves to touch a plucked bird with all that ghastly stuff," Steve said with a wide, toothy grin as the flies danced around headless naked chickens hanging on wires near the entranceway. Around the town, chickens wandered everywhere, and horses, cows, bulls, and mules roamed outlying fields. In the humid afternoon heat, cocks chased coral hens. Some defended their right to the hens in one-on-one clashes with challenging cocks, generating flying feathers, squawks, and then a clear winner with the right to service the hens.

Back aboard later in the day, a group wearing street clothes and official-looking name tags boarded again without permission. They entered the main saloon, looked at the basket of onions and potatoes for one minute, spent ten minutes filling out forms, scrutinized our passports, collected twenty dollars, and drank a can each of cold cran-grape juice that I offered in friendship. It was over. *Scooter,* her owner, and crew had officially cleared in to the Dominican Republic. I lowered the yellow quarantine flag from under the Dominican Republic courtesy flag flying from the starboard main spreader.

Adventures in Luperón, to be remembered as Pooperon, began. A single, narrow, nearly dried up stream, its mud banks littered with cast off crates, barrels, a fractured porcelain sink, and other large debris, drained past the town into the small bay. Insufficient tidal action in the harbor allowed the black and gray water from the many anchored yachts to putrefy. Cool early morning air depressed the sewage vapor close to the water's surface. A local fisherman zipped along, lifting the gasses in his wake as he passed. The light breeze carried the foul odor to our boat and down into the interior. Later in the morning the sea breeze filled in to flush the stench inland. Many cruisers became ill and sought care at a local infirmary. Some thought they had worms or dysentery. The doctor dispensed antibiotics for a fee. Our collective backgrounds helped us figure out that the sicknesses were caused by the poo stew that adhered to dinghy painters and dock lines. If not using a hand cleaner, touching a face or eating a snack after holding a wet line was the gateway to a serious sickness. Poo stew could transfer into the cabin, coat boat interiors, and saturate clothes, bedding and cookware. I suspended running the desalinator while anchored in the harbor and found that locals sold tap water from somewhere by the ten-gallon jug. They even poured it into the water fill at no charge.

Our daily routine consisted of riding *Jazz* ashore to the partially submerged dock on Avenida Duarte, sometimes to the Puerto Blanco Marina, but mostly to the Luperón Yacht Club perched on a hill overlooking the bay. The club had a kitchen, a large bar, and a small dance floor surrounded with tables and chairs. One afternoon, a fellow cruiser told a story about his clearing-in, saying that when he was asked if he had any guns on board he responded yes and presented his new revolver in its box. He was told he needed to obtain a permit from the port captain, who directed him to visit a specific town to have firearms papers completed and fees paid then go to another town for more fees and paper stamping and back to the port captain for final paper processing and fee collection. The entire procedure would take a full day of bus riding in unfamiliar locations with the gun in its box if he started early the next morning. The captain's office would be closed by the time he returned, making the clearing-in process a two-day affair, during which his wife would be marooned on the boat. The port captain noticed his astonishment and asked if he would sell the gun. He enquired as to how much. The port captain made an offer that was nearly what he paid for the revolver. He took the deal thinking that it was a good trade-off versus the time and risk to obtain the costly permits. Table talk bounced around opinions that perhaps the port captain had a collection of firearms negotiated away from cruisers using the same tactic. And that he may have been in the used firearm business to supplement his government income.

As the shadows grew long and I found a place for the next mug of Presidente among the table debris of past bar orders, a drum rhythm beat out from the bandstand behind a small dance floor. A flute appeared from a box near me. At another table, a man pulled a violin from a case. A trumpet came into view at the bar. Music began to the delight of the spectating cruisers. The dance floor filled. Home-schooled cruising children swayed in time with the music at the side of the small dance floor, amusingly watching with big eyes as mom and dad danced. Table

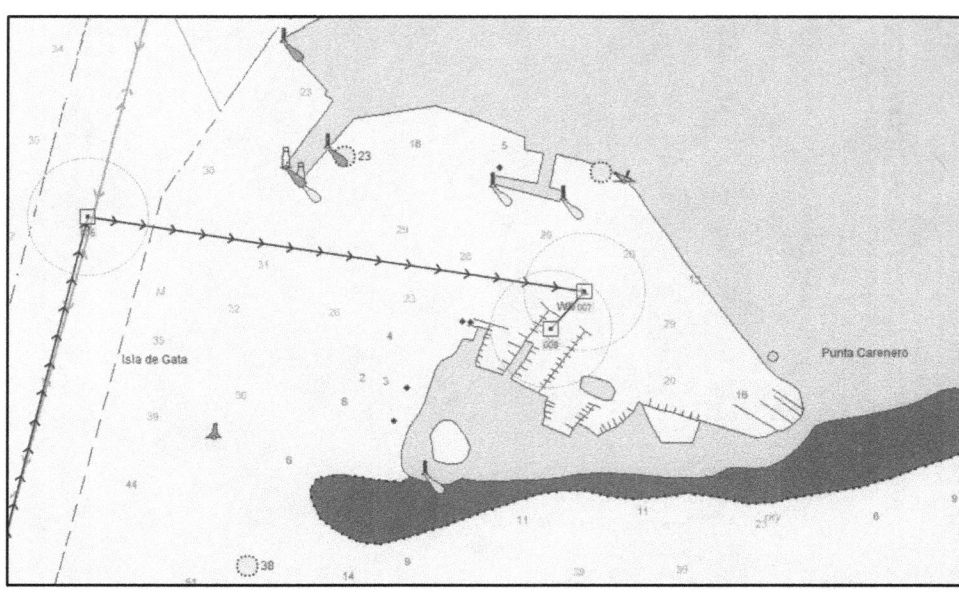

Ponce Yacht and Fishing Club

conversations flowed among groups of cruisers about taxi-bus rides to nearby cities, weather predictions, and taking a Sunday bus ride with cruising couples to spectate at a government sanctioned cock fight in a small town an hour away.

We joined the group going to see the cock fight, and Lynn handled the spectacle amazingly well. Then, while trying to dance among the crowd to the rhythm blaring from the ceiling high speakers, we confirmed the adage that unsensual gringos cannot dance the merengue.

Tropical storm concerns pressed me to move forward and cross the Mona Passage to Puerto Rico, a passage I was cautioned by bar stool gushings to be very difficult and sometimes dangerous. My Caribbean guide books spun stories of unpredictable currents, night thunderstorms, and challenging wave sets unless the crossing was attempted in an extended weather window. Clicking on the Nobeltec chart's ground track from the Luperón anchorage to the Puerto Rican west coast town of Boquerón, I noted a track length of 247 miles. At six knots that would take forty-one hours at best. Chris Parker's morning report said there would be light trade winds from the east for three days and Buoyweather confirmed the same. It looked to be mostly a motor crossing. I decided to set out midafternoon in order to make a daylight landfall at Boquerón.

Clearing out of the Dominican Republic in the mobile trailer on cinder blocks required payment of a country exit fee and a port usage fee to cover garbage burning. With all that behind us, we strolled along Avenida Duarte past a huge, unburned pile in the garbage bunker on the way to *Jazz* at the rickety government dock. Someday, our garbage burning fee would be put to use. There was no sewage charge for pumping black and gray water into the bay. It was good to be on our way.

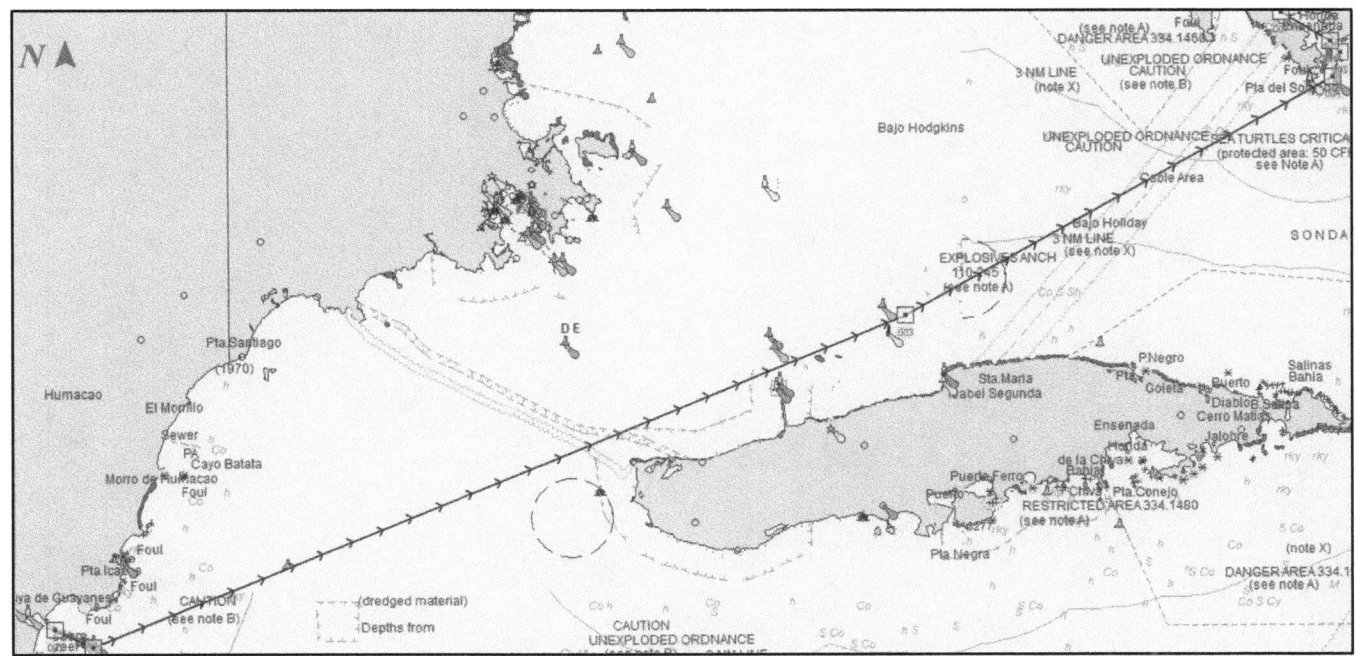

Yabucoa to Ensenada Honda, Culebra

On the fourth of April, we hauled anchor and motored along the island's north coast into a light breeze. After radar scans showed nothing, Lynn relieved my watch, and I managed two ninety-minute sleep cycles. Passing of the night was uneventful as was the first morning until a whale leaped fifty yards off the starboard side near the mountainous peninsula north of Samana Bay. East trades filled and at 1640, I rolled out the genoa and hoisted the main to assist Mr. Stink on a course directly to Boquerón, yet we were still in sight of the coast to starboard, with the rising half-moon off to port. Warm, moisture-laden air flowing onto the island grew cotton ball cumulus clouds into a wall of giant cauliflower-shaped towers reaching up into twilight. As the moon illuminated the clouds, a light-gray arch rose into the black sky from the north and back down to the sea in the south, my first moonbow. Chris Parker's weather forecast held as we motor sailed across the calm waters of the Mona Passage all night.

We locked *Jazz* to a dock at the Boquerón Yacht Club and processed in at the customs kiosk near the club. Uninformed American cruisers, surprised they were not permitted to use the customs kiosk to manage arrival because they had no document to support a customs decal like the one on *Scooter's* port saloon window, bused up the coast to visit the customs office in Mayagüez for processing. That afternoon and evening we roamed around Boquerón, seeing college kids frequenting bars, biker clubs trolling the streets, and high rollers driving expensive rides with convertible tops down to be seen.

Somewhat time pressured to make Grenada before hurricane season, I headed eastward along Puerto Rico's south shore and anchored at Caleta Salinas off Playa Santa for three days then sailed to Ponce, where I took a slip at the Ponce Yacht and Fishing Club, a private club that allowed cruisers to dock with limited club privileges. Centrally located on the south coast, Ponce became a day-trip hub. With a rented van, we, and a Portuguese cruising couple we met on the dock shopped mega supermarkets and big box stores.

I accepted an invite for dinner aboard the Portuguese yacht, but Lynn declined to go at the last moment. Not wanting to offend the cruisers, I arrived alone with a bottle of wine and excused Lynn's absence with a story of her not feeling well. Lynn's reluctance to socialize with cruisers paralleled her resistance to participate in boat management, docking, and sail trimming, causing me to surmise that, while sailing to Trinidad, she limited herself to galley duty. My concern grew when I lifted one of her backpacks stowed in the forward head while making rounds and heard the castanet sound of pill bottles rattling in unison.

She responded to my questioning by saying, "Oh, they're prescription meds I take routinely for my allergies."

"What allergies?"

"Pollen, mold, dust, and anxiety."

"Anxiety? From what?"

"It's complicated."

"How often do you take them?"

"Every day."

No wonder, I thought. That's why she was up one day, down the next, and sideways on others. Compromising our collective safety to enjoy her companionship could lead to

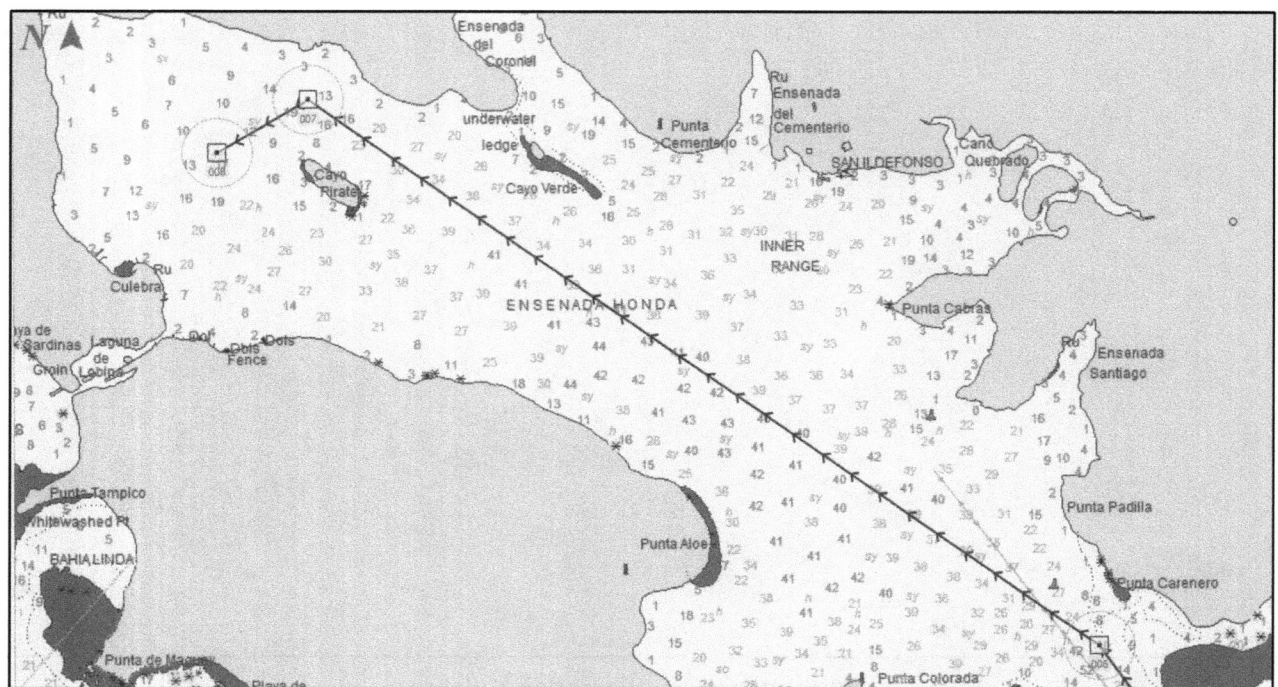

Ensenada Honda

disaster, and I began thinking about how to kindly end the relationship.

Seven days after arriving in Ponce the east trades calmed. We motored along the south coast to stage for the passage to Isla de Culebra and anchored off Yabucoa Harbor south of Playa Guayanés on Puerto Rico's east coast. The next day, I kept the sails covered while Mr. Stink pushed *Scooter* for six hours over glassy water, past Isla de Vieques.

Ensenada Honda extends nearly two miles into Isla de Culebra from a narrow entrance flanked by reefs uncovered at low tide. We anchored *Scooter* behind an island named Cayo Pirate far back in the bay. The island's hill had been constructed by pirates who mounded piles of rubble on the small island to hide their ships from view of the British sailing past the bay entrance. Piracy, or the Sweet Trade, flourished in Culebra, St. Thomas, St. Croix, and St. John because the governors thought it best to negotiate than be killed. After exploring the town, we bused to Bahía Flamenco on the north coast to snorkel in the deep, clear waters. With some coaxing, Lynn swam with me on the surface halfway to the towering rocks and back to the white sand beach.

We played for five days in the Spanish Virgins then sailed to St. Thomas, anchoring off Ruyter Bay near Water Island. I rented a car, and we made daily excursions around the island, becoming familiar with the streets of Charlotte Amalie. In a way it was like being at home, with the hustle and bustle of people and traffic. Because the open-air buses kept tight schedules all over the island, I returned the rental while Lynn waited on the boat. Riding *Jazz* back to *Scooter*, I reflected that a once-in-a-lifetime adventure around the planet with Lynn would put her at risk if something happened to me. She would be unable to sail to safety alone. We had to separate where she could fly home, and St. Thomas fulfilled that need.

We moved *Scooter* to Charlotte Amalie Harbor, a short zip on *Jazz* to the ferry dock near the bus stop at Vendor's Plaza. When I felt it was the right time, I spoke my mind. "Lynn, there's something we need to talk about." She turned from the galley sink, looked at me sitting on the starboard divan, scooched onto the port divan alongside the saloon table, and waited. "You know, safe cruising requires both of us to be capable of managing the boat. For three months, I've offered to help you grow basic boat management and sailing skills, even plotting courses on the laptop, and every time you had some reason to put it off." I paused, waiting for a response, but she gave none and I continued. "You know that if something happened to me, you would not be able to just get the boat to a dock. You wouldn't be able to call for help if I was not able to operate the radio. So, I have to ask. Are you interested in learning to do all that, or are you more interested in just enjoying the ride?"

"Do you want me to leave?"

Relieved with her comeback, I said, "I don't see you enjoying yourself with other cruising folks. This lifestyle is not working for you."

"I don't have . . . I'm different."

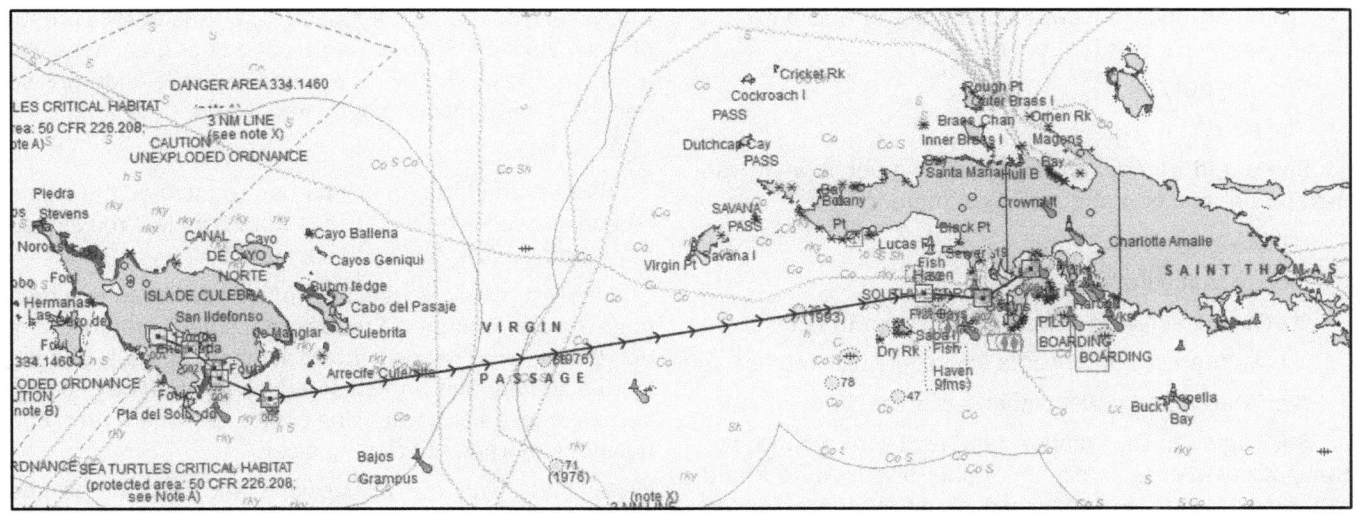
Culebra to St. Thomas

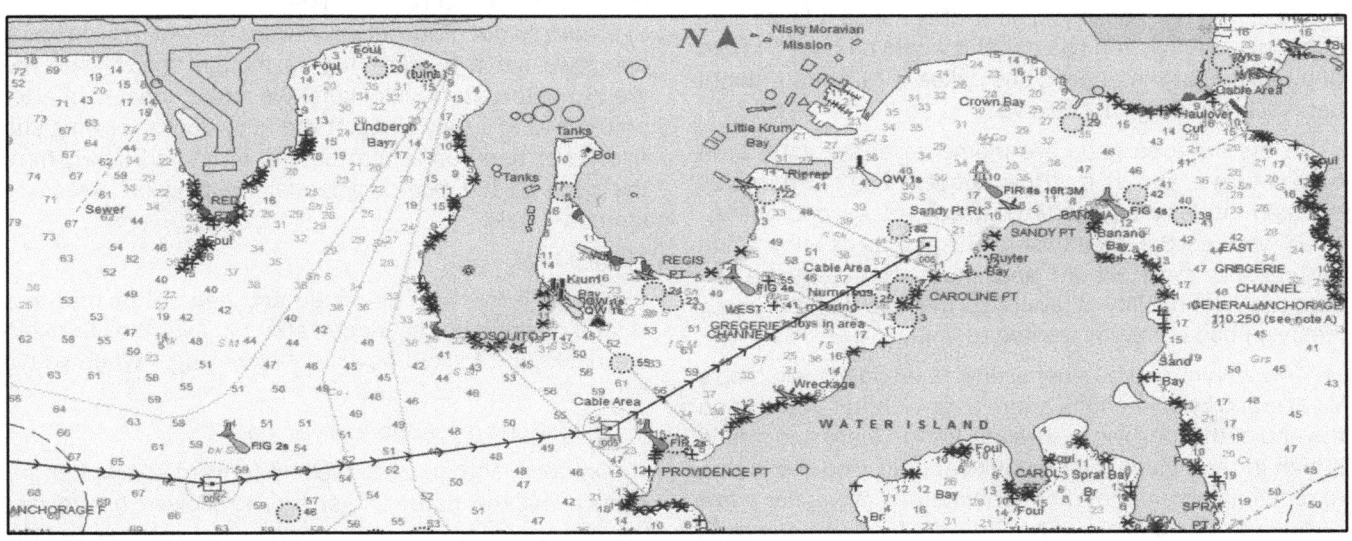
Ruyter Bay, St. Thomas

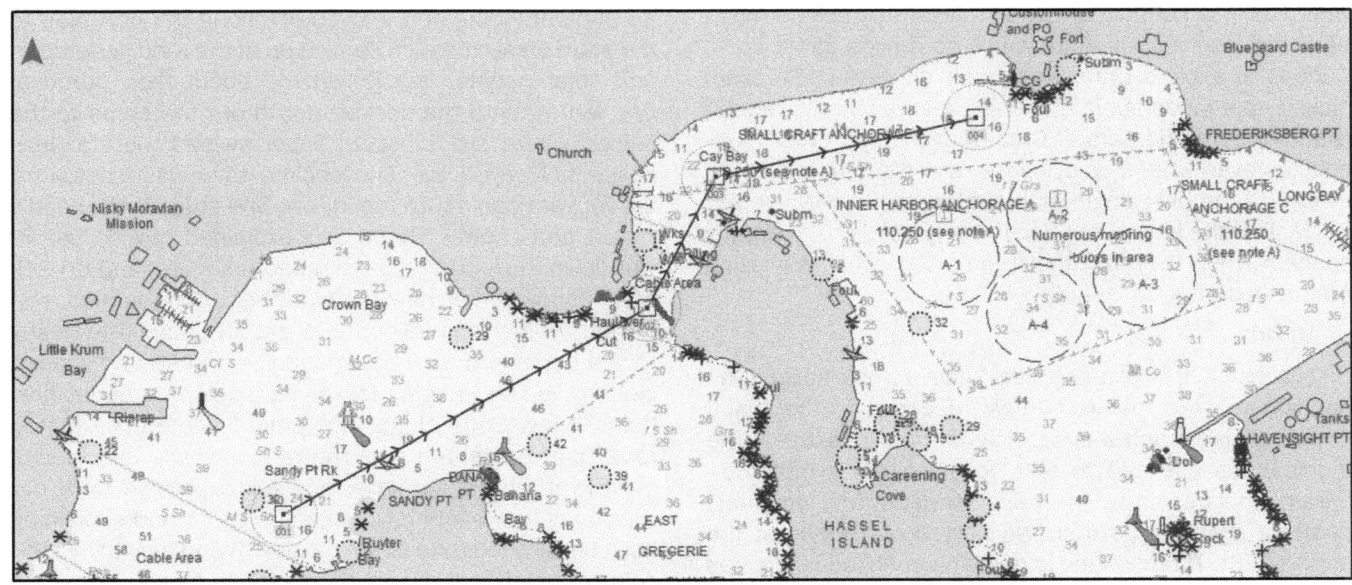
Charlotte Amalie Harbor anchorage

Choices • 45

"This has been an eye-opener for you and it's ok. I think it would be best for both of us."

"Are you sure?"

"I'm sure."

She sat in silence, probably thinking about what was next for her and how she would get there.

"I'll buy your ticket home."

"You're that sure?

"Let's look at flights. Where do you want to go?"

"I have friends in Minnesota who could pick me up."

"Let's talk about it over dinner, say at the Greenhouse?"

She agreed. Our dinner talk revolved around her thoughts of visiting family in Virginia and New York and returning to work. She declined my offer to pay for the flight. Two days later, with all her things packed into a soft suitcase and her backpack, she softly asked if I was sure about her leaving, and I said that it would be best for both of us. Again, at the airport, she asked if I was sure about her leaving and again, I said yes.

In the dry-eyed good-bye moments at the gate, Lynn turned to me and said, "How about a hug?" She softly thanked me for the good time. It was the second of May. I had entered the relationship wishing to develop a life partner, but time aboard and situations foreign to her exposed her inability to adapt to the easygoing cruising lifestyle I had earnestly wanted to enjoy.

The evening of Lynn's departure, I expanded the laptop's Wi-Fi reach by connecting a wire to an adapter antenna on the end of the long-range wireless LAN PC card and strung it high in the rigging. The modification allowed the laptop to reach an antenna at a bar on Veterans Drive. For a few bucks a week I could surf the Internet from the nav desk and make Skype calls. Only profiles in coastal US cities where sailing, boating, or ocean adventure seekers might be living received my inquiry, but no replies came back. Curious to explore the islands, I sailed over to St. John, picked up a mooring off Lind Point, and reconnoitered the island streets and bars of Cruz Bay for three days. I saw couples everywhere, enjoying the island's magic, and felt awkward, the only single man seated at the bar. I sent a SailMail to the kids about what was going on to avoid any concern when they saw that Lynn's sign-off was missing on the next email.

Hi kids,

Just as night follows day, I am again a single sailor. Lynn had asthma and severe allergic reactions to the island flowering plants and was seasick on many passages. The medications she had to take to mask the symptoms—breath inhalants and pills—made her dopey and incapable of being a sailing partner. We parted as friends at the airport in St. Thomas. She is doing ok in Philadelphia, has rented a new Pontiac, will visit relatives at home, then go to Alaska to do a job for her medical contractor for a breath of fresh, cool air. *Scooter* and I wished her happiness. I'm in St. John's USVI. This place and these islands are so beautiful, it is difficult to put it into words.

Love Dad

Back at Charlotte Amalie harbor, I continued the online search and received a message from Connie. "You looked at my profile. Why didn't you say hello?"

I replied, "Well excuse me! I must have been in a rush to go ashore. Your profile reads great. Thanks for following up." Connie and I Skype chatted at length for days, sharing our life stories. She worked at a desk in an office building, earning enough to cover living costs, apartment rent, and bus rides to work, not owning a car.

Euphoric with our discussions and the photos she emailed, I offered to pay her round trip to St. Thomas and waited at the concourse to meet the person in the emails. She waltzed out of the jetway toward me with a wide smile and gave me a riveting hug as though she missed me greatly, entertaining onlookers. We made nonstop chatter on the bus to *Jazz* waiting at the ferry dock. Knowing she had never been on a boat before, I motored slowly from the dock to the boarding ladder hanging off *Scooter's* starboard side.

"It's big."

"Enough for two," I quipped and tied the painter to a cleat. I climbed up the ladder, stepped over the life rail to the deck, and looked down at her, saying, "When you're here, take my hand."

"I don't need your hand. I can do it."

On deck, she instantly walked forward sliding her left palm along the hard dodger top. I followed her toward the bow, pointing out rigging parts then summarized the operation of the anchor windlass. She acknowledged with an understanding nod, moved aft along the port side to the stern under the arch, looked up at the wind generators and solar panels, and grilled me about their purpose. She led me into the cockpit and down the steps to the saloon where she stopped, finger swiped the stainless galley sink, eyed the Eno cooker, then dashed toward the forward cabin with me in tow. She studied the head's faucet and shower nozzle as I explained how to use it: wet down, turn off the water, soap up, rinse, and dry off. After I showed her how the watertight door worked, she moved through the saloon into the aft cabin. The neatly folded items in the aft cabin cubbies and equally spaced clothing in the hanging locker said volumes about how I was living. Back at the nav desk I booted the laptop for a brief presentation of the racy pics she sent during our Skype chats. My show and tell expanded from her questions into booting Nobeltec software and explaining how the GPS fed data to the display. "What's all this?" she said gesturing with an open hand to the panel holding the automatic identification system (AIS), VHF, SSB, CARD, two

GPS units, and CD player. "And that?" She nodded in the direction of the EPIRB.

"I'll show you how they operate when we sail. Are you hungry?"

She turned toward the galley saying, "Oh, good, where do I start?"

"No, no, no, no. We'll cook something tomorrow. There's this great place in town."

Her ease of communicating with waiters and patrons in the joyous atmosphere at the Greenhouse Restaurant and Bar gave credence to the skype stories of her past life. Hours later, shortly after reboarding, I opened two folding cushioned deck chairs and placed them on the aft cabin top under the mizzen boom, giving us a view of the city lights and the stars while sipping wine.

She asked up close, "And you live like this?"

I leaned close and whispered, "You could too."

I fell under her spell when she shifted over me and delivered a long, passionate kiss that started a groping adventure until she said, "Someone would need a good pair of binoculars to see us here."

"That's if they were on deck intentionally looking around."

"It would be fun to give them something to remember."

"Right here?"

Ashore the next day, we toured stores selling jewelry, watches, souvenirs, and high-end art and inspected restaurants and bars open to corridors painted with Caribbean pastels. Crowds of portly cruise ship passengers congested the narrow sidewalks, passageways, and store entrances. Connie led me into an apparel shop where she picked up a colorful bra from a display stand and asked what I thought. Trying to match her speed of wit I slid out, "Oh that's too big. You need something much smaller." Holding up what looked like dental floss with patches of material dangling down she responded, "How about this?" and glanced around to see if anyone heard. Pleased that she captured a few patrons' attention she placed it with the others and catwalked toward the doorway.

Way down Dronningens Gade, we turned into a shop after seeing a wine display and joined a cluster of cruise ship shoppers. Through my Maui Jim's I noted a tanned lass in a white bikini covered with a near-see-through whatever. Her white sombrero-like hat contained more material than the sheer cover-up she had on beneath it. Connie and I circulated with the crowd and chose our wine. While standing at the counter with our selection next to the register, the beauty under the white sombrero appeared to my right. I peeped down to see her gazing up at me with wide-open eyes and a teasing smile, grinned back, then swiveled my gaze back to Connie, who, as though she had just read my mind, circled around behind, and squeezed between the sombrero and me.

That afternoon I demonstrated working the Magma grill, baking with the Eno stove, and how the desalinator made fresh water. The next morning, she soaked up my radio operation review and projected confidence while making a call to "any boat" for a radio check during the motor trip to Cruz Bay on St. John's island. I hooked *Scooter* to a secluded mooring out of view of the town and a good distance from Solomon Beach. We zipped ashore on *Jazz* after I showed her how to stand to stay dry and guided her about the island town, making frequent beverage stops until late afternoon.

While tying *Jazz* to a stern cleat I suggested we take a dip before dinner. A short time later, I backstroked away from the hull and watched her climb down the ladder, turn, and without hesitation, splash out of sight, pop up, and wipe her face. She sculled around toward *Jazz*, looking like she was dancing in the water, then stretched both skimpy swimsuit pieces out on the pontoon top. I spun around to scan the beach for tourists. Seeing only sand and scrub brush and not to be outdone, I joined her water party.

The eve of her departure we talked at length about an ocean adventure, and a plan developed to unwind her lease and meet me in Grenada. I had to sail nearly five hundred miles to Grenada before the end of June to be in reach of Trinidad should Grenada find itself the target of another revolving tropical storm. She committed to the adventure when she arrived home. A day later, I provisioned, topped off the diesel, chatted with Chris Parker, cleared out of the US, sailed to Road Town, and cleared into the British Virgin Islands. At the end of a three-day tour of bars and shops I sailed to anchor off Prickly Pear Island across from the Bitter End Yacht Club, where I loitered for two days until clearing out.

Unpleasant wind-driven rain forced me to anchor in the lee of St. Kitts two hundred yards from shore after only thirty hours of sailing from the Bitter End. Not wanting to spend the time to clear in and out, I flew a yellow quarantine flag under the courtesy flag until the weather cleared. Martinique, the next stop, took thirty-two hours of sailing in the eastern trade winds before anchoring in that island's lee while flying the quarantine flag under a courtesy flag. I repeated the courtesy flag process while anchored off St. Vincent the next night. A day later, in the Grenadines, I zipped to the beach in Tyrell Bay with boat documents to visit customs and explore the town. Still green at island hopping, clearing in and out, navigating shallow water, weather fax interpretation, anchoring, and ocean-going female relationship building, I looked forward to one more day sail to Martins Bay just south of St. George's, Grenada, where Connie would soon join my ocean adventures.

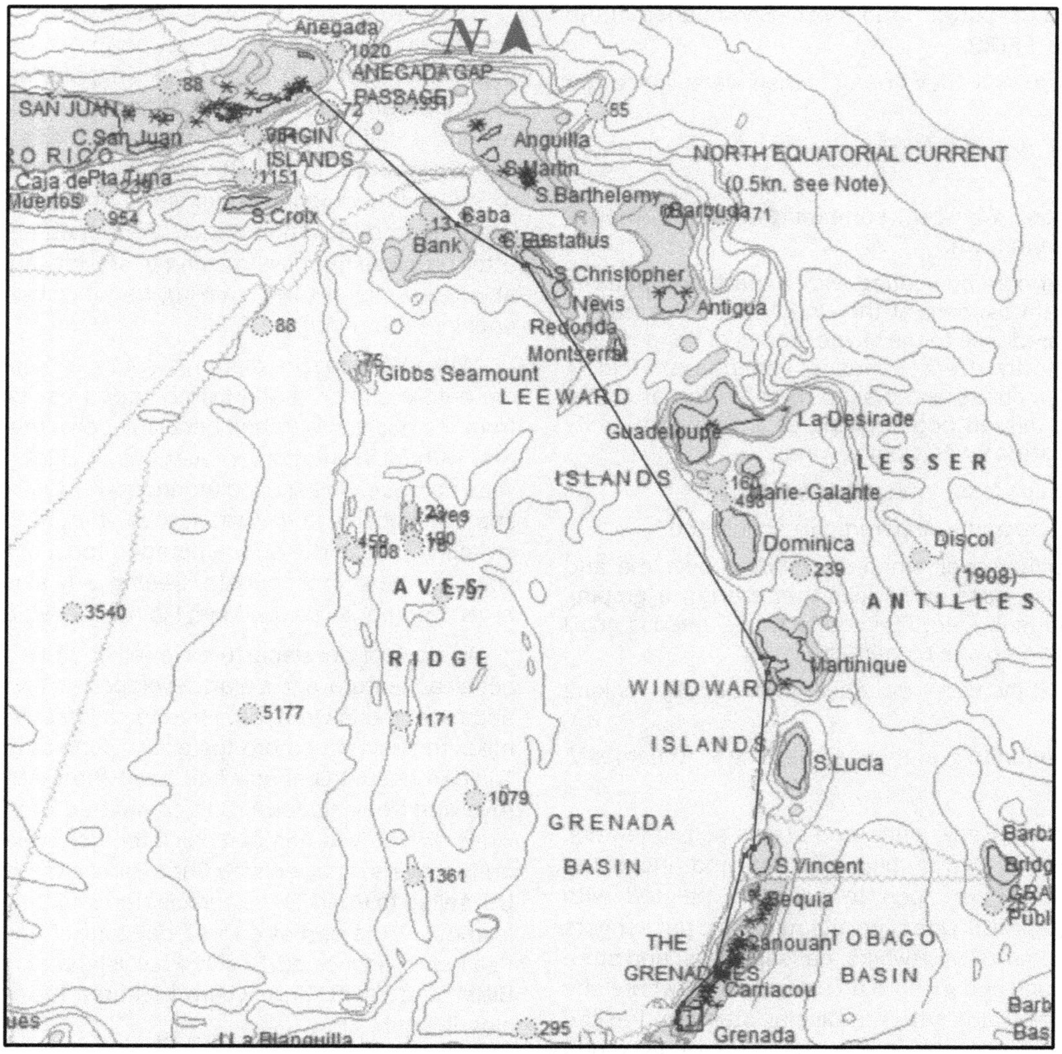

Virgin Gorda to Grenada

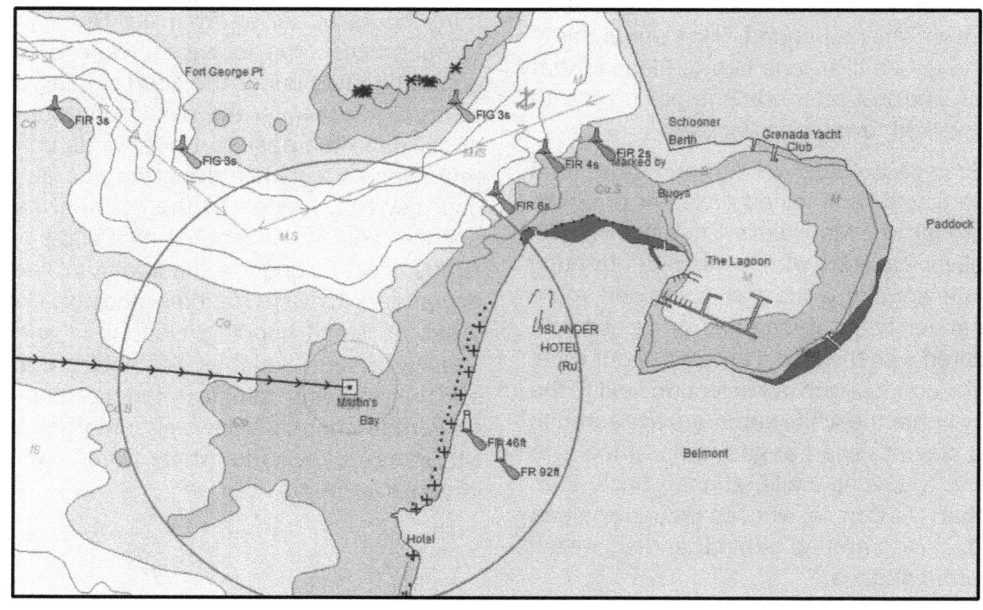

Martins Bay, Grenada

Enchantment

With her small soft-walled suitcase at her feet, Connie stood in *Jazz* and held the bow painter taught while I wrapped my arm around her waist and cracked the throttle open to zip us away from the Grenada Yacht Club dinghy dock to *Scooter* at anchor in Martin's Bay. With her gear stowed, I prepared and served dinner on the cockpit table, cleaned up the galley, unfolded deck chairs for viewing the evening sunset, and followed her suggestion about how to begin our ocean adventure.

The bar at the yacht club up the hill from the dinghy dock became a waypoint on journeys inland and sometimes the destination. One morning, a retired navy doctor and his cruising mate climbed into bar chairs next to us. After greetings, we shared island adventure plans while waiting for the barkeeper. By the time he arrived to unlock the register and take orders the room buzzed with chatter. The barkeeper quickly refused service to the athletically built doc who sported a tank top, referring to the dress code posted next to the door. Bar buzz fell to a whisper as heads turned to watch the scene. The doc apologized, left his cruising mate at the bar, and walked down to the dinghy dock. Bar buzz resumed while Connie chatted with the doc's mate next to her until the doc reappeared in the doorway wearing his navy summer white uniform, cap, bars, ribbons, and shiny laced shoes. Standing in the doorway he spoke above the buzz, "Barkeeper, do I meet the dress code, sir?" Heads turned, bar buzz ceased, and a roar of laughter erupted while the doc joined his mate.

Throughout her first five weeks of living aboard, Connie delivered on her boast made back in St. Thomas about

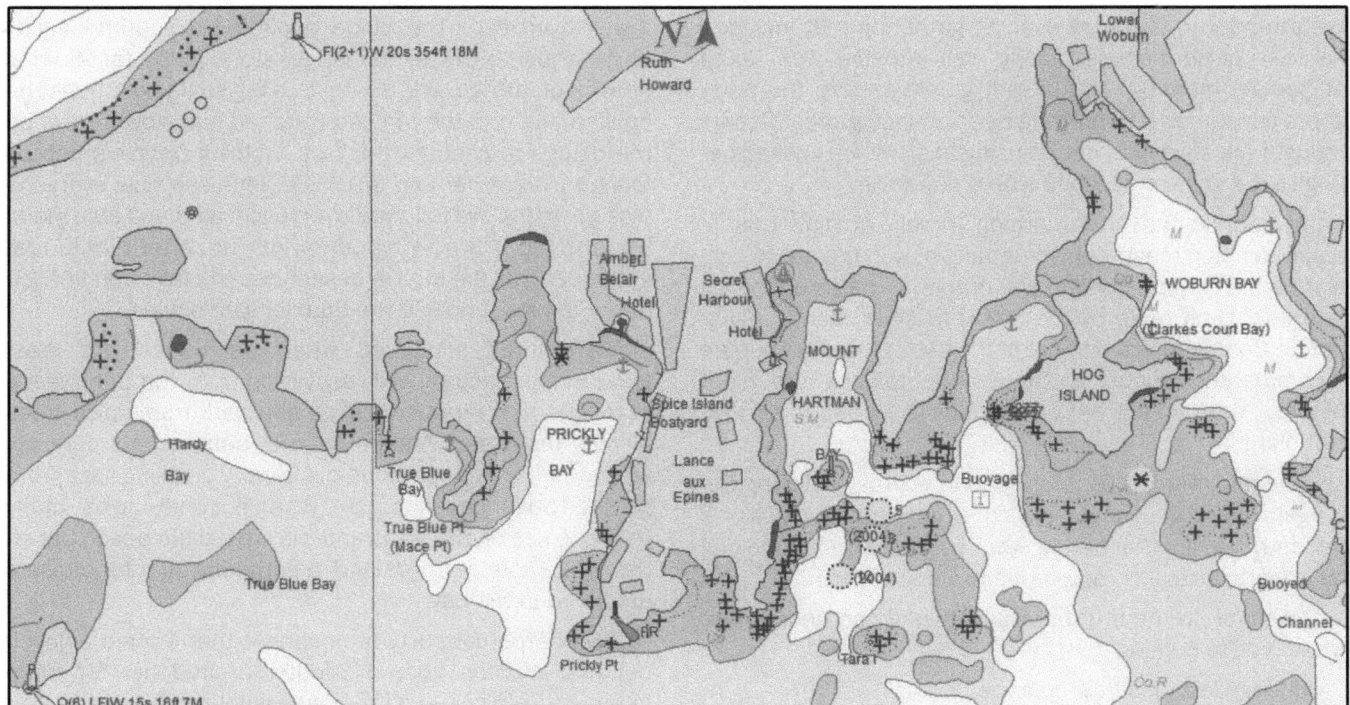

Grenada Bays

mastering anything she set her mind to do. With manuals, guides, and my coaching, she learned radio operation, ran the Nobeltec Admiral program on the laptop, and plotted GPS coordinates on a chart. In the galley she brought her creations from imagination to the table. Ashore, untraveled back roads had to be toured to see where they led and what waited for us when we got there.

We hauled anchor for a day of sail training that ended at Prickly Bay, where our pathway to and from the island destinations ran through the Spice Island Marina bar. I chose to anchor at the bay entrance away from the cluster of yachts anchored close to the marina, making for a long ride on *Jazz*. Exploring the nearby bays with *Jazz*, we found a very secure anchorage at Hog Island and decided to join the crowd of anchored yachts. Connie managed the helm while I operated the windlass, giving hand signals. Shortly after anchoring, a cruiser motored over in his dingy, grabbed the handrail, and introduced himself as the Hog Island commodore. He volunteered at the medical school acting as a patient pretending to have specific symptoms he rehearsed with professors. That association and his wife's work as an administrative assistant in a government office earned repeat visa renewals. They had been living on their American-flagged yacht for years and shared their vast knowledge about the island, its people, and where to have fun, such as at the small, secluded beach on the island's ocean side out of view of all but infrequently passing boats.

A short zip on *Jazz* took us to the nearby Whisper Cove Marina in Woburn Bay. Located at the foot of a steep driveway leading uphill to a bus stop, the marina became another beverage stop to and from island adventures. We attended a Saturday evening gathering that included karaoke performances lasting well into the wee hours of Sunday morning. The later it got, the more the party goers consumed, intensifying performance gaffes. Connie thought the show was not amusing at all. When I asked her to give it a go, she declined with a coy smile.

At sunrise the next morning, I woke to find Connie eager to begin mastering something new in the galley. Egg and bacon burgers, coffee, and orange sections appeared on the cockpit table by the time I finished rounds. Right before Connie took a bite out of the thick breakfast burger, I commented about her reluctance to sing the night before. "You had a great opportunity to please the crowd last night."

She munched, rolled her head in ecstasy savoring the burger, swallowed, and said, "It's not that doing that's beneath me. It's that I know what I can do. I'm not looking for cheers, atta girls, or to out-show any of them."

"Well, ok, you put it that way. I think I can understand where you're coming from."

She smiled, "It's how I planned living."

It came to me that morning that her involvement aboard would intensify. Cruising offered new challenges to conquer and activities to perfect to feel the rush of accomplishment.

We partnered with two cruising couples for an inland fresh water adventure that required notice that we would get wet and that it could be difficult. The minibus driver and guide pointed out historical sites along the way to a narrow trail in parkland under a thick jungle canopy. Wearing only swimsuits and tennis shoes, the party of six followed the guide into a rushing stream. Connie and I held hands in the knee-deep current, ready to follow the guide upstream. We obeyed his commands, sometimes navigating shallow water near the bank to avoid rapids and other times moving through knee-deep slow-moving water. "Looks like this is it," Connie said when a waterfall came into view. The guide gestured to follow him up the rocks into the cascade falling from above. Connie and I joined the other couples looking up at the guide nearly half way up the falls, water splashing off his shoulders. Connie chided, "I hope your suit stay on," bringing laughter from the group. One couple began their ascent and when nearly at the top, the other couple attempted the climb but took a different route. It looked easy enough to reach the top, and it was.

The next plateau presented more of what we negotiated before, calm pools then rushing rapids with rocky sides and another waterfall that we all slowly climbed. We were waterfall pros by the time we faced the big challenge. Out from a huge hole in a rock wall, water rushed to fill the pool at its base. Standing inside the cavern we saw white water gushing from high up that splashed off a ledge an arm's reach overhead. The guide applied his youthful agility and crabbed over the first ledge, stood in the fast-flowing downpour, turned, and said with a big smile he thought he could make it to the top. We watched him slowly crawl up the deluge to conquer the falls. Holding Connie's hand, I leaned toward her and said, "Uh, let's see how everyone else goes up." We followed everyone's lead and also made it to the top still wearing our swimsuits. After a brief rest in the pond at the top we descended the falls and flushed out of the giant hole in the boulder with smiles.

Adventures continued when we visited the West India Spices factory, still recovering from the prior year's hurricane that stripped leaves and bark from spice trees all over the island. Another journey satisfied our curiosity when touring a generations-old factory distilling juice from pressed sugar cane into rum. When not enjoying the many things to see on the big island, we visited the beach bar on the west shore of Hog Island, a gathering spot for cruisers anchored in the bay.

The perpetual party atmosphere that Connie enjoyed her first months aboard *Scooter* excited her for more intense levels of fun. Often, we visualized places to visit and experiences to be had with *Scooter* as our home base anywhere salt water could take us. Our conversation drifted to fantasies many times, but I was able to pull her back to the reality of how prudent ocean sailing depended greatly on the weather. I explained the benefits of sailing with the trade winds, the concept of weather windows, and that February of the next year would be the best month to begin sailing the South Pacific. We could head west to Panama from Grenada; however, a long-standing part of my sail plan involved visiting the KISS wind generator factory in Chaguaramas, Trinidad, to buy backup generator blades. It would be an easy overnight sail for me but the first overnight sail ever for Connie.

We moved Scooter back to Prickly Bay to get ready to depart and joined the group of anchored yachts near the customs office. The Spice Island Marina bar again became our pathway to the bus stop for inland adventures and our refreshment stop on the way back to Scooter. Every afternoon we found cruisers clustered around barroom tables. One afternoon we shared our sail plans, which resulted in a warning from a salty senior skipper; "Beware clearing in at Chaguaramas in other than normal working hours. When you clear into customs, the officer will ask you about the time you entered the Bocas. If your answer is before 0800, he'll add an overtime charge even though the office is closed until 0800." The story held first place on my clearing-in precaution list.

Expecting that challenge and the possibility of future demanding clearing-in episodes, I assembled a three-ring binder containing every scrap of vessel information available that might be requested at the time of clearing: vessel description; photos of Scooter in and out of the water; engine and propeller specs; machine space contents; rigging specs; type, number, and size of sails carried; professional sailing licenses; life raft information; data about onboard electronics, medicines, and pyrotechnics; and extra passport photos.

After dark, Connie followed the radar beam swiping around the screen, and when it flashed a bogie, she read off the distance and bearing data and popped up on deck, looking in the correct direction to confirm its location. She learned the sound of the CARD when it screeched the presence of an incoming beam and knew how to interpret a vessel's broadcasted position, speed, and course on the AIS. She showed no fear of being alone and self-reliant at sea. I set a four-hour watch rotation but followed my ninety-minute sleep cycle to see how she managed her time, answer questions, and offer supporting suggestions. At dawn, we sailed through the Boca de Monos, dropped sails, turned to the east, motored north of Little Gasparee Island, and tied up at a dock in the Crews Inn marina. We dressed dock lines and tinkered about below, making all spaces presentable, anticipating a customs inspection. I locked the hatch, and we went off to poke around the marina, stopping to review restaurant menus and wander in and out of the shops until we discovered the customs office on the second floor of a building far from Scooter.

I told the clerk, officer, or whatever he was, behind the counter that we passed the Bocas at 0900 with a straight face after he asked the expected question. He then told me to fill out the forms without saying where they were. Connie found a pile of forms at the far end of the counter next to the wall. When I asked for a pen, the officer said he did not give out pens, turned quickly around, and shuffled papers on his desk. I strolled back to the boat to get a pen, leaving Connie holding the blank clearing-in forms and Scooter's three-ring binder. After returning and completing the forms, I turned the pile to face the officer and slid it across the counter. The clerk said he wanted copies. I saw no copy machine in the room and asked where to make copies. Without saying a word or making eye contact, he turned his back to me and pointed with his pen to the corner where Connie had found the blank forms. Connie lifted the forms folder and discovered a folder containing carbon paper buried at the bottom of the pile. I made a copy of each form and slid them across the counter. The clerk picked them up, thumbed through them, and said he needed three copies of each page. I smiled while gritting my teeth, and fulfilled his request. He was known as the Pencil Nazi among the Chaguaramas cruising community. Some thought he was the son of a government official.

We swung on a mooring the first night and moved to a slip the next day to begin a nine-day sightseeing adventure around Chaguaramas and Port of Spain. I found the KISS wind generator plant conveniently located a short walk from the marina.

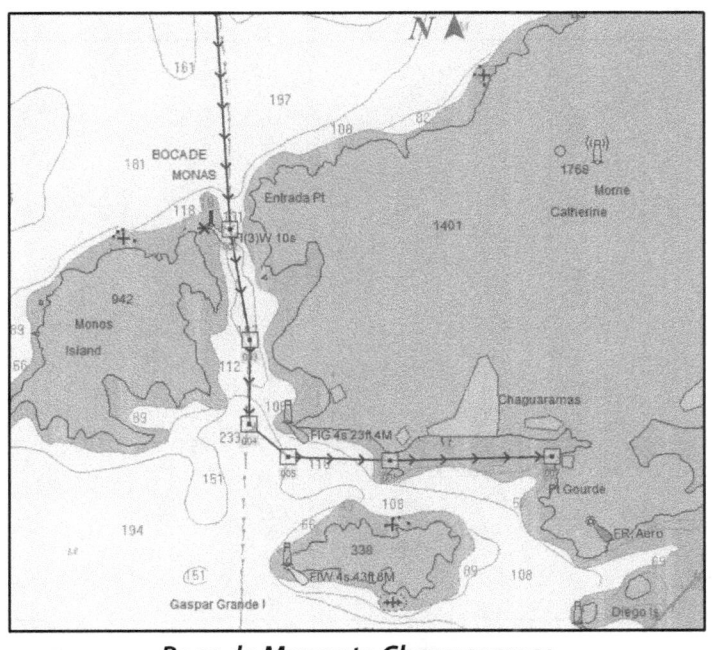

Boca de Monos to Chaguaramas

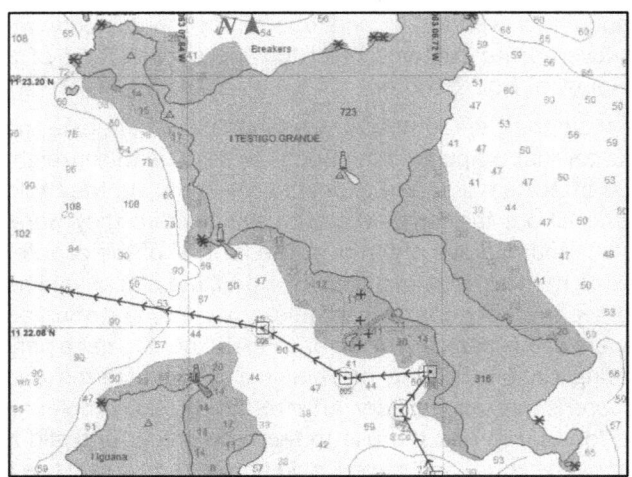

Isla Testigo Grande

Key West Island, north of Cayo de Agua

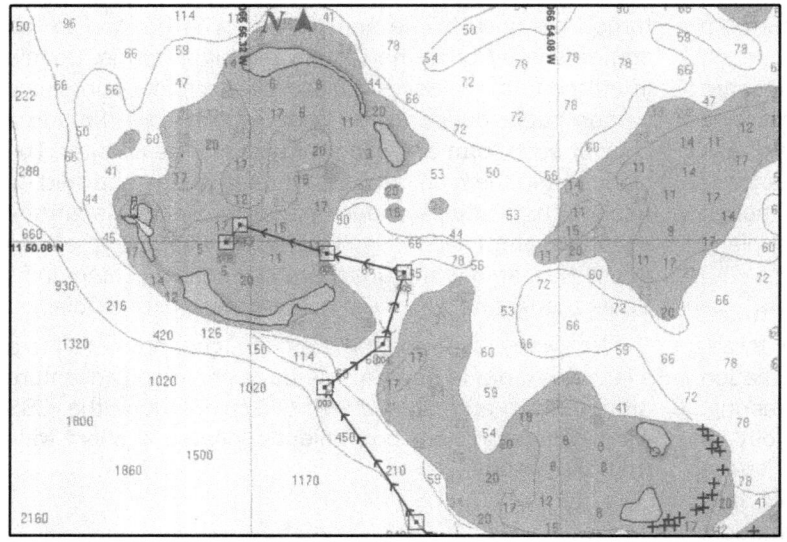

Los Roques

That September, Hurricane Ernesto formed northwest of Trinidad and tracked north. Below latitude 15° N, east across the Atlantic, opportunities for tropical storm development looked weak, easing my concerns. We sailed westward from Trinidad to relish the uncluttered island beauty of Isla Testigo Grande for two days while anchored in Balandra Bay, eighty-three miles from Trinidad. At the end of another a two-day sail, we followed the Nobeltec chart and picked our way into the Los Roques Archipelago and saw no other yachts. We anchored at Key West Island and zipped ashore to explore the isolated dunes. By that time, I appreciated Connie's appetite for anything that would tease her pleasure, including reaching out to fondle a woman's earring while seated around a table and commenting on how beautiful it was as her fingers softly grazed the woman's neck and swept slowly through her hair to see

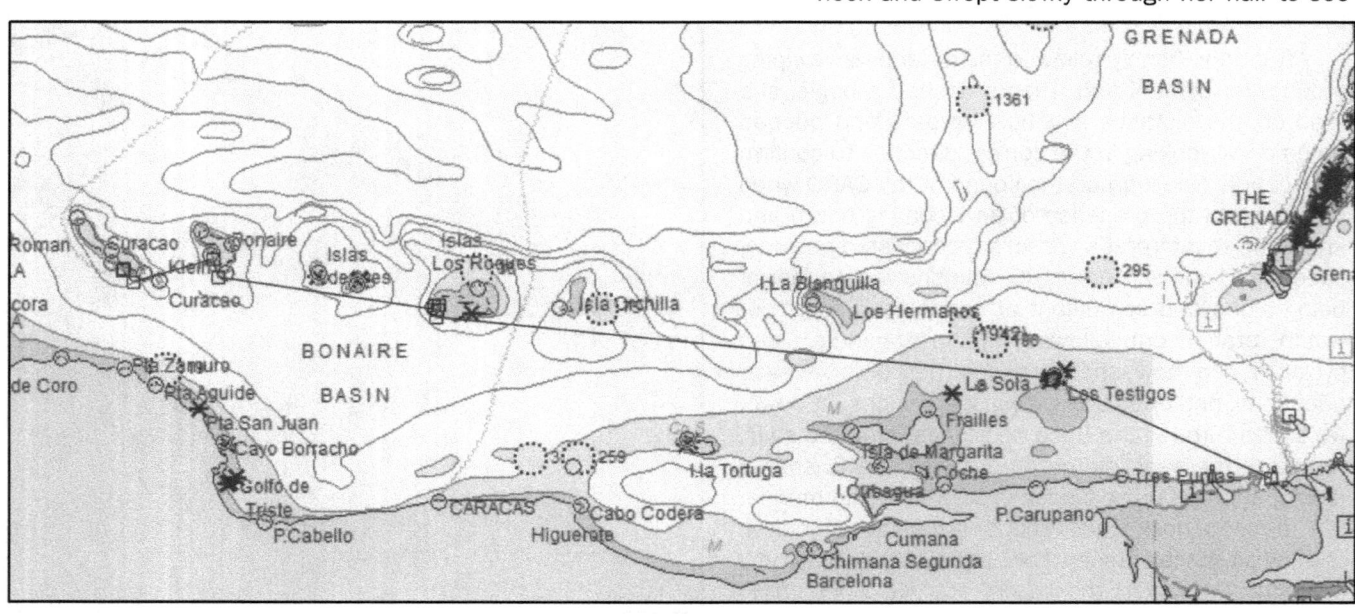

Trinidad to Bonaire and Curaçao

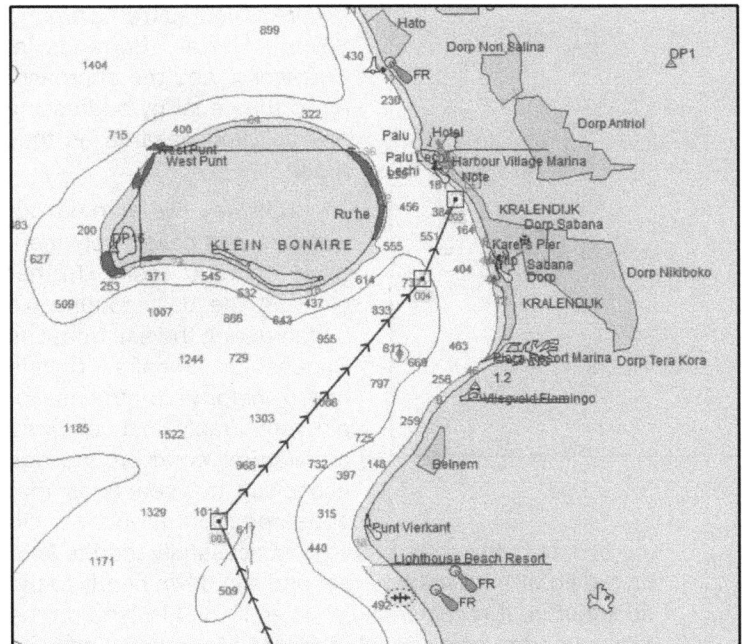
Bonaire

her response. I was not surprised when Connie flipped her bikini off, climbed the dune, and called for me to join her. Together we raced in the buff along the beach to the island's end then followed our footprints back to *Jazz*.

At the end of a day sail from Key West Island, I looked into five meters of water south of Harbor Village Marina on Bonaire to see two huge cement blocks with cables reaching up to yellow and white floats on the surface. Connie held *Scooter* into the wind while I slipped lines through loops on the floats' ends. Clearing in was unremarkable until returning to *Jazz* tied to the side of a cement pier. Three navy officers stood on the pier looking down at *Jazz* filled with water. They had seen a fishing boat back into it and motor out to sea. Once aboard, I found the starboard pontoon ripped from the transom to about a third of the length of the hard bottom. The navy men knew the owner of the fishing boat from Curaçao and offered to contact the owner to have him pay for the repair. I declined, not wanting to devote the days it would take to deal with the owner and asked about a repair shop, knowing the backup to *Jazz* would get us ashore. With a repair location and plan in mind we limped *Jazz* back to *Scooter*.

I unrolled the eight-foot soft-bottomed Zodiac inflatable boat that first floated off *Margetta* at the Ventura Marina in California fifteen years before. I pumped it up, plopped it overboard, assembled the two paddles, and rowed it to the steps at the quay about four boat lengths from *Scooter*, where I locked it to a cleat. After a fifteen-minute walk, we chatted with a worker at the Harbor Village Marina repair shop, learning he could repair the damage I described and would fit it in with other jobs. The next day we towed the Zodiac to the shop with *Jazz* and moved the fifteen-horsepower Mercury to the Zodiac for the trip back to *Scooter*. While motoring slowly along the waterfront the bottom's center seam split open the full width of the boat in a heartbeat. I lifted the bottom panel to keep it from scooping water, and we made our way back to *Scooter*. That evening, I thought about gluing the seam but speculated that other aged seams could split open at any time.

We inflated plastic trash bags containing a towel, shorts, shirts, and flip-flops and floated them ahead of us while we swam the short distance to the cement steps that extended from the sandy bottom to the quay top. Ahead of me, Connie negotiated hazardous marine life on the steps, rising to another new challenge. We dried off, slipped into our shore wear, each slung a bag with a towel over a shoulder, and began the day's island excursion. When *Jazz* was good to go, we slowly motored the Zodiac to the repair shop bailing all the way. I moved the Mercury to *Jazz* and we towed the Zodiac back to *Scooter*. That evening, I abandoned the deflated Zodiac in a heap on the quay. It disappeared overnight.

Planning to stay a week at Curaçao, we motored through a narrow inlet from the southwest shore and anchored in Spaanse Water, an inland bay. Leaving *Jazz*

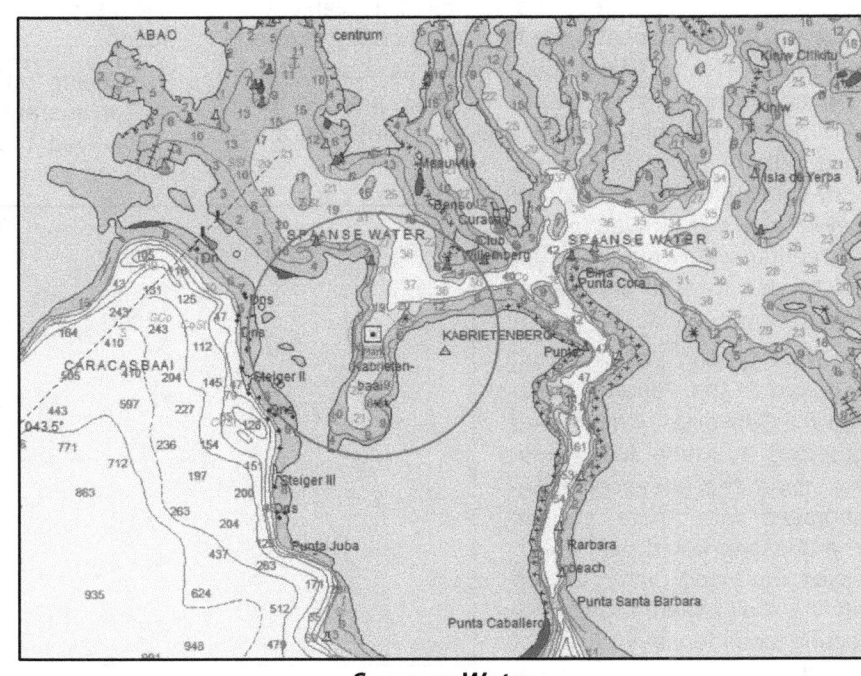
Spaanse Water

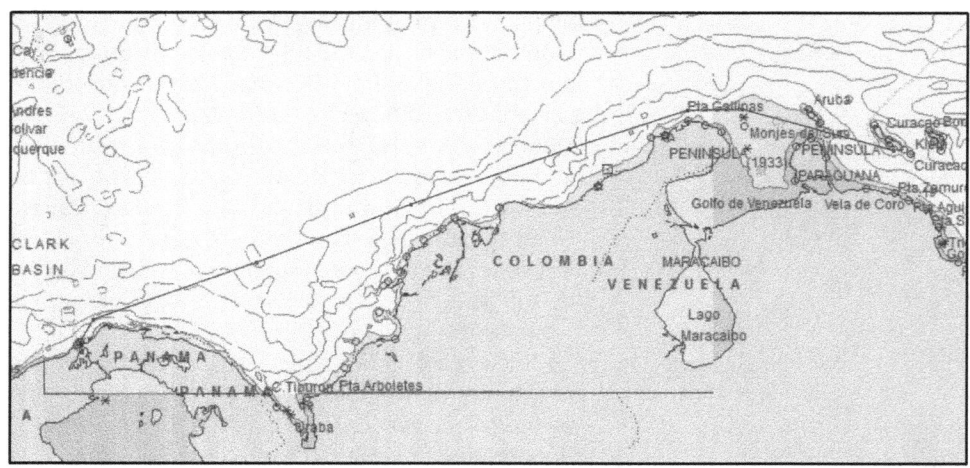
Curaçao to Panama

locked to a marina dinghy dock, we bused to Willemstad, lunched, explored, and worked our way back in time for dinner aboard. On the third evening, a couple stopped their dinghy near *Scooter* and invited us to join a group of cruisers at the nearby boat club bus stop the next morning. Connie thought it would be helpful to explore with those who had different experiences ashore. The next morning, we zipped over to the club at the appointed time and walked halfway up the sidewalk toward a group of five couples standing around the bus stop and paused to take in the boat club scene. A stately couple arrived, tied their RIB to the dock, and strolled with an unblinking forward stare past Connie and me holding hands. A very short white wraparound skirt hung from the lady's hips, balancing the white sleeveless blouse tied with a bow high above her deeply tanned waist. They stepped off the sidewalk, attempting to go to the head of the line, when a puff of wind off the water lifted her wee skirt high enough to reveal the two pieces were the extent of her wardrobe. Her mate, unaware of the show, walked alongside. Connie noticed me noticing, squeezed my hand, glanced at me with her right eyebrow raised, and said, "Let's get a seat next to them." Sadly for Connie, they sat with others and got off before the bus arrived at the city center, where our group got off to visit favorite shops and restaurants.

The ground track from Curaçao to the Panama Canal ran for 685 miles. I dismissed stopping at Aruba after reading about the absence of anchorages with shore access. The passage would take five to seven days and nights at sea off the Columbian coast. Projecting confidence in front of Connie, I talked about managing the expected traffic around Santa Marta, Barranquilla, Cartagena, and the approaches to the canal by addressing any collision hazards as they arose.

Underway, we worked our watches and collectively managed onboard tasks, further evolving the daily routine we began during the sail from Los Roques to Bonaire. Connie had transformed into a sailor girl remarkably fast, enjoying the natural world around her, especially the sea birds that appeared from nowhere to circle *Scooter's* two masts. One unsuccessfully tried to land on the jib with its webbed feet and slid down nearly to the deck before it regained flight. Then it tried to land on the fully extended solar panels forward of the spinning wind generator blades but slipped off the panel's slick surface. Persistence paid off on the third pass when it got a grip on the solar panel's aluminum frame where it rested for hours.

About three hundred miles from the canal entrance jetty, the knotmeter needle dropped to zero, while the GPS showed ground speed roaming from six to seven knots. And like any other failure I thought out the possible causes: a failed knotmeter display, impeller, or wiring. Could I repair it myself? Where in Panama would I find a repair shop? Could I order one online and have it shipped to Panama? Connie quietly observed my calm reaction to the discovery and my digging about the boat in diagnostic mode.

Closing on the Panamanian coast while flying the yellow quarantine flag below the Panama courtesy flag, I reviewed the rigid Panama Canal Authority controls,

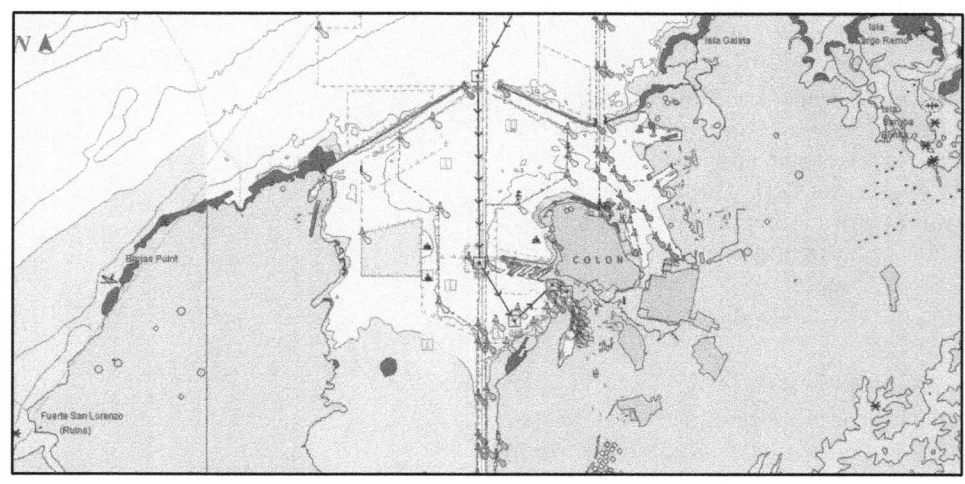
Limon Bay

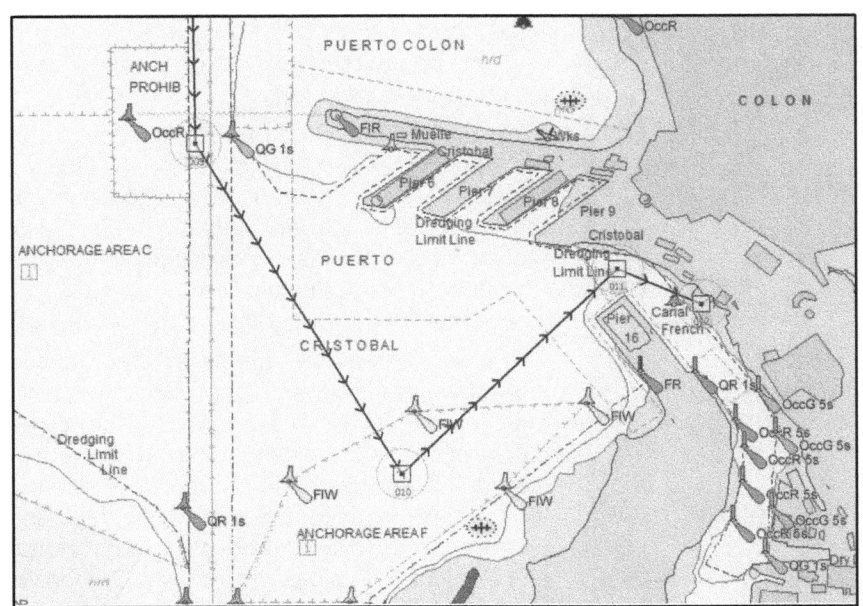
The Flats to the Panama Canal Yacht Club

rules, regulations, and protocols that applied to all vessels regardless of size. We lowered sails and motored past a dozen ships anchored north of the breakwater to follow the channel marking through the wide opening and headed for The Flats, a designated anchorage in Limon Bay. The anchor quickly set, and I returned to the guidebook for the locations of the buildings we had to enter on our pathway to clearing in. After neatening up below we closed *Scooter*, zipped to the Panama Canal Yacht Club, padlocked *Jazz* to a dock cleat, worked our way through the club bar, and crossed a wide paved area laced with railroad tracks leading to a large container storage area at the ship pier. Unlike other clearing-in episodes, this one required walking briskly with purpose in our step from office to office in various buildings, always looking over our shoulder, never pausing in the crime-ridden city. We made it back to the yacht club in Cristóbal and zipped back aboard without incident.

At that time of the year massive thunderstorms drifted westward over Central America. Lightning flashes illuminated ships anchored nearby in The Flats when bolts hit their high steel structures. Even though *Scooter* took no direct hits thanks to the static dissipaters on the mastheads, sometimes the strong electromagnetic pulse energized and activated the Leica GPS as though I had switched it on. The collision avoidance radar detector failed after one flashing squall. I emailed the CARD representative and after a lengthy discussion ordered a new antenna. He advised that to prevent energy in the air from damaging the new antenna, I should cover it with a metal can grounded by wire to the keel. An empty can of peaches got the job done.

In between the storms and visits to the marina, I removed the knotmeter head from the instrument panel next to the steering wheel. Bits of one gear fell out of the housing. Another gear crumbled when I tapped it with a screwdriver. I surmised that exposure to a high concentration of epoxy paint vapors during the many weeks of deck refinishing seventeen months earlier caused them to degrade, or maybe they just wore out.

Space for *Scooter* became available at the end of the yacht club fuel dock the first week of November, starting another marina life adventure, and I emailed the yacht club address to Seth for mail forwarding.

I knew my professional maritime licenses would expire the next year while I sailed the Pacific and had planned to complete the renewal paperwork, get a physical exam somewhere, and send the reissue applications to the Coast Guard in Miami and International Yacht Training in Fort Lauderdale. That changed when a letter arrived in the package from Seth informing me that the newly created Department of Homeland Security changed the license reissue procedure, requiring all mariners to return to the continental United States. I called the US Embassy in Panama City to see if I could process the documents through them and listened to the person read the same letter word for word. I had to return to Florida before sailing the Pacific and considered whether that time could also help resolve the knotmeter issue. We put *Scooter* to sleep, traveled on the bus system to the international airport in Panama City, arrived in Miami, rented a car, and checked into a hotel in Hollywood with a pool on the rooftop to Connie's glee.

I chased the US license reissue pathway—physical exam, eye exam, and paper processing. At the same time, I moved through the reissuance of my International Yachtmaster license and chatted with staff about how I applied that training to passing the USCG Masters exam, certifying to instruct American Sailing Association courses, delivering yachts, and arriving safely in Panama. They processed the application the same day I submitted the paperwork and handed me my second issue. The Coast Guard had to process the final document from an in basket somewhere to an out basket somewhere else and send it to my Islamorada mail address.

Between shopping at marine stores and beach walking we located Lauderdale Speedometer that fortunately had an exact duplicate of the VDO Sumlog. Knowing how easy auto odometers could be adjusted, after seeing that the Sumlog's odometer gearing was remarkably similar, I asked the technician to set the new display to read the

Plasma TV in Panama

sum of the failed odometer plus three hundred, which he did while we waited.

After we returned to Panama with suitcases full of parts and the new Sumlog display, we joined the yacht club bar crowd every afternoon. Cruisers waiting to transit the canal and eager for shopping and entertainment tips, like us, listened to stories by seasoned cruisers while snacking and sipping. We learned that the wide paved area laced with railroad tracks to the shipping container area between the club gate and Avenida Bolivar placed us in prime robbery territory. From high in the apartments across the street, bad actors could watch cruisers depart the club gate and cross the tracks toward the covered bus stop. The bandits had plenty of time to exit the building, cross the street, and mill around on the tracks tossing a softball. Unaware of any danger, cruisers walking in groups of two or three with their guards down passed the bandits with smiles before being knocked out from behind. Robbers first searched shoes for hidden money. I asked if anyone came to their rescue and heard, "You will be left to make it back to the club on your own unless another one of us could help. But that's risky."

"What if you have to go somewhere?"

"Take a taxi if one's parked outside the gate."

The couple on the other side of the table commented that if no taxi was available, they would abandon the trip when they saw someone walking about the tracks or take a chance and double time shuffle over to the bus stop when the coast was clear.

"But what about returning with packages?"

"Wait for a taxi to come by."

"Oh, of course. Just wait," Connie said, looking wide-eyed at me.

In a flash, I recalled the business card of a taxi owner given to me by an eastbound cruising couple way back in Grenada stashed away in the chart table drawer. Those cruisers highly recommended the taxi man, adding that he took pride in his nickname, Dracula, because he looked much like the character in the old movies.

Hensley profitably marketed his cursed looks. Owning his cab as a second income to his main job with the Canal Authority, he showed us places of interest, the post office, police station, restaurants, supermarkets, and mall stores. In town, we noticed the exterior of high-rise apartments had a latticework of white horizontal and vertical PVC pipes strung up to windows. Hensley said that the buildings' pipes failed after the local government required apartment building owners to reduce rental fees below what was needed to maintain them, leaving upkeep to the renters. They had erected the pipes to supply water. Some building owners even abandoned their investment. In that environment criminal elements prospered. From then on, we planned our shopping around Hensley's taxi schedule to keep us out of harm's way. He helped me locate and transport a very affordable portable air conditioner from the store to the boat on the day motorcycle police chased bank robbers around the city streets. A week later, he found a parking spot under the extended roof in front of a large mercado and waited while we shopped. Returning to his taxi, we saw him standing near the corner of the covered area next to a police car with flashing blue lights. He said a bandit tried to take a camera from a man entering his rental car after shopping. When the man resisted, the thief shot him dead right in front of the patrons pushing shopping carts. The ongoing Wild West rerun kept our situational awareness finely tuned.

The canal elevated Panama from a typical Central American economy to a crossroads of global commerce. Huge warehouses in the Colón Free Trade Zone stored goods from around the world. International buyers examined products in large showrooms and arranged purchase and transportation to retailers globally. At one warehouse showroom, I asked about a camera on display in a glass counter. After a lengthy product demonstration, the sales rep enquired about how many I wanted. I asked how much one cost. He lifted a clipboard from the glass countertop and asked if I wanted one case or one container. We continued shopping and found a wine warehouse we had to revisit the next day.

Planning the sail to Tahiti, we calculated our daily wine consumption. I thought that maybe it would be a

Señor Meza directing rafting

Waiting to enter the locks

The Gatun Locks

week to the Galápagos and perhaps four weeks from the Galápagos to Tahiti. Two glasses each with dinner, basically a bottle a day, was a lot of bottles, but they would make great ballast. Red wine on the port side and white wine on the starboard side could be stored in the space below the main saloon deck along with liter cartons of soy milk. When the delivery truck arrived after we placed our order at the wine warehouse, we wheeled cases down the dock on the collapsible hand truck. I packed the bottles tightly with socks, preventing them from moving about, not wanting to hear *whoop, whoop, clunk* as the boat rolled while trying to sleep.

A new model plasma TV on display at a local retail store had a mounting system on its back side made for *Scooter*. I installed it on the bulkhead forward of the saloon table and connected it to the DVD player while the air conditioner kept me cool. I gave the small TV purchased years before to Hensley for his children's bedroom.

In between adventures in town and movies on the new TV monitor, I examined cruising guides for Tahiti in detail and highlighted important paragraphs in yellow. They recommended obtaining visas prior to making landfall in French Polynesia to speed clearing in. That led us on another group of eyes-wide-open bus rides to visit the French Embassy in Panama City to process the necessary documents. From there, we bused to the Port of Panama City in Balboa, found the customs and immigration office where we would clear out after transiting the canal, visited a refueling dock, and scrutinized anchorages described in the Panama Canal guide.

Scooter previously transited the canal as *Meg*, but the owner left no admeasurement documents aboard. Had they been available, I would have avoided processing most of the forms. Included with the physical measurement paperwork to be completed by canal officials, a written release of the Canal Authority for any damage to *Scooter* had to be signed. The local business Yacht'n'Oceans Services made a good revenue by renting lengths of heavy duty ropes they called warps required by the Canal Authority to be used during transit. They also rented protective fenders fashioned from cloth-wrapped tires. And they charged for paperwork processing time.

With two couples as volunteer line handlers, we anchored on The Flats in Limon Bay and waited for a transit advisor to board. At sunset, a motor launch came alongside. Señor Meza climbed over the rail and directed us to raise the anchor and make for Gatun Locks. After driving Mr. Stink at full throttle to make time, he ordered me to stop about one hundred meters off the lock gate until lock line handlers secured the ship ahead of us. While waiting, we assisted a sloop in rafting to us on our port side then, much later, after dark, a uniquely configured cabin cruiser rafted to the starboard side. Once secured together, the three vessels moved as one

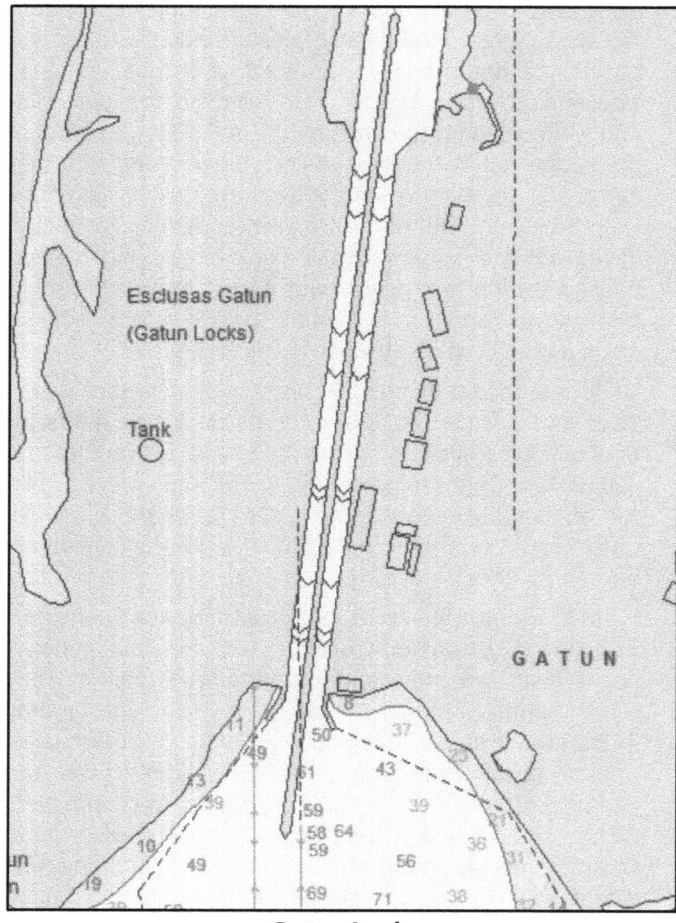
Gatun Locks

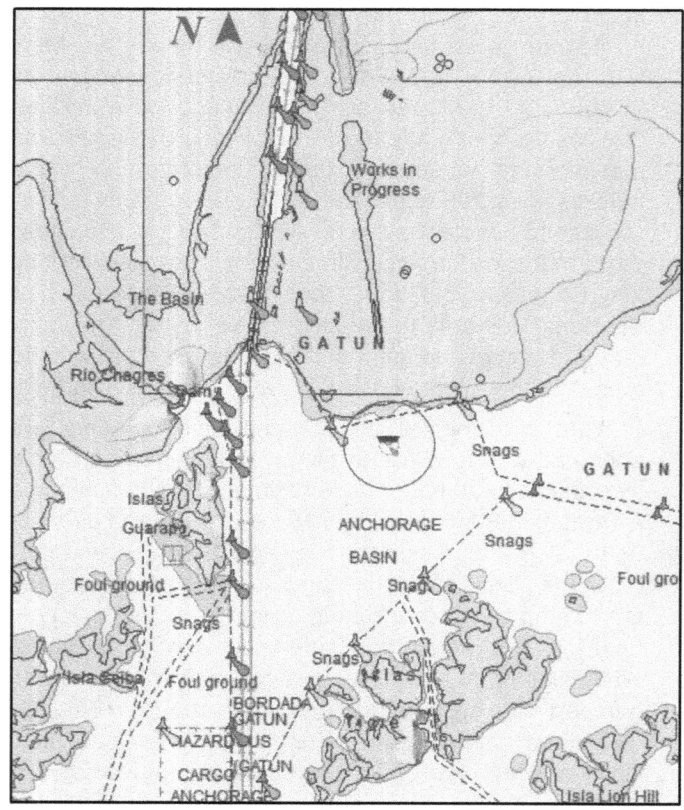

under Mr. Stink's power into the center of the first of three lock chambers behind the ship ahead.

Line handlers standing on the edge of the lock wall far above threw down thin heaving lines with baseball-sized knots called monkeys' fists tied on the end that bounced across the decks. Line handlers on the boats rafted to *Scooter* received instructions from their transit advisors to tie the light line with a slip clove hitch to the large eye spliced into the end of each warp positioned on deck. The lock line handlers pulled the heavy warps up and looped the eyes around bollards, then the boat line handlers slipped the loose ends around deck cleats.

Together, the boat line handlers trimmed the warps around deck cleats, keeping the rafted boats centered in the rising, swirling water. When the lock filled to the same level as the next chamber, the doors opened, the ship moved forward, and the lock line handlers lifted our warps from the bollards. The boat line handlers pulled the warps back to the boat, leaving the light line tied to the eye in the warp. While I motored *Scooter* and the rafted boats forward, the lock line handlers walked the light heaving lines at the same pace up the lock sides onto the next chamber's walls behind the ship. After the rafted boats passed the lock doors, the lock line handlers pulled the warps up and hooked the eyes around that chamber's bollards. The doors closed behind us, the water rose, and the boat line handlers trimmed the warps. Repeating the process a third time lifted us to the Gatun Lake level twenty-six meters above Limon Bay, where the lock line handlers untied the light lines and the boat line handlers pulled the warps aboard after the ship ahead of us cleared the lake lock door.

I motored *Scooter* with the two rafted boats into the lake. A good distance beyond the chamber doors, the

Canal

<--- *Gatun Lake overnight*

Party boat

Line handlers

transit advisors ordered the boats to separate. Señor Meza directed me to a large ship mooring in the anchorage basin and began speaking on a handheld radio. Moments after our crew hooked a line to the mooring, a motor launch came alongside. Señor Meza stepped over the life rail to the launch while telling me to be ready to move the next morning at 0800.

As a favor to our crew, we slept in the main saloon letting our guests enjoy the forward and aft cabins. All were up for an early breakfast, anticipating the day's adventure on

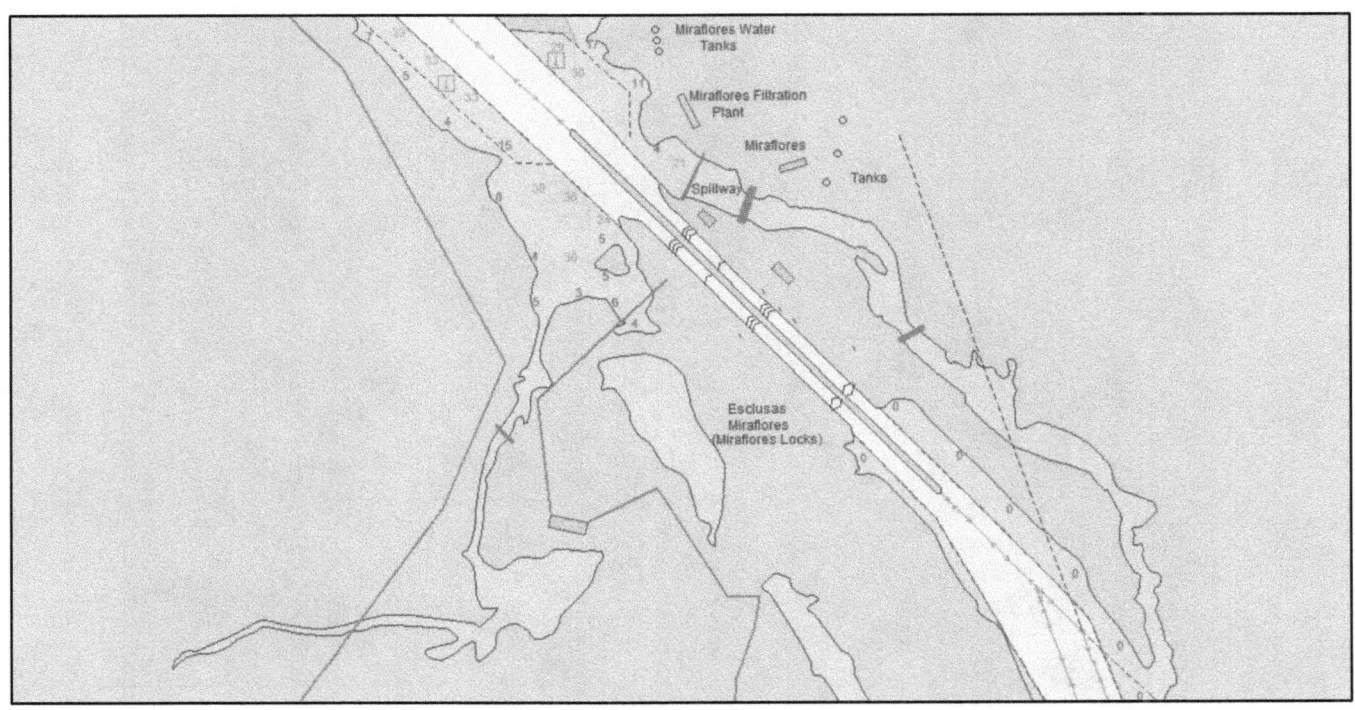

Miraflores locks

Miraflores second lock opening

Rafting with the party boat

Miraflores Lock at Pacific Ocean level

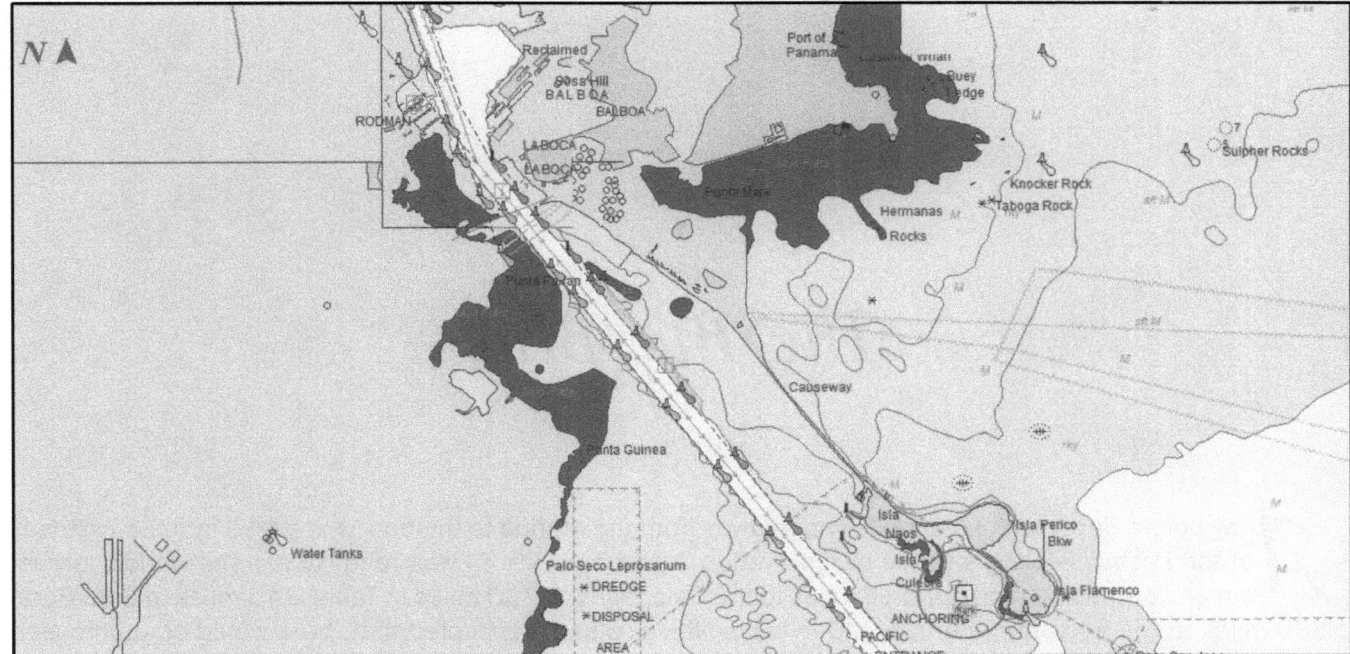

Balboa

the canal, and the wait for Señor Meza began. Long after the time to be ready, we saw a launch heading our way. I brought Mr. Stink to life and our companions prepared to slip the mooring line back through the large mooring eye. With Señor Meza aboard, our crew released the mooring, and I piloted *Scooter* twenty-eight miles in the still waters of Gatun Lake and the Chagres River past a remarkable number of ships to the Pedro Miguel Lock. There, lock line handlers swung monkey fists aboard and the crew tied the light lines to the warps. The lock line handlers pulled the warps over to the lock wall and dropped the large eyes around bollards. We watched the lock walls grow to nine meters above us while our crew eased the warps around cleats to keep *Scooter* in the center of the lock on the way down to Miraflores Lake. I pushed *Scooter* at seven knots over the mile long lake to the first Miraflores Lock, where Señor Meza directed me to lay up alongside a touring boat. Those dining inside pretended we were not there during the descent even though we smiled and waved while the lock walls rose above us.

The lock doors opened. I motored away from the party boat and waited for it to be repositioned in the second lock before I brought *Scooter* alongside for rerafting.

We watched the walls grow until the lock doors opened, revealing another extensive waterway and a long high wall to starboard. I followed orders to slip away from the party boat, but this time I motored slowly past the open gate, not having to rush as fast as Mr. Stink could push *Scooter*. When passing container cranes on both shores the Pacific came into view framed by the Bridge of the Americas. At 1500 our crew tied *Scooter* to the fuel dock at the extreme end of the Balboa Yacht Club pier where Yacht'n'Oceans Services personnel waited to receive the warps and tires. Our group of seven walked the long pier to the parking lot, where I signed off on paperwork and thanked Señor Meza for his courteous directions. The timing was perfect for our volunteer line handlers to catch a bus to the Grand Terminal in town and exchange for one routed to Colón. After they boarded the bus, we turned to make the long walk back to *Scooter*, nearly out of sight at the pier's end. A stranger stepped forward from a small gathering and said, "Hello, there. Did you just go through the canal?"

I cautiously answered, "Uh, yeah," wondering why anyone would ask that question.

I shot photos of a boat with an American flag while we were at the visitor's center. What's your boat's name?"

"*Scooter*."

"That's the one."

What fortune! After exchanging greetings, email addresses, and thanks, Connie and I began the long trek down the dock to the boat. "Can you believe that?" I said. "How many have photos of their boat in a Panama Canal lock?"

"Maybe it's more than luck."

"Oh?"

"The way the universe works."

With the business at the Balboa Yacht Club finished, I motored *Scooter* south to anchor off Punta Culebra. The next day, Connie and I zipped into the small resort marina, padlocked *Jazz* to a cleat, and bused around Panama City to sightsee and do some last-minute provisioning.

Enchantment • 61

The Big Blue

A day before departure, I stopped *Jazz,* midway from the marina to the boat and gazed into the vastness of the Pacific. Feeling a sense of reservation, I asked myself if I was ready to sail the world's largest ocean. It would be nine hundred miles to the Galápagos, 3,720 miles to Tahiti, 145 miles to Bora Bora, 1,680 miles to Fiji, and, from there, 1,220 miles to New Zealand. I accepted that there would be unforeseen dangers ahead, and that I would have to call on life's experiences to make the correct judgment at the time.

Exactly a year to the day since departing from St. Petersburg, I motored *Scooter* away from Central America, steered around anchored ships east of Taboguilla Island, and proceeded south to find enough wind to sail. By 1800 the genoa, main, and mizzen lifted us along on random puffs on a wandering course somewhat east of south. Twenty hours later, conditions allowed sailing more toward the Galápagos. Connie stood watches and entered data on each line of the new supplemental logbook I developed in Panama. It had four lines for each day to record information on weather, wind, current, sail combinations, and remarks at 0600, 1200, 1800, and 2400 or as close to those times as conditions permitted.

We wandered down the ground track in light air adjusting heading to keep the same sail set while reading, cooking, storytelling, and goofing around to fill our daylight hours. We had seen no sign of life around us for days. In that isolation, we set watch at dusk. A single red florescent lamp above the nav desk cast a soft glow around the saloon with enough illumination to see all instruments and allow stepping up into the darkness of the cockpit without the instant blindness that would occur if going on deck from bright white light.

Halfway to the Galápagos, I rose from my second sleep cycle in time for Connie to come off her four-hour watch. After I reviewed her 2400 log entry, I watched the green line rotate around the radar screen without a ping, switched it off, and popped into the cockpit saying, "I have the watch." She looked up from her book propped behind the steering wheel and said, "Nothing seen but stars. Sails look good and we're on course."

I slowly scanned the horizon out of habit after switching the dodger's red dome light off and wished her sweet dreams. She turned the aft cabin light off, extinguishing the sharp white light coming through the hatch starboard of the mizzen mast. I moved from the helm seat to the port cockpit seat, propped myself up with a cushioned deck chair, relaxed, and searched above the horizon for anything moving in the sky. *Whoops!* I caught myself nodding off, shook my head, shifted my position, and relaxed again. *I better check below*, I thought and found the clock had moved a half hour. Seeing the AIS screen displaying no vessel data, I set the alarm clock fifty minutes out, placing it in front of the instrument array forward of the helm and stretched out on the port cockpit seat.

"What the hell are you doing! You aren't sleeping, are you? Yes, you are! What the hell! You talk and talk and talk about the watch and talk about safety but you sleep."

All I could get out was, "But I . . ." as I focused on Connie's dark silhouette glowing in the hatchway's red light.

"What's this? Alarm clock? Don't give me any 'but I's.' Do I have to check on you? Will I have to worry about you sleeping? It matters; our safety matters; it matters that you are awake on watch."

"No, No, No. I didn't think it unsafe to nap. We haven't seen a thing for days," I yelped in the direction of the silhouette in the red light while rising to sit at attention.

"So, I can sleep on watch? How about we both sleep in the cabin all night, huh?"

"Ok, ok, my bad. Won't happen again. Go back and get some sleep."

"You better not. I'll keep an eye on you. You won't know."

Panama Canal to the Galápagos

"I won't do it again."

"I'll check on you," she said, backing down the steps into the red glow. Moments later the aft cabin light blared through the small hatch onto the starboard cockpit seat.

"Ok, ok, it won't happen again. Get your sleep." I moved the soft chair to the bench seat starboard of the mast where I could see Connie rolling onto the bed and said, "I'm right here where you can see me, ok?"

"I'll be a squirrel on your shoulder."

She switched the light off leaving me in darkness. *"How stupid. I'll hear about it at breakfast and maybe all morning,"* I thought. A heartbeat later, *"She really asserted her importance as half the sailing team."*

Nine hundred twenty-one miles of water passed under the keel before we set the anchor in the bay off the beach of Baquerizo Moreno on the island of San Cristobal. We padlocked *Jazz* at the end of the San Cristobal Main Dock and followed the guidebook map to the customs and immigration office. "Your visas please," said the officer behind the desk in a heavy Spanish accent.

"Visas? What visas?" I said, which immediately brought a light speed Spanish scolding while he flailed his arms and his face twisted. Catching a few words I could understand, I realized we should have obtained visas from the Ecuadorian Embassy as we did for Tahiti from the French Embassy. I turned away for a second to see Connie on my right glancing around the room at the officers, who quietly admired her between glancing at me in my moment of reprimand. I knew the tourist trade heavily supported the islanders' standard of living. I pulled the Galápagos guidebook from my three-ring binder, opened to the map, pointed to markets and restaurants circled in yellow, and asked him for recommendations. He slowed to a conversational rate, looked at the map, and said in understandable English, "All good" and processed a limited ten-day stay with the understanding that *Scooter* would be restricted from sailing to other islands in the archipelago.

Seals are in charge

The Big Blue

With a lot to see and do in the short time we had to do it we visited the markets circled on the map. Tired from the walkabout and in need of a good night's sleep after the nine-day sail we arrived at the ramp from the Main Dock down to the floating dock to see a seal stretching its body the full width of the ramp, blocking our way. It looked up at us like a pet wanting to be stroked and cooed over. Connie bravely led the way, talking to the critter as she would a happy puppy. When she got close enough to step on a flipper, it barked and waddled off the ramp.

Seals owned the bay and the beaches. At dawn one morning, a woman's sharp screams jerked me awake. Up on deck I looked around for the source of the ruckus. Movement on the stern of a catamaran anchored off the bow caught my attention. I watched a seal lumber its way down the starboard hull's transom steps. It stopped at the lowest step, looked back at the screaming woman, barked in her direction, and slid into the water. I thought that it probably had heaved itself onto the transom steps, made its way to the wide aft deck between the hulls and into the open sliding door to greet the boat lady when she came up to the galley to make her morning coffee. It may not have been the seal's first catamaran exploration.

From our learnings in Grenada and Panama about taxi owners' willingness to be tourist guides for a day, we spoke with the first one we saw, resulting in a multiday island tour. At the first stop, we cautiously climbed a steep rope-suspended wood-plank ladder to inspect a tree house bed and breakfast before having lunch at a village café. That afternoon I knelt next to the huge tortoise for a photographic moment. Another day we strolled grassy fields around a crater lake only to find huge piles of past picnic trash in waist-high grass waving in the breeze.

Planning the westward passage, I shaped a ground track to Tahiti with the Nobeltec Admiral program to sail north of the Tuamotu Archipelago then southwest to safely weave through the archipelago's western atolls. Buoyweather and a weather fax suggested little air movement to the west, showing isobars far apart. By the time we departed I had photographed turtles, seals, iguanas, birds, and plants, missing only the sight of a strutting Blue-footed Booby.

When the VHF radio stopped squawking Spanish the first day out of the Galápagos, I switched it off. Our daytime watch rotation became pretty casual with one of us on deck most of the time as our route took us far from commercial ship lanes. Nothing seen on the horizon equated to no need to look again for another hour, yet we habitually glanced around, and Connie continued to be a stickler about entering data in all the columns on her watch. We balanced daytime hours below with reading while seated either at the helm or next to the mizzen on the cushioned deck chair, where we could quickly check the horizon and saw only sky, clouds, and water. At night we read under the dodger dome light when not spectating the planets and twinkling stars arching overhead from horizon to horizon. They seemed close enough to touch. No aircraft strobe lights flashed at night. No jet contrails streaked overhead by day. No bogies blipped on the radar, and the CARD stayed silent.

The only sense of humanity alive over the horizon arrived when we listened to broadcasts from English-speaking stations around the world on the single-side-band radio, or we found an email waiting when we linked to SailMail. Connie learned that when a radio announcer said fifteen hundred hours Coordinated Universal Time that it was 3:00 p.m. at Greenwich, England where global time starts. We were at longitude 097° W and had to subtract seven hours from UTC to realize our local time.

In the absence of spectators around us we chose to comfortably live in our skivvies while moving about *Scooter* at a rhythm ruled by the light wind and long undulating waves. Between housekeeping, movie time, book reading, standing watch, and play, I pressed coffee after grinding beans and Connie creatively delivered aromatic dishes listed on the two-week preplanned menu rotation. Oatmeal with frozen berries for breakfast meant that lunch would be bland, but dinner would be something pulled from the freezer, thawed, and grilled with potatoes, beans, and veggies or sauerkraut and the like from cans. Cleanup happened directly after the meal.

When not searching cookbooks for recipes calling for ingredients aboard or moving about with ease while *Scooter* sailed in light air on easy rolling seas, Connie followed me about below making rounds. She learned where to place her finger on each through hull or valve to check for leaks and what to look for in the machine spaces containing all the water pumps. Sometimes living slow and relaxed gave way to times when high wind speeds drove cresting seas or vacillating wind whipped up crossing seas, calling for quick responses and jumping up our speed of managing the entire vessel. I dubbed it living at ocean speed, and Connie began to understand the vibrant meaning.

Sailing into our second week, she said, "Let's get the sheets and things washed," after cleaning and toweling both heads. We waited for the freezer compressor to cycle off, started the desalinator, and sampled the fresh water flowing from the special faucet at the galley sink with a handheld gauge. When it tested pure, I turned a valve under the sink from faucet to tank. I pulled a yellow plastic five-gallon bucket holding spare halyards from under the port cockpit seat and filled it with water using a short hose from the cockpit's single tap. Sitting next to the starboard primary winch I watched her add soap and pump sheets up and down then helped her wring them out and pile them on the port seat. I added water and we repeated the process with skivvies then again with the towels. The rinse cycle followed, consuming more water, until the bucket was free of soap bubbles. Together we hung all the laundry on lines strung from the main shrouds to the mizzen shrouds. With everything hanging in the rigging we used the hose to wet down, lather up, and rinse off and sat in the cockpit to air dry.

Two weeks into the sail we had seen windless days turn into rain blowing horizontally, demanding fast action by taking a reef in the main and working together. Connie closely observed my every move while setting a second reef when the wind jumped again, driving three-meter seas. When the seas and winds allowed us to be comfortable in the main saloon not having to move fast to grip our way around or stand ready to scamper on deck to shift sails, we snuggled on the port divan in front of the big screen.

Scooter sailed westward downwind sometimes with the jib held off to one side with the spinnaker pole and the main to the other, a sail set I explained to Connie as wing on wing. Other times all sails were set on the same side sailing on a broad reach with the wind and seas coming in at an angle off the stern. Scrambling to make the sail shifts and setting reefs and shaking them out during the frequent wind speed changes to maximize boat speed would work against the calm life at sea I wanted to present to Connie. I dropped the mizzen, set the first reef in the main, and accepted a slower boat speed in light air guaranteeing a slower pace of living at ocean speed, more relaxed. About that time, weather forecasting devices aboard showed air moving rapidly in a southwesterly direction far north of our latitude, creating waves that rolled far beyond the wind to bring our first ever experience with huge seas in light air rolling the boat, flogging the sails fiercely. I lowered the main, rolled the genoa in, and called Mr. Stink into action. The sea state could have been a predictor of heavy wind in the future as it was for the early Polynesians.

Along with doing the laundry, watching movies, and routine cooking, I created *Scooter* Chili. The shifting aromas drifting up from the galley to the cockpit as I added ingredients delivered a living texture far different than all that was going on around, below, and above us. I started in the early morning reducing minced garlic, then chopped onions and red bell peppers into a large pot. When the bouquet of their browning filled the saloon, I added ground beef, cooking it fully. I stirred in tomato paste, water, mild chili powder, and oregano and let it simmer until midafternoon. Nearly done, I stirred in black and red beans, sorted and soaked overnight. A few hours later, after the beans were tender, I finished it off by adding a cup or more of Merlot. The odor of the sea, if there was any, had disappeared long ago into an unremarkable nothingness compared to that of the below deck spaces laced with the essence of *Scooter* Chili.

Sailing into our fourth week in what felt like a big blue bubble, we had seen a number of weather and sea conditions but not sustained winds over thirty knots. We had finished playing with the fishing line when it happened. Murphy's Law, "If it can fail it will fail and at the most inopportune time," proved true aboard *Scooter*. I thought that I had smartly engineered Murphy off the boat, but somehow, when I was looking away, he snuck back on and stowed away until I started Mr. Stink to motor southwest between Manihi and Takaroa, atolls of the Tuamotu Archipelago. Murphy couldn't have picked a better place to force an electronic navigation program relied on for its impressive accuracy to fail, requiring immediate action. While the autopilot held a course of 215° compass as darkness closed in, Connie plotted future positions on the paper chart toward Tahiti, keeping Rangiroa to starboard, and I disconnected and reconnected cables that delivered data to a SeaLINK interface adapter. When that failed to fix the problem, I removed a panel behind the nav desk giving access to bus bars where the fine wires in the SeaLINK connected to the GPS data-feed wires. I scraped them with a pen knife until they shined and reconnected them. It worked! Visual electronic charts appeared again on the laptop, and I keyed in destination dead reckoning waypoints that Connie had noted on the paper chart, finding that her calculations were spot on. That morning, a superyacht rose from the sea directly off the bow and disappeared over the horizon within an hour, making it the only vessel of any kind seen on the water or in the air since departing the Galápagos.

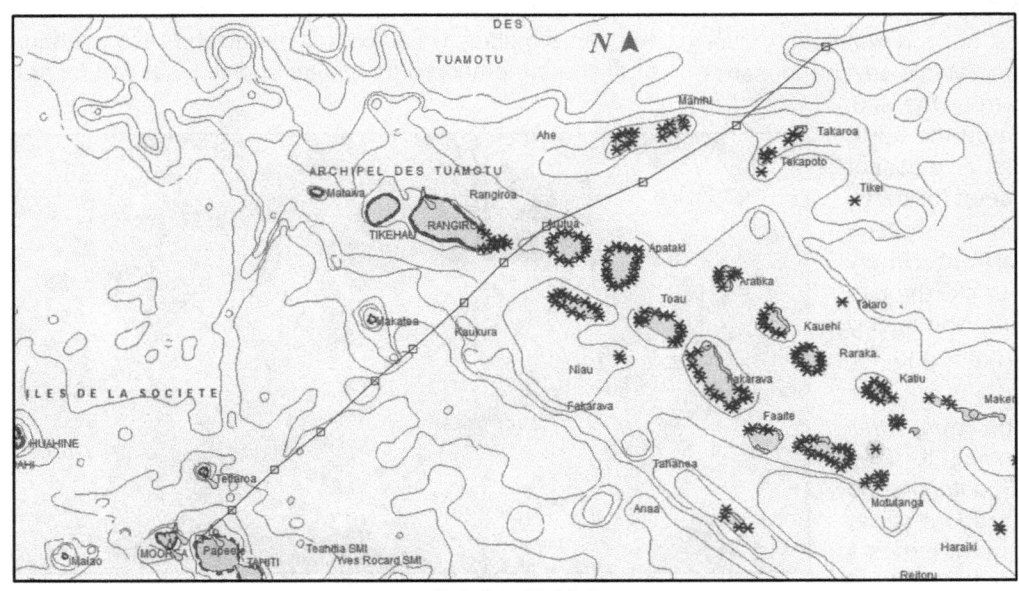

Raising Tahiti

Approaching Papeete Harbor

Diesel fuel reserves had become a concern as the consumption rate increased. On the glassy sea, Scooter could not make over five knots regardless of RPM. At 1,900 RPM she should move at six knots. I had no inkling that the stuff I cleaned from the untreated knotmeter impellers could grow on the expensive bottom paint.

By then I had planned and replanned passages through the reefs under sail and zoomed in on the Admiral chart of Papeete's harbor to lay out a ground track through the reef to anchor in Nanuu Bay near the quay, also under sail if needed. Sailing through a current-swept reef channel required good wind from directions that would give a beam reach. If the wind was light or would not allow a beam reach, I planned to sail Scooter away from the reefs until conditions were just right. Not wanting to excite my mate, I kept my concerns to myself.

The sun sprayed over the horizon reflecting silver shards off the wave tops when Tahiti's seven-thousand-foot mountain, Orohena, rose from the sea. The abundant shades of green on the north slope of the mountain made a pleasant change from the blue on blue seen for thirty-five days. Motoring outside the reef around Point Venus, we took in the waterfront scenery while following the chart's track through the Passe de Papeete. Entering Nanuu Bay opened a view to cruise ship piers and the Quai des Yachts.

After motoring toward the quay wall scanning the bottom and finding it deep enough for the rudder, I circled Scooter around and out to where I thought it prudent to set the plow anchor far from the quay. Fenders hung over the transom. Stern lines and aft-led midship lines were draped over the aft stainless handrail under the arch, ready for deployment. I brought Scooter to a full stop, hurried forward, and lowered the anchor until the chain went slightly slack and asked Connie to ease out the chain as I backed Scooter to the quay. Connie released the windlass gypsy clutch with the operating arm to control the speed of the chain runout, matching Scooter's sternway speed toward the quay's cement wall. Before bumping the wall, I shifted to forward for a moment to slow sternway to a drift then shifted to neutral, hurried aft to see the transom fenders lightly touch the quay wall, threw the coiled lines to the quay on both port and starboard sides, and stepped through the open stern rail gate onto the quay. I grabbed the lines and fast walked to the quay cleats, looped the line around each, stepped back aboard and signaled Connie with my right fist held high swirling my index finger. She locked the gypsy drum to the motor with the operating arm and depressed the windlass's up button with her foot to retract the chain, edging Scooter away from the quay. I trimmed the stern lines until the transom looked to be about a meter from the quay and signaled Connie to stop rolling in the chain. After making the final passage notes in the logbook, I deployed the boarding gangplank, and we walked together on land for the first time in five weeks.

Together we stood looking past Scooter's bow to the cruise ship pier. I turned to my right to survey the curve of the quay against land and felt dizzy. Not dizzy enough to sit fast and prevent tripping over my sandals but enough to know that after thirty-five days of constant motion I was on land. It moved under my feet as I stood still, glancing back over the water to the pier that appeared to float up and around and back into place. Connie experienced the same malady while looking about and held my hand until she remembered the ginger cookies stashed for just

Quay, port side

Quay, bottom worms close up

Stern to quay starboard side

Stern to quay port side

that feeling, scampered back aboard, and returned with the sealed FoodSaver bag slit open at the top. We stood on the quay munching until the world around us stayed in one place.

The unexpected sight of worms wiggling from tubular shells attached to the bottom paint around the aft quarter, on the boot stripe, and on the hull above, where the sea had washed for weeks, grabbed my attention. They appeared to be shipworms, a species of saltwater clam that resembled a worm, historically prevented on wooden sailing ships by copper plating below the waterline. No wonder *Scooter* could not make a decent water speed while Mr. Stink turned above 1,900 RPM. The bottom paint applied two years before sloughed off or simply failed to prevent the growth.

Looking up from the wormy bottom to the immediate cityscape beyond the wide boulevard, seeing cars rolling past shops and restaurants, reminded me of Charlotte Amalie. We walked along the quay to find customs and immigration somewhere beyond the cruise ship pier with the necessary clearing-in documents obtained in Panama ready for presentation in *Scooter's* binder. An official in the port captain's office copied information from our papers onto forms in French and gave Connie a form that had to be stamped at a bank and returned, proving that she had arranged a refundable bond covering her flight expense to the US. Visitor policy considered her to be crew that could be stranded without the financial ability to leave the island. Owning *Scooter* relieved me of that requirement. He slid our passports and visa papers into a desk drawer and gave directions to a bank in town.

Across the boulevard next to the quay, we waited at a window while the teller processed a special account for Connie with funds from my credit card, signed and stamped the bond document, and, at my request, counted out a hundred dollars' worth of French Pacific francs. Back in the office beyond the cruise ship pier, the port captain stamped, signed, and recorded the bond document and stamped our passports and the visas obtained in Panama City, making us legal French Polynesia visitors.

At the quay

Scraping the worms off the bottom became job number one. The clear, warm water made it an enjoyable task for a couple of hours a day until the bottom felt slick. Within two weeks we had entered almost every retail store, restaurant, and grocery store within a day's walk, and I had not seen the Tahiti I read about in my youth. Costs of provision amazed us after converting French Pacific francs to US dollars. A box of chicken nuggets was over eleven dollars, and the cheapest wines started at twenty dollars. Connie let the folks back home know about her experience on the South Pacific Ocean and keyed an email I sent by SailMail:

We experienced extremely light air for most of the almost 4,000 miles, which was exciting as we didn't have the fuel capacity to motor the entire way. There was a lot of sitting and drifting, looking over at a squall and thinking "I'll bet there's some good air over there! Should we aim for it?" When a squall did catch us, we had a nice 15 minutes of 25 knots or so of wind. So, we did some replotting to shorten our course by weaving through the atolls as we got closer to Tahiti. Needless to say, this was the time our electronic chart software decided to bite the dust. We had been charting our course on a paper chart from GPS readings anyway . . . so we just kept doing that and kept a sharp eye out. Capt. Bob actually got us closer to the atolls so we could finally get a glimpse of some land. It was thrilling to see.

Thirty-four days out at sea we saw nothing but ocean, sky, and each other. We don't have a lot of pics of the passage, but all to see is ocean and sky. You know, it's big . . . and it's blue. It certainly is quite an experience, though, to adjust to living on a sailboat on a passage like that. Although we had light wind, we had very big waves, 15 ft and higher, which really tossed us around. Both Bob and I got tossed onto the deck of the cockpit on our watches a couple of times. Ouch. After about 10 days of that you kind of want to stop the ride and get off, but you have to keep going. You get used to it, and learn to wear asbestos outfits when cooking in the galley. I highly recommend martial arts classes to learn the proper stance for balancing yourself below! The weather was beautiful – the occasional squall was harmless and gave us a cool breeze and moved the boat. Capt. Bob was able to motor us as far as possible, stopping to set the sails when we actually had wind, and got us into harbor with 109 liters of fuel to spare. We started with 580 liters.

We entered Papeete harbor and anchored stern to at Quai des Yachts, which is a wharf right up against the main boulevard. We have people walking, traffic whirring, and it's exactly what we needed after the sensory deprivation out on the Pacific.

Paying weekly at the port captain's office for the space at the quay motivated me to motor out of Passe de Papeete, south along the reef, through the Passe de Ta'apuna, and into the Lagon de Punaauia, where I slipped the anchor off the bow as Connie managed the helm. Protected from the ocean swells by the Tepuahano Reef, we were in awe of the stunning sunsets over the island of Mooréa to the west. The Marina Taina dingy dock, south of Pointe de Tata'a, a short zip away on *Jazz*, became another waypoint to island exploration.

While reading one afternoon in the shade of the dodger, light air carried the words, "Ahoy aboard," from somewhere off to starboard. Looking in the direction of the voice, I saw a guy motoring a dinghy about the anchorage. He approached a boat, called out, and moved close to talk if he heard a response. I had seen that in the past—vendors selling all kinds of stuff or offering services that may include protecting the yacht while the owners were ashore, intimidating the owner to pay for protection. I watched him motor toward me sitting in the cockpit. About three meters away he waved and introduced himself as the owner of the Riverside Drive Marina in Whangarei, New Zealand and asked if he could come alongside. Once he knew my plans to visit his country, he cautioned me about the strict clearing-in formalities. After I told him that I would look into that when in Fiji, he held out a pamphlet, suggested I give it a good read before sailing, and invited us to stay at his marina. When he motored on to another yacht I stowed the package in the chart table.

Formalities package

Curiosity inspired us during a morning trip into town to check out a large sloop with an American ensign that arrived overnight at the waterside pier next to the superyachts. We strolled the pier and ogled the rigging and deck accessories, seeing she was out of California. Looking down into the open hatches we saw in plain sight unwashed cookware, piled dishes, strewn clothes, spilled backpacks, open bedrolls, and personal items littered about. The mess said much about the sailors and crew. The next morning, while riding *Jazz* to the dingy dock, we saw a group of young men and a young woman on the yacht's stern deck, but on our return ride to *Scooter* the boat looked vacant. The memory of the conditions on the yacht persisted.

In pursuit of rural Polynesia, we sailed west to Mooréa and anchored inside the reef at the entrance to Cook's Bay in twenty-seven meters of water with nearly all ninety-two meters of chain rolled out. The long zip into the village of Paopao at the south end of the bay gave us a spectacular view of shoreline homes before we beached *Jazz* and walked the village streets and alleys for hours soaking up another culture.

Zipping back, we noticed a family bathing naturally off the beach in front of their home in Piha'ena meters away from *Scooter* at anchor. After four days of exploration, we motored back to Tahiti to resupply with the knowledge that Mooréa would be a pleasant waypoint on the sail to Bora Bora, where we could clear out to head west, continuing our journey.

When ready, we returned to Mooréa for a night then comfortably sailed 105 miles overnight to arrive off the east reef of Raiatea at dawn. With the sun rising over the stern, I piloted *Scooter* through a narrow reef passage. Oohing and aahing at the tropical island, we motored north inside the reef, around the small landing strip on the island's north side, then west to pick up a mooring near Apooiti Marina. After dinner at the marina restaurant and a comfortable night on the mooring we motored north to circle anticlockwise inside the reef around Tahaa Island. Small reef islets north of a town named Patio summoned us to drop anchor and reconnoiter aboard *Jazz*. Two days later we motored south, anchored near the main island, and zipped on *Jazz* a quarter mile west to play in clear

Apooiti Marina

The Big Blue • 69

Tahaa islet

water above the white sandy bottom between uninhabited islets at the reef's edge. When we were ready to slip over the side, a stingray visited and circled for the longest time, encouraging us to beach *Jazz* and let ours be the only footprints on the sand. We walked in wonder at the unspoiled natural beauty and the sight of a coconut lying where a high tide had swept it against a vegetation plateau. A stem had grown out and up from an eye, and from another eye a root had made itself fast to the moist sand below just the way they had populated ocean shorelines around the world for ages. I had finally reached the Polynesian island I had read about.

Midmorning on the fifth of June, we motored *Scooter* out through a narrow cut in the reef to blue water and good air to begin our passage to Bora Bora. Six hours later, we rolled in the blue gennaker, lowered the main, navigated the only deep-water passage to the inner lagoons, and hooked a mooring at the Bora Bora Yacht Club.

We found the dingy dock at a French Polynesian bank to be a safe place to leave *Jazz* while searching for the customs office, where clearing out of French Polynesia could be managed days later. While exploring, we found an ATV rental company and decided to return to rent one for a drive around the island to see the cannon sites left after the Pacific war. After riding out heavy winds for two days,

Raising Bora Bora

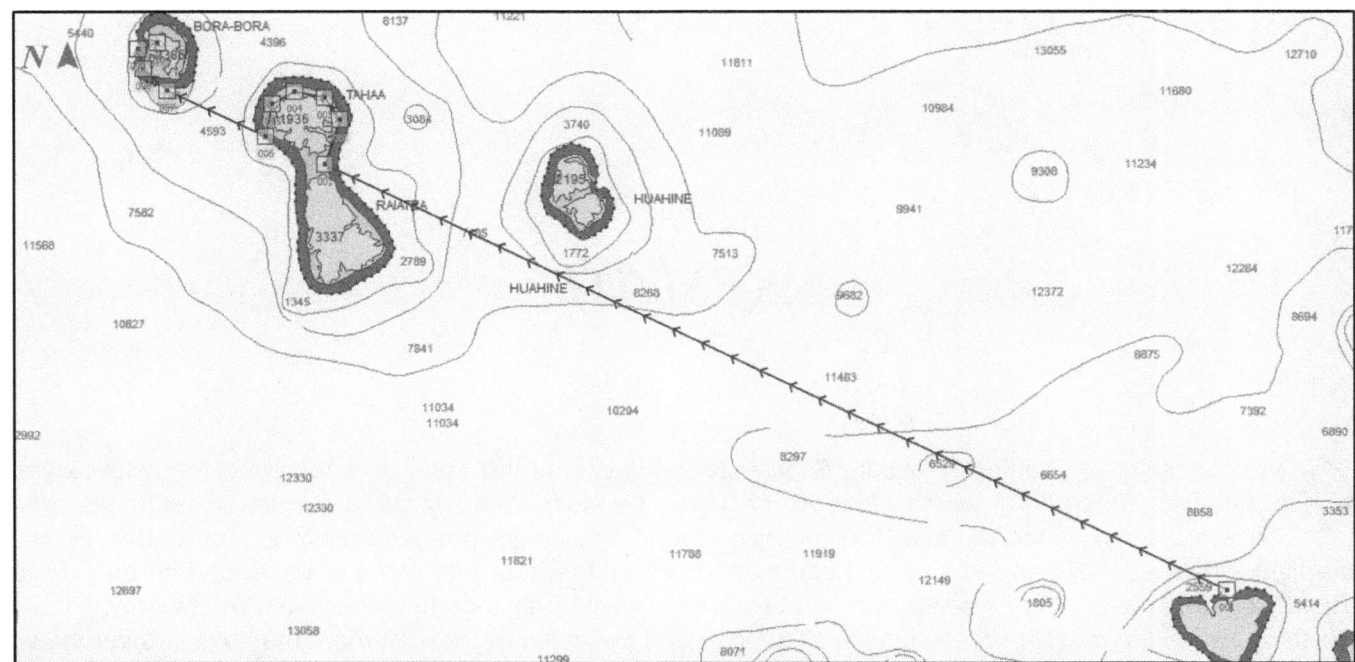

Mooréa to Bora Bora

swinging on the mooring, we zipped ashore for the big adventure.

Following the buggy rental owner's directions, I turned onto a dirt road that narrowed to a steep, stone-covered trail. The incline increased to the point that I thought the buggy would flip over backward and I stopped. I rolled in reverse down the trail and found a spot to leave the buggy while we hiked up the trail. We paused to catch our breath where the grade flattened into an open field. There, I remembered that I had left our passports and wallets and cash in a backpack in the buggy next to the cooler filled with beer and sandwiches. I thought that they would be safe in this missionary-anchored paradise and decided against returning down the steep grade to make a recovery only to climb back. The buggy was well-hidden from the main road.

On the hilltop we found a panoramic view of the barrier island and the airstrip but no cannons. The sound of a motorbike climbing the lower part of the steep trail pierced the rustle of bushes in the breeze. I gave it no thought but had yet to discover that the missionaries had not been successful in changing Polynesian attitudes away from thinking that what's yours was also mine. After snapping pictures, we headed back down the steep trail. At the buggy, only the cooler remained with contents untouched. We reported the theft at the poste de police and learned that the nearest consulate where passports could be reissued was back in Tahiti. That afternoon, sitting at a picnic table on the yacht club restaurant's sand floor, I linked the laptop to the Internet and canceled my credit cards.

Our hopes were high for a fast sail back to Tahiti as the forecast was for twenty knots. The genoa, main, and mizzen pulled *Scooter* at good speed, but when the wind died down the expectation of raising Mooréa before dark faded. With no moon that night, the deck glowed under starlight against the black water. I had no intention of negotiating the passage through the reef to the lagoon off Tahiti nor into Cook's Bay after dark, so I decided to lie north of Mooréa with sails down and wait for sun-up. The light breeze made the sea state easy. We managed a two-hour watch rotation, monitoring *Scooter's* icon on the Nobeltec display, drifting on the tidal current until daybreak, and found anchorage again in the familiar Lagon de Punaauia back on the west shore of Tahiti.

Humbling myself in front of the consulate's wide mahogany desk, I listened to him agree with my opinion about stupidity before he delivered his passport responsibility lecture. Long minutes later, he got to business renewing our passports. Waiting for the replacements, we revisited shops, restaurants, and places of interest, enjoying them more than when we first explored the island. It felt similar to returning to familiar streets and shops at home after a long time away. Twenty days later, we were legal again with temporary passports, new credit cards, and driver licenses.

Chatter on single-side-band radio nets about the ongoing political issues since the fourth coup in Fiji suggested I rethink my desire to visit that island nation at this time. I looked to Tonga as the next stop and created the 1,400-mile ground track. I reviewed charts, researched clearing-in requirements, checked the weather, and prepared to sail west.

Restart

Before sunset on the Fourth of July, *Scooter* sailed back into the world of blue above and below, westbound for Tonga on a course far south of Bora Bora. At the horizon the two blues shifted color tone where the sky joined the sea 360 degrees around. That night the deck again glowed under intense starlight. The speed of living at sea changed sometimes by the hour just as we experienced on the sail to Tahiti. Connie proved to be the perfect first mate after twelve months aboard, capable and trustworthy. Should anything happen to me, I knew she could sail *Scooter* and me to safety. Now, at more than a year together we had worked through the ups and downs in our relationship as many couples do.

One morning she said, "I've a urinary tract infection. I'm worried it'll really get bad before we get to Tonga."

"I'll check the med kit for something that'll take care of it."

"I can't take just any old thing, especially sulfa drugs. I'll get sick on those."

I grabbed the kit at the bottom of the forward cabin hanging locker and pulled out three antibiotics. She chose ciprofloxacin hydrochloride after recalling she had taken it for the same problem before. Holding the plastic bottle, I read the directions, "Ah, twice a day at the same time for fourteen days. Did you have any diarrhea, stomach pain, headache, weakness, nausea, or vomiting back then?"

"I don't know. It was years ago."

"Oh wait! Says here not to take it if you're pregnant."

"That's stupid. Give me that. I'll decide."

Her symptoms disappeared two days later, and I reminded her to follow the remainder of the fourteen-day routine. While she rested, I managed nighttime sailing by cycling through sleeps on deck after radar scans. Occasionally during our straightforward talks, she went on about the rent control law at home that protected only those who continued to rent from price increases, but I missed asking why the concern, being focused on working the boat and navigation to Tonga. I shaped a course around Vava'u, Tonga's north island, and south to enter a protected bay from the west that we would motor through to the customs dock at the town of Neiafu after thirteen nights at sea.

We found Tongans to be just as Captain Cook observed on his first landing, naming the island group the Friendly

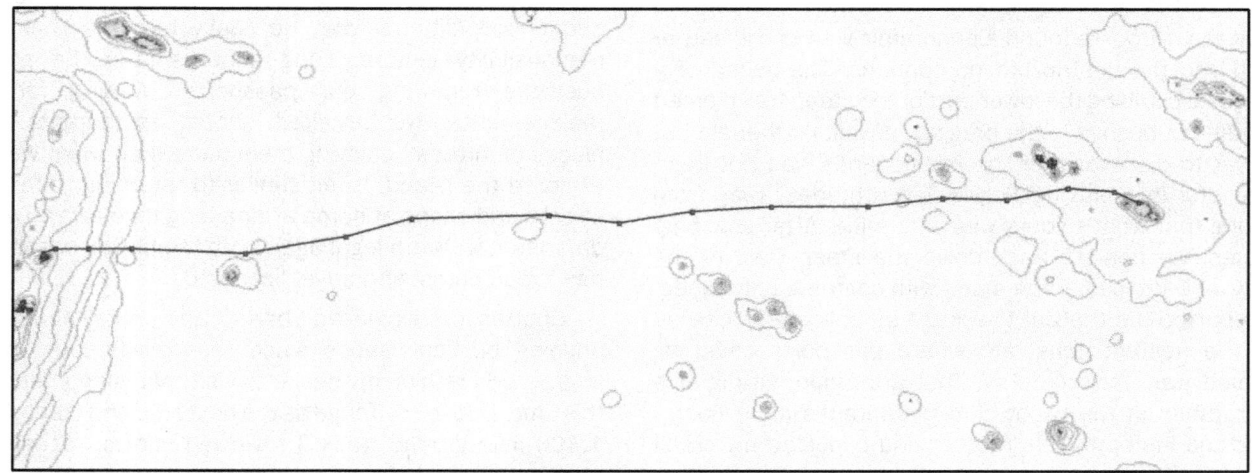

Tahiti to Tonga daily plots

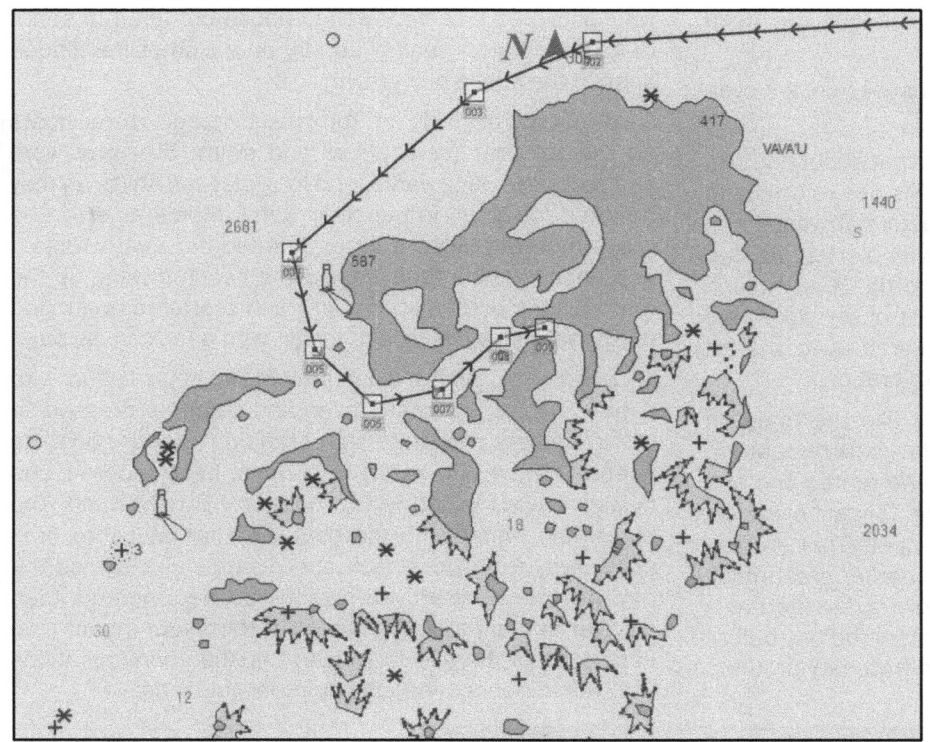
Arriving Vava'u

Islands, and enjoyed that friendliness while we cleared in by following a suggestion found in a cruise guide to offer cookies, cakes, pies, and the like to those who board to conduct entry formalities. Paper and document stamping moved along at a cordial pace. Quarantine stayed in effect until the Ministry of Health and Quarantine stamped forms at the local hospital, where we waited, standing on a painted concrete floor at a nursing station counter, feeling the warm breeze flowing in through open windows. I signed a Certificate of Pratique on which I guaranteed that the vessel and all aboard were healthy and that if a quarantinable disease broke out aboard while in Tongan waters, the certificate would be voided and all would have to immediately leave the Tongan archipelago aboard *Scooter*. On another form, I agreed to keep all garbage in leakproof containers and take no foodstuffs ashore. That done, I removed the yellow quarantine flag flying under the Tongan courtesy flag and motored to pick up a mooring in Koko Bay. The jellyfish swimming near the surface in the murky bay water alerted me that bottom cleaning and watermaking would have to wait.

The cruising guide spoke to the extreme religious doctrines, dress codes and social customs brought to the Pacific islands during the missionary Christianizing years. That way of life persisted in Tonga unlike other island nations that had since blended the light of Christianity within their cultures as social values changed. Tongan businessmen customarily wore a black shirt, full length black skirt down to the shoes, and a wide palm dress belt of woven palm fronds that looked more like a cummerbund. School-age children wore blue uniforms. The shoulders of women and men had to be covered, and public displays of affection, even hand holding, were considered disrespectful. Topless or nude sunbathing could be enjoyed only on uninhabited islands. Lady visitors were urged to not wear short shorts or miniskirts for dinner or evenings out, and men had to be seen in slacks and a shirt with a collar. Shorts and T-shirts passed scrutiny in town during the daytime but not in church.

Day-trips into town carried us through either the Mango Café, where locals and cruisers gathered, or the dockside restaurant owned and operated by a young couple from San Francisco living aboard their sloop moored in the bay. We walked Fatafehi Road from the farmer's market near the customs dock to explore Neiafu restaurants, markets, cafés, the ANZ bank, St. Joseph's Cathedral, the Post Office and went to Paradise Hotel Vava'u for an enjoyable meal.

Our search around town for beef turned up only one lonely dark gray steak sitting on a shelf behind a glass door at a small meat market. Sharing our beef search story with cruisers brought us a tip about a Tongan with connections in New Zealand who processed select cuts at his house. We strolled the narrow streets until we found the address over the door of a small house on a corner lot. A large wood-cutting band saw stood in the shade under a rickety lean-to somewhat attached to the street side of the house. From the street we could easily see decayed meat debris covering the entire exposed saw blade and table, which was swarmed with flies. I commented to Connie that it looked like we would visit the open-air farmer's market often. The sight sold us on avoiding any meat products not in a can. Perhaps that's why corned beef in cans was sold in every store. Not the little tuna fish-sized cans but the type found at food warehouses. Some mini grocery stores displayed cans from small to giant size stacked the full length of double-high shelves. The sight made us speculate that corned beef was the major protein source for the islanders and might be why they were remarkably tall and large.

Provisioning included selecting choice wines at affordable prices that we consumed before, during, and after evening meals. One morning Connie said, "You got really loud last night. You scared me."

"You drank as much as I did and—"

Restart • 73

"I didn't get angry. I can hold mine, you can't. You need to stop that."

"That was last night. We both got testy again. It's over. Let's have a good day."

I discounted it as just another rapid spat about nothing. We had been having them occasionally since returning to Tahiti unlike during our time together before arriving there. Her comment about my evening behavior alerted me that something more serious could be troubling us, as no one before her in my life had surfaced that observation. We cleaned up the breakfast dishes, squared away the aft cabin, and set out to resume island exploration.

A group of all-terrain vehicles just like the ones on Bora Bora sat in the yard next to the dockside restaurant, waiting to be driven about the island. We rented one and joined a group with a guide, learning Tongan historical facts at each location the caravan stopped. That evening at the Paradise Hotel, while enjoying another great meal, we acknowledged the young men and a girl seated at a round table nearby. We encountered them the day before at the Mango Café, learning they were fraternity brothers

Buggy rental

out on a summer break aboard a dad's sailing yacht out of San Diego and skippered by a professional captain. We had seen the boat at Marina Taina in Tahiti.

Adventuring to explore a less inhabited nearby island might ease whatever relationship issues were floating around us, I thought. So, I suggested we motor south through the bays to anchor near the shallow sandbar between Nuku and Kapa islands, recommended in a comprehensive cruising guide for the Kingdom of Tonga. There, on our second Friday in Tonga, we zipped on *Jazz* to explore Nuku Island's long sandbar beach. Walking about, we discovered a cement-walled house but felt it best not to approach after seeing laundry on a clothesline hidden deep in the jungle overgrowth.

Saturday, a group of Tongans beached three boats on the sandbar for a picnic and swim. Everyone wore street clothes, long pants, and long-sleeved shirts as they frolicked for hours in the clear water. Moments after the group motored away, a silver-bearded old man wrapped in a neck-to-ankle robe walked the beach picking up the many plastic bottles and other trash scattered about and disappeared into the island jungle with a full canvas bag.

Sunday morning a boat arrived on Kapa Island with a man at the outboard tiller and another dressed in black trousers and white shirt standing near the bow. He hopped off the bow as the boat made beach contact and quickly walked inland with a book in his right hand. The other man waited with the boat. An hour later they both sped away from the beach and disappeared across the bay. Another boat arrived and the scene repeated, then another and another. The island of thirty-four inhabitants had seven of the eleven Tongan Christian denominations with worshippers in need of spiritual guidance.

That evening, we were back on the mooring in Koko Bay sipping wine after dinner. I must have said something stupid that set off another quarrel, which accelerated until Connie stood under the open saloon hatch and screamed out a long, loud, "Hellllllp!" I stopped, wondered who may have heard the scream carrying over the still water, and went up to sit on the aft cabin top next to the mizzen. Looking forward through the hatch I could see Connie, motionless on the starboard divan. Minutes later a dinghy pulled alongside with two men aboard. One grabbed the handrail saying, "We heard a scream for help. Is everything ok here? Sometime the stresses of living closely together brings friction."

"I did," Connie said rising up the saloon steps."

"Are you ok?" the dinghy man asked.

"Uh, yeah, I'm ok."

"We know all about the tensions two people can have confined aboard a boat. I can help by taking the lady to the hotel for the night."

Connie held me in a steady gaze and said, "Take me with you. I'll get my things."

The sight of Connie climbing down the ladder into the dinghy and fading into the darkness replayed many times that night while I tried to understand our relationship breakdown. Not knowing how I would be received at the Paradise Hotel the morning after my restless sleep, I straight out asked the guy at the desk for her room number. He said he would see if she was up and disappeared through the beaded curtain behind the desk. He returned a few minutes later and said, "She will be out soon."

Connie walked with determination as we followed a path out to the dock and stopped to sit on a bench in the shade of a palm tree. "What's troubling us?" I said.

She looked straight into my eyes and said, "I'm not going to sugarcoat anything. You scared me again last night, really bad. I don't feel safe. I've nowhere to go to get away when you drink. Don't get me wrong, I love the freedom of sailing. I've learned so much, but now I have to feel safe. I have nowhere to go here, and home is so far away. I don't like being trapped."

Taken aback, stumbling for something to say and at the same time recalling how we matched each other's wine, glass for glass, I looked away. Saying I was sorry or promising to do better would not address the issues that had festered. Whatever it was would only get worse for her and for me. Separation was the only way to move forward for both of us.

Before I could speak, she snapped, "My apartment will cost so much more. I'll have to get work right away to make ends meet." That worried her far more than I had previously sensed. As with Lynn, I wanted to pay for Connie's flight home, but this time I felt compelled to go further and offered a $2,500 cash gift to help her jump-start her life back home. The frustration in her voice faded as she accepted release from her fear. While the morning shadows moved along the dock, we planned her journey home. That afternoon, she collected her things and packed her travel case while I purchased a next-day flight ticket at Teta Tours and obtained an advance from my credit card in US dollars at the ANZ bank. We shared that night together at the Paradise Hotel, and over breakfast talked about her plans to reengage friends at home. Taking full control of her future, she bused alone to the single-runway airport on the north side of the island.

I stood in front of the hotel on Fatafehi Road watching the bus carrying her away until it vanished over the hill into town. Her first hop would take her to Fiji, where she would change to a larger plane to New Zealand and then jet to California.

Reclined in the cushioned deck chair on the aft cabin top I recalled the words of dinghy man about the tension that can build between two people in confinement aboard. I wondered if our egos had collided, both of us being quite full of independence and self-determination, inhibiting compassionate compromise under stress. Yet, thirteen months with Connie had immersed me in what heretofore had been an unknown lifestyle. Chasing thoughts further, I had to be aware of the bad effect of more than one glass of wine, something never experienced during my time with Lynn or Cindy or before with Donna. That thought powered me further inward to see that I may not have finished grieving over losing Cindy, and that perhaps wine had become a way to wash the grief away.

Shifting my focus, I had to plan sailing through the many island groups to clear out at the capital, Nuku'alofa, on the southernmost Tongan island of Tongatapu. From there I would sail to New Zealand as previously planned. On that passage, I would be self-reliant for days and nights at sea for the first time, unlike the easy day sails island-hopping from St. Thomas to Grenada. Confident of my sailing and navigation skills and with the formidable upgrades aboard *Scooter*, I pondered what to do to fill my time alone at sea. Inventorying the entertainment aboard, I counted 120 full-length feature movies on DVD and ninety-nine music CDs, including rock, classical, country, rhythm and blues and jazz. I rediscovered early radio recordings, *The Shadow* being my favorite, and whole seasons of several TV series. *Scooter's* library shelf stored unread books by Clancy, Baldacci, Crichton, Ludlum and Patrick O'Brian's entire collection of sea stories ready for a reread. With spare time management resolved, I searched for where I put that folder about clearing into New Zealand.

A Wi-Fi tower at the dockside restaurant linked my laptop to the Internet after I rigged the card purchased in St. Thomas to a wire hoisted in the rigging. Gremlins immediately bypassed the laptop's security package but were eradicated at the restaurant by a computer specialist. His primary business revolved around virus removal and device protection at local Internet cafés. Tongans, very trusting people, rarely considered that bad actors could be tracking Internet searches wanting to infect software for the thrill of it. Connie's email thanking me for the adventure and the stipend filled me in on her journey home.

My beaten path to shore became the Mango Café, where cruising couples and others engaged in conversations. Surrounded by the frat boys, I saw the single gal was the center of their attention at the bar when I walked my order to a table. A man ordered a beer at the bar, walked over to the long table where I sat, and started to chat about his reason for visiting Tonga. He made a living buying and selling boats that owners had to get rid of after having terrible ocean experiences or finding that "sailing the dream" fell short of expectations. Boat owners wanting out of their boat, many in a hurry, flew home leaving the boat with a local broker to manage the sale. After I disclosed my reason for being in Tonga alone, our table talk ended with us wishing each other luck with the search.

Meeting people, provisioning, and journey planning filled the days. Mail arrived from Seth containing no surprises. On the way back from the Post Office to board *Jazz*, padlocked at the café's dock, I said hello to the yacht buyer in passing. He stopped me and enquired if I would like to meet two women he had met the day before. I had been very focused on solo sailing to New Zealand in the southern hemisphere's spring weather window before the tropical cyclones popped up, but what the heck. I agreed to be introduced.

A tall, blue-eyed blonde named Erin accompanied a petite, dark-haired, dark-eyed Fran, who was wearing a great smile when we met the next morning. I had no energy for another involvement and committed myself to just making small talk. They were on a grand adventure away from their Australian homeland. Erin's parents, American expats, joined an Australian commune when she was a child, and Fran, a professional photographer, wanted to expand her talent into underwater photography. After introductions and chats that morning, unexpected encounters with them happened at various shops, bars, and restaurants as the days passed.

Erin carried vials of water blessed by her spiritual mother. Sprinkling the water onto aches and sprains relieved pain. So, she said. However, when I watched her drip the water onto a woman's neck, place one hand on her shoulder near her neck and the other high on her back, mumble some words, and shout, "Out!" while rapidly moving her hands upward, my eyes opened wide. *Really!* I could not believe that people would pay for that treatment. Surprisingly, the woman, seated on the other side of the picnic table from me, said her neck pain was gone! *Hmmm. Is this for real or are they all working together to trick a bystander into paying for a healing?* Fran stood by smiling, camera in hand.

Between episodes of the Erin and Fran show, I studied the requirements and restrictions for yachts arriving in New Zealand. My enthusiasm for visiting faded the further I read. I thought about everything I'd experienced thus far clearing in and out of countries and looked at the New Zealand demands as way over the top. On the Border Agency's information sheet in large bold font I read, "Greetings and welcome to New Zealand." Below that, I read in a slightly smaller bold font, "Prior to arrival the master of every craft is required to give forty-eight hours' notice to the New Zealand Customs Service and Ministry of Agriculture and Forestry of the expected port of entry and time of arrival." Next in the folder I scanned the Supplemental Customs Fact Sheet Number 32, seeing, "Arrival of yachts and small craft in New Zealand." It warned, "Failure to comply may result in prosecution and a penalty of up to twelve months imprisonment." I read further; "Report directly to a customs port of entry;" "Fly the international Q-flag once you have entered New Zealand territorial waters (12 nautical miles)." Following that, a list of required entry documents appeared:

Advance Notice of Arrival

Inward Report

Import Entry Documentation—for yachts and small vessels

New Zealand Passenger Arrival Card—for each person on board

Valid passport containing a valid permit visa—for your intended length of stay for each person on board

Border Cash—cash in excess of NZ $10,000 must be declared on this form

Last Port Clearance and Master Declaration

That seemed easy enough. No problem. The next three pages of the fact sheet asked for information that I had not yet thought to gather in my clearing-in binder. The form entitled "Don't Bring Hitchhikers to New Zealand" caused some concern even though I checked the bottom monthly. Then I came across the forms to complete for advance notice of arrival, which spelled out the forty-eight-hour advance notice requirement, including how to give that notice and what to do if my estimated time of arrival changed. The Inward Report for Small Craft form contained four pages. The Import Entry for Temporary Small Yachts form had a yellow onion skin copy. The Outward Report for Craft was five pages. A single sheet required advanced notice of Departure of Yachts and Pleasure Craft. Had there been an animal aboard, I would have to disclose the pertinent information and the pet would be put in caged quarantine ashore. The New Zealand Ministry of Agriculture and Forestry form required itemization of the meat on board—type, weight, the country of origin, country of import, and where it was loaded. *No problem here*, I thought, *I'll just eat down the fresh food inventory on the way and jettison extras overboard before arriving.* Reading on, I had to certify on a form that no garbage had been thrown overboard from the vessel within the outer limits of the territorial waters of New Zealand. Another form had thirty bullet points identifying restricted bio-security hazards under the heading, "Prohibited and Restricted Items," and noted, "WARNING, failure to make a correct declaration is an offense punishable by imprisonment and may result in removal from New Zealand." A departure form headed, "Important Note" read: "You are required by law to leave New Zealand before your permit expires. If you do not do this, Immigration New Zealand has the power to make you leave." A listing of arrival ports showed that the northernmost and closest to Tonga was the town of Opua on New Zealand's northeast coast, and I made that my destination. I planned to leave Vava'u on August 30th to meander and explore south to Tongatapu Island the next week.

I shared my frustration about the mountain of requirements and restrictions with Erin, who chided, "Wait till you go to Australia." It was apparent to me that Erin and Fran were not looking for men to pay for their adventures or take care of them. Erin obviously earned money from selling spiritual pain relief, and Fran seemed to be self-funded somehow. They shared stories about their time snorkeling with humpback whales on a government approved and escorted expedition in Tongan waters. I thought that it would be fun to carry their adventure in Tonga to another level and offered *Scooter* as an exploration platform around the north islands. I invited them aboard to look around. Both liked the accommodations and agreed to the adventure.

They arrived with bags of provisions, followed my food storage directions, and unpacked their kits in the forward compartment. Chatter about our backgrounds brought us together sibling-like while I motored the channel south toward Kapa Island and the anchorage at Port Mourelle. We created meals together and watched sunsets and sunrises, all the while eagerly anticipating what waited for us on the next dive or island exploration.

Two days of snorkeling, beach walking, and exploring Swallows Cave—where sailors had painted ship names on the cave walls for centuries—gave way to relocating to the island of Taunga for another day of water play. Erin demonstrated how to open a coconut she found under a tree by stabbing the coconut eye with a chef's knife and twisting the handle. She popped the knife point clean off.

The girls wanted to snorkel the vertical side of a reef. Following depth markings on the chart I moved to north of Vaka'eitu Island's wide, crescent-shaped beach and worked *Scooter* to anchor with the forward scanning sonar, getting close enough to swim to a reef from the boarding ladder. After lunch we coasted *Jazz* onto the bright white sand. The girls jumped off and made a beeline to a giant banyan tree and straddled the huge roots, feet almost touching the heavily charred sand that gave testimony to the many fires made by past generations of Tongans. Thick aerial roots grown into new trunks gave the tree the appearance of a colossal green pergola covering an area the size of a soccer field. Erin hugged the banyan tree for the longest time, slowly mumbling, while Fran and I wandered up a winding, overgrown path. Erin caught up and our little explorer band discovered ruins of an old open-air restaurant, aged picnic tables, counters, fire pits, and barbeques that peeked above the jungle undergrowth. I had found another Polynesian island paradise long searched for. Banana plants grew everywhere.

Fran disappeared down a bank to my left and Erin vanished into the jungle on my right. I wanted to shepherd them back aboard *Scooter* and navigate the passage to the mooring on Koko Bay before dark. As soon as I got them corralled one inquisitively wandered away and disappeared behind huge green leaves. When the shadows had grown long, I was able to convince them of the need to leave the jungle and return to the boat before sunset.

Sitting on the helm seat while steering *Scooter* toward Koko Bay, a pain in my right knee sharpened, prompting my recall of the injury years before while unstepping the mast on the Flying Scot for the first time. Surgeries performed in Michigan and California to stimulate cartilage regeneration had been successful enough for me to lose the incident in memory until that long walk up and down the island's steep jungle paths. Rubbing the knee with my right hand had no effect. The sharp pain continued. Erin observed my stress and offered her treatment. She splatted drops of blessed water from a small vial onto my knee and the ache immediately stopped. I thought I had been conditioned to that response by observing how the water worked on others and that

Swallows Cave

Humpback and calf

my mind had tricked me. But the pain really went away! I was and am still baffled.

At dusk, we hooked to the mooring in Koko Bay, and as a thank you for the adventure, Fran gave me digital copies of the photos she shot while they were snorkeling with humpback whales before the new underwater housing her boyfriend gave her began to leak.

The day after the memorable Erin and Fran adventure I made rounds below and on deck, reviewed provisions, and plopped into the soft deck chair on the aft cabin top to witness the beauty around the bay and the cotton clouds drifting above while pondering where to restart my companionship quest.

Tonga whale dive

Ocean Solo

While planning the sail from Tonga to New Zealand I felt no apprehension shrinking my courage to sail the distance alone. Relieved to have no one to be responsible for at sea except myself, I slipped the mooring in Koko Bay to work my way south through the Ha'apai group of islands toward the southern Tongatapu Group. I spent the first night at the familiar anchorage between Kapa and Nuku islands. It served as an attitude-adjustment stop at the beginning of my first ever long-distance ocean solo challenge.

From Nuku Island, good air lifted *Scooter* south to an anchorage off the village of Pangai on Lifuka Island in the Ha'apai group. The next morning, I zipped ashore and wandered the streets of the town in search of a been-there souvenir and found a black T-shirt with "Mariner's Café, Ha'apai, Tonga" emblazoned on it. As usual the planned one-day stop turned into two days with a second café visit.

Wanting to walk the sands of an uninhabited island, I anchored off the west side of Nukupule Island, launched *Jazz*, and followed a sandy-bottomed passage between submerged coral cliffs. I tossed the anchor over and snorkeled along the coral walls with the colorful fish. Because none were large enough to take with my speargun, I motored to the beach, set the anchor high on the white sand, and walked along the water's edge on a stroll around the island. Repeated heavy thuds from off the blue water drew my attention, and I saw a humpback whale smacking its pectoral fin on the surface less than fifty meters from the beach. Picking up shells, inspecting sprouting coconuts trees, and looking for signs of humanity, I weaved my way from the water's edge to the foliage line and back as I trekked around the island until *Jazz* came back into view. Before I closed the island-circling loop, I spotted high on the beach at the jungle's edge a pile of huge, rusted corned beef cans. Bright paper labels wrapped around two shiny metal cans showed it had been a short time since Tongans had taken a meal break from fishing in the nearby shallows.

Moving on, I anchored and snorkeled Tungua Island's reefs for two days and repeated the fun at Nomuka for another two

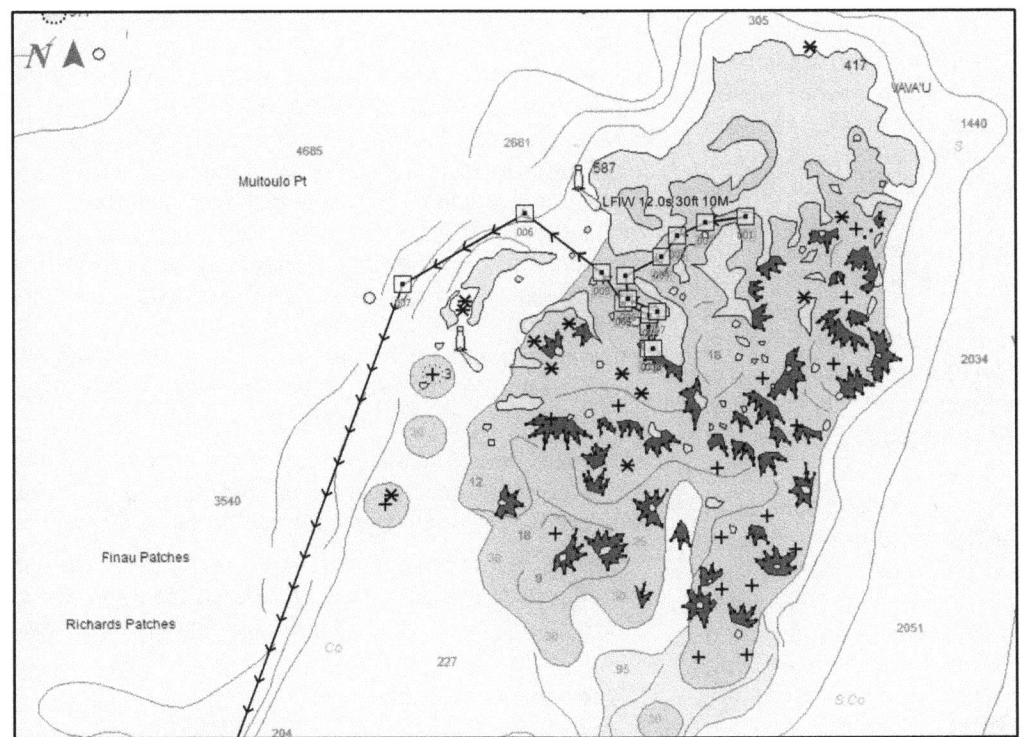

Departing Vava'u group

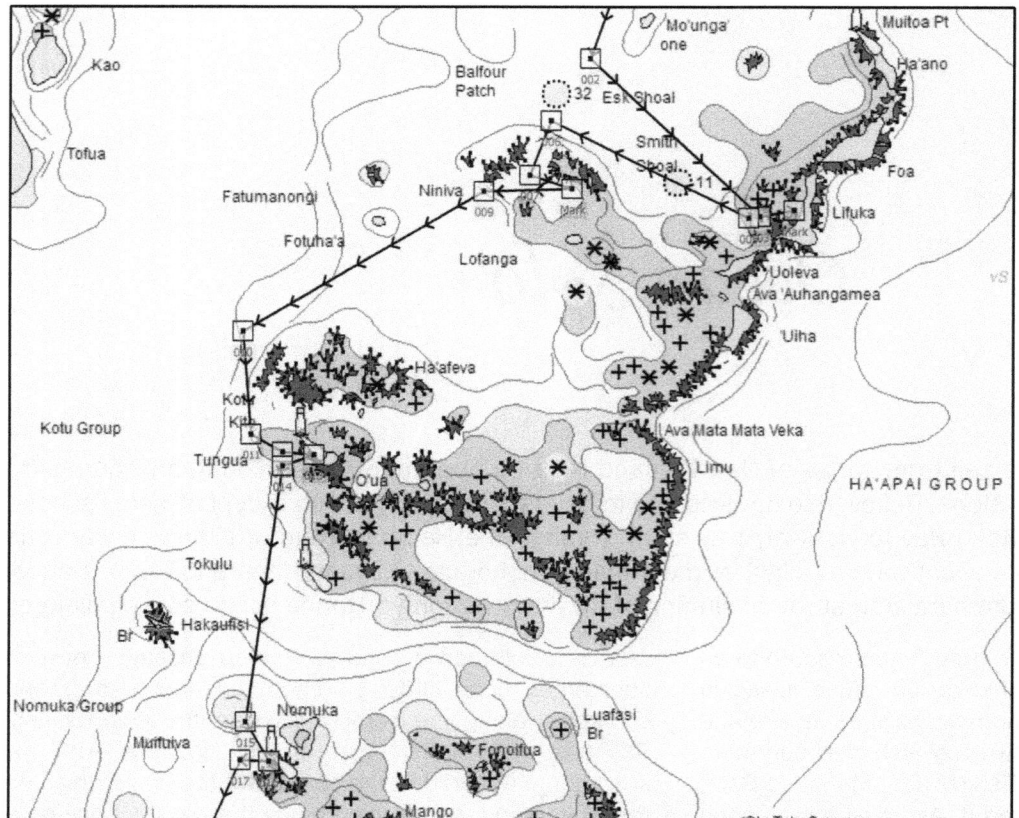
Ha'apai group

days. A day's sail later, I anchored southwest of tiny Pangaimotu Island a little more than a mile north of Nuku'alofa, the capital of the Kingdom of Tonga, on the southern island Tongatapu.

Standing on *Jazz,* I zipped the mile to the small boat quay behind the Queen Salote Wharf. In town, I visited an Internet café and shopped at small markets. My walkabouts led me past burned-out structures and charred concrete slabs where buildings once stood. A shopkeeper recounted, after I enquired about the devastation, the movement that occurred against the conservative king's son, who inherited the throne after his father died in November of the prior year. The parliament went into recess for the rest of the year instead of voting on democratic reform proposals and the opposition rioted, overturned, and burned police cars, and looted and burned major stores, including the large food market. Six people died in the melee.

After learning my way around town, I moved *Scooter* to anchor off the breakwater near the wharf but away from the ferry boat's charted route. It shortened the long and sometimes wet ride on *Jazz.* Early one morning while reading on the starboard cockpit seat I heard what sounded like a ruptured high-pressure air hose wheezing. I looked up toward the waterfront where the sound seemed to originate but saw nothing unusual at the wharf. Then the loud sound repeated close up. Reaching for the handrail, I stood, looked down, and there it was: a whale about as long as *Scooter*, slowly moving next to the hull toward the stern. I moved to the stern rail and watched it circle around the transom to the port side, where it moved slowly toward the bow. I walked forward on the port deck, chasing the clear sight of it moving next to the keel until it joined a larger whale waiting motionless in the deep, clear water, its nose about to touch the anchor chain that dissolved into the depths below. They blew warm, misty breath right in front of me and inhaled before they swam westward side by side. I speculated that they had echolocated the water-filled keel and, sensing that it may be alive, approached to satisfy their curiosity.

My time in Nuku'alofa happened to be the same month of the meeting between Polynesian nation leaders. As a security measure, a Tongan Royal Navy vessel arrived and anchored off my port stern while I provisioned in town. Upon returning, I secured *Jazz* to a stern cleat and noted some of the ship's crew on the bridge, watching me with large binoculars. I stored my provisions, returned to the cockpit, and positioned myself on the helm seat in a comfortable pose, looking aft toward the wharf while glancing out of the corner of my eye at the crew on the bridge watching me. I went below, returned with my long eyes, and focused in on the large lenses protruding from the ship's bridge, returning the scrutiny, but held back from making a smart-ass wave. Two sailors lowered a launch and headed directly to *Scooter's* port side. After I greeted them, one handed me two papers, the first dated July 19, 2006 read:

You are hereby notified that you are anchoring in the prohibited area according to our Standing Orders and Code of Practice which was enforced on July 1, 2006.

Please do remove your Ship from this area and anchor outside the prohibited or moor at the Faua Basin. Otherwise, Port Authority will take action to remove your Ship.

The second page read:

Fishing and anchoring are prohibited in the area enclosed by: A straight line joining the following points:...

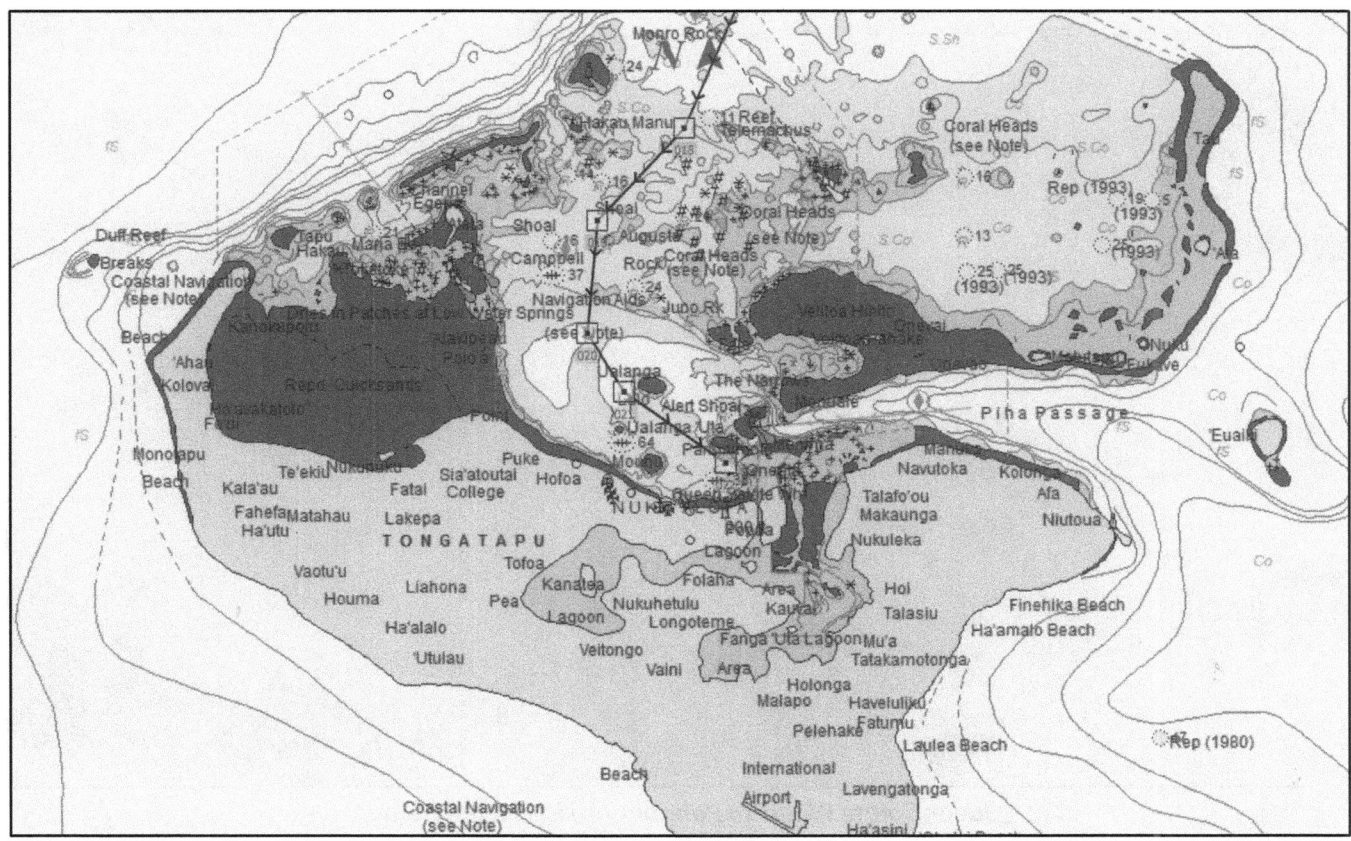

Arriving Tongatapu

The listed eleven latitude and longitude points were not noted on my paper chart, guidebook chart, or the Nobeltec chart, but challenging that as a guest in the nation would be a waste of time. I pulled anchor and moved back to Pangaimotu Island, committing to lengthy *Jazz* rides to and from town.

Bashing into sharp waves on the way from the small boat quay to *Scooter* a few days later, the motor slowed as though a hand had grabbed the prop. Puffs of steam spit from the exhaust where there should have been a steady outflow of water. I jerked the lanyard around my wrist to pop out the emergency shut off plug. Running my mind over the possible causes while the motor head cooled, I paddled toward *Scooter* about a half mile away, straining to keep *Jazz* headed into the wind and the sharp whitecaps. Sometime later, the motor started and ran, but the coolant outflow sputtered with no steady water stream. Cycling between paddling while the engine cooled and running it until steam puffed, I got to the boarding ladder before dark. After stowing provisions, I removed the outboard, fixed it to the mount under the arch with the prop facing the aft cabin deck, lifted *Jazz* to its secure position with the arch bow, and located the Mercury's service manual. Comfortable with my mechanical abilities, I fixed dinner, watched a movie, and retired, leaving outboard servicing to the next day.

With the prop off, the lower unit came apart per manual instructions and the new impeller, fresh from its plastic wrapper, fit without issues. The original impeller in my hand looked new, showed no wear, and puzzled me. To check it out, I lowered *Jazz* to the water and clamped the motor on the transom. It ran but no water flowed from the exhaust port. The problem was far more serious than I had thought. Fortunately, the service manual had detailed disassembly instructions and diagrams showing water flow from the pump up a tube to the cylinder block where it circulated in cavities, removing heat on its way to exit at the bottom of the cylinder block. The failure of the new impeller to pump water through the system suggested that obstructions existed upstream from the pump. After transferring fuel back to a red gas can, I slowly disassembled and laid each part on a canvas tarp stretched across the aft cabin top until the lower strut, drive shaft, and motor block lay bare for close inspection. All coolant passages from the pump to the block exit were occluded with a hard white substance. It took a full day to scrape out the calcium-like material in the passages using dental tools and another day to slowly reassemble the engine following the service manual instructions. Fortunately, I had in my spare parts kit's rolls of various types of gasket material from which I could cut gaskets to replace those damaged during disassembly. A search of outboard motor Internet sites revealed that I

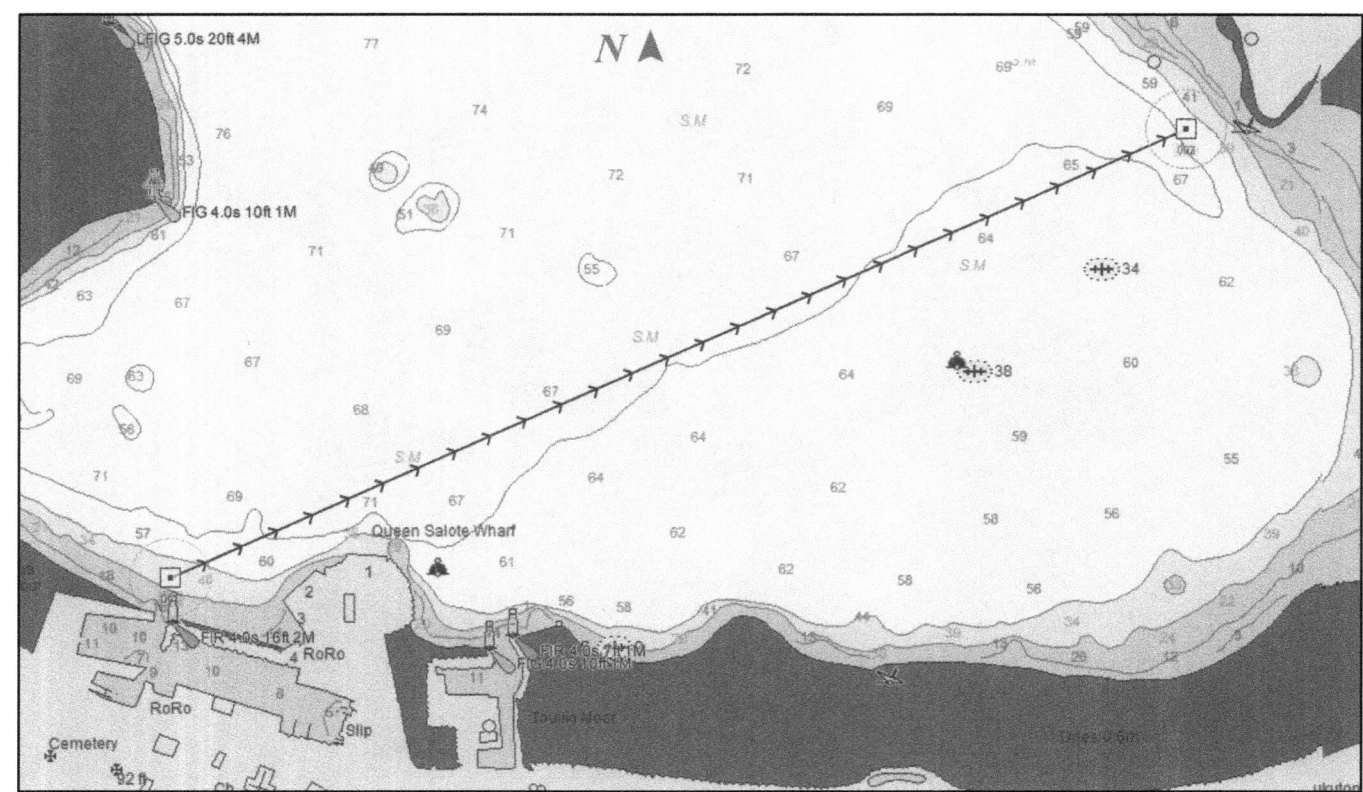
Queen Salote Wharf to Pangaimotu Island anchorage

had purchased a freshwater model in Michigan, and that those sold around the coast were equipped for salt water.

Trips into town included time at the Internet café to check emails, inspect weather sites, and join a New Zealand dating site. Connie's emails trumpeted joy about finding an affordable apartment and visiting with her old group of friends. My son and daughter were doing well in Michigan. Eileen had moved to a continuing care retirement community in Bay City, Michigan, owned and operated by a woman medical doctor who had been a student years before at the high school where Eileen had been an administrator.

Continuing my search for ocean going companionship on the New Zealand dating site, I messaged with Kora, who shared an intriguing story about being homeschooled aboard the family yacht sailing the Pacific. At eighteen she struck out on her own and after several failed relationships now managed the construction of upper-income homes near Auckland. I revealed most of my sailing life story and thought that Kora would be an interesting person to meet if she could spare the time.

Buoyweather and a synoptic weather fax chart showed a disturbance moving with the eastern trade winds south of Tonga. The Southern Ocean tropical cyclone season ran from October to April, and Tongatapu, at latitude 21° S, was in the path of damaging winds. My study showed that when tropical storms arrive at New Zealand's north island, at latitude 35° S, their intensity is generally reduced to tolerable rain and high winds. I had to sail south out of the high-risk area, hoping that the early seasonal disturbance would be short-lived and manageable.

From the laptop, through the Pactor modem, to the single-side-band radio, I communicated the required New Zealand customs information, thinking I would confirm my arrival time three days before, again two days before, and at the time I entered the twelve-mile zone. New Zealand customs responded to the message, documenting my compliance with their requirements. I was confident I could meet the long-distance solo ocean challenges square on as I studied the one-thousand-mile ground track to Opua. Seeing no shipping routes to cross or run parallel with along the ground track relieved collision worries, but the exposed tip of a seamount eighty-six miles south of Tonga at 22° 20.2' S and 176° 12.2' W near the ground track had to be avoided. In the unlikely event of light or no air, Opua could be reached under Mr. Stink's power alone. I SailMailed New Zealand customs with an estimated time of arrival at Opua, processed outbound clearance with Tongan customs, and exchanged Tongan pa'angas for New Zealand dollars at the ANZ bank.

When the anchor hooked over the bow roller, at 0815 on October 23rd, I packed Play-Doh around the chain in the hawsepipe and motored around the northwest point of Tongatapu to run a course of 204° true. The barometer read 1017 millibars, and the visibility was unlimited. With

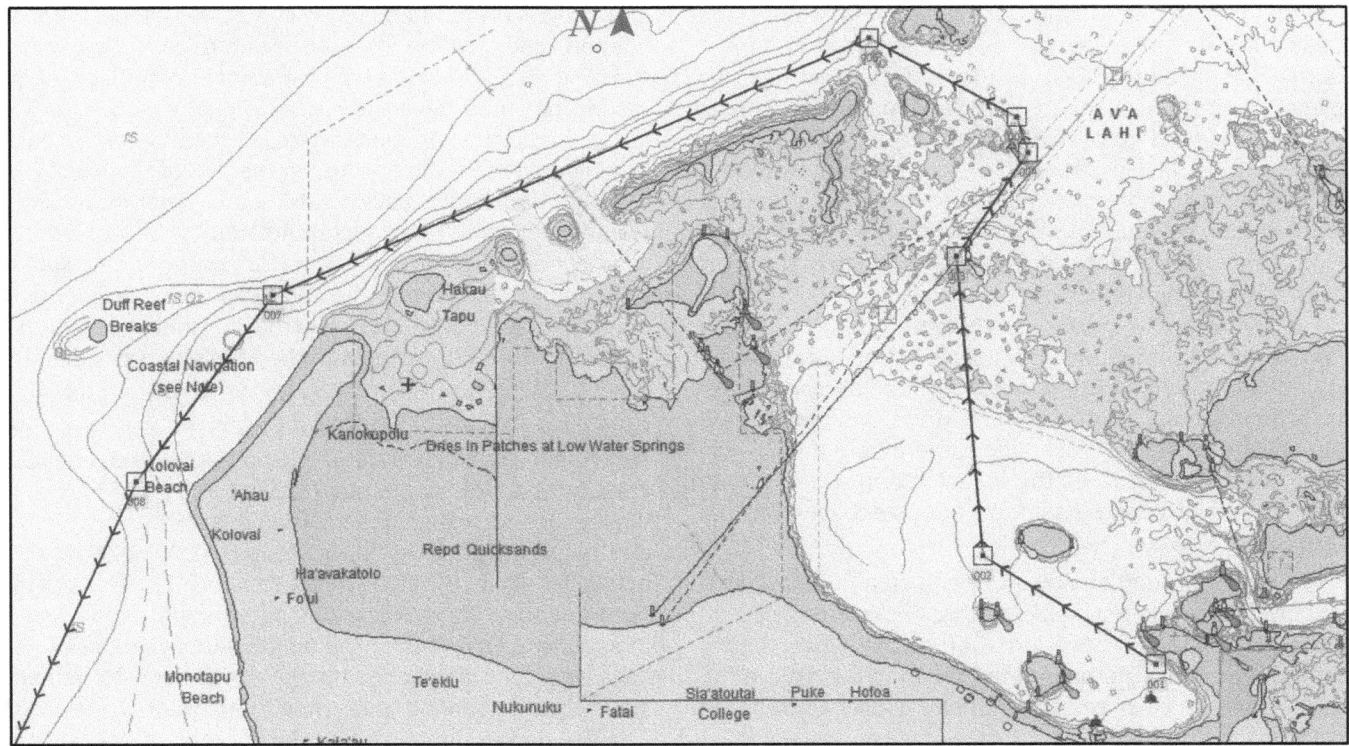

Departing for New Zealand

the number one jib, a double reefed main, and a full mizzen, Scooter clipped along at seven knots in east wind.

To keep the same sail set in changing wind direction the first night, I altered course to starboard and sailed west of the ground track, leaving the seamount well off to port. That day's weather deteriorated as the barometer fell fast from 1013 millibars to 1007 millibars, warning of foul weather to come. Undaunted, I spiked the bland ocean air with the heavy scent of fried bacon and French toast while watching *Dr. No* on the big screen before running my overnight sleep routine.

The next day, the wind speed jumped from sixteen to twenty knots straight off the port beam, and heavy rain pelted the deck, but the cockpit stayed dry inside the clear side curtains. After dinner without a movie, I moved about quickly on deck while tethered to the jack line, pulling down and securing sails as forty-five-knot winds blasted Scooter's beam in surprisingly consistent seas. Thankful that the pilot bunk's lee board kept me in place, I repeated the ninety-minute sleep routine while Scooter lurched from wave peaks to troughs. On the awake side of the sleep cycle, I made all-around visuals from the cockpit deck and watched the radar sweep the screen between bright clusters indicating returns off wave tops.

At daybreak, I had Scooter sailing at six knots with the number two jib, double-reefed main, and full mizzen in light air from the east. Wind speed jumped before noon to twenty-six knots and clocked to the southeast. I quickly struck the main to sail jib and jigger (jib and mizzen only) and altered course to 240° compass, maintaining a port beam reach. As the afternoon progressed the barometer rose to 1015 millibars, and the wind settled to under twenty knots from the same direction. All that day, Scooter sailed at over six knots on a parallel course, five miles west of the ground track.

Rain fell at midnight before Scooter passed from west longitude to east longitude early on the twenty-sixth, but no change had to be entered in the log. I had crossed the International Date Line just before arriving in Tonga. At 1800 the air backed twenty degrees and fell to twelve knots. I hoisted the main, bringing boat speed back to six knots. That night, the wind speed dropped to nine knots, the clouds parted, and the full moon stretched my shadow to follow me while making rounds on deck.

At latitude 27° S on the fifth morning, the temperature had fallen to 20° Celsius (68° Fahrenheit), the barometer held at 1014 millibars, visibility was ten miles, and the air moved easy. I enjoyed the various aromas of chili ingredients as they filled the saloon interior while reminiscing about my youth as I swayed to Mom and Dad's favorite big band sounds from the fifties. That afternoon, for some unknown reason while seated on the starboard side of the mizzen burning through another Tom Clancy novel, I looked up from the book to starboard. About a quarter mile away, I saw a steep wave ready to break, but after squinting it looked to be an island. In less than a heartbeat, Clancy flipped out of my hands, landing on deck, pages fluttering. I moved forward to the helm seat but saw no island off the bow. I spun to my right. The wave stood dead still. I zipped below, grabbed the long eyes, returned to the cockpit, and focused on the wave to see a massive pile of small stones heaped up about a meter and more in places. The black-rock island stretched a great distance north and south, no sand, no palm trees. Astonished, I ran below and scanned the paper chart, seeing only water depth markings south of my last fix notation. I booted the laptop and opened Nobeltec, seeing no island in that part of the South Fiji Basin. *Scooter's* icon at 27° 29' S, 177° 54' E, showed only water depth markings, confirming I had made no navigational mistakes. It could only be an island of lava pumice stones belched from an underwater volcano, floating with the current. Radar beams skipped right over the pile. I retrieved the camera from the forward bunk locker and recorded the sight thinking how fortunate I was to have escaped a near disastrous encounter with a rare ocean anomaly.

In late afternoon on day six sailing on a port tack with jib only in twelve knots of air, weather data warned of wind backing to the east where dark overhead clouds rushed in from the horizon. The barometer began to rise as did the wind speed. In clear air, the wind slowly backed from the south toward the southeast. I lazily tapped the autopilot port course change button, attempting to keep a broad reach in the backing air. Wind speed jumped to twenty-six knots and continued to back. Rain streaked across the confused seas off the port stern quarter. I continued to tap the port button, changing course degree by degree to keep pace with the backing wind. In a flash, the air backed way past the stern as though I had sailed through an invisible anticlockwise spinning cyclone to strike hard on the starboard quarter. In that instant, the jib slapped to port with a loud whump. Pulsing thirty-five-knot wind vibrated and loosened the retaining pin in a starboard solar panel support tube until the pin popped out, releasing the panel to swing up and be impaled by a spinning wind generator blade. The panel stayed straight up with the blade piercing it. I switched the autopilot off, took the helm, turned hard to port driving the stern through the eye of the wind and watched the jib slap back to starboard. Later in a steady twenty-knot wind, I reengaged the autopilot, switched the wind generator off in the engine compartment, strapped on a harness, snapped the tether to the jack line, and gripped my way forward to lower the jib. I then went aft and extracted the solar panel from the wind generator blade.

Scooter lay beam-to in twenty-five-knot winds and large seas sweeping in from the east until 0730 the next morning. I sent a SailMail to New Zealand customs as required, advising them of my intended port of entry and ETA, and they responded with a confirmation email. No more shorts and T-shirt because it was 15° Celsius when I rigged the jib and jigger again. By midafternoon, twenty-four knots of air from due east lifted *Scooter* along on a firm broad reach at speeds over six knots. The air pressure was 1024 millibars, and visibility reached the horizon under a 45 percent cloud cover. I scanned radar, monitored weather, prepared and cleaned up after meals. Making rounds below deck I checked through hulls, and on deck I checked sails, shrouds, stays, blocks, and winches. Satisfied, I filled time reading while seated in the cockpit. Every now and then I looked into the wind to see the crest of a wave appearing as a vertical wall rising from the southeast to lift and roll *Scooter* far over to starboard and back to port as the swell slid between the keel and skeg.

That night the howling wind continued in the twenties, driving *Scooter* at six knots or better even though I had double-reefed the mizzen. High seas slapped the port side rhythmically when I set the alarm clock for the third time and rolled over the leeboard into the pilot's bunk. Shortly after I fixed my position with the pillow there came from the port hull midship right near the galley stove a piercing *BOOM* that violently shook the boat. I sprang over the leeboard and stood for a moment immobilized. What just happened? A few heartbeats later on the cockpit deck, I looked to port then

Floating island

aft seeing nothing that Scooter could have hit and turned to see only darkness off the bow. Below, I opened the roll-out locker under the galley stove, checked under the port bunk then in the dry locker aft of the cooker. Thankfully, all spaces were dry. Had Scooter hit or grazed floating junk or a whale? If it had been a weather buoy, I would have known about it and had it plotted on the chart. I delayed the sleep cycle for an hour while I sat at the nav station with my back to the desk, listening for bilge pump sounds and thankful that Scooter continued sailing.

Only 170 miles remained on the ground track to the

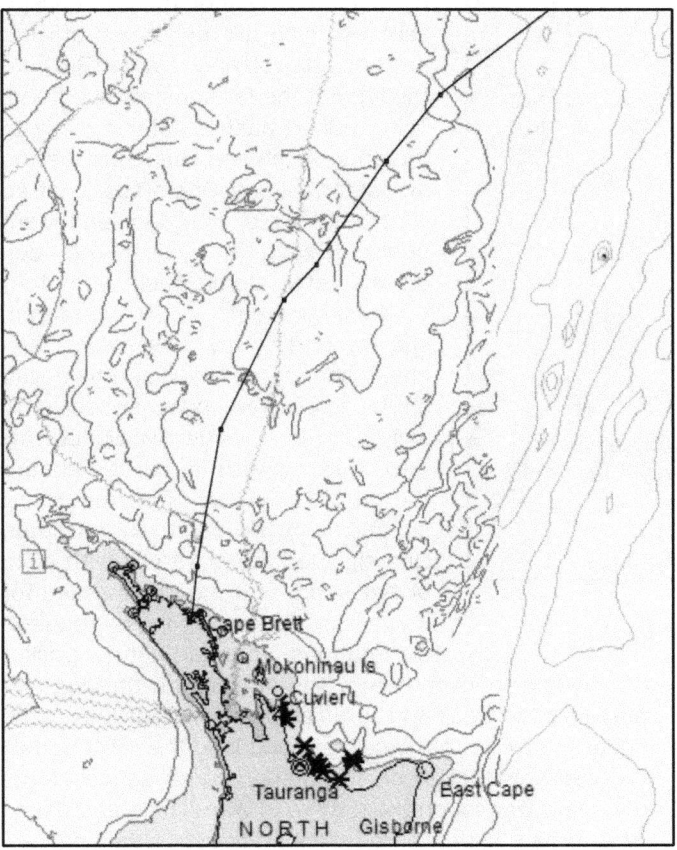

Tonga to New Zealand

designated waypoint twenty miles off the New Zealand coast that crispy morning. Before midnight, the wind speed fell to fourteen knots but stayed directly out of the east. In the friendly sea state, I hoisted the main with a reef, lifting boat speed to over seven knots while sailing a course just west of due south and focused on my New Zealand arrival.

As in the past, clearing-in preparation consisted of cleaning all spaces below, hanging clothes neatly spaced in the closet, and folding and neatly stacking others inside lockers just as I'd done in boot camp forty years earlier. I looked about to wipe up any spills on the hull in the undercabin storage spaces of the sole and adjusted food containers to make an orderly presentation for when the decking would be lifted for inspection. Items on the navigation table, generally in disarray from active use, got rearranged to make all radio licenses and maritime certifications visible under the Lexan cover. Making the master stateroom bed completed the squared away appearance. I rolled into the pilot's bunk at 1800 that afternoon 145 miles from the waypoint. Four sleep rotations later Scooter had reduced that distance by thirty-seven miles.

At sunrise, I calculated arrival at the waypoint off the Bay of Islands to be late that afternoon if conditions prevailed and debated whether to wait overnight to make a daylight landfall or navigate the narrow channel after dark. Fixed wing aircraft had zoomed low from bow to stern and over the wake for miles the day before, confirming the nation's intention to enforce what I had read in the customs documents and possibly looking for anything that may have been jettisoned overboard. Not wanting to risk an encounter with New Zealand coast guard assets while floating offshore overnight, I decided to risk making landfall in darkness.

Approaching the waypoint, I lowered and secured sails but kept them ready to hoist just in case Mr. Stink had issues. I called Russell radio on VHF channel sixteen to revise my ETA, followed the ground track line into the Bay of Islands, passed Frazer Rock at dusk, and motored on to the first aid to navigation (ATON) at the Veronica Channel buoyage. There, I had a chance to test the accuracy of the Nobeltec chart, knowing the Leica GPS displayed four digits to the right of the minutes decimal making the GPS antenna on the arch accurate to 18.5 centimeters on the water. I steered close to the first flashing beacon marking the channel and looked from the helm seat down to the laptop on the nav desk to see the boat icon appeared to graze the charted beacon at the moment the antenna passed confirming the Nobeltec chart accuracy at that spot. Motoring forward only fast enough to manage the currents in the increasing darkness, pinpoint lights on shore, some colored, some flashing, blended with the navigation lights I needed to follow. Trusting accurate beacon placement on the Nobeltec chart ahead, I keep the boat icon in the channel on the screen until the curved, isolated customs and quarantine jetty came into view bathed in bright lights from the large marina off Scooter's starboard side. Docking port side too would leave Scooter bathed in marina lights, making it a better choice than on the other side of the jetty in the dark near the channel. I flipped fenders over the port handrails, led the breast line back to the cockpit, and looped it over the handrail near the cockpit ready to be grabbed.

Gliding halfway along the jetty's length, I clicked the transmission into reverse to bring Scooter to a stop. Sensing a fast flood current pushing her forward, I revved up, matching the current speed, brought her to a stop against the jetty, hopped off with the breast line, and made

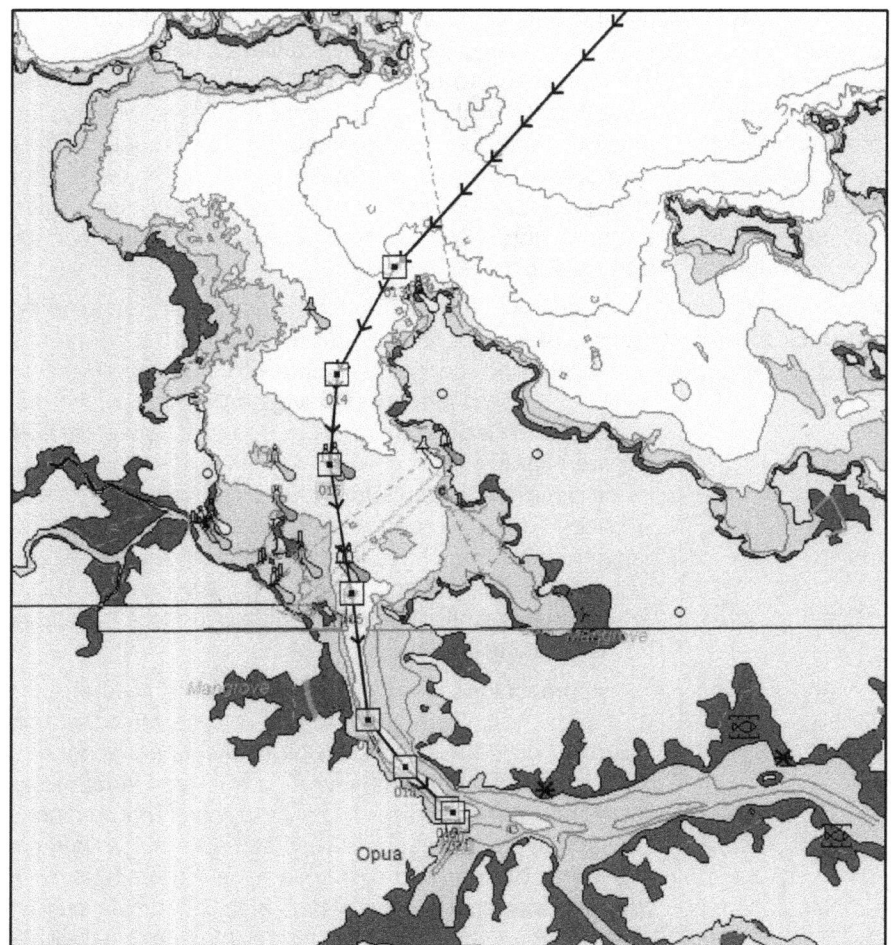
Arriving Opua

it fast to a cleat. Back at the helm, I shifted to neutral and turned the wheel to port, making the rudder thrust the stern to port in the current, pressing the port quarter hanging fenders to the jetty. I tossed stern and bow lines onto the jetty, stepped down to the dock, and cleated the lines while judging the jetty's condition, its distance from the illuminated marina docks, and the silence beyond the sound of *Scooter*'s exhaust. After putting Mr. Stink to sleep, I scolded myself for not considering the possibility of current in a tidal bay at the mouth of a river.

Signage on the jetty directed vessel owners to wait until customs and immigration arrived during normal working hours. The jetty even had a head at the far end. Examining the port hull at midship with a dive light, I found a foot-long gouge arching from the water line up and aft. A very hard object had grazed the hull the night of the boom. It could have been a devastating blow well below the waterline. However, *Scooter* was safe and secure after nine remarkable days at sea.

While breaking out a snack, I heard commotion on the dock and stepped up to the cockpit deck to see a ketch about *Scooter*'s size immediately off the stern. On the bow, a man held a line while standing on the foredeck and spoke to a woman dressing a line around a jetty cleat. I climbed over the port rail and stepped to the jetty to offer assistance. The man returned to the cockpit when the lady started to chat it up with me, asking unexpected personal questions about my past, my wife, and my future sailing plans. My brief narrative flowed until her mate called her back aboard.

Ready for customs inspection the next morning, I sat on the port cockpit seat watching two uniformed officers and a dog step off an unmarked RIB onto the jetty at the far end near the head. They walked past *Scooter* directly to the other ketch and began processing arrival formalities. One officer chatted with the couple, boarded, and went below, leaving the officer with dog on the jetty. Comfortable with how I would present myself—showered, shaved, and neatly dressed in clean khaki shorts, collared short-sleeved shirt, scuff free boat shoes, and white socks—I patiently waited my turn. Finished with formalities aboard the other yacht, the officers casually strolled along the jetty toward *Scooter*. One signaled the dog to sit with a flip or her hand, and the other asked for my arrival forms with the required declarations. I handed her my packet and invited them to board. The officer with the dog told me to wait on deck and came aboard. The lively dog came under the rail, into the cockpit, and lead the officer down the steps into the saloon. In a friendly conversational tone, the agent waiting on the jetty read every page and asked where I had been, where I planned to stay, how long, why I was sailing alone, what I planned to do in New Zealand, and other casual but probing questions. Our tête-à-tête, I thought, revealed my veracity as she circled around to ask similar questions in a different way, all the time observing my body language. The officer with the dog, I assumed, would be looking for restricted items and signs that more than one person had been recently aboard. The dog eventually climbed up the steps to the cockpit followed by a smiling customs officer.

With my processed documents, I had a three-month visa and a stamped passport. I only lost a jar of mayonnaise produced in a South American country where chicken eggs were suspect, but I could only speculate why the dog boarded *Scooter* and not the other yacht. I launched *Jazz* and motored around the marina looking for a dingy dock.

The Long White Cloud

What had I been worried about? All I had to do was comply with the customs and immigration formalities. It took far more time to transmit notices of arrival, prepare forms, and get ready for the clearing-in inspection than the clever scrutiny at the customs dock. I locked *Jazz* to a cleat in an open space between a row of dinghies and walked about until I found the main office. While introducing myself to the counter person, I pointed over to *Scooter* at the customs jetty and briefed him about my sail from Tonga.

"Well, good on ya, mate," he said, my first but not the last encounter with that phrase.

Soon after berthing *Scooter* at the marina, I found the recommended Marina Shop Limited, specializing in the required insurance to legally sail New Zealand waters, and purchased a Lloyd's of London policy. With that vital job done, I began fulfilling immediate needs: car rental, road maps, provisions, phone SIM card, and Internet connection. I learned how to safely drive on the left side of the road before I clicked on the laptop to announce my arrival to the potential oceangoing companion I chatted with before leaving Tonga.

Kora arrived in her Mercedes convertible with curly blond hair windblown from her drive from Auckland. I must have met her expectations. She parked and asked to see the boat. My casual presentation of the spaces below deck and demonstration of how to operate the shower and head conjured up memories of doing the same with Lynn and Connie. *Scooter* was very different from what Kora recalled of her parents' yacht.

While dining locally she proudly expanded on her life story. I listened in amazement about her quality lifestyle and how she worked her way up in society after leaving her parents' boat. She worked as a cocktail waitress in Las Vegas, met and married an attorney, stayed with him for some time before divorcing, moved to England with the settlement money, and purchased a flat. Later, she rented the flat, returned to New Zealand, and divorced after a second marriage. Single again and living in the house as part of the settlement, she began constructing another house with the proceeds from the London flat rental. Upon completion, she sold the first and moved into the new home. Managing the construction of luxury homes moved her up the wealth and social ladder.

By the time she had educated me about where she fit in society, she said it was too late to drive back to Auckland, and asked if she could stay overnight sleeping in the forward cabin. Back aboard, she went on about the universal healthcare scheme, that those with money pay personal physicians outside the system, and that medications unavailable in the government's formulary were sourced from other countries. She could travel anywhere in the world for medical services, as could her friends. I nodded with understanding until it was time to turn in and wished her a good night on my way to the aft cabin. Midway through the night, she woke me in a frenzy, complaining about the sound of the water lapping on the hull, and accepted my offer to share space next to me.

Kora returned to Auckland the next day and the phone became my tool to see where a relationship might go between our few visits. She had shared the photo snapped of me on *Scooter's* deck the day we met with her special friends seeking their opinion of my fit with her group. They agreed that I looked to have a good ten years left in me, but Kora recommended a facial plastic surgeon who would guarantee long-term youthfulness should we become mates. Our values were far apart and my interest faded. I had arrived in a land of adventure that had been praised by many cruisers I met along the way, and I planned to experience as much of it as I could.

Between chats with Kora, the fraternity-boat girl seen last in Tonga appeared on the finger dock with a large smile and introduced herself. *Hmm*, I thought. I had seen her in Tahiti, Tonga, and now New Zealand! Amused by it all, I invited her aboard and opened a bottle of wine to see what she had in mind. The frat boys were back on campus, leaving her to search for her next ocean home. Her lack of interest in sail handling and boat safety shined, and instead of pouring a second glass of wine, I ended the interview with a fabricated story about an afternoon appointment.

While I was reviewing road maps spread out on the cockpit table, the woman from the ketch, who chatted it up with me at the customs jetty the night of my arrival, appeared on the finger dock. Marge, more mature than the frat boat kid, delivered a story about her years-long sail around the planet on other people's yachts as crew after renting out her house in Maine. She had crewed aboard the ketch before the owner's wife departed in Fiji and decided to stay on for the trip to New Zealand, where she could find another crewing opportunity. Marge had no interest in presenting herself as an attractive woman and was as plain as a sand dune beach. After I showed her around *Scooter*, we met for dinner to talk about arrangements, and I agreed to give it a go, valuing companionship above soloing. She moved aboard the next day and quickly adapted to *Scooter's* below-deck spaces.

On the sixth day since arriving in New Zealand, I sailed with Marge out to the Bay of Islands and overnighted in Otaio Bay. After tacking around Cape Brett, we sailed down the coast to where wind and rain drove us to anchor in Mimiwhangata Bay for the night. The next day we rounded Bream Head, and Mr. Stink pushed *Scooter* up the Hatea River to the Riverside Drive Marina in the town of Whangarei, which I soon learned to pronounce FONG-ga-ray.

In the town of thirty thousand residents, I found everything I could want within an easy walk from the marina, which offered haul out, long-term boat storage, an enclosed paint building, a machine shop, a small marine store, and family-sized shower chambers next to the restrooms. A coin in the shower meter brought hot water long enough to get wet and soap down. Four coins at a time avoided the need to leave the shower, transit the dressing bay, and feed the meter. A covered picnic area adjacent to the dock entrance housed a barbeque and large picnic tables. Wide shelving lined one wall, accommodating dishes brought to share at Friday evening gatherings. That became the place to meet marina residents not seen on the docks, spin sea stories, share recent town adventures, and discuss future sail plans. My tasty pot of *Scooter* chili got scarfed up faster than all other dishes.

An American expat couple lived aboard a large sloop berthed in the slip next to *Scooter*. The lady of the boat, a retired special education teacher, learned her experience was in high demand in the merit-based New Zealand immigration system. Meeting the requirements, she quickly obtained a position to teach in a government-sponsored school for gifted and challenged children. Her husband's sailmaking skills contributed to the economy at a local sail loft. Over the following weeks, I met many others, like Peter and Ginger aboard SV *Marcy*, whose paths I would cross many times in the years to come.

Avid coastal sailors and regatta competitors from San Diego, Bill and Millie struck out on a circumnavigation adventure with their race boat. Layers of duct tape around the boat's deck hatches suggested the deck flexed greatly not being engineered for rigorous ocean wave action. An inverted bottle of fluid taped to the top of the helm had a clear tube linking it to the helm pedestal, indicating the hydraulic system leaked. It also hinted that the possibility of a leak was not considered, and that spare parts and perhaps special tools for the job were absent. The morning after their arrival in Whangarei they washed bed sheets in the marina laundromat and draped mattresses over the boom to dry after hosing them down on the dock. Millie, a very attractive woman, modeled long, straight blond hair, perfect nails, and perfect makeup. Bill knew all about sailing fast. A few weeks after they arrived, only Bill attended the Friday dish sharing. I asked about Millie's whereabouts. Bill said she flew back to visit her sister in San Diego. When he skipped the next Friday meal, I gave it no further thought until I spotted a "for sale" sign hanging from his boat's bow lifeline. Amazingly, the man who introduced me to Erin and Fran in Tonga had arrived that week and parked his rented camper in the

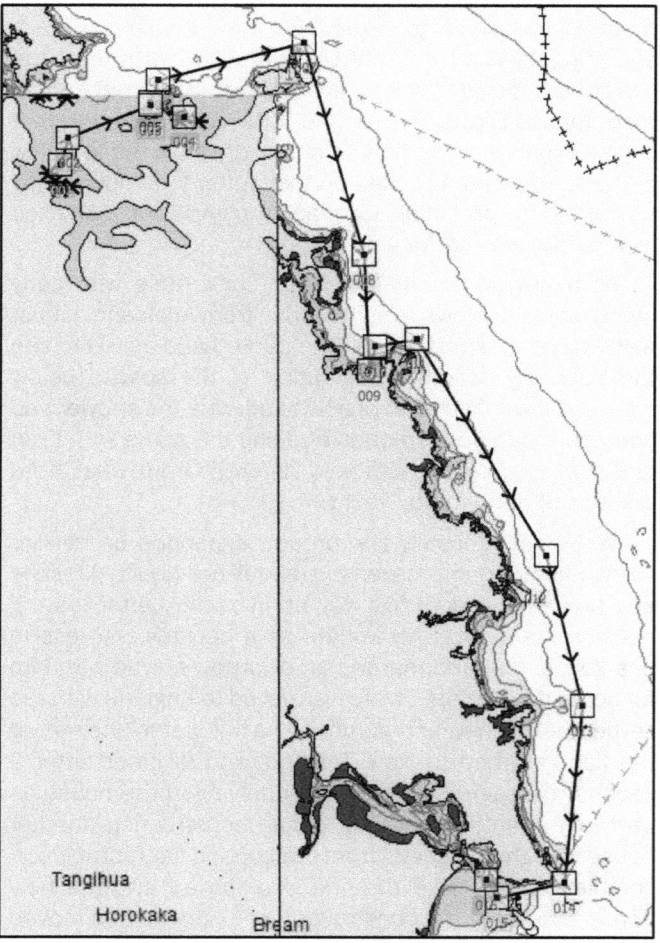

Opua to Whangarei

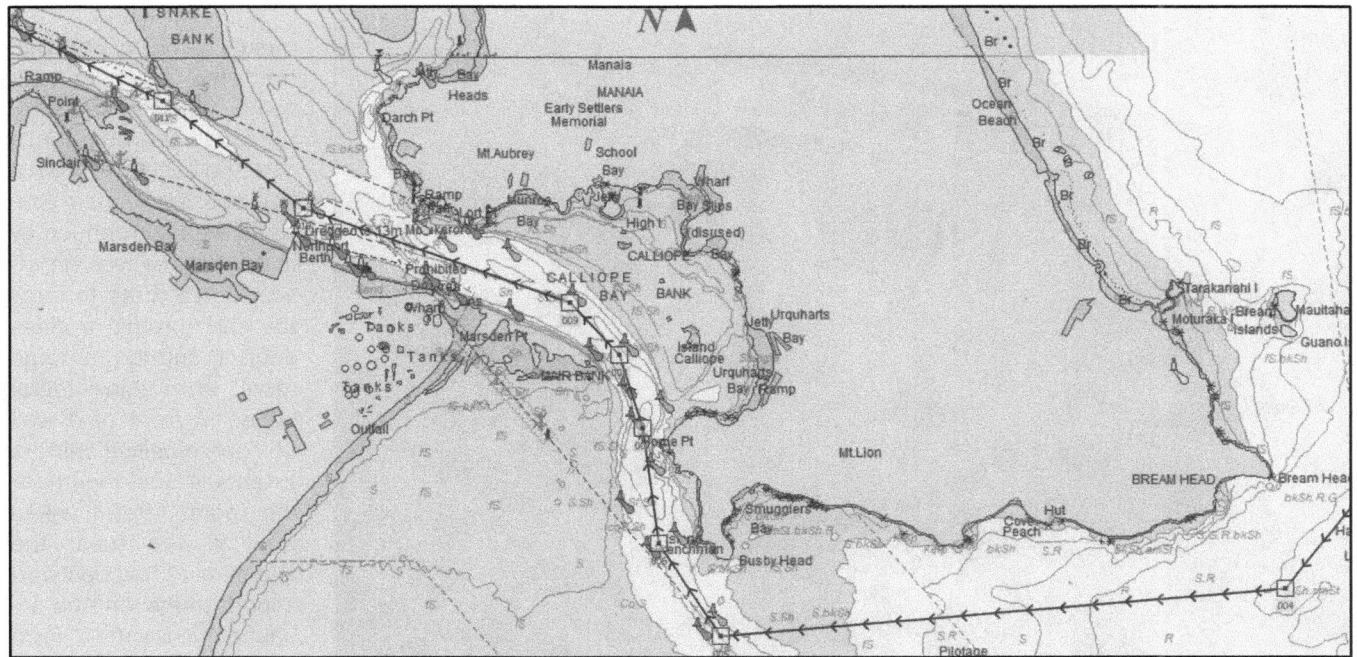

Rounding Bream Head

marina parking lot to use the facilities and continue his search for abandoned sailboats. Bill and Millie's boat soon disappeared.

Early in my stay, I realized that I needed more than three months to thoroughly explore and interact with New Zealand culture. Because my visa could be extended one time, I decided to enjoy a half-year adventure under the "Long White Cloud," the term used to describe the island by the Polynesian ancestors of the Maori nine hundred years ago. With an extended visa in hand, I chose to find a used car that could be quickly sold before I departed instead of renting one all that time. After a brief newspaper search, I discovered a 1988 Nissan Cefiro sedan. It had a clean interior, no body damage, and the valve tap let me know the engine was running. It took some time to build the muscle memory for shifting the stick with my left hand.

The two-page to-do list, the longest ever, lay open on the nav desk, challenging me to get it done. Local marine stores had everything needed but the prices far exceeded those on the West Marine website. A 13 percent VAT made the costs more extreme. Closing in on Christmas, I emailed my daughter and asked her to receive and store items I ordered online before I visited for the holidays. She loved the idea and received water pumps, overhaul kits, an alternator, a barbeque burner plate, a wind generator blade, a water maker osmosis tube and pump, a fuel filter housing to replace the one that started to leak in Tonga, and other

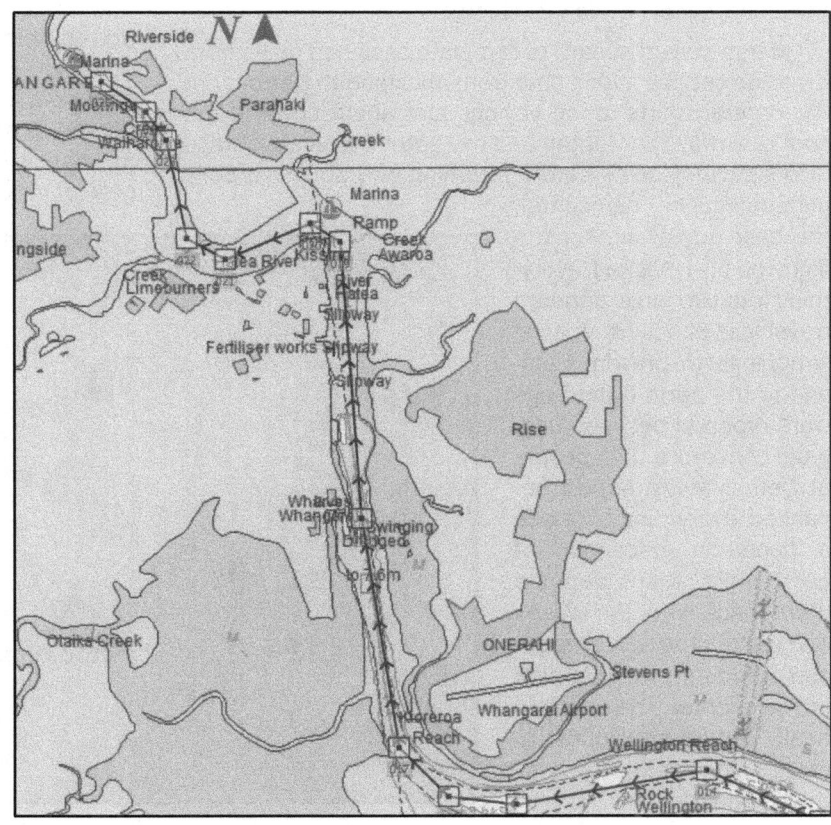

Hatea River to Whangarei

Riverside Drive Marina

In Auckland, the queue to claim baggage from the carousel took some time to traverse. I stacked the bags on a cart and pushed it down a long passageway to a spacious area surrounded by glass walls where an officer ordered me to push the cart through a glass door. I entered a large room with shiny metal tables in front of a wall of floor-to-ceiling mirrors extending the length of the room. After I asked why all the fuss, the agent said I had declared import items on the inbound customs form while aboard the plane. I must have checked the wrong box. I unpacked and laid all the parts on a table for inspection. A customs officer entered through a mirrored door in the mirrored wall and said that a goods and services tax had to be collected on the imported items. I responded that the parts were for my US documented vessel and that the US and New Zealand, as members of the International Maritime Organization, had agreed to not levy duty on parts brought into the country for vessels from other IMO member states. I handed him a copy of my document, visa, and clearance papers and told small items. I looked forward to time with my kids during the holiday and to shopping for over-the-counter medications unavailable in New Zealand.

Marge stayed aboard to complete assigned tasks from my to-do list. It's a long time from Auckland to Detroit, but the ordered parts' price savings just about covered the cost of airfare, car rental, and the hotel. I took advantage of postholiday sales before returning and bought a Sony high-definition camcorder, the best buy of all. For the flight back, I packed everything into two large zippered travel cases, using special wrappings to prevent damage to the parts if the bags were dropped between baggage conveyors. TSA people at Detroit Metro Airport unpacked everything to make a hands-on inspection of each part then dumped them back into the cases and stuffed the wrappings in as I stood on the other side of the counter. They sarcastically denied my request to repack the parts the way they found them.

View downriver

View upriver

him customs could verify my claim by calling the Riverside Drive Marina in Whangarei. He said he would check on it and went through the mirrored door.

A woman at a table behind me wept quietly while standing next to items she removed from two bags. Many minutes passed. The agent reentered and returned my papers, saying all was ok. He offered to help repack the bags. Outside the arrival terminal, while waiting for the shuttle to the remote parking lot, the red-eyed woman approached and stood nearby holding one bag. Back aboard *Scooter*, I found that Marge had completed nearly all the assigned tasks.

A solar panel ordered through KISS and shipped from China arrived at customs. After a brief presentation of *Scooter's* papers and copies of IMO regulations, I carried it to the Cefiro. It just fit in the trunk with the back seat folded down. I installed the solar panel and replaced the damaged KISS blade with the one brought from Michigan, keeping the three purchased in Chaguaramas as a backup set. Attacking the to-do list, I climbed the masts using the Mast Mate climbing system to check every upper rigging part. I inspected all components in the engine compartment and the space under the port settee while the machines operated. I changed the transmission fluid, cleaned the transmission cooler plate, and had the diesel engine's fuel atomizers serviced locally. The yellow paint on two meters of anchor chain, marking every fifteen meters of runout, needed recoating. I rolled all ninety-two meters on the dock to get the job done. While that dried, I cleaned the chain locker and disassembled the windlass, checking for wear.

As the to-do list shortened, we had more time for inland adventures. We walked about Auckland for a day then shared a room at a hostel. Restrooms with showers were at the end of the hall. Youths on what New Zealanders called an Overseas Experience, mostly from Europe, filled the main lounge near the lobby. After graduating from university, that travel exposed youths to societies different from home. Many wore necklaces dangling a whale tail pendant signifying their traveler lifestyle, similar to that of whales known to travel all oceans. Youths traveled everywhere in New Zealand, hitching rides, toting backpacks, and moving from one WWOOF (World Wide Opportunities on Organic Farms) to another. Farm owners provided a bunkhouse and three meals a day for those who worked the farm. A mini phone book found at the hostel listing the type of WWOOF, its location, the work to be done, and the phone number became a useful reference.

I bought a four-person tent with a porch along with air mattresses, sleeping bags, a camp cooker, and a chilly bin (New Zealand slang for a cooler), thinking the kit may find service in future travels. I set out with Marge for however long it would take to explore the North and South Islands, first pitching the tent at a lakeside holiday park noted for its black swans. A hot spring bath in a shed off to the side of a camping field attracted campers for soothing dips. I set up the tent nearby. Partially submerged in the hot water, I chatted with bathers while Marge walked about the area. Later she led the way on paths through heavy brush to the black water lake, where I wanted to video black swans. Whenever I panned toward her, she turned away or dipped into the heavy brush. At day's end, I had not captured a second of her facing the camera to balance the scenes of swans and bubbling sand holes. She persistently avoided the lens while exploring around other campsites during the following weeks. When I asked why, she returned a blank stare and shifted to talking about something else.

For a change, we worked a WWOOF and quartered in a bunkhouse room with only two beds and no other furniture. Restrooms with showers were near a space with a table and chairs. There was no kitchen. I mowed while Marge pulled weeds in a large garden. At no time did she accept any suggestion about how to do anything from me or anyone else. No matter to me. I had someone to talk with, an explorer companion, even if it was becoming one-

WWOOF bunkhouse

sided with little conversation, mostly short answers to my questions. I wondered how far this association would go after we no longer talked about sailing north to explore Pacific islands.

The WWOOF owners prepared meals we enjoyed in their large dining room. During our first evening meal the lady of the house asked Marge why she pulled the seedlings in the garden along with the weeds. Marge expressed surprise then simply said, "They looked like weeds to me," and asked, "What do you need done tomorrow?" without blinking. The lady of the land looked inquisitively at her husband for the answer. To break the silence, I asked how long they'd had the farm and the table talk turned to a time long ago when they sold their farm in England, sailed to New Zealand, and became citizens. They moored their large catamaran at the riverhead on the property and lived aboard while they established the farm and constructed the main house. As the farm prospered, they built the WWOOF bunkhouse. Over the years, with lack of use and attention, the catamaran decayed and was overgrown by trees and brush. During a coastal surveillance flyover, photos of the dilapidated catamaran looked like a drug smuggling operation hidden in the vegetation. Drug enforcement agents raided, took them in handcuffs to jail, and searched the property. After finding nothing of interest, the police returned them home, free to tell the story.

Continuing our travels, we rode the Interislander ferry to South Island, drove past kilometers of grape vines in various stages of growth, and camped our way south through the mountain range to Invercargill, the home of the hero of *The World's Fastest Indian*, the name of a movie at the time. The main character, Burt Munro, started his notable life adventure in Invercargill with an Indian motorcycle and rode that adventure all the way to win speed records repeatedly at Bonneville Salt Flats. At that holiday park campsite Marge smiled and chatted while leading an artsy crayon class for campsite children, an interaction far different than she ever had with me. To make the time in Invercargill memorable, I motored to the southernmost point possible and snapped a photo of the handheld GPS recording the furthest south latitude reached at the time.

While trekking a steep trail routed over large rocks on a western mountain near a campsite, painful irritation developed in my right knee. Returning downhill, I had to side step all the way to prevent the ice pick-like pain from piercing my knee. The pain lingered all night into the next day. I dropped Marge off at another trailhead, drove around the mountain, and waited for her to appear hours later at the exit.

Further north we set up the campsite at a holiday park near Fox Glacier. Marge returned to the tent after using the Wi-Fi connection in the park kitchen as she had done wherever we camped and proudly announced that she had agreed to be flown to Santiago, Chile, at the expense of another sailor to crew aboard his yacht for a sail up South America's west coast. That was when I realized my need for female companionship had clouded my judgment. She had used me for a free everything over the past months while searching for the next more immediate ocean ride. Alone again, I explained her absence aboard and how we met to the many cruising couples I befriended at the marina.

After all those weeks of trekking around the mountains my right knee randomly popped out of joint anytime, or anywhere. When it happened, I stopped moving, planned the next step, and moved just right to unlock the joint. Knee replacement came to mind along with thoughts of how to blend that with my aspiration to sail the Pacific rim. I wanted to explore the Solomon Islands, Palau, where Cindy's dad served with the marines; Guam; the Northern Mariana Islands; the Philippines; and perhaps even visit Saigon—with a compatible partner if I could find one online.

I looked for amusing things to do other than boat jobs and exchanging books at one of the many used bookstores.

While shopping at a large grocery in town I stopped in the produce department at the sign "Capsicums" hanging above a wide box of red, yellow, and green bell peppers. Prepacked jars of red peppers were unavailable wherever I shopped. I envisioned pickling and stowing a batch below the saloon deck. Exploring around town I found a supply of Ball jars at a general store operated by a Chinese expat. The Indian owners of a spice shop at a mall advised I use an assortment of their spices to flavor my vinegar mix. The pickling process proceeded for days until I filled all the jars, giving me months of sandwich and scrambled eggs additions.

I happily made an online connection with a woman who claimed to be a body builder from Kansas. She posted photos of her competitions and described her timeshare in Christchurch where she suggested we meet. We shifted to email and shared personal details. Her photos presented a well-toned athlete. I decided to give it a go, anticipating a fantasy week after the celibate time with Marge, drove north to the Kaikohe airport, and boarded a flight to Christchurch. Late that afternoon, I waited for her to appear at the foot of the arrival gate's outdoor steps to the parking lot as planned. Hearing, "Hello Bob," I turned and looked up to see a plump, gray-haired, flabby-armed woman leaning over the rail at the stair top. Why should I be surprised? Her photos must have been twenty years old. *Ok*, I thought, *I'm here. No plans for a hotel, just ride along and get out tomorrow.* I smiled and helloed back. We walked the beach in front of her timeshare and dined at her favorite eatery. The next morning before breakfast, after a night on the couch, I mentioned that this would not work for me, borrowed her phone, called a taxi for a ride to the airport, and fortunately secured a seat on the morning northbound flight.

On the drive from the airport back to the marina, I joined a long queue of vehicles after getting flagged to the curb by police. I crept forward to where an officer held what appeared to be a small microphone close to my mouth asking where I lived. When I answered, "At the Riverside Drive Marina on a boat," she told me I could go. The microphone-like tool was a Breathalyzer. On the other side of the car, an officer noted the date on the inspection sticker. Moving away from the stop, I passed a vehicle hauler loaded with cars then a small bus filled with occupants. The random checks for driving under the influence kept me from barhopping in search of companionship.

Internet searching resumed with the keywords "sailor," "sail," and "sailboat," with "Auckland" as my hometown. A profile mentioning sailing experience captured my interest enough to chat online and then by phone. She enquired about my past and my current intentions, pausing often to allow me to question her in return. Passing her scrutiny, she invited me to stop by her office, a short walk from the super grocery store parking lot in town. From behind the only desk in the small office a forty-something woman looked up at me with a huge smile when I said, "Hello, ah, Sefina?"

She placed her pen on the desk blotter, stood with her eyes fixed on mine, and rounded the desk saying, "Hello, Bob." Waving her left arm to the small table and two chairs next to the desk, she said, "This is where I discuss my patients' concerns." She sat in a chair and crossed her legs, which were neatly clad in khaki slacks below a buttoned dark-blue jacket covering an aqua blouse.

I slid the other chair away from the table and quipped, "What's a person do to be a patient of yours?" Sefina smiled and spoke about her holistic healing practice. Patients that the universal health care scheme rejected kept her busy helping them adjust their lifestyle, diets, and exercise to overcome ailments.

Within a few days our chats led to cocktails at the open-air restaurant overlooking the river,

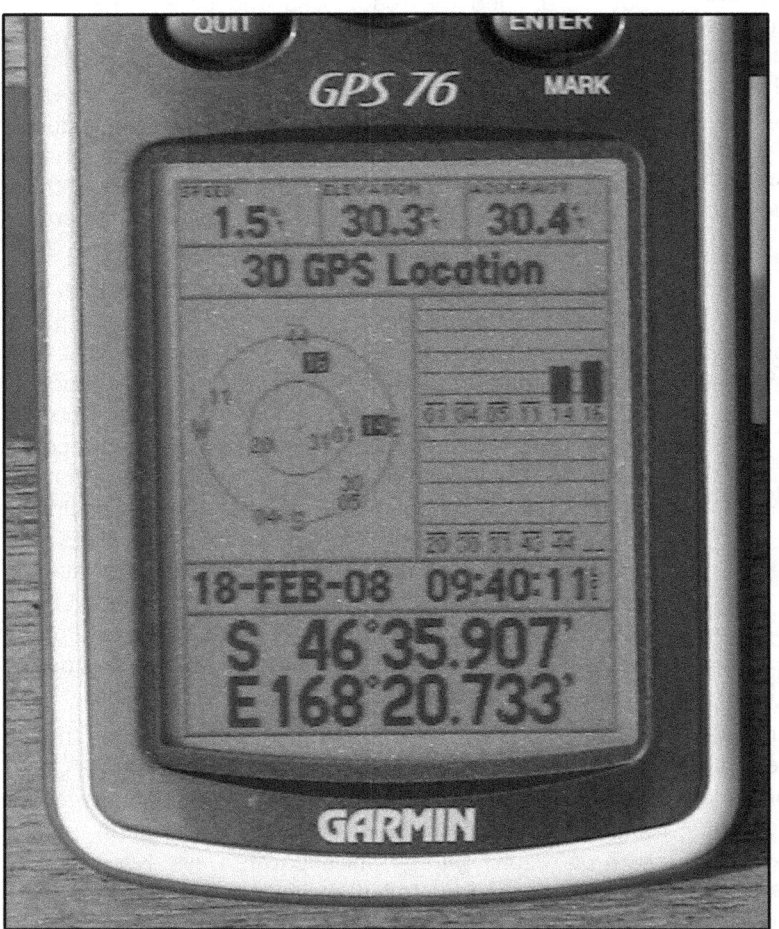

GPS at Invercargill dock

more phone chats, a dock walk to inspect *Scooter,* then an invitation for dinner at her house. Her directions led me to a long, steep downhill stony driveway off an unpaved road that rose into the hills from a two-lane highway. The driveway hooked left at the bottom to reveal a wide turning area in front of a brick staircase leading to a round single-story structure. Sefina, standing in front of an open multibay garage at the far side of the drive, waved me over. Entering the garage, she led me through a laundry room and kitchen to a spacious living room enclosed by a series of linked glass panes in the curved exterior wall. She strolled toward the glass and said, "Come see it from here." At her side, I looked out over a green valley to a tree-covered ridgeline receding to the east. The valley sloped below the ridge down to caress the blue sea beyond a curved white sand beach in the distance. "Nice, isn't it?" she said, touching my arm.

"Stunning."

Moments after taking in the extensive view, she led me toward the center of the circular house where glass panels, rising from floor to ceiling, created a transparent silo. She moved through a narrow opening and gestured for me to stand at her side on soft carpet surrounded by large pillows propped against the glass walls. From there, I had a full view out the panoramic living room windows. She looked up to a clear glass skylight. "This is my calming space. Passing clouds by day. Stars at night." I stood beside her, feeling the tranquility in the hub of the circular home, lost in time until she led me to see more. I followed her past the bedroom to a patio curving around the valley side of the house with a set of brick steps running down to the driveway.

Seeing the bricks imbedded with seashells I asked, "Where did you get these?"

She nodded toward the sea to the east. "I collected the shells on Sandy Bay Beach and mixed them into the bricks."

"Did you do all this?"

She turned away to look at the distant sea. "My mate and I built it years ago."

"What happened?"

Seconds ticked until she said, "He's gone," in a tone I would have made if asked about Cindy. I moved on to chatting about the landscape splendor cascading downhill from the patio to the valley below, all the time sensing the inner peace she projected in voice and manner, much like Cindy. Returning to the kitchen, I asked about the large glass cylinder sitting on the counter. It contained sand and rocks and had a spigot. She said it filtered water from the rain catchment system. Rain flowed off the roof to a small cistern near the garage where a pump pushed the water up to a large tank on the hillside above the house. Gravity flowed water from the tank into the house, supplying all needs. Water had to be hand-poured into the cylinder on the counter to make it potable. Over dinner, when we shared stories about our children, she described her autistic daughter's life in an Auckland care facility.

Driving back to *Scooter,* I reflected on the afternoon and evening hours and how our values aligned. Her sense of well-being, good health, and life-fulfilling aura mirrored the spirit I lost four years before.

Our next time together we enjoyed a passionate flash of life not experienced for a long time. Her visits aboard *Scooter* stimulated hours of delight as we shared past memories of times under sail and visualized a sailing future together. When alone, I wondered if this was truly happening, a partner who knew how to manage sails, was ocean savvy and capable, and wanted to join me. I was on top of the world. I could see us together over the horizon years into the future as global travelers like the many couples I had met. Every morning I anticipated the joy of her company. As time passed, that euphoria played on while pushing a lawnmower around the valley hillside of her home, knowing what waited for me when I was done.

Issues around New Zealand citizenship and where to obtain a knee replacement intruded on my thoughts during those happy days. I did not doubt local surgical abilities, but I examined the roadblocks and pitfalls that would be experienced while I negotiated a health care system where precious medical resources were rationed. I could just put it off and have the cost covered later in life when we sailed to the States. Then to Sefina's surprise, a doctor determined that her autistic daughter, under the care of the state and living in a special state home, was three months pregnant. Sefina felt strongly obligated to care for her future grandchild and not abandon her to state care.

The next week, a mail package arrived from Seth with a letter announcing that health care benefits for General Motors retirees would terminate on December 31, 2010. The loose plan to put off the knee replacement suddenly had an ending date. I could fly to Florida, sort out who and where to do the needed surgery and where to recover, return to New Zealand, then fly back to Florida for the surgery. Recovery time would be uncertain as would the hotel expenses for the months of follow-up visits and physical therapy, draining investment savings already severely depleted by the ongoing US housing market bust. *Scooter* would be unattended in a rented slip or stored on the hard at the Riverside Drive Marina. My visa was due to expire soon and a timely decision had to be made.

I wrestled with the complexities of what life had thrown each of us. After deep reflection, I shifted my dream of global sailing with Sefina to a dedicated solo sail homeward. We shared our concerns during a long conversation, ending with us resolving to go our separate ways. Knowing that we had a finite time together energized us to make every moment from then on intensely memorable.

Homeward Bound

When not enjoying time with Sefina I planned my journey home. Sailing across the Pacific to the Panama Canal and up the Caribbean to Florida would deliver an experience similar to the return to Tahiti from Bora Bora, but to make that a comfortable downwind passage I would need to sail north of the equator in the westerly trades toward California then hook south to the canal. Surgery in California would be possible, but that would put me in a very expensive place for recovery compared to Florida. Taking advantage of the southern hemisphere's easterly trade winds, a gentleman's downwind sail westward across the Indian Ocean to Africa would offer the benefit of an African safari that could be another once-in-a-lifetime adventure.

The westbound ground track I structured on the laptop ran north to New Caledonia, west to Australia, up the Great Barrier Reef to the Cape York Peninsula, and across the Arafura Sea to Darwin. From there, it stretched across the Indian Ocean to Mauritius, south around the Cape of Good Hope, north to Trinidad, and straight through the Caribbean to Port Everglades, Florida. It was 15,600 miles in total. Averaging six knots boat speed it would take

Launch day, Whangarei

2,600 hours at sea, almost four months nonstop on the water at a minimum. I considered that the North Atlantic hurricane season starting in thirteen months could tweak the arrival time in Florida but decided to deal with that in Trinidad. In all, I had time to haul Scooter for a needed bottom paint recoat.

Living aboard on the hard, I sanded the bottom and rolled on coats of a super-high-copper-content paint unavailable in the states and applied a special antifouling coating to the propeller. To avoid delaying departing due to an unsold car, I listed it for sale when the bottom work started. Priced to move, it had a new owner a day after Scooter returned to the water.

On departure day, my collection of memories accumulated over the six months of interacting with friendly New Zealanders made me think that, of all the places traveled to on my sailing adventure thus far, this was the one I would revisit. The last time I saw Sefina was at her office in town. In our final minutes together, we agreed to stay in touch, sharing our adventures as we journeyed forward. After I released our extended hug, thankful for the joy she gave me, I walked out the door not looking back. I strolled over the Victoria Bridge and down the Hatea Loop next to the river on my way to Scooter imagining that if destiny allowed Sefina to be available in two years, I could easily sail the second time around.

I had Scooter ready to go with 580 liters of diesel, a refrigerator and freezer stocked with meats, and every item on the meal planner spreadsheet stowed for a three-week passage to Australia. Shortly after settling up with the marina, I motored down the Hatea River, docked at Marsden Point, visited the customs office I had previously reconnoitered before selling the Nissan, and cleared out of New Zealand. Mr. Stink pushed Scooter out Calliope Bay and around Bream Head. I switched him off after hoisting sails in good east air. Within an hour, a New Zealand coast guard vessel closed fast from astern and hailed on VHF sixteen. The radio voice wanted to know where I had been, the number on board, and my destination. The cutter followed for some time after I answered the voice, mentioning that I had cleared out at Marsden Point a short time before. I waited patiently until the voice broke the cockpit silence, approving my departure for Nouméa, New Caledonia.

Foul weather closed on the horizon while sailing north along the coast. Rain began to fall from very dark, low clouds. The sun, if it could have been seen, hung low in the west. As Scooter approached the southern land prominence of Sandy Bay, a beam of sunlight streaked through a small break in the thick cloud, and a rainbow appeared directly off the starboard bow. With the camcorder in hand at the time, I recorded myself saying, "There must be some kind of magic off Sandy Bay," and looked upon the rainbow as a message saying, *Sail safely my friend*, mystically beamed by Sefina, the holistic healer in my life.

East flowing currents around New Zealand's North Island blended with light air from the same direction to make for smooth sailing with three sails up. On the second midnight the wind changed direction to the northeast, becoming so light the seas turned glassy. I held position, lying ahull, waiting for low pressure to bring squally weather, rain, and hail. At first light I woke up Mr. Stink, and by noon he had powered Scooter through heavy squalls to

Port Moselle decal

where I could sail wing on wing right up the ground track, cooking along at over seven knots in twenty-five knots of air out of the south. About noon on the day of arrival off New Caledonia, the air backed to the east at twenty-six knots and remained constant until I sailed into the lee of New Caledonia's southern hills.

The memory of a bright-yellow customs seal peeled off the freezer lid while updating refrigeration years before in Michigan and the Port Moselle decal under the nav table's lid piqued my interest in visiting New Caledonia. Visiting the island would ease the long passage to Australia and allow me to experience another French overseas territory, where I could spend the remaining bundle of French Pacific francs. Online completion of arrival documents uncovered restrictions similar to New Zealand. Quarantining pets on board to protect the island from rabies topped the list.

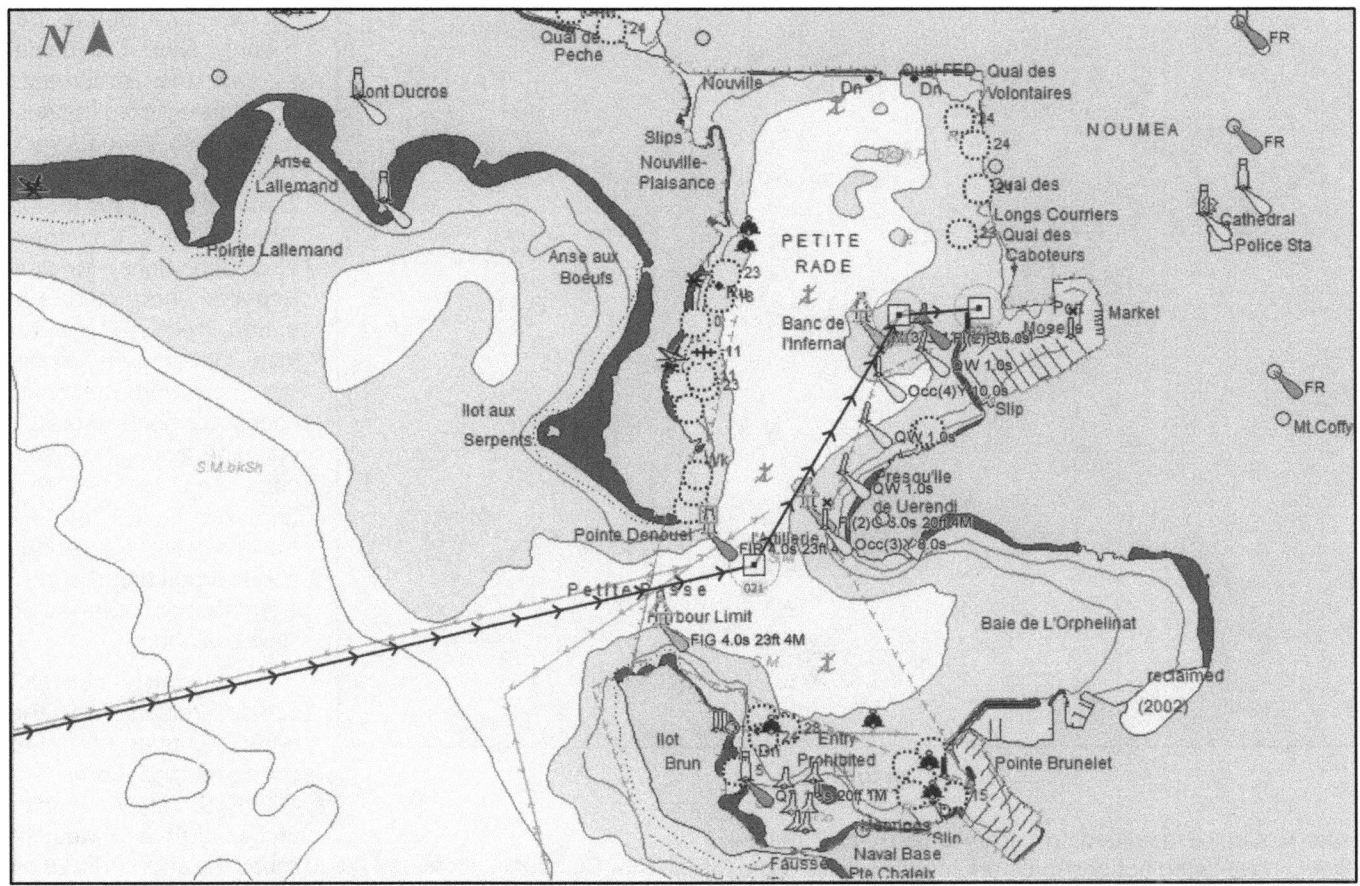

Arriving Port Moselle

While sailing, I printed the documents I found online that had to be delivered to the marina office within an hour of docking.

Arriving before sunset, I anchored in Baie des Citrons off Nouméa flying a French courtesy flag over the yellow quarantine flag with plenty of time for dinner and a movie. The next morning, I made a VHF call to the large marina complex in Port Moselle and obtained directions to a slip. After securing dock lines, I found the dockmaster's office and delivered my arrival documents and gathered that an officer would soon inspect the boat.

A woman wearing a pressed kaki uniform boarded *Scooter* with a black-plastic garbage bag in one hand and a clipboard loaded with forms in the other. She inspected the aft and forward cabins, looked around the main saloon, opened the refrigerator, flipped down the freezer door, saw frozen shrimp in its original package, and asked in French-laced English to see my certificate of origin. When I told her that I had not seen a certificate of origin while processing arrival documents online, she started to fill her bag, saying that she had to remove and dispose of all meats without a certificate. I pointed to the label on the frozen shrimp clearly noting it's origin, the South China Sea. She shook her head saying, "No certificate; I must take it." That triggered me to open the large freezer under the TV monitor and toss onto the port divan other meats with New Zealand labels. I walked back to where she stood at the galley sink and asked her to have the most senior customs officer come aboard and show me, using my laptop, the certificate on their website and to tell me who would be authorized to make the certification. I stared steadily at her, waiting for her response. She stood in silence, looking down. Long moments later, she said she could seal the freezer, but it had to be unbroken when inspected the day of departure. From deep beneath the bundle of papers on her clipboard she extracted a long yellow tape seal. I repacked the meats and closed the freezer lid. Not saying a word, she peeled the backing off the yellow tape, stretched it across the lid and down the seat face, and handed me documents. She climbed over the rail to the finger dock with her clipboard and an empty black-plastic bag.

Reviewing the clearing-in documents, I noticed in the center of the sanitary certificate, which she referred to as the certificate of origin, the words "certificat sanitaire insuffisant." She had drawn a line through the three words and written below in English, "Meat consigned in the freezer, Tel:> 7826.81 before departure." I considered that if the customs procedure was legitimate, the form would have been on their website with information about

Insuffisant

Two days before departing New Caledonia, I read the documents downloaded from the Australian Visa Bureau website while I was in New Zealand: Long Stay Tourist Visas, Eligible Countries, Visa Conditions, Medical Requirements, and Required Proof of Funds for Visa Obtainment. Wanting more information, I checked a handy cruiser's planning guide, Noonsite.com, and realized that Erin was right. The Australians were as serious about protecting their environment and citizens as New Zealanders.

Scuttlebutt between some cruisers on the dock cautioned that charts of the Coral Sea failed to show hidden atolls north and west of New Caledonia. It caused me to recall the chart printed on a dinner table placemat from a Nouméa restaurant that I found in the chart table aboard *Meg* years before. My paper charts for the Coral Sea published by the Australian Hydrographic Service clearly showed many reefs by name. They had been updated prior to purchase with paper overlays pasted where changes were needed per Australia law, which restricts the sale of out-of-date charts. The reefs on the Australian charts corresponded with reefs identified on my Nobeltec electronic charts. I speculated that perhaps a local restaurant had continued printing Coral Sea charts on placemats.

The port of Cairns became my Australian landfall destination, as it would afford a shorter sail north through the Great Barrier Reef along the Cape York Peninsula to the Torres Strait. Arriving at Bowen or Mackay, farther south on the Queensland coast, would be a shorter sail from New Caledonia, however, that would require a longer sail north inside the dangerous reef. On the Nobeltec chart, I structured a route northwest of New Caledonia, around a reef cluster in the Coral Sea, and to Grafton Passage east of Cairns. Zooming in on the Grafton Passage chart, I spotted navigable water around the coral reefs and islands, easing my concerns about making a night passage if needed. At 1,300 miles in length, and averaging six knots, I calculated a nine-day sail.

Planning my third ocean solo, I recalled the events of the Tonga to New Zealand passage and the easy sail from

who would be qualified to certify origins, and the form would have listed actions to be taken: remove for disposal or sealed onboard. My imagination quickly conjured up the devious intentions that could have been in play. Over the next few days, I met many cruisers on the docks and in the marina compound. When the opportunity presented itself, I casually brought up the Certificate Sanitaire topic, learning they all gave up fresh meat upon clearing in.

Along with searching for souvenirs in the many shops near the port, I walked the docks, meeting global cruisers. Carlos, the skipper of the sailing yacht birthed on *Scooter's* starboard side, said he retired from banking in Portugal to become a global wandering minstrel. Another Amel Maramu ketch a few years newer than *Scooter* appeared the day after my arrival in the slip on my port side and looked to be in excellent condition. The Amel couple invited Carlos and me aboard for dinner. Carlos entertained with songs about the romantic Pacific islands he visited while strumming his guitar. The next morning, he gave me and the Amel couple CD recordings of his island songs. The other slip next to Carlos held a sailing yacht occupied by a woman who had just been told by her husband that his time with her and the boat had ended, leaving her to sell it or sail it. Carlos relayed the story, suggesting I meet her at another dinner aboard the neighboring Amel. Dithering around with a potential female cruising companion who had just been marooned for some reason had no place in my fast-track mission. I declined the invitation and when encountering her on the dock, politely said hello.

New Zealand to New Caledonia. I committed to staying on top of weather forecasts. Three-day forward plots on Buoyweather revealed that I would be motoring in light air from the southwest before the wind backed and filled in the Coral Sea north of New Caledonia. Continuing forward weather study would guide my route around the reef hazards. Comfortable with the sail plan, I completed customs departure documents and settled up slip fees in the marina office. The officer said there was a message in my mailbox. It read, "It's not necessary to wait quarantine tomorrow. You are authorized to open your freezer."

Clouds warmed by the morning sun towered over the island as I motored in a warm onshore breeze out the Passe de Boulan at the reef's edge west of Nouméa. Turning to a course of 302° true, I easily slipped into the routine of living at the speed of the sea. My time ashore must have been too short to establish land legs that would take a day to transition to sea legs. Maybe the smooth water rippled by the light breeze aided the shift.

Mr. Stink pushed *Scooter* for a day and a half up the coast until the wind backed to come off the starboard quarter at ten knots. I ran the main and mizzen full up, rolled out the genoa, and put Stinky to rest. As had been my practice, I rigged the main boom preventer. On a starboard tack, the preventer block and tackle ran from an under-boom pad eye to a block at the port toe rail, with the line extending to a cleat just aft of the port primary winch at the cockpit. A similar system fixed the mizzen in place as well. I rigged the spinnaker pole off the starboard side of the mainmast, fixing it in place with a halyard and fore and aft guys strung aft to the cockpit, giving me the ability to shift the pole angle without going on deck. With that in place, I hoisted the number two jib. At all times on deck, I wore a harness tethered to a jack line. If I lost my balance or the deck moved out from under my feet, I could save myself if I flipped over the life rail.

Unlike the prior two solo ocean passages, when I chose to change course to hold a consistent apparent wind angle instead of shifting sails, I wanted to stay on my planned ground track around the charted reefs. Reef avoidance dominated my daily solo routine, jumping my speed of life at sea as I shifted the jib and main from starboard tack to port tack and back, sometimes shifting the jib, main, and mizzen; sometimes reversing wing on wing; and sometimes flipping only the jib flying alone. I monitored the Nobeltec constantly instead of every six hours, and the changing weather conditions around the reef induced me to frequently plot positions on the paper chart.

Midmorning on day four I sailed through a squall, then into clear air, then into steady rain in the afternoon. Before passing the first set of reefs, I switched the Leica MX420 Navigator System to an alternate page that displayed a 1.3 knot current running at 19° true, setting me westward closer to the reef. Thankful I had that immediate information, I altered the autopilot, heading further north.

Scooter sailed into day five under clear skies in twenty knots of air from the east, but the southbound current increased to 1.6 knots, setting a more westward course made good and demanding another northerly course adjustment. Shifting or trimming sails, reading on deck, quick meals, listening to music, and watching the cockpit side curtains fend off the salty sea spray happened at a speed dictated by changing ocean air and sea conditions.

Gusty twenty-knot winds drove *Scooter* into day six, swimming over seven knots on a starboard broad reach. That morning I sailed with two reefs in the main set far to port with the preventer and the jib poled to starboard. Seas smashed the aft quarter, splashed under the side curtains into the cockpit, and drained through the scuppers twice. I kept the vertical hatch fully up and the slider hatch closed to prevent flooding the saloon. *Scooter* bashed along pitching port to starboard while I shot videos of the rolling seas as the wind carried a Carlos song from the arch-mounted stereo speakers into the cockpit. At noon I had to change course from 302° true to 280° true to stay

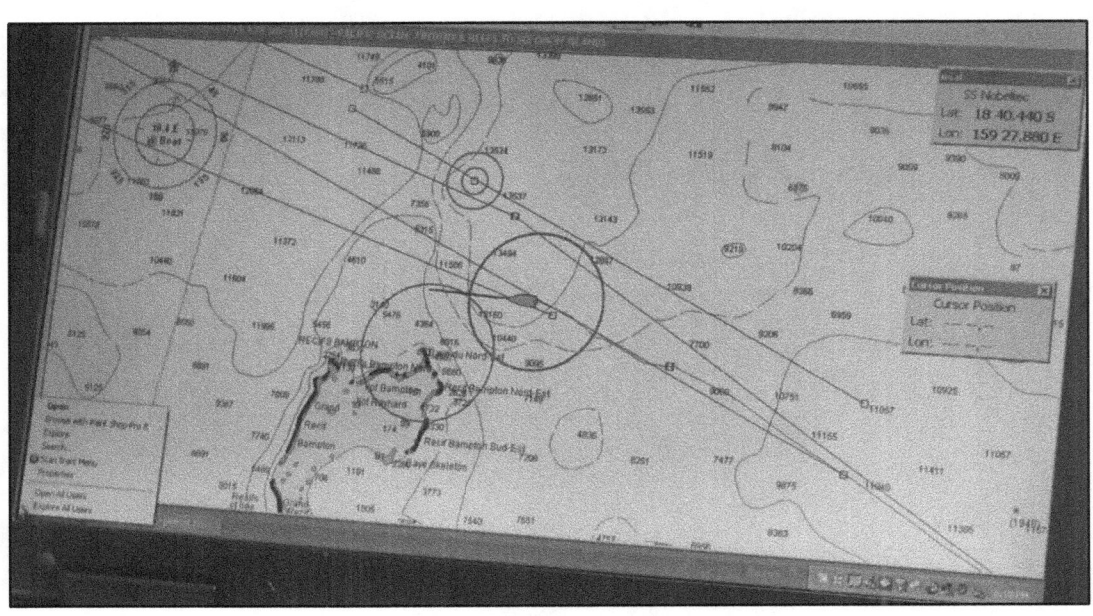

Getting by the reef

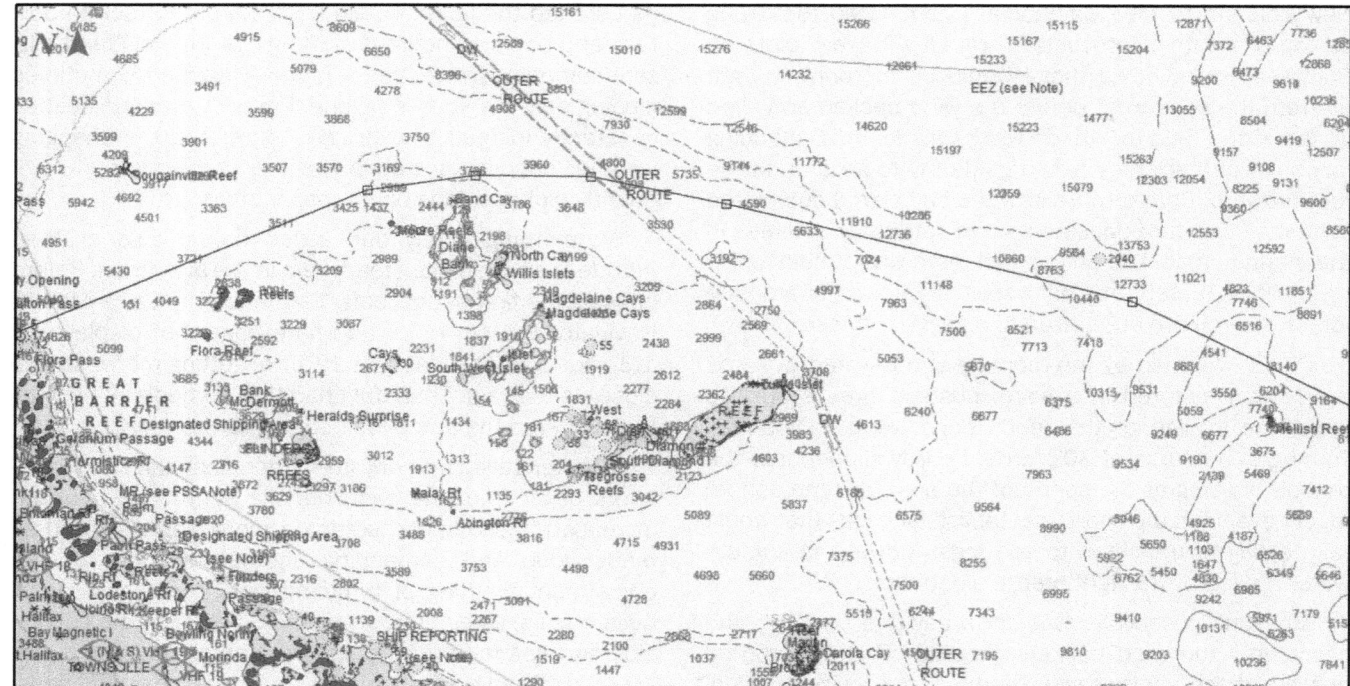

Reef to port

on the ground track and prepare for the twenty-knot wind that was forecasted to arrive soon. Gripping around deck for most of an hour, I struck the jib from the pole, replaced it with the storm jib set to starboard, and jibed the main, bringing Scooter to a port broad reach, ready for the wind to move the point of sail forward. When the wind changed direction the speed of living on the Coral Sea slowed from extreme to just fast. By 1300, I was dry again, sipping hot coffee and monitoring the Nobeltec. That night and all the next day Scooter managed the seas, current, and wind

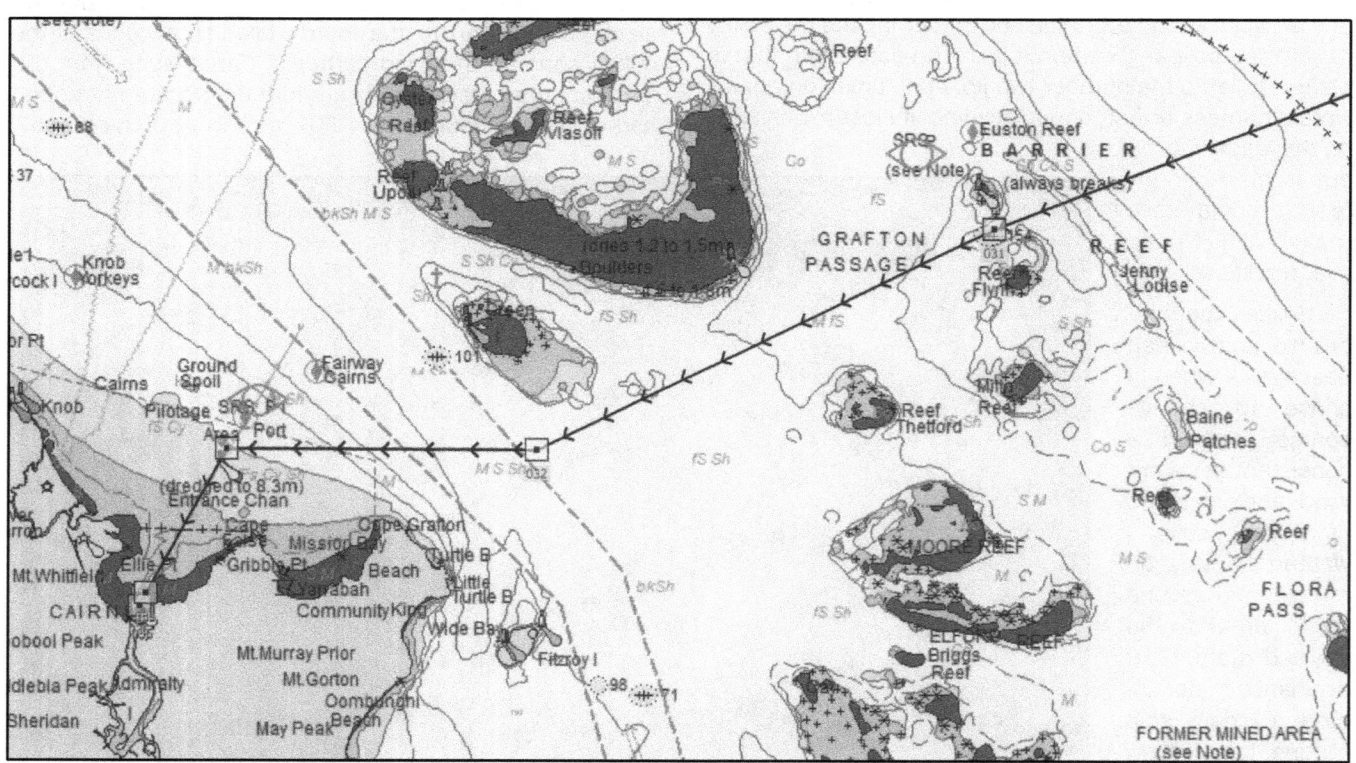

Grafton Passage through the Great Barrier Reef

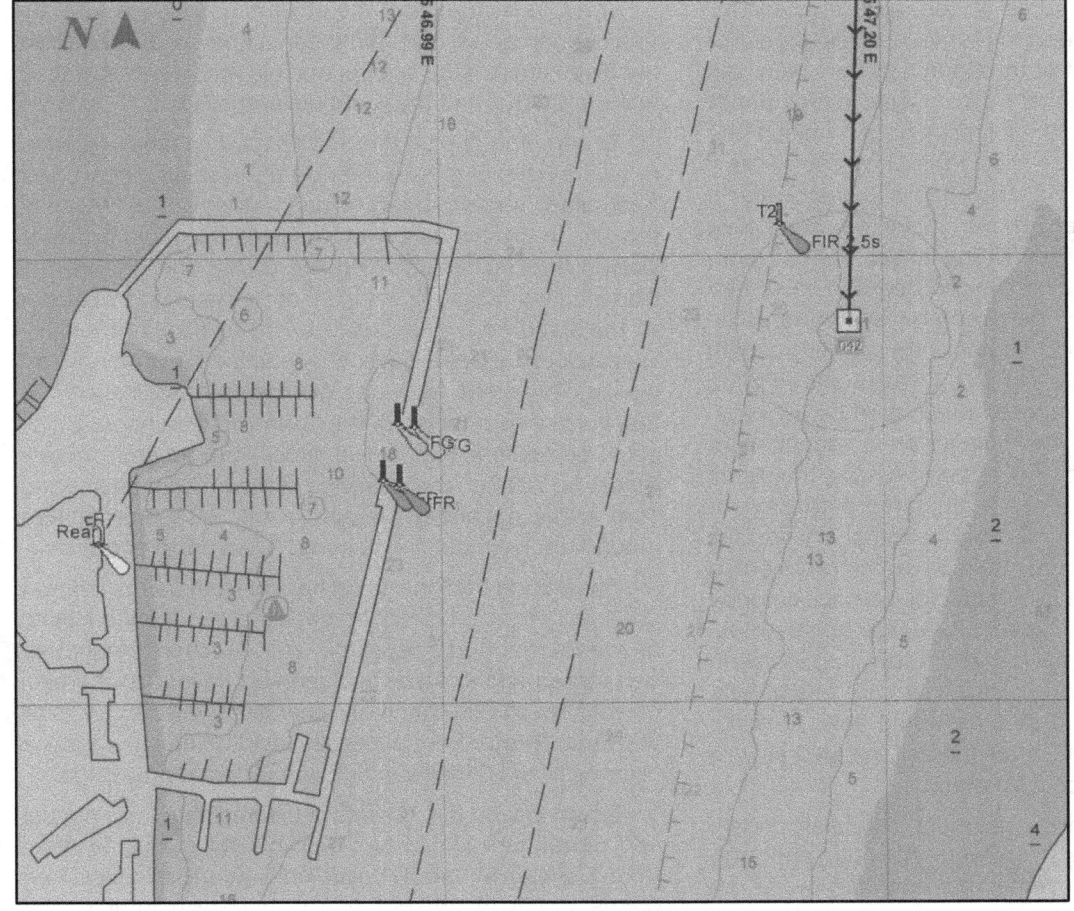

Marlin Marina, Cairns, Australia

as expected, allowing me to have restful sleep cycles and hours of spectating the sea and sky from my perch in the protected cockpit.

Dawn on day eight cracked with Scooter rounding reefs to head toward Grafton Passage, a marked entrance into the Great Barrier Reef on a course of 245° true. Sailing seven miles north of Sand Cay at the upper end of the Diane Bank while sitting at the helm with the long eyes in reach, I watched the laptop chart at the time of closest approach. Four hours after passing the cay, I rounded Moore Reef seven miles to the south. At 2300, I was up from a sleep cycle while skirting Holmes Reef to port.

At the eastern edge of the Great Barrier Reef, I navigated Scooter between the Euston Reef Light and Flynn Reef, followed Grafton Passage through the reef, turned due west, and crossed the shipping lanes to enter the Trinity Inlet off Cairns. There, no one answered my VHF calls on channel sixteen to the Marlin Marina. A listener on a boat in the marina responded that the office had closed at 1700, and that the town name was pronounced kerns not karens. I anchored out of the channel east of the marina breakwater, ending my third long-distance solo ocean sail on the fifteenth of June and noted in the supplemental logbook that the Sumlog recorded 1,467 miles.

Rest came easy that night. There would be no surprises with customs. I had processed an Australian Electronic Travel Authority while in New Zealand three days before departing for New Caledonia and received a temporary visa, the fee for which would be collected when I cleared in. They also acknowledged that I intended to arrive at Cairns. While underway, I received a message confirming receipt of my changed arrival time. Nothing could go wrong. I had given notice of my intended arrival date while in New Caledonia and the day before landfall.

At anchor the next morning, I made preparations below deck to present Scooter and myself to customs, immigration, quarantine and marine enforcement. I called the marina office on VHF, followed directions to an assigned slip, opened an account with the dockmaster and returned to Scooter. Minutes later, two customs officers requested permission to board. I welcomed them to the main saloon to process formalities. A casual conversation began covering all things to do with customs, immigration, and quarantine in an open-ended interview similar to that experienced in New Zealand. One officer asked if he could look around and followed the passageway to the aft cabin while the other officer, seated at the end of the saloon table under the TV monitor, continued the interview. The officer who inspected the aft cabin returned to the main saloon, paused at the nav table, studied the US and international sailing licenses, the radio license, and the EPERB registration forms displayed under the Lexan then asked about the food on board. My provisions passed scrutiny until he asked about spices. I slid the panel above the galley sinks to the right, exposing the rows of identical bottles with alphabetically ordered labels turned ready for inspection. He looked into the bottle marked "Bay Leaves" and plucked them into a plastic bag. As expected, they conversationally assessed my intentions, background, and honesty while I sat on the starboard divan recounting times in ports, adventures at sea, and my plans for future landfalls. One handed me a faded black-and-white photocopy of a mini-chart of the Coral Sea from New Caledonia to Australia on which he instructed me to pencil the route sailed to Cairns. Once I recognized names of the atolls, islands, and reefs on the faded photocopy, I drew my passage line, confirming that I had complied with requirements to not stop anywhere on the way from New Caledonia. When the officer sitting under the TV monitor asked about the medications on board, I presented my medicine kit inventory. He raised his eyebrows as he read down the page. I told him about my navy corpsman wound-suturing experience and that I was prepared to do minor suturing with the supplies prescribed by my physician, and that copies of the original prescriptions were available should he want to see them. Among the items in the ship's medicine kit were antiemetics to prevent vomiting, three antibiotics, two antibacterial analgesics, two antidiarrheals, a decongestant, a bird flu treatment, a malaria prophylaxis, three injectable anesthetics, suturing materials, hypodermic syringes and needles, fungus infection cream, arthritis treatments, and potassium iodide in case of the unimaginable—nuclear fallout. He hesitated a moment after reading and said he would have to make a call for a medical review. After the call, he said all was good and nothing would be restricted.

When the interview and document stamping ended, I commented about how I enjoyed the talk, and they responded in kind. Both remarked that they were not looking forward to the next interview. A yacht had arrived that morning without following prearrival formalities. One officer asked if I knew the boat. His description matched a yacht I'd seen back at the Riverside Drive Marina in Whangarei.

As the second officer took the final step up to the cockpit deck, he looked to his left into the open shelf above the entrance to the aft passageway where I kept a stash of pepper spray and bear spray canisters reachable from below in the saloon and from on deck. He looked down at me and casually enquired if there were personal defense items like . . . defensive sprays aboard. I had completely overlooked the sprays and pointed to where they were located. Both officers returned to the saloon table and listed them on a Receipt of Goods Removed used for firearms, erotic books, and DVDs, and other restricted items. When all was done, an Australian Certificate of Quarantine Clearance (pratique) and a visa were issued. The needed Control Permit to Operate in Australian Waters would be issued when I submitted the required sail plan for Australia identifying all places *Scooter* would go listing name, latitude and longitude coordinates, and number of days planned to stay for each location. It looked to be a time-consuming job. Given up in the clearing-in process were cans of illegal pepper gel and Alaska Bear Repellent and a pinch of bay leaves considered to be "organic risk material surrendered for destruction."

Later, I saw the yacht the officers had issues with, the one I remembered from Whangarei. I never learned about the disposition of the skipper and his wife, never saw them while in Cairns, and the yacht never moved.

To complete the required sail plan document, I worked in reverse, moving the curser on the Nobeltec chart from Australia's westernmost territory, the Cocos (Keeling) Islands, in the Indian Ocean to Darwin. I would arrive off Darwin after sailing 1,075 miles across the Arafura Sea from an anchorage off the town of Seisia on the west side of the Cape York Peninsula. Seisia looked as though it would be an excellent place to anchor for a day or two, waiting, if needed, for wind from the east. Sailing with the fast current over the tip of the Cape York Peninsula, Seisia could be made in four or five hours from an anchorage in Blackwood Bay on the west side of Mount Adolphus Island. That island anchored the end of my Great Barrier Reef ground track almost five hundred miles north of Cairns.

The ground track north in the reef from Cairns followed the ship lanes that threaded between and around islands and reefs. I plotted a dozen day sails, each to terminate at designated anchorages, and marked bailout anchorages on each leg should conditions change during the day. In all, the Great Barrier Reef passage would be much like island hopping in the Caribbean but with far greater hazards.

Indian Ocean pilot charts projected that July, August, and September would be favorable for sailing to Africa from Darwin. My study revealed I needed to sail from Cairns within two weeks to reach Darwin in July. That would be enough time to manage boat projects and provisioning. The next morning, I submitted the sail plan and added my copy of the Control Permit to Operate in Australian Waters to my Australian formalities folder, the fourteenth such folder containing every scrap of customs and immigration papers signed and stamped since sailing away from America twenty-eight months before.

Early morning light cast long shadows across the marina when I brought Mr. Stink to life and slipped dock lines back aboard on the twenty-first of June. I motored *Scooter* over to the floating fuel dock along the pier and made her fast with a breast line. Eager to start the sail up the reef, I impatiently waited for the dockhand to unlock the pump. Eventually, from out of the shadows where the ramp from the floating dock rose to the cement pier, a vertically challenged guy in neat coveralls approached, looked at his clipboard then up at me, and asked if I had registered an appointment. "Appointment for fuel?" I asked. He pointed to a sign at the foot of the ramp. Once there, I read that all fueling required an appointment. He looked up at me and said that the signs were everywhere and everyone knew it. I would have to wait until he could fit me in on the register. Even though there were no other boats at the fuel pier, he scribbled on his clipboard, turned, and walked away. I sat in the cockpit for an hour after digging out the "Welcome to Cairns" packet and read the Marlin Marina

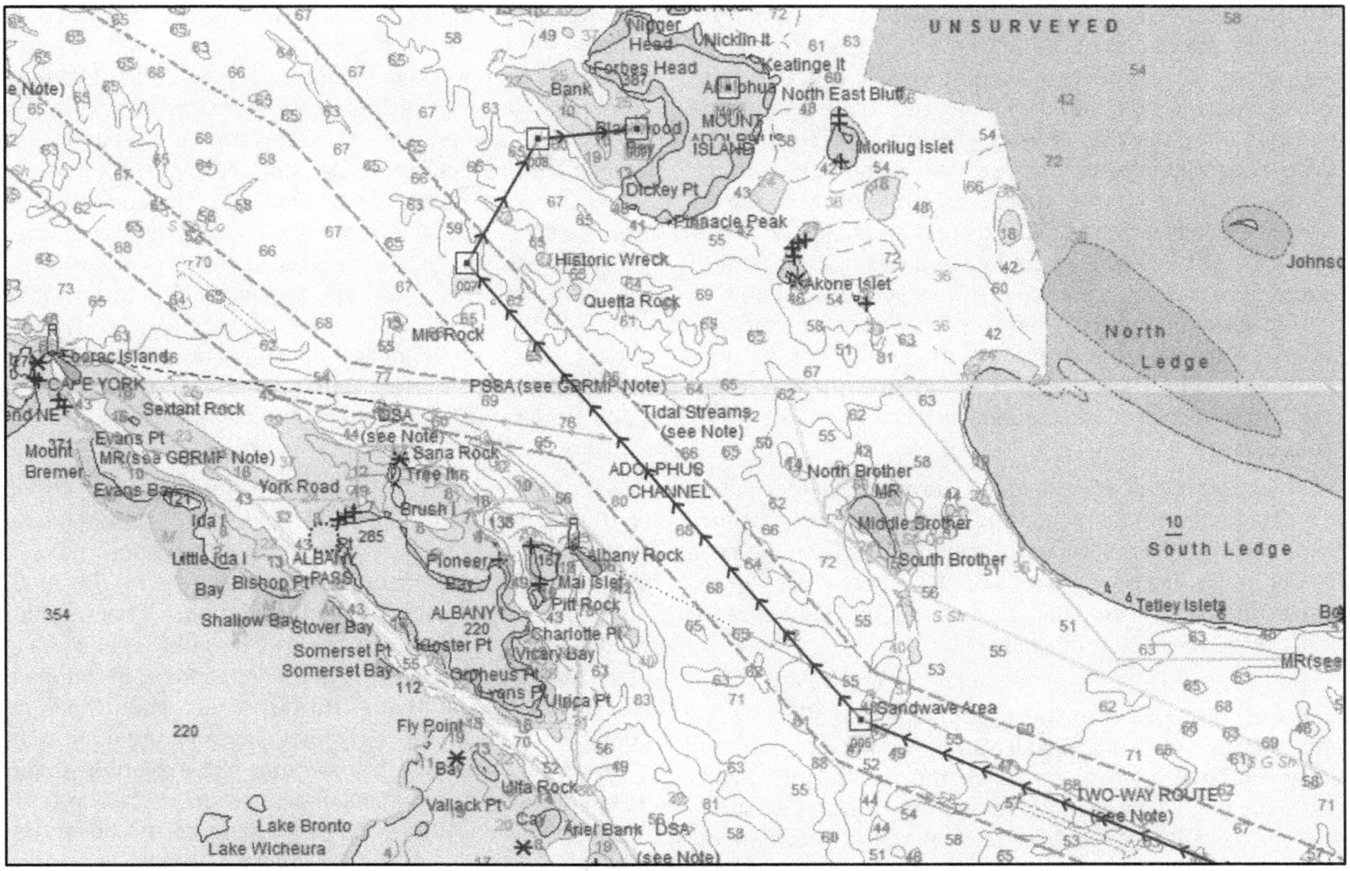

Mount Adolphus Island

brochure completely for the first time. There it was in plain sight: "Bookings are essential for all refueling requirements." My bad, but for the little man, rules were rules. My journey restarted when he unlocked the pump. I topped up the tank while *Scooter* remained the only boat at the pier.

The evening of the first passage, I switched the VHF radio off after anchoring. Later, I heard a fixed-wing aircraft buzz loudly overhead. From the cockpit, I watched it circle back and dive directly at *Scooter,* bear away, circle around and begin another dive. I got the message and switched the VHF on to hear a commanding voice. "Sailing vessel *Scooter,*

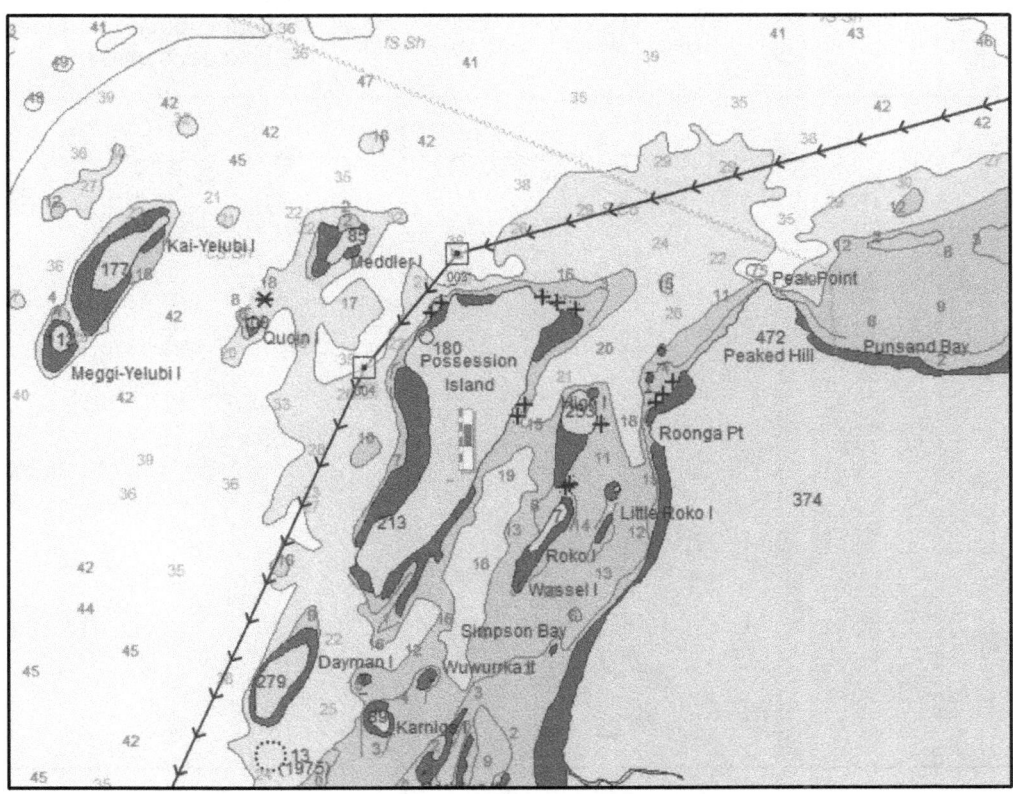

Possession Island ground track

Homeward Bound • 103

Scooter, Scooter. Over." After I answered the flying voice's questions about my name, intentions, number aboard, last port of call, and intended port of call, it wished me safe sailing and headed north along the coast. From then on, I monitored the VHF all waking hours and answered the same questions often before sunset. Some days, strong southeasterly air lifted *Scooter's* speed and my speed of living while sailing close to islands and reefs, and on other days light air allowed slow and easy times aboard. At the end of each sail, I made sure the plow anchor hooked the bottom hard by making sternway until *Scooter* stopped moving. Each evening, I studied the next day's ground track and current arrows on the Nobeltec chart mile by mile and reef by reef and listened to local marine weather broadcasts.

Favorable weather conditions permitted bypassing a few designated anchorages, and on the afternoon of the ninth day from Cairns, Mount Adolphus rose from the sea off the starboard bow. Hours later I anchored *Scooter* in Blackwood Bay, successfully completing the long passage north in the Great Barrier Reef.

From Blackwood Bay, *Scooter* sailed across the Adolphus Channel, over the tip of Cape York Peninsula, and through the Endeavour Strait southward toward Seisia under a clear blue sky on the second of July. It made my day when I sailed close enough to the western shore of Possession Island to photograph the monument to Captain Cook's journey through the strait on his first circumnavigation back in 1770.

South of Possession Island, Mr. Stink pushed *Scooter* toward a sandy beach off Seisia while I kept an eye on the forward scanning sonar. SV *Marcy*, last seen in Whangarei, swung on the hook with other yachts, and I joined the group at a safe distance. It turned out to be a three-day wait for the trades to fill. I chatted with Peter and Ginger, read another book, reviewed the ground track across the Arafura Sea to Darwin, and plotted waypoints to reach on the sail over the shallow banks southwest of Prince of Wales Island. From there I laid out a westward ground track with a planned bailout anchor spot in the lee of the west shore of Cape Wessel should trade winds turn foul. From there the track continued west past Cape Croker, above the Cobourg Peninsula, and extended south to Popham Bay, a perfect location to stage for a day sail to Cape Hotham followed by another day sail to Fannie Bay off Darwin.

On the morning of departure from Seisia, strong southeast wind offered up a westbound broad reach over the shallow banks and into the waters between the Gulf of Carpentaria and the Arafura Sea dotted with container and passenger ships heading east. Buoyweather predicted increasing but tolerable wind speed as I approached Cape Wessel. I set a second reef in the main and sailed past the cape. On day three, when the wind consistently blew over thirty knots, I struck the main after a preventer block shattered—more like exploded—under stress. *Scooter* swam along at over seven knots flying only the jib until Cape Croker's light flashed on the horizon at midnight on the eighth of July. Midmorning the next day, I rounded Cobourg Peninsula and sailed into Popham Bay on the northwest tip of the peninsula, repeated the after-anchoring routine with the voice in the sky, and reviewed the next day's passage to Cape Hotham.

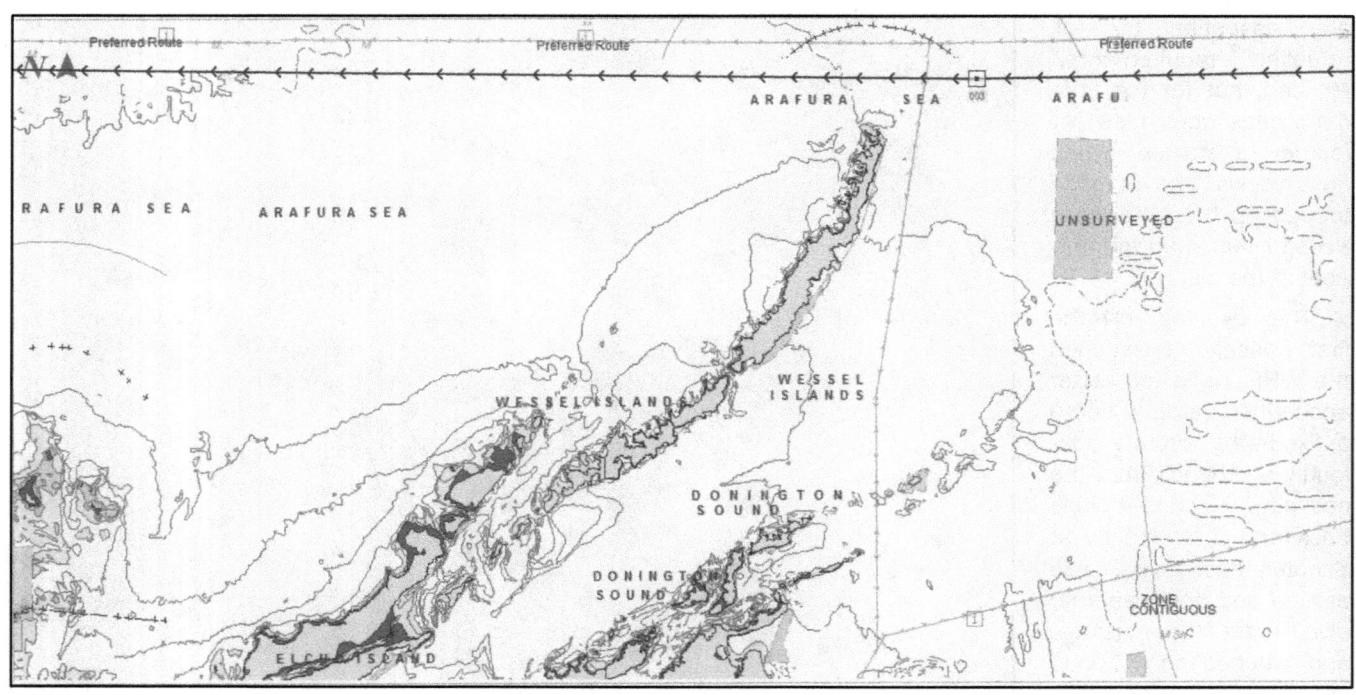

Cape Wessel

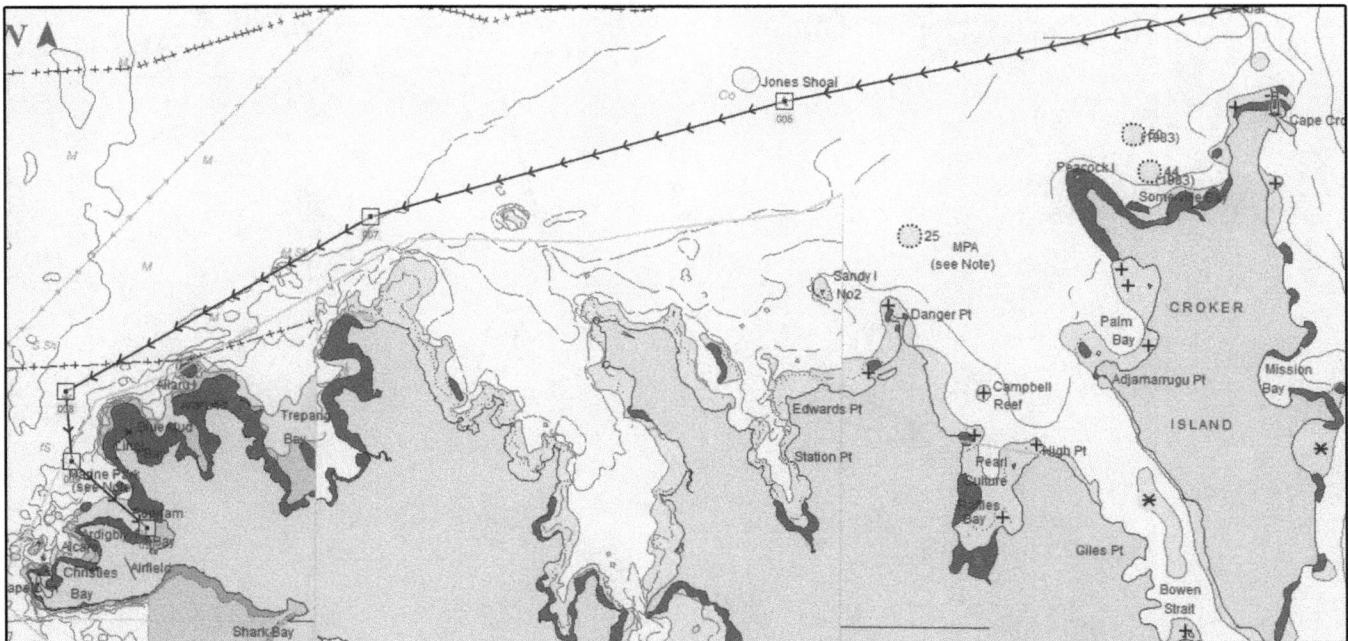

Arriving Popham Bay

Because I felt no rush to get underway to make the few hours sail to Cape Hotham, I dragged out the morning routine, started Mr. Stink, casually rolled in the chain and secured the anchor. That lazy routine suddenly changed when Mr. Stink stopped with a loud bang the moment I shifted into forward. No smoke rose from the engine when I lifted the hatch, but while lowering it, I saw the starboard jib sheet leading off the toe rail stretched tight against the hull. The image of a sheet wrapped around the prop came to me, and I rushed forward to reset the anchor.

Australian guidebooks warned of crocodiles in Northern Territory waters as well as fast-swimming box jellyfish, bluebottles—local slang for a blue Portuguese man o' war, and of course sharks. To top that off, Popham Bay enclosed a marine sanctuary. I recalled reading somewhere that saltwater crocks missing a meal opportunity would return to the same spot at the same time the next day to check if the missed meal returned, and that beach landings with a RIB should be made at different locations at different times of the day to avoid encountering a crock lying in wait.

My choices were clear: leave the line wrapped around the prop and sail away to remove the line in safer water, risking disaster if I needed auxiliary power during the passage, or get wet now, knife in hand, and cut the line from the prop. I dug out my ankle-sheathed dive knife, mask with snorkel, and thin wet suit and suited up. I positioned the boarding ladder down the starboard side and tugged on dive boots that fit into my dive fins, only to realize there could be an additional hazard. Should I spot a crock or shark while in the water, I would want to get up the ladder fast with no time to remove the fins. After walking the decks and seeing no crocks, jellies, or bluebottles, I lowered myself slowly down the ladder trying to not make a ripple. I slipped under, looked around, and

Alert for crocs

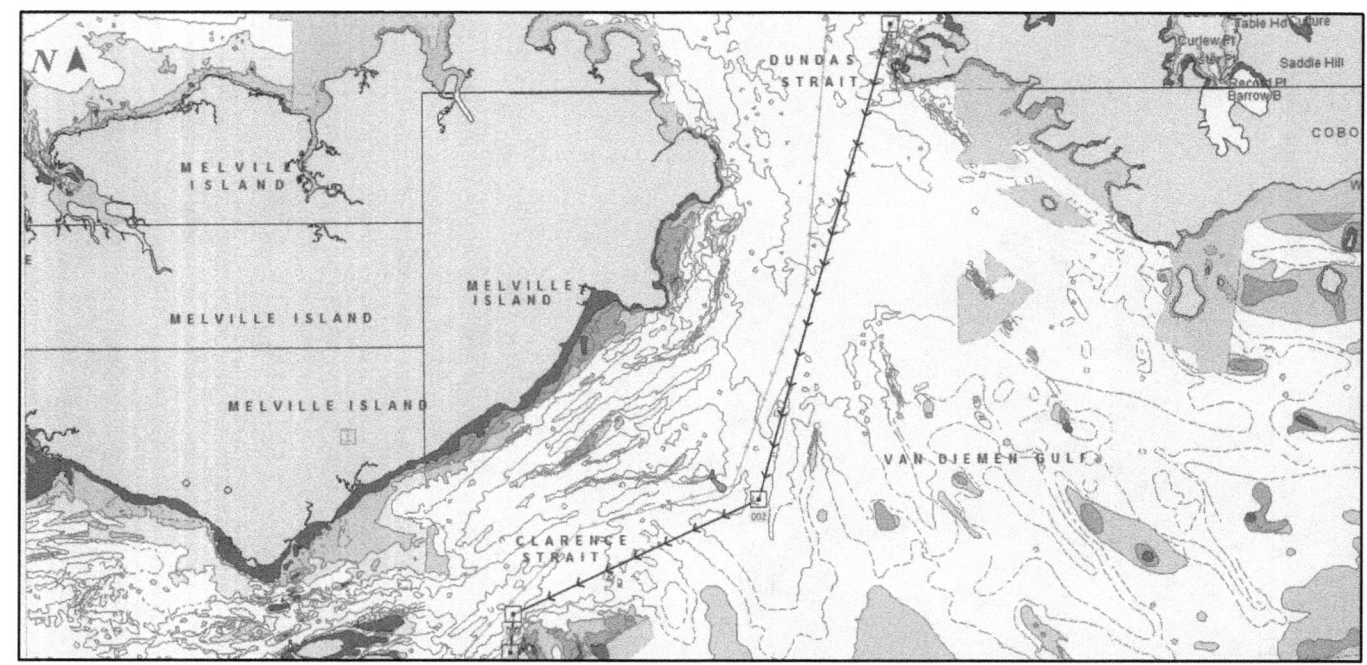

Popham Bay to Cape Hotham

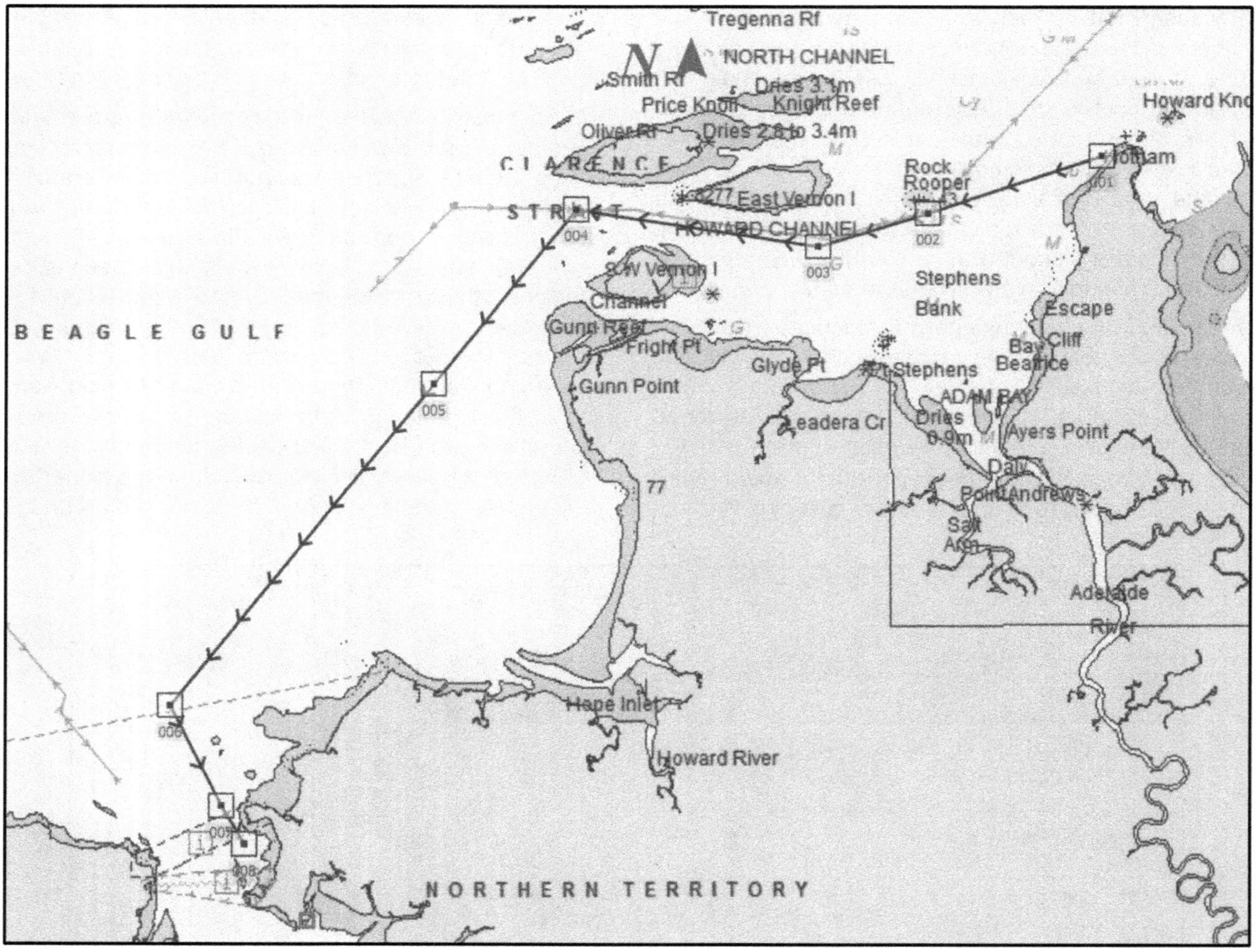

Cape Hotham to Fannie Bay

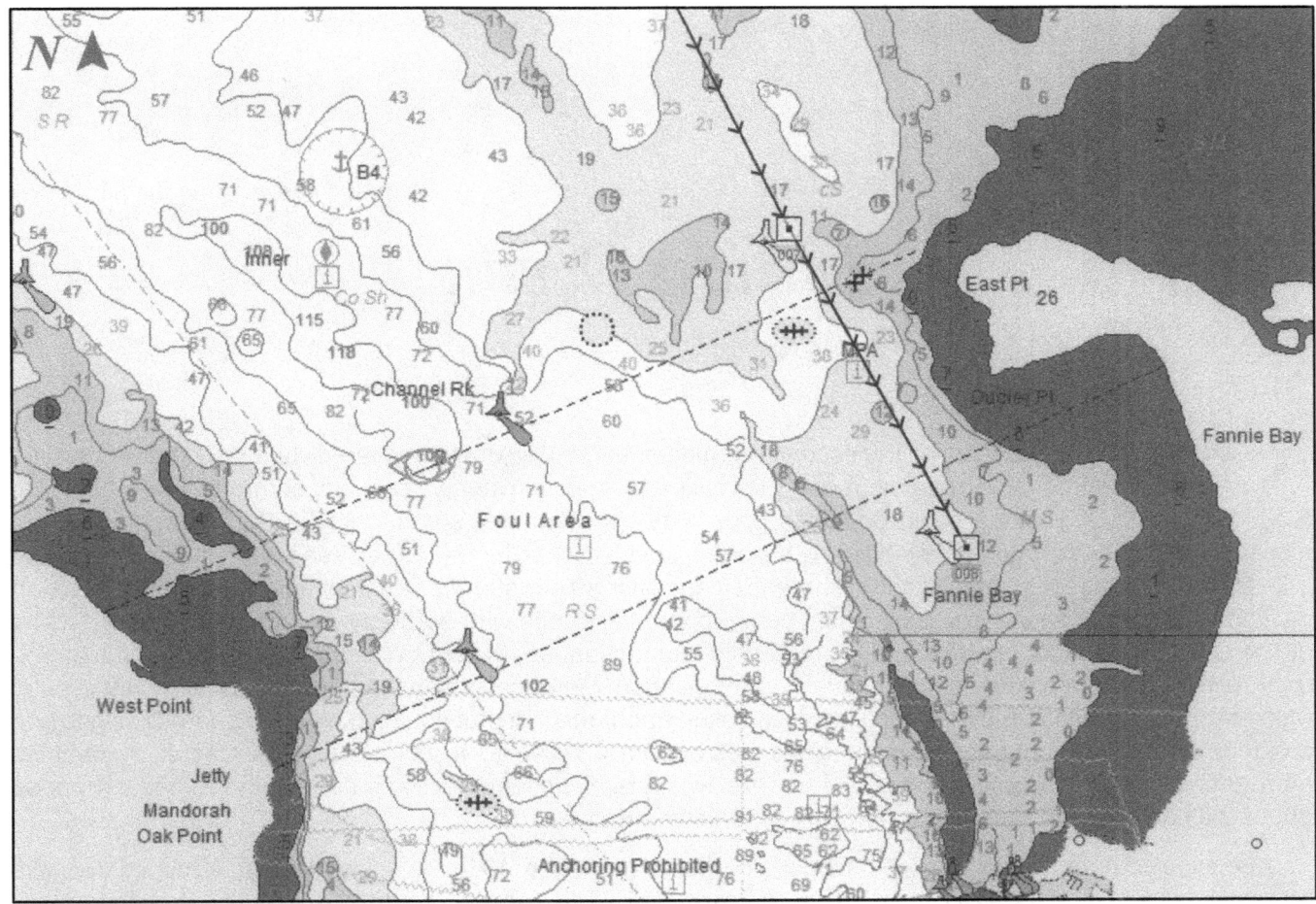

Arriving Fannie Bay

seeing nothing, surfaced to take several deep breaths. I submerged and swam with knife in hand to the prop and found it wrapped by the jib sheet, forming a large tangle. Cutting as much as I could on one breath, I looked around in the clear water that blurred to murky gray at the bow and returned to the ladder to reoxygenate. Back aboard, breathing easy with cut sheet sections strewn on the deck after several dives, I peeled the boots and wet suit off, started Mr. Stink, hoisted the anchor, and set sails for the run to Cape Hotham under a cloudless blue sky.

From Cape Hotham, I navigated currents and dodged huge, floating sea weed patches in the Howard Channel between the Vernon Islands, sailed south, and set the hook on the west fringe of a large group of yachts anchored in Fannie Bay. On the day after arrival, I heard a ship's horn and rose to the deck to see sailboats tacking and jibing around *Scooter*, giving me a front row seat for the Saturday morning regatta. That welcoming sight launched a three-week adventure in Darwin to marine stores and marketplaces.

Before crossing a grassy park to the bus stop beyond the beach to start my explorations, I had to account for the sometimes five-meter-tides in Fannie Bay. Arriving at low tide, I had to run the painter with anchor and chain far up the beach and mark its location with driftwood stuck vertically in the sand, prepared, with a swimsuit under my shorts, to wade out to it when I returned. Abandoning *Jazz* at high tide could require dragging it a good distance to the water's edge after six hours ashore. For three weeks, I walked or bused as much of Darwin as could be fit into the daylight hours and spent the evening planning the passage across the Indian Ocean to Mauritius. Ashmore Reef, west of Australia; Christmas Island, south of Java; and the Cocos (Keeling) Islands, west southwest of Christmas Island, all Australian territories, became waypoints along the 4,350-mile ground track.

On the second of August, I sealed the anchor chain hawsepipe with Play-Doh and motored northward in Beagle Gulf to catch enough wind to fly three sails and make way against a tide current in two-foot short-period waves, beginning my westward passage across the Indian Ocean, a passage that would vigorously test *Scooter's* engineering, my sailing skills, my self-reliance, and my resolve.

Indian Ocean

Scanning SSB frequencies on the second morning out from Darwin, I discovered voices aboard westbound yachts participating in a radio network they called the net, delivering a sense of comfort to members that assistance, if needed, could be called upon. The net controller, a volunteer for the week, opened the morning net at a designated time delivering his or her specifics: position, weather, sea state, and vessel course and speed then called on each yacht to share their specifics so all listeners could factor the data into their own navigation planning and safety decisions. The net controller spoke with authority, no humor, no banter, as he or she called each yacht on the list. Once all yachts had responded, the controller closed the official net saying that the frequency would be open to casual communication. Members enlightened others about recent events. Men offered solutions to maintenance issues or joked about the fish that got away. Women shared recipes and chatted about a variety of sailing women's issues and joys. Vessel-to-vessel radio chatter lasted sometimes more than an hour. The net's call sign, Zebra One, was retained even after the member who coined it dropped out of the flotilla to explore another faraway ocean adventure.

That morning radio chatter balanced the quiet peace while motor sailing on the placid sea, so I decided to join in and gave the net controller *Scooter*'s specifics and the number aboard. When the morning net closed, I made slow and relaxed rounds on deck and tossed back the flying fish that landed overnight.

After a 460-mile sail in light air, I spotted Ashmore Reef, a common waypoint for Indian Ocean travelers, an hour after dawn. As predicted, the wind spiked when I reached the southern side of the reef, requiring me to quickly lower sails getting ready to find my way into the reef. Peter and Ginger from SV *Marcy*, regular Zebra One

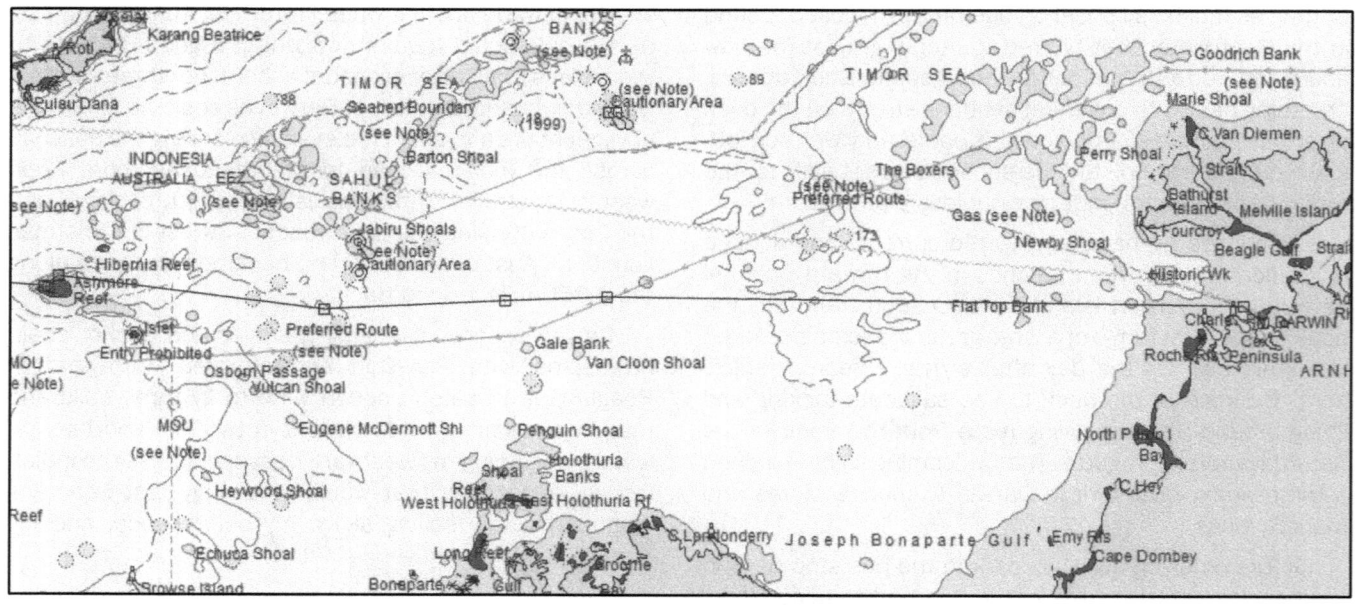

Darwin to Ashmore Reef, noon plots

Ashmore Reef, Source: ParksAustalia.gov

radio net participants, had already attached to a large ship mooring just north of West Island. Knowing I was sailing alone, Peter motored a dinghy alongside to help me slip a line through the eye atop a huge mooring buoy in the stiff breeze. It was illegal and not prudent to anchor on the hard coral bottom of the small bay bounded by exposed coral to the north, east, and south with overnight winds predicted in the high teens. I checked in with the customs officer stationed aboard the Australian cutter moored in the West Island lagoon and began my evening routine.

Two days later, I slipped the mooring for the 1,027-mile sail to Christmas Island in heavy east wind. The next morning's radio net chatter contained the faint voice of a woman on the sailing vessel *Floatingpoint*. I listened closely to her broken transmission, deciphering that she was sailing solo in the same rough and lumpy conditions that demanded much from me. The eastern trades blew in the upper teens, and *Scooter* sometimes rolled far over with the force of the seas. Angry ocean waves collided from three directions: Fast-moving trade winds drove large waves westward that crossed with very large and long-period swells traveling at an angle toward them from the southwestern Indian Ocean. Rollers from the northeast smashed into the mix creating a chaotic sea state.

Converging waves pestered *Scooter* and disrupted my comfort aboard until sailing over the 4800 meter depth contour line at around longitude 119° E where the sea state settled into a long, westward roll. Perhaps water depth had affected the sea state. However, the next morning, the seas again violently peaked from multiple directions. Some net participants experienced the same conditions and talked about dealing with the chaos below deck

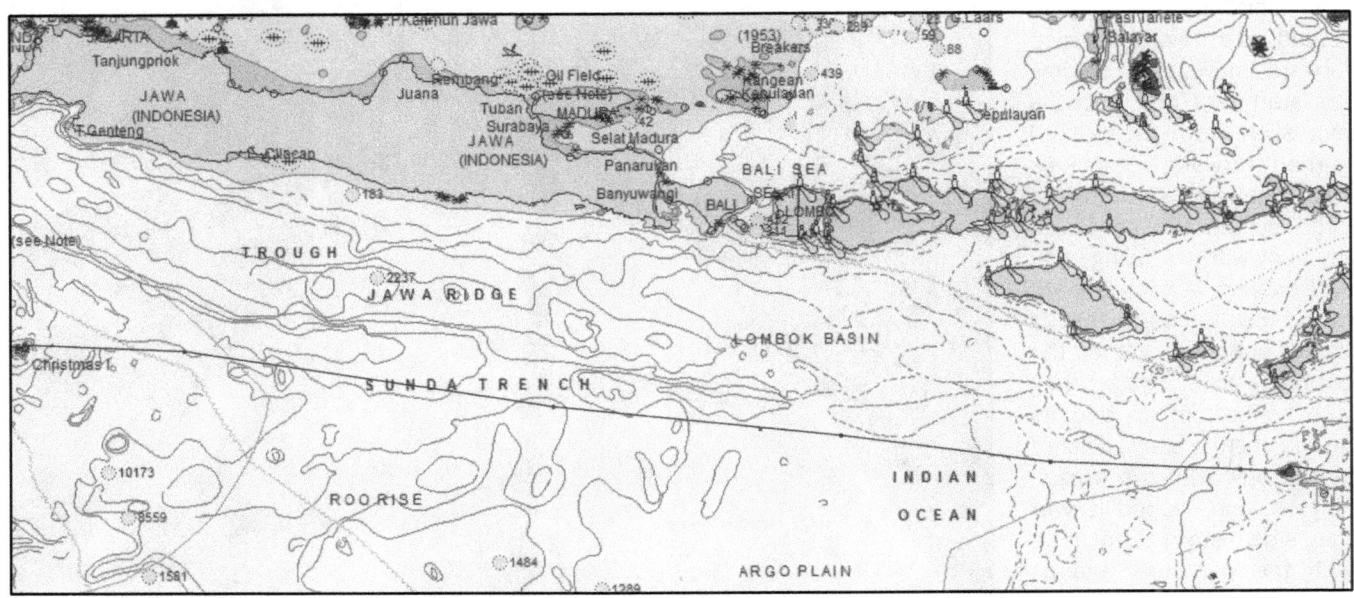

Ashmore Reef to Christmas Island, noon plots

Indian Ocean • 109

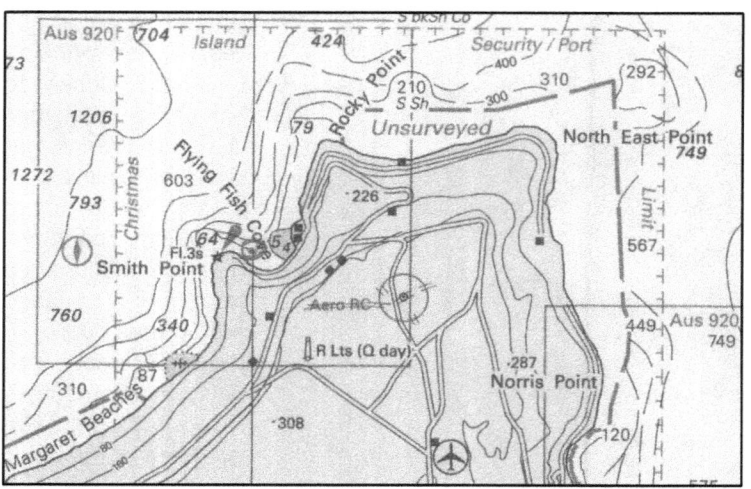

Flying Fish Cove
(Not to be used for navigation)

during the lumpy ride—except for Carolyn, *Floatingpoint's* skipper, who cheerfully said, "All is well."

Christmas Island's rocky shoreline, two hundred miles south of Indonesia, rose from the confused seas after sunrise on August 16th. I rounded the north shore of the Australian territory, where phosphate mining operations, the sole reason to inhabit the island, came into view. Conveyors from a large complex on a hill moved ore above the main road near shore and out over the water on the northern prominence to waiting ships in Flying Fish Cove.

In light air, I motored *Scooter* past orange mooring buoys tethering cruising yachts until I spotted a vacant one close to where the cove met the cliff on the south shore. It looked to be a risky lee shore, but it was the only one available. After shifting to neutral, I revved up in reverse to stop forward movement, placing the starboard bow about a foot away from the buoy. I hurried forward, slipped a spare halyard through the large eye in the center of the buoy with a fending pole, and snaked it back aboard for a quick temporary tie. At the aft cabin top, I rolled the Sunbrella cover off *Jazz* lying with its bottom up and its bow facing the stern, hoisted by the bow with the mizzen halyard, and slipped it over the side, stern end first, with the pontoons against *Scooter's* hull. After letting the halyard slip around the winch until the pontoons touched the water, I let the halyard fly, and *Jazz* hit the water with a hollow thump.

Aboard *Jazz*, I pulled myself, hand over hand, along *Scooter's* starboard side to the bow, where I grabbed a special-purpose heavy mooring line staged on the bow deck. Long before, I had threaded the line through a length of clear vinyl tubing, returned the bitter end to the line, and spliced it, creating a loop protected from chafing. I slipped the loop through the eye in the center of the buoy, snaked the free end through the loop, and led it over the port bow anchor roller, hitching it to the large deck cleat. I then replaced the halyard with a length of dock line that would serve as the last line to be retrieved at the time of departure.

I floated *Jazz* aft, tied the painter to a midship cleat, climbed up the boarding ladder, shut off the engine, and returned to the bow. To protect the mooring lines from chafe where they ran through chocks, I slipped tubing, previously split lengthwise, around them and pressed the package into the chocks. Seeing that the heavy line rubbed on the anchor at times as *Scooter* swung in the breeze, I lowered the anchor down to swing just below the surface. Confident that the lines would hold *Scooter* in high wind and that the buoy chain and whatever it was fixed to below were well-maintained, I rolled onto the aft cabin bunk for a well-earned nap.

Back on the forward deck, when panning the long eyes over the tethered yachts in the bay, a large ketch came into view. On her reverse-sloped transom, a wood banner routed and inlaid in white identified *Floatingpoint*.

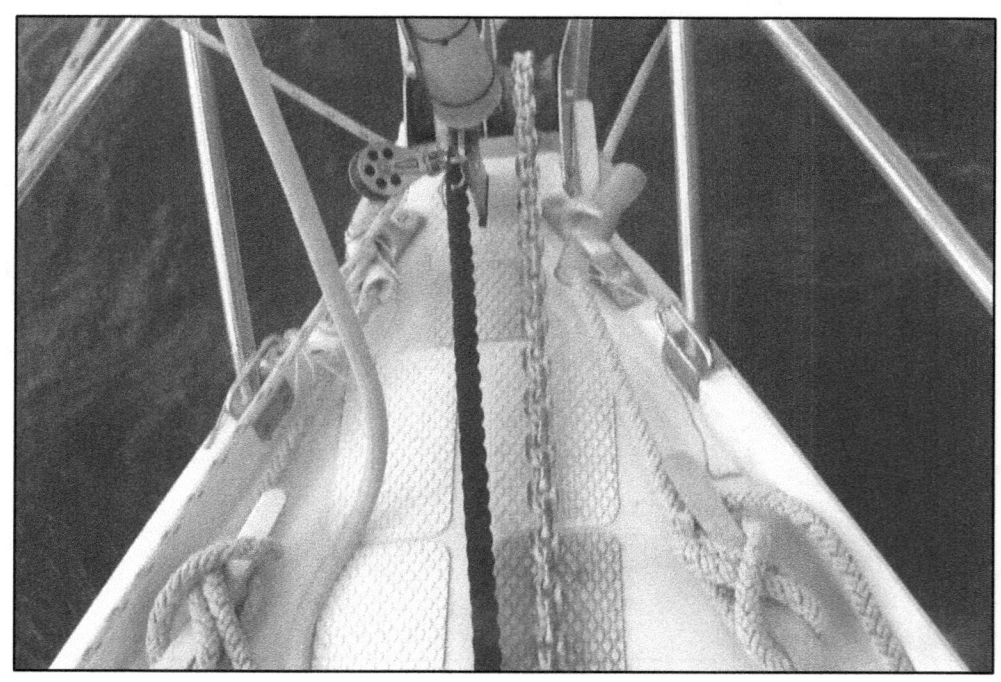

Buoy lines secured

Below, a similar wooden banner read "East Lansing, MI." The yacht had no davits extending off her stern where a dingy or RIB would hang. Lines overlaying a folded tarp on the long cabin top between the main and mizzen masts suggested the place where a dinghy would ride inverted while sailing. Panning the long eyes right to search for places where Carolyn may have gone ashore, I spotted a pier that extended out to deep water from a sandy beach. A dingy floated under a ladder hanging down from the pier. Seeing the pathway for going ashore, my attention shifted to reviewing engine and machine spaces, maintenance requirements, and provisions. With those tasks finished, I prepped *Jazz* and zipped straight for the pier.

The land end of the steel pier connected to a narrow sand-blown road, Jin Pantal, becoming Gaze Road up the coast at a roundabout near the phosphate conveyors that rattled overhead. Back in 1887, discovery of phosphate on the uninhabited island led to bringing in two hundred indentured Chinese to work the mines along with other Asians and some Europeans, all administered by the United Kingdom through offices in Singapore. Captain William Mynors named the island after the day he discovered it more than two hundred years earlier in 1643. Australia and New Zealand bought the mining company in 1958, transferring the sovereignty from Singapore to Australia, and operated it until 1987, when the mining operations were stopped for environmental concerns. In 1990, mining restarted after modernizing at the direction of a restructured ownership.

North of the roundabout, I explored the small but adequate Christmas Island Supermarket offering frozen meats and even fresh vegetables. Islanders spoke English, the official language, many with strong Asian inflections. Further up Gaze Road in the Internet café, I opened the laptop on a small table and plugged the converter into a 230-volt power socket on the wall. It took minutes not seconds to transmit an email that flowed by cable to Australia before being beamed to a satellite. Zipping back to *Scooter* with a canvas bag full of veggies, I circled *Floatingpoint*, seeing a dingy tethered off the stern but no one on deck or in the cockpit. Out of respect for her privacy I refrained from calling out. My curiosity persisted about the person sailing the ketch, who had such a commanding voice on the radio, and why she was sailing solo.

When steady winds out of the east returned five days after arriving, I removed the heavy line holding *Scooter* to the buoy and secured *Jazz* on the aft cabin top. I brought Mr. Stink to life, retrieved the anchor line from the mooring, perched myself on the helm chair, and piloted *Scooter* northwest, away from the rocky shoreline. Rejoining Zebra One, I chatted with familiar westbound voices during the five-hundred-mile sail to the South Keeling Islands. Four days of westerly air at twenty-five knots carried *Scooter* faster than planned. Nearing the island at dusk, I lowered the mainsail to the boom and secured it with sail ties leaving it quick to hoist if needed. The wind speed dropped to seventeen knots that night, guaranteeing that sailing with only the jib would delay arrival until after dawn.

Midmorning sun welcomed my approach to Direction Island, one of the many Cocos (Keeling) Islands in the westernmost Australian territory. A brilliant white sand beach framed by green palm trees surrounded the sparkling clear water where I laid the anchor on the sandy bottom in Port Refuge. It was difficult to imagine that such a beautiful island could have been a WWII seaplane base.

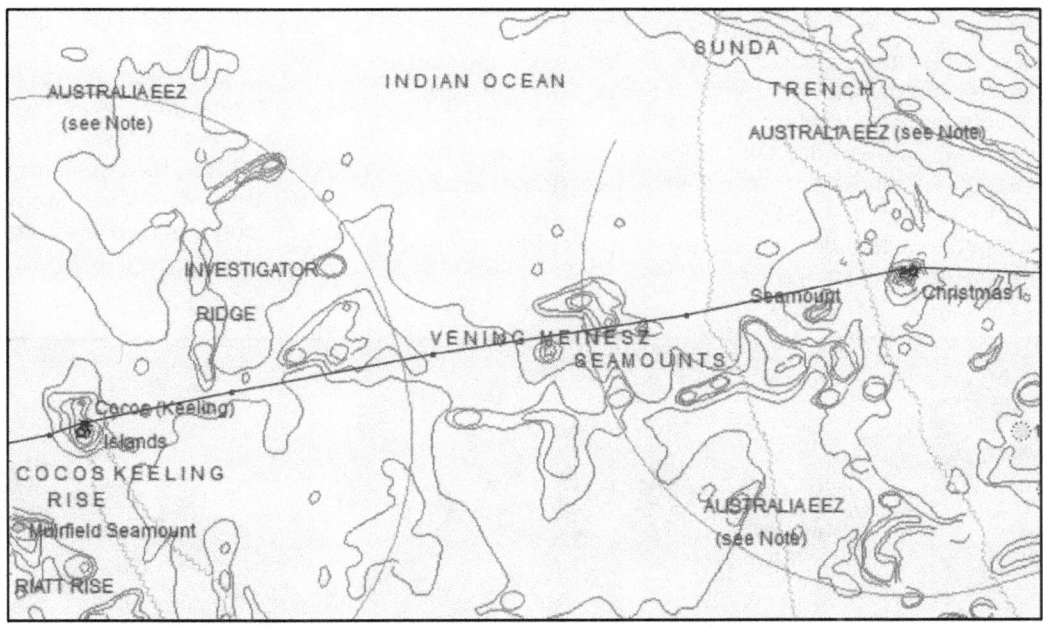

Christmas Island to Cocos (Keeling) Islands, noon plots

SV *Marcy* floated at anchor along with many yachts participating on the Zebra One net. On the beach, a shelter supported by vertical steel posts shaded picnic tables and a large hammock. Driftwood, fenders, fishing net floats, and other salty things inscribed with vessel names and dates hung overhead as testaments of passage, creating a nautical environment where net participants could interact face-to-face. Nearby, a stone fire pit and a water cistern flanked a barbeque grill. Conversations encompassed

Indian Ocean • 111

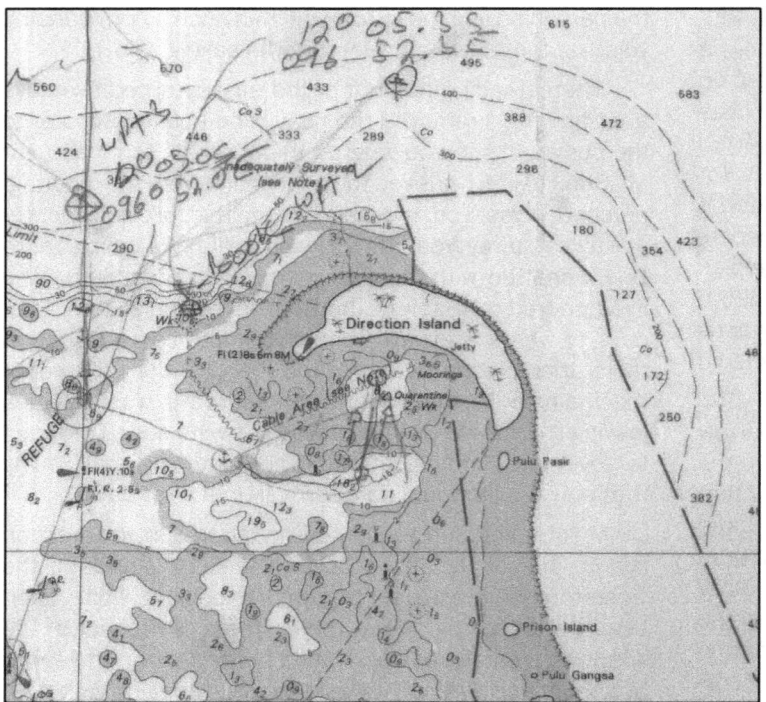

Direction Island, Cocos (Keeling) Islands,
(Not to be used for navigation)

Exploring the fast-flowing tidal passage dubbed "The Rip" between the southeast tip of Direction Island and the small islet Pulu Pasir where snorkelers flushed east to west in the rushing flood current, I saw *Floatingpoint* maneuver into the anchorage. At that distance I could see a white-haired woman of small stature move rapidly from the helm to the foredeck. From a dingy that arrived alongside, a man boarded, helped her set the anchor, chatted a while, then departed and motored to SV *Marcy*. Chatting it up with Peter and Ginger under the shelter that afternoon I learned that Carolyn wanted to rest and not join others ashore.

Every day, cruisers arrived and departed the island, a waypoint on their passage to somewhere. Among emails from the kids one arrived from Sefina about her wait for a grandchild soon to be delivered and other happy events. Five days after arrival, forecasts predicted heavy east winds for many days to come. They exceeded the Indian Ocean pilot charts' observations over my planned course for August, showing southeast air at force five on the Beaufort scale (seventeen to twenty-one knots) for over half the years observed. I prepared *Scooter* for more than two thousand miles of heavy-weather sailing. On a Friday, I zipped on *Jazz* south to Home Island with the *Scooter* binder in my shore bag and processed final clearance out of Australia. With the port fees paid and the passport, visa, and Certificate of Clearance stamped for departure the next day, I secured and covered *Jazz* on the aft cabin top.

past adventures, places visited, visions of the next landfall, marinas, coves, island beaches, towns, societies, favorite recipes, and the never-ending boat project to-do list that grew every day at sea. Joyous interactions among the self-reliant sailors, some who were homeschooling children, continued daily during the pleasant pause from fast-paced action on deck or slow and often boring times floating on windless water.

Implementing my departure routine, I copied the 2,300-mile ground track to Mauritius from the Nobeltec chart to an Indian Ocean Routing Chart published by the hydrographer of the Australian Navy. Long-range weather opinions heard the next morning professed moderate to heavy air out of the east southeast, suggesting a port-tack run. It looked like I would be living at the high end of ocean speed. Making rounds on deck, I rigged the spinnaker pole off the port side of the main-

Cocos (Keeling) Island's marks of passage

mast after leading a sheet from the storm jib bag on deck through the pole's open end and back through a fairlead block on the toe rail to the port cockpit winch. I snapped the jib's sail hanks onto the inner forestay leaving the jib flaked in the bag secured to the forestay deck fitting and led the other sheet around the shrouds and back through a fairlead on the starboard toe rail. The job finished when I rigged main and mizzen preventers.

Shortly after sunrise, I fixed the anchor in the bow roller, packed the chain hawsepipe with Play-Doh, and motored northwest of Horsburgh Island. At my Nobeltec waypoint, I turned into the wind and set the main with a double reef. After keying the autopilot to the westward course, I eased the main sheet, allowing the main boom to swing out to starboard as *Scooter* rounded to course, and trimmed the preventer line, fixing the boom in place. Making way on course, I pulled my harness tether along the port jack line, removed the storm jib from its bag, and returned to the cockpit where I trimmed the sheet to bring the clue near the spinnaker pole end. Back at the bow, I shifted my tether to the starboard jack line, hoisted the jib, and walked the tether along the starboard jack line to the cockpit. With final sail adjustments made, *Scooter* sailed wing on wing along a 260° true ground track in seventeen knots of wind on large but slow southeast swells, a pleasant beginning to the long passage.

Overnight, *Scooter* sailed in winds of twenty-seven knots, with gusts of thirty-five knots. Large four- and five-meter seas rolled her up, over, and down deep troughs. Every now and then two steep waves came together, crested, and broke, sometimes smacking the port quarter hard. At dawn the eastern sky filled with low, dark clouds far off the stern that arrived overhead by day's end. Rain pelted peaked seas, spewing mist off battered wave crests.

Near daybreak the wind backed and fell to sixteen knots, having no effect on *Scooter's* course to Mauritius, which was being held true by the robust WH autopilot. Large waves soon arrived from the east under the chop, announcing heavy air heading my way. After the wind shifted to nearly off the stern, I altered course to 240° true to keep the apparent air close to thirty degrees off the port stern. I wanted to avoid being driven on deck in a fast-backing wind to manage jibing in those conditions. Plenty of sea miles stretched ahead, allowing *Scooter* to wander above and below the ground track with the shifting winds.

When below, I often had to be careful of my next step to avoid violent contact with a bulkhead or table corner as *Scooter* leaped with the waves even though the long roll from port to starboard had become a predictable regularity. Some morning radio chats captured my attention during less active moments. A few yachts were sailing in the same weather and others reported easy sailing farther north or just west of the Cocos (Keeling) Islands. Carolyn's voice seemed cheerful, reporting fair weather. I heated an easy one-pot noon meal of canned meat and vegetables as *Scooter* rolled, pitched, and yawed around its center of lateral resistance. That center happened to be located just forward of the galley's double sinks. It was exhilarating to stand at that point straight up, perpendicular to the horizon, and look forward while the saloon pitched up and down and rolled side to side, knowing that the boat was self-sailing with all systems performing as designed. I scarfed the soup from the pot with a large spoon while bracing myself against the galley sink and straightaway washed and stowed the cookware in the under-sink cabinet.

When rolling to starboard the boat's heeling motion would eventually slow then pause and begin to roll back to port where it slowed, paused, and returned to starboard. Transiting the narrow passageway from the main saloon to the aft cabin head and back had been managed many times without effort. Shortly after lunch, while gripping my way toward the main saloon, I noticed that when there should have been a pause ending the roll to port, the roll continued a little farther and a little farther still until the roll stopped way beyond where it had in the prior cycles. The recovery roll to starboard began and when the roll should have stopped, hesitated and returned, it continued on and on until the nav station seemed to be almost three meters below the galley stove. The passageway leaned to what I sensed to be about 90 degrees from vertical. Cookware under the galley sink clinked, refrigerator items clunked, and dishware clanged. The laptop leaped up off the nav desk to bang into the radios. I held on to the midship bulkhead opening next to the navigation station to keep from being thrown forward while watching the action as the loud sound of roaring water overcame the usual rush of the wind and swoosh of the seas. Lying on her starboard side, *Scooter* had almost stopped forward motion. I held my place in the passageway, eyes wide open, ears searching for familiar sounds, until she started to roll back to port, and I could sense forward motion again.

Damn, that's a knock down! Two or more large seas had come together, building a breaking wave, a rogue wave larger than the repetitive five-meter waves, and rolled *Scooter's* starboard rail into the sea, mast almost parallel to the horizon, keel almost in clear air. Everything stayed in place; all cabinets and below decks storage spaces held their contents. Had I been at the galley stove or on the head, I would have been thrown over to the starboard side a cabin-width below. It was good that the soup pot had been put away after cleaning and that nothing had been boiling on the galley cooker. What a disaster that would have been!

In an instant, I hopped to the third step at the top of the companionway, pulled the barrel bolt that held the vertical door locked in place, dropped the door, and slid the hatch open. Rising to the cockpit, I saw *Jazz* still lashed to the aft cabin top handrails. Solar panels and wind generators looked good. I spun around to see the double reefed mainsail set with a preventer and the storm jib full and drawing off the port pole. I unzipped the starboard clear-vinyl sea curtain from the hard dodger, looked along the deck, and was relieved to see that the lines securing the jerry cans to the stainless-steel handrail had held, but the rubber mats under the jerry cans to prevent chafing of the starboard deck were gone. Even the boarding ladder, suspended outboard of the railing, held its place though it must have experienced the full force of water moving at seven knots.

Navigation station

I momentarily visualized that monster wave passing under and around the keel, the skeg, and the rudder as the boat rose up the steep wave face to the crest, where the heavy keel fell over the back side of the wave, bringing her upright again. Had I been on deck without a harness, *Scooter* would have automatically sailed onward to become a ghost ship, laying up on some island or African beach. I descended the steps to the saloon, secured the hatch and companionway door, and checked the electronics for operation.

While waiting at the nav desk for the radar to initialize, a trickle of water wandered across the desk top from under the vertical panel at the hull side of the nav desk. Long ago during restoration and upgrade projects, I fixed a sheet of marine plywood to the hull behind the panel with an array of wire connector bridges to link electrical components in an orderly fashion. The panel filled the space behind the nav desk up to the underside of three cubbies backed by mahogany panels, each holding electrical switch plates. Should the need arise, each of these panels could be unscrewed and tipped out to gain access to the wire runs behind.

I removed the lower panel and found water dripping onto the bus bars from above then unscrewed and tilted the cubby switch panels out to follow the flow. With a mirror and flashlight in hand, I spotted the leak source, right at the seam where the deck had been epoxied to the hull the full length of the boat on both sides. By that time in my solo sailing life, I had gotten good at talking with myself and whispered, "Yup, has to be from that repair after the truck smacked the toe rail in Ohio. The repair guys missed sealing it, dammit. It's still dripping! The rub rail's gotta be holding water, letting it drain through." I conjured up seeing the damage when the boat was delivered to Port Clinton, Ohio, and remembered the weekends Cindy and I spent getting it ready for sailing the Great Lakes as I realized there was no way I could repair it at sea. I stowed the lower panel in the forward compartment, leaving the circuit panel uncovered, and left the switch plate panels unattached to watch for future leaks.

Scooter bashed along at close to eight knots in winds of twenty-five knots and gusting. Below deck, it continued to be an uphill climb from the navigation station past the galley sinks to the cooker high to port. Sometimes I would shuffle downhill in the same direction, looking for handholds in case my bare feet failed to grip. The heavy weather had not reached Carolyn yet according to her conditions report that faded in and out as she spoke with others far over the horizon. After the morning chat, I tucked myself between the mizzen and starboard cockpit seat to witness the angry seas fomenting to the horizon, skipping the morning log entry. At noon I gripped my way below to scribble, "Weather. Rain. High seas." Long hours later, low dark clouds swept fast overhead from the east as daylight transitioned into darkness, dissolving the eastern horizon and the large swells earlier than usual. It looked as though the nasty weather had no end. I made rounds on deck as the radar initialized. The green screen displayed no bogies when *Scooter* stood at a true vertical attitude. When not at vertical, the screen displayed scattered fuzz on one side as wave tops reflected the beams. My customary evening activity of a movie after dinner gave way to overnight sleep cycle preparations.

The night passed without incident although the wind and seas continued thrashing *Scooter*. I filled time between breakfast and lunch making rounds, checking progress, monitoring net chatter, and reading on deck. Midafternoon, while standing next to the galley cooker dumping coffee from the grinder into a plastic container, a huge sea again rolled *Scooter* starboard at a rapid pace. I rose to almost directly above the nav station and grabbed the solid safety bar in front of the cooker with both hands. The open container of coffee grounds flew up to kiss the overhead as *Scooter* rolled way to starboard and paused.

Looking down at the nav station, I watched the airborne coffee grounds ricochet off the overhead and land right on the nav table, into the open laptop keyboard, onto all the exposed nooks and crannies about the area, and, of course, into the delicate wiring bus bars on the uncovered circuit panel. It was an instant mess. *Scooter* returned upright as she rose over the wave crest and accelerated on course.

Without an injury, I rushed again onto the cockpit deck to check on rigging, sail set, and all things lashed. The starboard sea curtain was ripped its full height from the cockpit snaps to the dodger roof. I easily unzipped it while swirling water in the cockpit drained through scuppers. The jerry cans remained in place but the boarding ladder had been unseated from its stowed position and dragged alongside, banging against the hull in the rushing water. From the evidence I could see, the wave rolled *Scooter* farther than the last time.

At the nav desk, I watched seawater flushing coffee grounds down the exposed bus bar panel and sopped up the mess before it seeped under the desk lid to make another mess. The speed of living on that angry ocean had taken a major leap. Safe boat handling required fast responses made from experience. Time spent thinking about how to resolve an immediate problem could have disastrous results. I was grateful that this had not happened back in the green days as I grew my confidence sailing between Caribbean islands when the speed of living at sea was slow and easy. Squalls and four-meter breaking seas kept me busy that day. Seas calmed somewhat overnight, peaking less frequently.

I volunteered to be the Zebra One net controller for a week and listened closely to Carolyn's fading broadcasts until I had copied Floatingpoint's specifics on my check sheet. The reason for her easy sailing leaped right off the Nobeltec screen after plotting her position. Her departure from the Cocos (Keeling) Islands three days before me placed her four hundred miles farther west, sailing in ten knots of air from the southeast, well ahead of the storm I had been living through. Hours after she said she would put into Port Mathurin on Rodrigues east of Mauritius to rest, the storm winds following me for two weeks diminished to twenty knots from 120° true. I sailed again on a comfortable broad reach, spending less energy tending to vessel management issues and living at a much slower pace. The next day when the wind backed to 80° true dead astern at twenty-four knots and driving consistent three-meter seas, I dropped the storm jib, fixed the number two jib in place on the port set spinnaker pole, hoisted the main full up, moved the boom far to starboard, and adjusted the preventer.

Wing on wing

Mauritius Commitment

While Carolyn rested at anchor in Port Mathurin, I sailed north of Rodrigues toward Mauritius and continued as the net controller. Of the group, I would be the first to arrive in Port Louis, the capital city of Mauritius. Feeling kinship with another solo sailor, I mentioned to Carolyn after closing the net that I could brief her on my customs arrival experience before she entered the port and received a quick "That would be fine" in response.

Wind speed stayed at just over twenty knots, but the seas became regular, signaling lighter east trade winds to follow. North of Mauritius, Serpent Island slowly rose from the horizon off the bow followed by Round Island then Flat Island. Mauritius appeared to port while sailing anticlockwise around the three northern islands. There, in the lee of the main island, I lived at a slower speed, squaring away the deck and preparing myself and the boat for clearing in the next morning on the thirteenth of September.

Three days later as Carolyn approached Port Louis, I shared my clearing-in experience with her on the VHF radio. Upon my arrival small fishing boats tied to the floating wood dock extending from a seawall at the customs, immigration, health, and coast guard buildings made the dock unapproachable. To the right side of the dock, a seawall topped with a white-painted guard rail rose about two meters above the water. I coasted *Scooter* in a tight clockwise circle midchannel between the dock and the navy ship moored on the far side, rigged fenders off the port side toe rail, and lay up to the seawall. My first throw easily whipped the breast line around the lower part of the railing. After hitching it to the midship cleat, I tossed bow and stern lines up over the railing. *Scooter* sat there

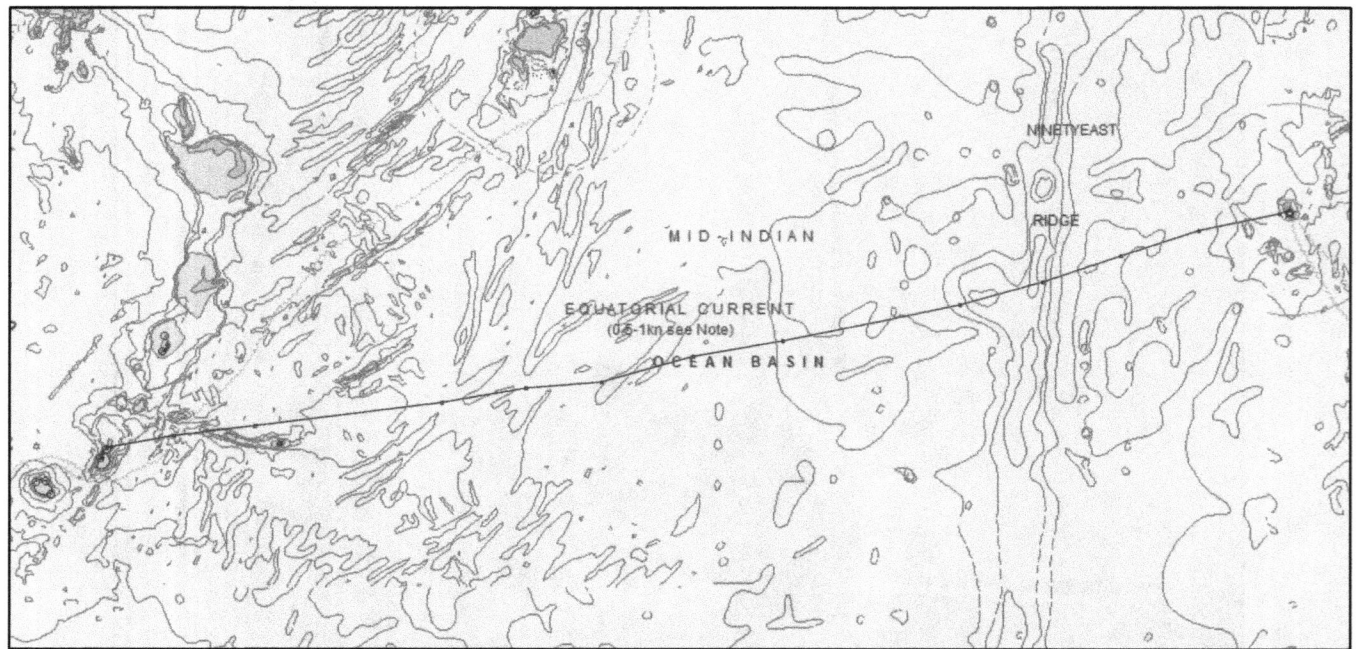

Cocos (Keeling) Islands to Mauritius

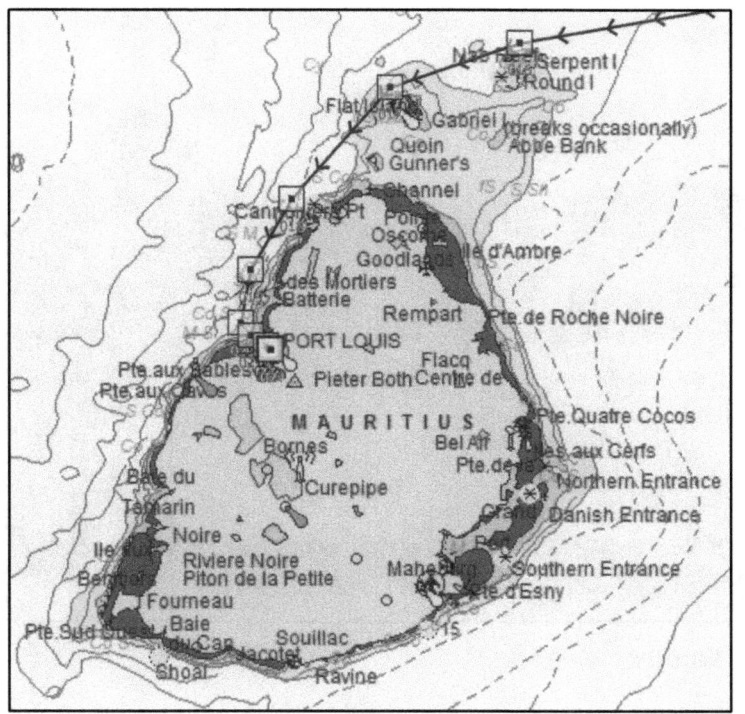
Mauritius

Carolyn's professional-sounding VHF radio call to port control requesting permission to enter the harbor alerted me to grab the long eyes. A dozen or more commercial fishing vessels rafted together mid channel blocked my view of the harbor entrance. *Floatingpoint* appeared from behind the fishing fleet, motored toward the customs dock, and circled to stop at the seawall topped with the guard rail. A woman gingerly climbed from the deck up over the railing with a small bag slung over her right shoulder, secured lines, and walked with purpose into the covered passageway. Sometime later, she climbed back the wall, pulled in dock lines, and moved about at the helm.

Standing on the pier above two large tires forward of *Scooter,* I waited while Carolyn piloted *Floatingpoint* toward me with intense focus on her destination. She shifted to neutral, allowing momentum to carry *Floatingpoint* on. A few meters before the bow sprit would contact the pier, she spun the wheel hard to starboard, shifted into reverse, and throttled up. *Floatingpoint* slowed. The bow sprit swung to starboard and the stern swung to port. She gunned it in reverse, then eased off the throttle at just the right moment to settle her port side gently against two tires, bringing her yacht to a full stop. At the moment of contact, she tossed a midship line directly at me from behind the wheel, which I caught and made fast to the supersized cleat on the pier. While I bent the cleat hitch, Carolyn, standing at the helm, tossed a coiled stern line in the direction of where *Scooter's* bow

in no wind or current but chop from passing commercial boats bounced her around while I shut down Mr. Stink and locked the main hatch. With my shore bag slung over my shoulder, I climbed up to the top of the wall and hitched the lines to the guard rail.

In an office under a shaded portico a few paces from the rail, I completed form after form, watched the customs officer rubber stamp each in a professional, unintimidating manner, and slid a copy of each into the *Scooter* binder. Before leaving, the officer requested I move *Scooter* to make space for other vessels with customs business and gestured toward the outer wall of the pier that protected the nearby small Caudan Marina from harbor traffic. Looking over to the pier, I saw that it would give me a clear view of the harbor entrance, the inner harbor, and the customs dock. Hanging down the pier wall were huge earthmover tires to fend off tugboats and large fishing vessels. They appeared to be difficult to manage, but it was the only place to tie at the time. I unhitched bow and stern lines and motored *Scooter* down the seawall to lay up to the pier. With dock lines hitched around huge cleats, I trusted my marine-store fenders, deployed between the tires and the hull, would hold air under the oscillating pressures of the wakes thrown by passing vessels. I set off to find the marina office and join the waiting list for space in the basin.

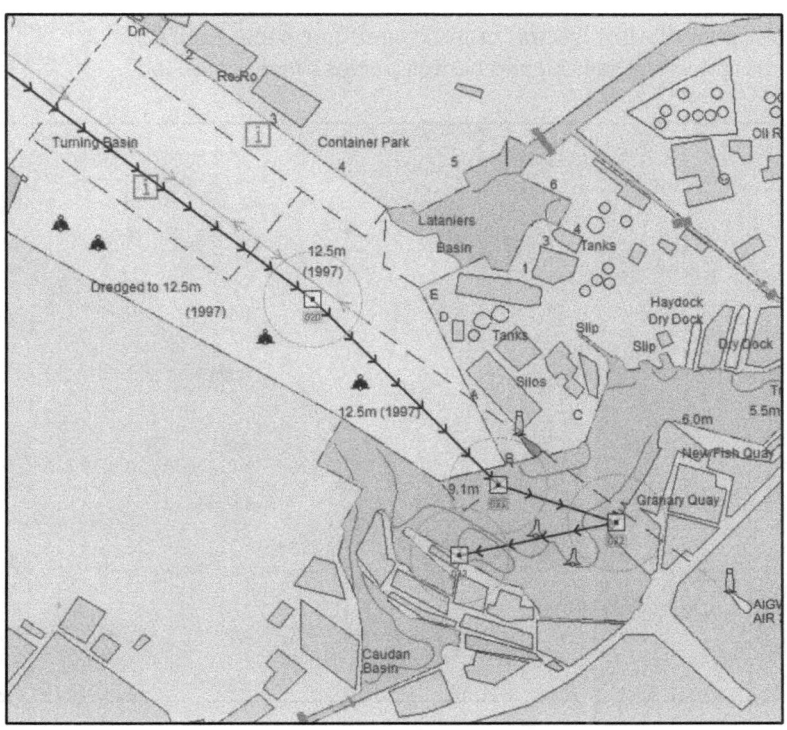
Caudan Basin

Scooter

line wrapped around a large cleat. She scurried forward on the port side deck to midship, picked up the coiled end of a staged bow line from atop the inverted covered dinghy, and threw it forward up to the pier. By the time I hitched the bow line to a cleat, Carolyn had climbed atop the pier to begin bending the stern line over *Scooter's* bow line. As her hands moved the line around the giant cleat horns, she fixed her eyes on me until she finished the hitch. She rose to stand a little more than a meter and a half tall and walked slowly toward me. She wore a sun-faded boonie hat pushed back so the brim covered her neck. Bobbed straight white hair hugged her full, tanless face, caressed by adjustable hat cords. White running shoes capped with white socks, khaki shorts, and a white T-shirt made up her sailing attire. With her eyes still fixed on mine she stopped, extended her right hand, and said, "I'm Carolyn. Thanks for the customs tips."

"Welcome to Mauritius. Good to meet the face behind the voice," I said, needing to know why this senior woman sailed the Indian Ocean solo.

She smiled. Her hardened grip confirmed she had long ago committed to sailing. Somehow, she had managed to protect her China-like complexion from weathering. We

Floatingpoint

looked down at *Floatingpoint*, and after I explained the wait list at the marina she said, "So, I've got things to do. Can we talk later?"

"Ok, I'll be here or out looking around."

In recuperation mode, we went our separate ways until we met to register at the dockmaster's office to secure space at the quay in the basin and explore the new marina shopping area between the pier and town, chatting all the way. Asked why she sailed solo, she said, "My husband started to act differently in Darwin. He got crazy. I thought he was having psycho problems."

"What happened?"

"I put him on a flight to get back home to see a doctor in Michigan."

"Any news?"

"They found he had an impacted tooth that infected his whole body. He's under treatment now."

"Wow, that's unusual. I saw you anchored in Flying Fish Cove at Christmas Island but never spotted you on deck when I went ashore."

"Oh, yeah. I was recovering from the ordeal getting there. A couple I met in Darwin wanted to crew and said they were experienced, but they ate all my special provisions, the best of everything while I slept off watch."

"What did you do?"

"So, I put 'em off on the island to let 'em find their way."

We chatted about sailing to the States and the number of things that had to be done to the boats before pushing on to the next port, where another list of repairs or maintenance items identified on that passage would be addressed. Carolyn's to-do list covered routine maintenance and provisioning. I needed at least four weeks to resolve three major issues. The large house alternator turned by the engine failed while sailing from Darwin to Ashmore Reef, where I replaced it with a spare, one of the many parts stored aboard. Wanting to always have backups, I planned to order a replacement from West Marine and have it shipped in. Before that, I had to figure out the customs protocol for bringing parts into the country. The second project revolved around making a permanent repair of the seam that leaked above the nav desk, and the third addressed repairing the ripped side curtain under the dodger.

The tiny dockmaster's office at the far side of the parking lot had a narrow counter with enough space for a person behind it and two, maybe three people in front. A curtain hung across the back wall. While standing in the queue outside the door to make the Friday guest payment, a gray-haired gentleman I'd not seen before walked up behind me. With a smile, I tried to be friendly and said, "Hey there, welcome to Port Louis. Where ya from?"

"Got in from the Seychelles."

"Was it a good ride for everybody?"

"A bit lumpy. Went with it. Quite 'appy alone."

"Me too. If you ever need a hand with maintenance, I'm on the Amel ketch."

"I'm good. Learnt to sail early. A sea cap'n's son."

We smiled in passing after I paid for the next week's berthing privilege. Minutes later, on his way to survey his assigned place on the quay, he spotted me standing on *Scooter*'s deck just as Carolyn walked by, giving rise to a three-way solo-sailor bonding moment. Three old salts soon made shopping sorties into the new waterfront commercial development and across Trunk Road, bordering the marina complex. The thriving economy and stable multiparty democracy revealed its success in high-end shops and restaurants, summoning deep exploration. With boat chores done, taxis driven by well-spoken island historians carried our trio around the island to visit marine shops, the post office, Internet cafés, the Citadelle, Muslim mosques, and Hindu and Buddhist shrines.

On one all-day excursion, we encountered two unique surprises. At a glass gallery we watched craftsmen dip metal tubes into melted glass, blow and shape the glowing globs into goblets, bottles, and almost everything else that was for sale in the shop adjacent to the factory. I captured the journey back in time with my camcorder to one day hopefully give my grandkids a view into the old-time glassblowing art. The driver responded to our request to take lunch somewhere expressive of local culture by delivering us to what looked like a home kitchen in a storefront off the beaten path. He waited outside munching a sandwich while we enjoyed the curried aromas wisping from the kitchen as two Indian women created the spicy meal. After lunch we toured a model ship factory. I had seen super detailed large models of seventeenth-century sailing ships at the gallery on the marina promenade a few days before but never expected that they were made locally. We followed the guide from table to table to see how craftsmen constructed a replica ship from scratch. From heavy large planks, workers cut small blocks and placed them in boxes next to the modelers. Looking through magnifying lenses attached to eyeglasses they carved exact reproductions of every part, following construction documents posted on boards nearby. Boxes of identical parts surrounded assembly benches where a ship model grew to completion during weeks of meticulous labor. Those exact scale models of seagoing vessels would become conversation pieces in museums, yacht clubs, hotels, and mansion entranceways worldwide.

Back at the quay I managed boat chores among occasional impromptu chats with locals strolling along the quay. Mauritius, a past British territory, became a republic in 1968. It is home to many races and religions, some being descendants of the slave trade from Africa and Madagascar and others from indentured Indian servants, all thriving without bias or hate. Strolling around the basin shopping area and out to the boats, Muslim, Buddhist, Hindu, and Christian families dressed in their own distinctive attire sought acquaintance with cruisers from foreign lands. I would hear "American," as they pointed to the ensign on the stern post and looked to see who was aboard, smiling, wanting to strike up a conversation. Responding to one spectator and his son earned me a day-long excursion on the island with a family proud to showcase their homeland.

Once I knew the arrival date of the backup alternator, I put the wait time to good use attacking the water leak over the nav station. I stood on *Jazz* floating next to *Scooter's* hull in the quiet water of the basin and removed the rub rail that ran around the hull-to-deck seam. It was held in place by nail-like pins piercing up through the rub rail's lower lip. I pulled the pins downward from the rub rail starting at the stern, removing them as I floated forward to where I knew the hull seam had been previously repaired. With the pins removed, I floated back aft and began working the rub rail loose, lashing it with string to the stainless-steel life rails above. Upon a very close inspection of the old repair, I found a minute fracture in the deck-to-hull joining. The rub rail encapsulated the seam well enough to prevent rainwater from seeping into the fracture, but when dunked during the knockdown it channeled water right through the fracture. Years before at GLSS events, I met fellow sailors the Gougeon brothers, creators of West System epoxies, and began using their products. From a plentiful supply of West System components aboard, I mixed a small cup of epoxy and injected the mix into the V-shaped groove I made along the fracture with a Dremel tool. The next morning, I reattached the rub rail confident that, should *Scooter* experience another knockdown, there would be no water leaking onto the nav desk. With that job done, I repaired the tear in the cockpit curtain ripped in the second knockdown with my Sailrite sewing machine. That day another email arrived from Sefina announcing the birth of her granddaughter, and I responded with a short story about my Indian Ocean adventure.

With the major to-do list jobs done, I structured a ground track to South Africa on the laptop. The passage would take me south of Madagascar and across the Agulhas Current, which flowed at speeds up to six knots south along the South African coast from the Mozambique Channel to south of the Cape of Good Hope in South Atlantic and Antarctic waters, where it turns back on itself. I studied a tattered, faded, and water-damaged photocopy of an Agulhas Current crossing guide left on board by the prior owner. It warned that the fast-moving current could peak to anomalous seas and monstrous freak waves sometimes eighteen meters high with steep troughs during northbound gales, resulting in the recorded breakage of ship midsections. The document called it the most dangerous ocean area on the planet. With that in mind, I selected Durban to be my port of entry to the Republic of South Africa while reading *Southern African Cruising Notes* by Tony Herrick. The harbor entrance could be seen long before entry. Coded lights on a signal tower visible to those entering from the sea reported harbor shipping movement, and the tower maintained a radio watch on VHF channel sixteen. Clearing-in formalities could be processed at either the Durban Marina, the Point Yacht Club, or the Royal Natal Yacht Club. Cruisers could attach to one of the two hundred swing moorings or one of the 350 pontoon moorings. After studying maps, the town of Durban appeared to be a good location to anchor an African adventure while preparing for the sail around Cape Agulhas at Africa's tip to Simon's Town. Feeling good about the plan, I copied the route to a planning chart on the cockpit table. Just as I finished, Carolyn appeared on the quay and said, "Bob, it's time I get going for Durban. I'll leave tomorrow. Everything's ready on the boat." Her worries about her husband ended earlier when he emailed about his positive response to treatment.

Looking up at her standing on the quay I said, "Hey there. You know, I'm headed that way too. I've been looking over charts but I can't leave until an alternator arrives next week."

She looked up at the sky saying, "I hope you don't have to wait too long, the weather's supposed to get bad by next month."

"You're right but it's only the second week in October."

The cyclone season in the southern Indian Ocean from November to April historically tracked southwest across Madagascar then down the Mozambique Channel right to where I planned to make my crossing, but conditions for that showed no signs of developing early and I asked, "Why not wait until I get the alternator, and we can sail at the same time so at least there's someone who might be able to assist should something happen."

She stood looking down, saying nothing, probably thinking out the impact of the delay on her plans. I pressed further. "Do you know of anyone else headed in that direction? Any voices on a morning net?"

"I haven't been listening, but I'm sure I can find one when I get going,"

"What if there's no one between here and Africa but ships. Ever chat it up with the night watch on a ship bridge just for grins?" I carried on after she said nothing. "Look, the part was shipped two days ago; we could sail out of here next week at the latest, well ahead of the storm season. It would be the safest thing to do, and we'll get to Durban by the end of the month."

She thought for long moments, then said, "So, I'll wait." As my gaze followed her along the quay toward *Floatingpoint*, a vision of Cindy with years of ocean savvy swelled and faded. How wonderful it would have been.

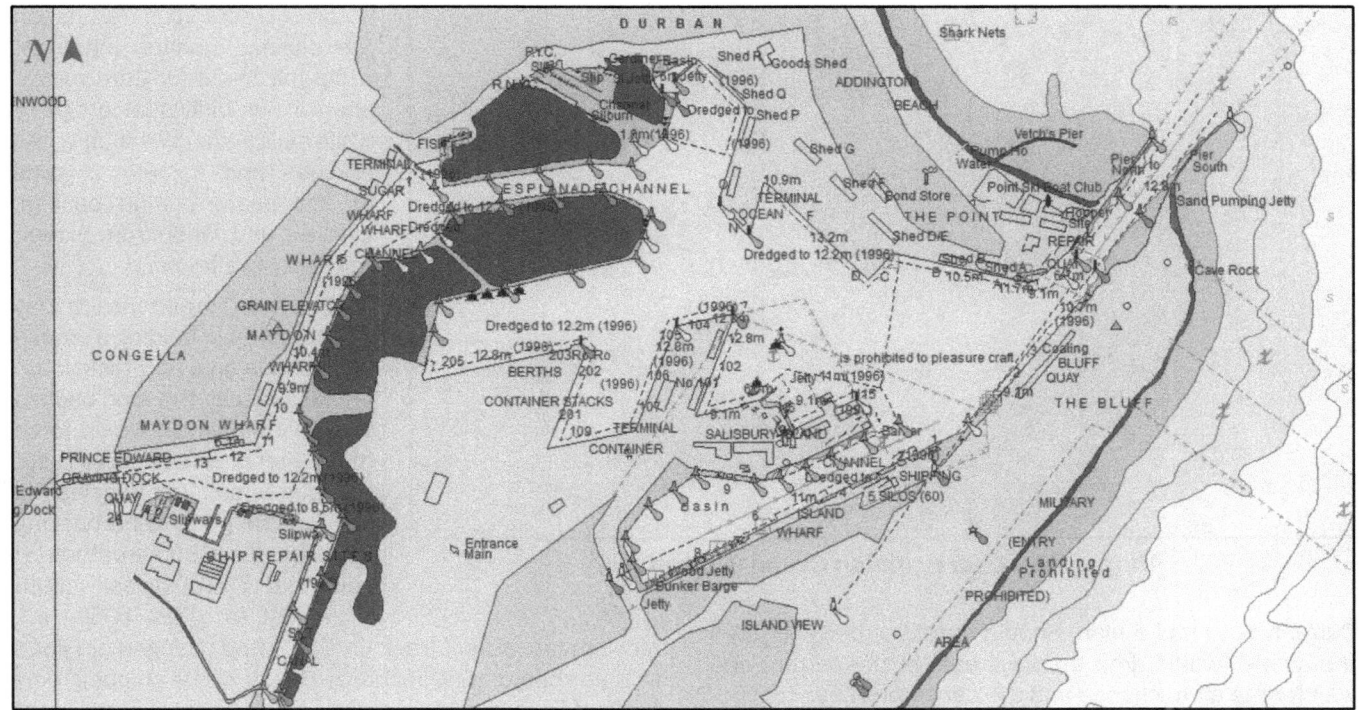

Destination Durban

My ground track to Durban ran far enough east of Madagascar to prevent being trapped in light air should there be west winds and far enough south of the island to also avoid potential southerly light air in the island's lee.

The next week I chased the alternator shipment from West Marine through customs and found that two unordered small boat ladders had arrived with it, both charged on the invoice. That mistake consumed a few more days of emailing and waiting for return shipping labels. All that time, weather reports along the ground track projected wind from the east. To make departure day different from arrival day, Carolyn and I cleared out of Mauritius at customs by walking around the city side of the basin to the office and back to the boats.

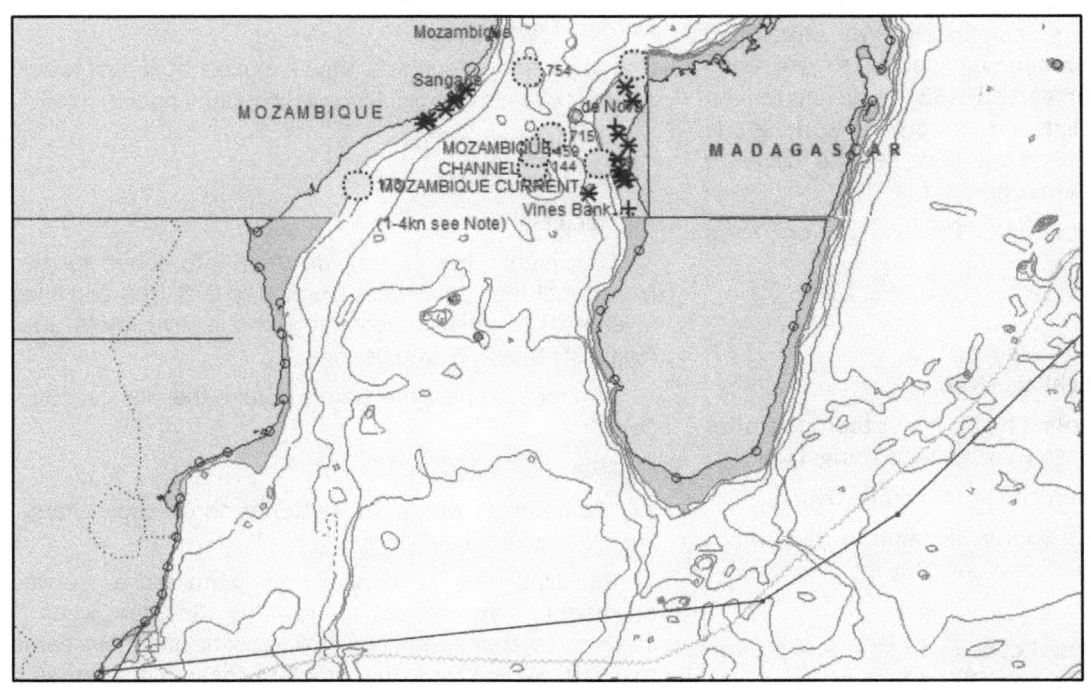

Planned ground track to Durban

The last leg of my solo passage across the Indian ocean, would be in moderate conditions per the *Atlas of Pilot Charts* for November that showed a high percentage of favorable easterly winds in the area to be sailed. The easy passage, I thought, would be a reward for dealing with the wild Indian Ocean although the atlas notes were sums of averages over many years and conditions could change at any time. My singular concern focused on crossing the Agulhas

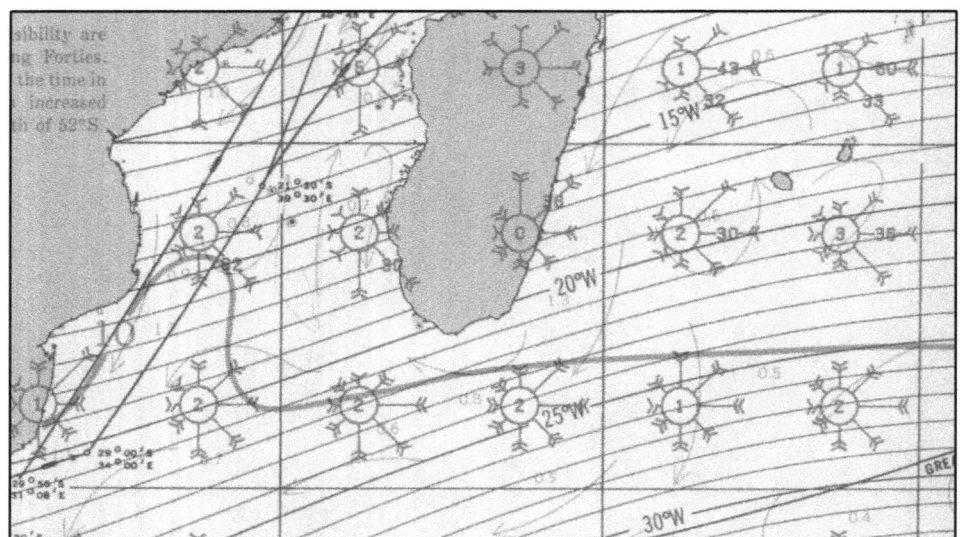
Atlas of Pilot Charts: Indian Ocean (November)

Current, but I had a plan. Should there be heavy air from the south I would drop the sails east of the current and wait for the air to change and the dangerous seas to moderate.

Carolyn and I motored in sight of each other southward along the west coast of Mauritius until we passed the Savanne Mountains, which blocked the easterly trades. There, in seventeen knots of air from 134° true, I set four sails on a beam reach and held a course of 224° true to stay east of La Réunion, the island to the southwest of Mauritius.

My next noon log entry showed that *Scooter* had sailed 150 miles. *Floatingpoint* sailing slower, followed over the horizon north of *Scooter's* position. Our VHF radios had become useless, their antennas needing to see each other. We shifted to our agreed SSB frequency for our scheduled noon chat, listened for others working the frequency and, if clear, called out. If we heard a voice, we would shift to a backup frequency.

I reached out to her saying, "Carolyn, you on?" and waited for a response.

"I'm here."

"How's it going. Over?"

"Oh, it's ok. Kind of light air. Over."

"Me too. Had light air last night. It's sixteen now after backing, and I'm running down wind. Nice going. Over."

"I'm good with the main and jib. No hurry. Over."

We chatted on about what ever came to mind and I closed saying, "Ok. Have a great sail. Out"

"You too. Out."

Life at that ocean speed consumed little energy. The noon radio chats gave me something to look forward to other than reading the next book, receiving and sending email, or screening reruns on the plasma monitor. I thought it did the same for Carolyn. We shared our individual progress while sailing southwest on broad reaches and sometimes runs as the easterly wind backed, clocked, and varied from sixteen to twenty-five knots.

Early morning on the fifth day from Mauritius, holding a course of 208° true on a port tack south of Madagascar, the wind backed to 040° true, which would force me to alter course to port if I kept the same sail set. Evaluating a continued wind-backing forecast on Buoyweather, I saw that I would sail south southeast for days, taking me far from the ground track until the wind changed or I jibed to a starboard tack. Richards Bay, a major shipping port north of Durban and my second-choice port of entry, lay at the end of my newly penciled prejibe plot. While standing in the center cockpit, I controlled the main's swing from starboard to port as the autopilot turned the stern through the eye of the wind then popped the jib over, ending the maneuver heading 285° true.

At noon I radioed. "Carolyn, you on? Over."

"I'm here. Over."

"I'm heading almost due west in a wind shift that could last for days and am scouting out Richards Bay instead of Durban. Over."

"Oh! I know Richards Bay. I looked at it last week. Another place to go. So, I'll go to the same course. Over."

"All ok with you? Over."

"All's well. Over."

"Ok. Out."

That night I had to call Mr. Stink into action for two hours until the light breeze clocked to 078° true and filled in enough to push *Scooter* at just over five knots after falling off to a 275° true heading.

At noon, the next day Carolyn broke the silence. "Bob. Over."

"Hey, how's it going? Over."

"Something's wrong. The batteries don't keep a charge. I'm looking for ideas."

Recalling how I applied my automotive service engineering experience to rewiring *Scooter* when I installed solar and wind power, diagnostic questions came to mind. Where was the problem, charging alternator, wiring, devices, or battery monitor? I glanced at my battery monitor above the chart table as my mind's eye scanned Scooter's electrical systems looking for answers and asked, "What do you see? Over."

"I, ah, the voltage goes down faster than usual after I run the engine to charge. Over."

"Well, I guess you ought to try switching each circuit off at the panel and see what effect that has. You can see amps draw? Over."

"Ah, yeah, amps. Sure, ok. I'll try that and watch amps. Over."

"Oh, let's keep the channel open. Over."

"I'll keep it on. Over."

"Roger, standing by," I said and replaced the mic in its mount next to the radio.

Less than an hour later she came back. "Bob. Over."

I closed the book I had just started reading and picked up the mic. "What did ya find? Over."

"I had everything, the refrigerator, the freezer off except for the nav panel, but the amp meter stays high. Over."

"Could it be the meter's having a problem? Over."

"Don't know. It's as old as the boat. I'll keep looking. Over."

"Standing by."

I thought more broadly about operating systems that could be overheating and called back. "You on? Over." No answer. "You on? Over."

"Hi. Uh, over," she said.

"I was thinking. What's still operated through the nav panel? Over."

"Well, uh, the radio, the navigator, auto pilot and, uh, I think that's all. Over."

"If you can, why not check and see if they're operating hotter than normal. It could be the cause of the problem. Over."

"Ok, I'll look around. Over."

"Roger. Standing by."

Early that night *Scooter* and *Floatingpoint* motored in light air and Carolyn called. "Bob you on? Over."

"Wait one. Over," I said as I clicked the remote putting the evening feature movie on hold. "What did you find? Over."

"So, I'm seeing a charge. I'm running the engine. Over."

"That's good news. I'll be down for sleep in about an hour. Over."

"Ok. Over."

"Standing by."

James Bond won in the end as usual, and I turned in for my first sleep cycle.

Shortly after daybreak, the wind clocked all the way to 145° true and blew in at over thirty knots as predicted. The speed of living rapidly increased as I shifted the sails while the wind drove the sea state higher. I made the noon log entry:

Double reef main. Riding north curve of hi pressure. Port beam reach. Speeds to 7.2 knots, SOG up to 9 at times. Much spray on deck.

The pilot chart was right. Nearly a two-knot current lifted *Scooter's* speed over ground. I set the autopilot to hold *Scooter* on course at 277° true and checked forecasts for what was to come that night and the next day, thinking that the weather front was wide enough to have captured Carolyn.

Midmorning Carolyn reached out. "Bob. Over."

"I'm here. Over,"

"I switched the radios and the nav computer off. The only thing that could be working was the autopilot, so I got down below to watch the autopilot ram move the rudder post tiller arm," she said, rapid fire, in one breath. She inhaled and said, "It's over to starboard but the boat's not turning. I looked at the amp meter. It swings high when I go over a wave. I think I've lost my rudder. Over,"

"No rudder! Did you hear any loud noise like you hit something in the water? Over."

"I was busy turning the boat in the wind shift. I could have but didn't hear it. The boat's still sailing but the course has changed off to port and wanders with the waves. Over"

"You're on a port tack and the compass course wanders; the ram wants to hold the rudder to starboard. Is that it? Over."

"Yes, it's not moving. Over."

"Did you try to turn the helm wheel? Over."

"I have to switch the autopilot off. Over."

"Ok do it. Standing by."

An excited voice came back. "The autopilot's off. The meter's back to normal. I turned the wheel but that didn't change course. I can't see the rudder post when I steer. Over."

"Can you see the rudder if you lean over the side? Over."

"I'll try. Over."

"Standing by." I ran my mind over what could hold the rudder to starboard—something like a damaged tiller arm or a failed autopilot ram.

Much later Carolyn called. "Bob. Over."

"Go. Over"

"So, I can see the rudder with a mirror. It's straight back. I tried turning it with a rope I hooked around the stern but it didn't work. Over."

"The rudder's there but neither the wheel nor autopilot turns it. Right? Over."

"So, what do I do now? Over."

Damn, she's not under command, unable to comply with navigation rules! A solution came to mind. "Carolyn. Over."

"I'm here. Over."

"What's your wind like? Over."

"From the south over twenty at times. Over."

"You oughta be able to steer *Floatingpoint* without the rudder. Try this. If you want to bear away to starboard, ease out the main then trim the jib. If you want her to come up on the wind to port, ease the jib and sheet in the main. Play both sails to keep your course as the wind changes. Over."

"Uh, ok, I'll try that. Out."

I grinned inwardly, thinking that the steering method demonstrated back in St. Pete teaching sailing classes may deliver her to Richards Bay. After more than an hour, an out-of-breath voice broke the silence. "Bob. Over."

"I'm here. Over."

"It worked . . . a bit . . . but . . . I wander . . . in the puffs . . . and over waves . . . Over."

"As long as you're heading westward in this wind that's good. Over."

"Oh, yeah . . . if the wind . . . keeps up. Over."

"Well, if it falls off, you could drag lines over the stern on the side you want to steer to, the heavier the better. Over."

"Right now . . . I can keep going. Over."

"Good to hear. Standing by"

Confident Carolyn would be able to keep *Floatingpoint* headed on a westward course all night sailing in the nearly constant air, I rolled into my sleep cycles. The next morning, our chat got deeper into controlling boat heading by dragging lines as the air lightened and boat speed fell, forcing her to motor sail. Carolyn set about finding extra lines and deployed one through a stern chock, leading a good portion of it to a primary winch where she could trim it in or ease it out to change the drag on that side.

"Bob. Over."

"How's it goin'? Over."

"It keeps the boat somewhat on course in the light air. Over."

"Add more line and, if that doesn't work, tie a chain to the end—anything heavy that can grab the water, even something like a dingy anchor. Over."

"Oh, yeah, I see what you mean. Over"

"Ok, let's get back on around noon, ok? Over."

"Ok. Out."

"Out."

Sailing one hundred miles farther west of *Floatingpoint*, I entered remarks into the log:

Jib, Full Main, Full Mizzen, waiting for wind to back & come from NE then N then NNW & shape course to Richards Bay while helping *Floatingpoint* (via SSB radio) not under command—damaged steering. 343 miles to Richards Bay, Weather forecast shows south wind 15-20 against Agulhas Current for 10/28 am. I could make the transit or may have to lie ahull.

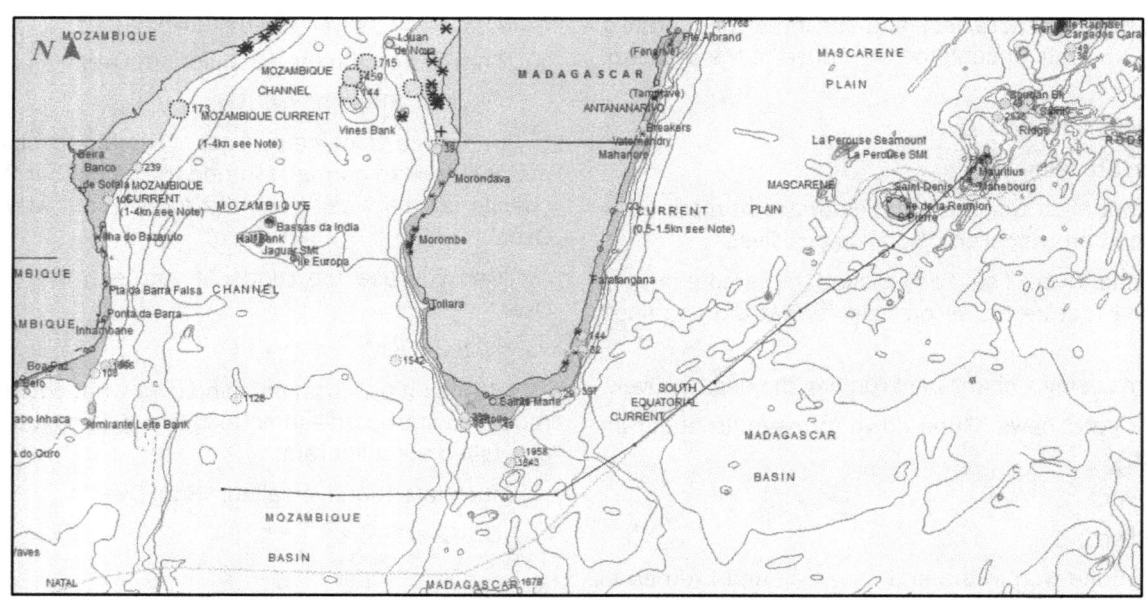

Day nine from Port Louis, noon plots

Duty

Steady winds drove *Scooter* on rolling seas toward twilight over Africa. I imagined myself high above, my complex yacht rushing westward only a speck on the blue, foam-streaked ocean. I considered sailing back to give aid, yet I took no action. Assisting Carolyn could involve subjecting *Scooter* to the risk of damage or loss. Additionally, should I go to her aid, I would be committing myself to the responsibilities of a salvor and subject myself to a plethora of associated legal and financial risks. Maritime legal squads could challenge a disastrous outcome should I implement it unsafely, cause environmental damage, decline assistance from more capable salvors, or take other action deemed improper.

In a radio communication only four hours earlier, Carolyn had said, "I'm making it. But if the ocean gets rough again, I'll have to stop and wait." Stretched out on the pilot's bunk, I pondered other ways to help her steer and considered a mariner's duty while the alarm clock ticked off precious sleep minutes. I thought of her saying as long as there was some air to work with and the waves stayed the same, she could sail. The whooshing sound of the sea streaking along the hull filled the saloon. I recalled past duties performed, some daring, some benign: completion of assignments, carrying out the pledge made to my country, rising from cover to aid battlefield wounded under fire, earning an education, managing assigned core work responsibilities, and financially supporting my children until they were adults. My duty to ensure the safety of my vessel and protect the asset I pledged to my co-owner children should I not survive the global adventure pushed against a mariner's duty; besides, others could give her aid if needed. Reasoning that should the wind die; it would fill and she could sail and steer by dragging lines all the way to Africa cemented my procrastination. At daybreak, the unchanged weather greeted my rounds on deck. Below, I hesitated with mic in hand before the call, wanting to hear good news about her overnight sail.

"You on?" Nothing heard. I called again and waited in the silence for her to pick up. *Perhaps she's early in her morning routine*, I optimistically thought and snapped the mic back onto its hook beside the radio.

A cup of coffee later I called, "You on?"

"I'm *here*," she said, breathing heavily.

"You, ok? Over."

With a fatigued voice she said, "I worked hours last night. Little wind. Over."

"Are you sailing? Over."

She dragged her words out in a way I had not heard before, "I motor sailed . . . until the wind stopped. Can't motor . . . and shift . . . lines behind . . . fast enough . . . to steer. I'm stopped. I'll wait for wind. Over."

"But are you ok? Over."

"Oh . . . I'll do ok. I'm tired . . . real tired. It's daylight . . . I should be up and about."

She sounded like she was at the end of her endurance. Flashing back to my suggestion in Mauritius that she wait for me to sail together for safety overpowered my procrastination. In that moment, I realized I would be committing an irredeemable life failure if she should not survive. The thought of having to live with that shame steeled my will to go to her aid and do my humanitarian duty. Energized, I said, "Carolyn, stop trying. Drop your sails, hold your position, and get rest. I'll come to get you. Over."

"Will you? Over."

"Where are you roughly? I need your latitude and longitude just to the minute. Over." With her rough position noted I said, "Ok, uh, looks about a day maybe more to get close. Get rest. Let's keep the channel open. Over."

"Ok, thanks, I will. Over."

"Ok. *Scooter* out."

Immediately after turning *Scooter* to get close to the reciprocal course to be sailed, I noted in the supplemental logbook:

10.27.2008, 0900 hrs local, 27° 53.6' S, 036° 51.3' E, COG 072T, SPEED 5.4, BARO 1021, VIS 10, CLOUDS 20%, REMARKS: Genoa, Full Main, + 1400 RPM, turned to assist *Floatingpoint* 52-ft Cherubini ketch not under command—disabled rudder.

I laid a ground track to her rough position on the Nobeltec display, giving me a real-time visual of our two positions. Shortly after noon the wind backed to the northeast. I headed close-hauled then tacked to sail a northerly course and made another log entry:

10.27.2008, 1330 hrs local, 27° 44.2' S, 37° 01.0' E, COG 319T, SUMLOG 50,882, BOAT SPEED 5.1, GROUND SPEED 5.1, WIND 12, DIRECTION ENE, TEMP 26C, HUMIDITY 53, BARO 1017, VIS 10, CLOUDS 0, REMARKS: Sailing north to get to *Floatingpoint* latitude then will tack to intercept.

My attention turned to towing gear, how to prepare it, the need to calculate fuel requirements, the sail set if there was good air, and how to do it all safely. The best way to transfer fuel, if needed, would be to throw a line to Carolyn, have her tie it to a jerry can and lower it overboard, and pull it back to *Scooter*. Visualizing that moved me to recall the South African deckie saying, "There's only one way to throw a line," while preparing aboard the sloop the evening before the Yachtmaster oral exams. His comment came after we learned the evaluator would ask us to demonstrate knot tying. Immediately a competition between the well-seasoned megayacht deckies began. Nautical knot tying became an instant challenge for me. After some muscle memory training time, I managed to tie a bowline behind my back. He then demonstrated how to prep a line for throwing it full length saying, "If you are right-handed, place the bitter end of the line in the out stretched palm of your left hand and grip it tightly with your thumb letting the line lay over your palm and down the side of you hand. Make a large loop to just shy of the deck then back up to your palm. Lay that line across your palm forward from where your thumb grips the bitter end and complete another long loop down and back to your palm. Lay consecutive loops across your palm until your hand is full to your fingertips. Wrap the rest of the line into a small, neat coil in your right hand. Stand facing your target and hold your left arm fully outstretched pointing your extended fingers at your target. Hold the bitter end of the line in your palm tightly with your thumb. Ensure that you have just enough line from the last loop in your left hand to the coil in your right hand to not impede your right-hand backswing. Make a fast underhanded pitch releasing the coil to fly up at a forty-five-degree angle. If you are throwing into the wind, wet the coil in your right hand to give it more mass. You can adjust the length of the loops and the number of turns across your left hand depending on the length of the line." Not since that event had I had to throw a line it's full length.

Another wind shift required tacking back to an easterly course, but hours later the air became too light to sail, and I woke up Mr. Stink. My speed of living slowed, but no movie played on *Scooter*'s big screen that night. The glassy sea rolled consistently from the east and nothing blipped a radar return. Restful sleep again eluded me. Lying awake on the pilot's bunk, I vacillated from planning to stewing. Pondering how to safely take *Floatingpoint* under tow, I thought about the sailing events that brought me to this place, with this boat, and how all of that came together to assist me in doing my duty. Uneasy about the distinctions between a contracted tow and a voluntary salvage operation, I resolved to plan each step carefully.

At dawn after less than restful sleep cycles, I entered the morning's log notes while Mr. Stink pushed *Scooter* on a course of 074° true at five knots in variable light air.

To brief Carolyn on my plan I made another call. "You on?" Hearing nothing, I called again. "You on?"

"I'm here. Over."

"How are things? Over."

"Ok, here. Light air. Over."

"Same here. Been motoring all night. I'm about six to seven hours away at this speed and have figured the fuel I have may not be enough if I motor with you all the way. You have extra fuel in cans? Over."

"I have four cans. Over."

"You have enough in the tank? Over."

"I fueled in Rodrigues. It's full. Over," she said, relieving my worries.

"Ok, how about I come along side, throw a line, you tie it to a jerry can, and I pull it back? Over."

"I can do that. Over."

"Good. Ok, anything else? Over."

"No. I'll get 'em ready on deck. Over."

"Ok. Well, I'll call on VHF when we're in range. Over."

"So, in about seven hours? Over."

"Roger, say seven at the most. Over."

"Ok, I'm out."

"Out."

Damn, I thought when I snapped the mic onto its mount. Like throwing a line, this would be the first time I'd have to apply my learnings from the towing endorsement I acquired for the US license. I dug out the spare thirty-meter length of anchor rope from the port bow lazarette. From a yellow bucket under the port cockpit seat, I pulled four fifteen-meter lengths of the same line, normally used as dock lines. I coiled one end of the long anchor rope around the aft deck winch, flaked the line out along the port side deck to the bow and back to the center cockpit then tied a bowline in each end. To create bridles at each end of the anchor rope, I tied the two shorter lengths with bowlines to the bowline at the end of the anchor rope on the aft deck, leaving them coiled separately, and tied the other short lengths with bowlines to the bowline laying in the cockpit. From way deep in the starboard bow lazarette, stored since departing Florida, I pulled two large turning blocks and shackled them at the toe rails aft of the port and starboard primary winches. After a short rest, I strung the bitter ends of the short-length bridles coiled on the aft deck through stern chocks, pulled them along the deck, looped them through the turning blocks, wrapped them around the primary winches on each side of the cockpit, and secured them to nearby cleats. With that done, I removed the bridles from the cockpit seat and flayed them on top of *Jazz*'s blue Sunbrella covering on the aft cabin top. Pleased with the plan, I sat on the helm seat reviewing everything step by step. I had a complete towing rig good to go. The mizzen jib halyard looked to be an excellent throwing line. I pulled it down and laid it on the starboard cockpit seat.

The AIS aboard *Floatingpoint* transmitted vessel speed, course, GPS location, vessel name, Maritime Mobile Service Identity number, and other data that described the vessel and received similar data from other AIS transponders. AIS devices, like VHF radios, communicated in the line of sight, but the unit I had could only receive data. I could "see" her but she was unable to see me as I approached. When her signal reached me, I knew we were within VHF radio range able to talk more securely than by using SSB frequencies that could be monitored far away over the curvature of the earth by bad actors in that dangerous part of the world.

Floatingpoint's masts rose from a gently rolling sea beneath a four-knot breeze. When her boat icon displayed on the AIS I called. "Carolyn VHF. Over."

"Where are you? Over."

"West of you. Just saw you on AIS. I'll come alongside. Over."

"Standing by."

When *Floatingpoint*'s hull rose, bow toward me, I steered to port and continued until her whole length was visible. Carolyn waved, walked forward on her starboard deck, and wrapped her left arm around a main shroud. I slowed, turned hard to starboard, circled back along her starboard side, and shifted to neutral. Facing *Floatingpoint* that close, I looked at her stern and saw the rudder rise with the hull as she rolled on the light sea. Carolyn behaved unlike a person who had recently lived through a bad dream at sea. She cupped her hands next to her cheeks and shouted, "Thank you."

She was upwind at the time but throwing a line with the breeze would be best. While I motored around *Floatingpoint*'s stern, Carolyn moved the cans to midship on the port deck. I brought *Scooter* to a stop about ten meters off. Slow-moving swells lifted *Scooter* then *Floatingpoint*. While slowly drifting together, I leaned against the starboard railing to manage my balance and prepped the halyard for the throw by laying more than half of the line in my left hand, letting it fall outside the handrail, and coiled the remainder tightly in my right hand. Because the rail prevented an underhand pitch, I made a strong roundhouse throw and let the small coil fly, aiming up at *Floatingpoint*'s main spreaders. The tightly coiled line flew upward, pulling looped sections off my left hand, and unwound, fully straight out, like a string tied to an arrow flying over her sail-draped main boom. Carolyn grabbed the line, tied it to a jerry can, lifted the twenty-liter can over the lifeline, and lowered it into the sea. Surprising me, it floated. Careful to not gouge my precious hull finish, I lifted it over the handrail and sat it on the side deck with just enough time to motor away before we drifted together.

A few minutes later, I had *Scooter* positioned for another throw, but it failed to make the distance. Noting my rate of drift toward *Floatingpoint* I circled around for another try. Sometimes a wave swept us apart just as I made the throw, or when I got the line fully prepped in my hands, we were too close to allow adequate time for the transfer. Failing often, we stayed at it for more than an hour until the last can came over *Scooter*'s rail. That time hull contact looked imminent. I dropped the can at my feet on the side deck, scampered to the helm, clicked the throttle lever forward, and then a little farther forward to slowly increase prop turns to get *Scooter* moving. Too much RPM at once would cavitate the prop, costing time and distance. *Scooter* drifted close enough to *Floatingpoint*'s port side that turning to port would swing her stern into *Floatingpoint*'s port bow. I held a straight course hoping that a wave would separate us just enough to avoid a collision. It did, but *Scooter*'s starboard stern slipped under the end of *Floatingpoint*'s long bowsprit as Carolyn's boat was lifted by a wave. Almost clear, the swell passed, and the bowsprit came down just missing the solar panel and antenna arrays but continued down to knock control knobs off the outboard motor mounted on the stern rail. Rebounding, the bowsprit almost jerked the outboard up off of its mount. I motored *Scooter* away as the lazy wave continued to lift *Floatingpoint*'s bow and lower *Scooter*'s stern. A minute later, I throttled back to idle and turned to take in the view of *Floatingpoint* rising on another wave and Carolyn rapidly moving along the deck toward the cockpit. She went below. I called with the bridge mic. "That's done. Over."

"Yeah, they're heavy. Over."

"The tow line's ready for ya. I'll throw a light line tied to two lines, one for port, one for starboard. Over."

"Ok, I'll be ready. Over."

"Oh, and when we're linked, I'll pull ahead slowly and you motor, ok? Over."

Towing Floatingpoint

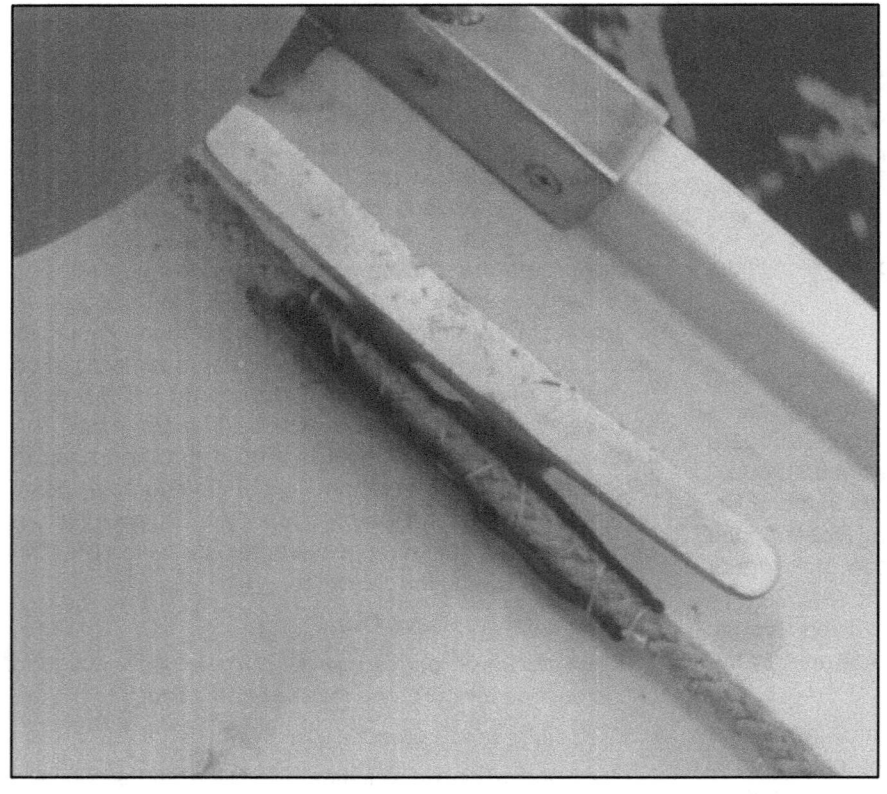
Chafe prevention

"I'll do that. Over."

Moving away from *Floatingpoint*, I snaked the bridles from atop *Jazz* out to the stern deck and around the starboard arch support and draped them over the handrails near the cockpit. Transferring the throwing line from the jerry can to the bridle bowline loops completed that end of the system. I stepped to the helm and circled back for another pass along *Floatingpoint's* port side. As *Scooter* drifted forward near Carolyn standing on the port bow, I made the throwing line ready in my left hand and held a tight coil of it in my right hand. At the moment the sea began to lift *Scooter*, I looked to check the bridle run from under my left hand all the way along the starboard handrail to the stern deck. All looked good and I flung the coil in my right hand as hard as I could. It flew, snaking the loops off my left hand and landed straight across her deck and lifelines. The moment Carolyn grabbed the line, I pushed the bridle off *Scooter's* handrail to fall alongside. Back at the helm, I looked over to see Carolyn haul in the line then the bridles, untie the line, and slip each bridle through a hawsepipe at the bow and secure them around the samson post. To ensure the bridles would clear the prop and skeg, I let *Scooter* drift forward until the remainder of the tow line slid along my starboard deck and off the stern. When in gear making slow turns the tow line straightened and I watched *Floatingpoint's* bow turn toward *Scooter's* stern. We were linked together and making way slowly. Not much damage. The boats were floating. We were aboard and well.

My task was to control *Floatingpoint's* direction of sail, not tow her dead weight. Turning toward Richards Bay, we increased speed to understand how the two boats interacted with each other on the long, lazy waves from the east. Our safety depended on keeping both vessels in step on the crest of a wave, on the face of a wave, or in the trough of a wave. Towing out of step could cause damage as the rapid increase in tension on the tow line could cause any component of the system to fail. To maintain proper distance,

I ground in or eased out the bridle around both primary winches, or Carolyn altered *Floatingpoint's* engine RPM.

Sometimes, *Floatingpoint* stayed far from *Scooter's* port or starboard side and other times she wandered back and forth, changing the drag on *Scooter's* stern. Checking the tow system for possible wear points, I noticed that just forward of the stern chocks the lines worked against the stern cleats as the changing load stretched and eased the lines. To prevent the lines from chafing through I stitched a leather wrap around each.

After growing accustomed to being linked together underway, I calculated it would take six days to reach the coast if the air stayed light and no heavy southerly air whipped up big seas in the Agulhas Current. Motoring in light air and easy seas that first night challenged us less than we thought it might. Taking turns standing watch with the VHF radio volume turned up, we illuminated the tow line with handheld narrow-beam lamps plugged into twelve-volt outlets. Before daylight, the wind clocked to the south southwest and cracked to over twenty knots. I launched the number one inner-stay jib at sunrise to see how that would work while I backed down engine RPM. It provided enough sail lift to give Mr. Stink a rest and maintain sufficient boat speed to lead *Floatingpoint*. Carolyn continued to adjust the engine RPM to stay in step and later set her main. We sailed on a port beam reach in step on large and long following seas driven by heavy air far away in the east, and at 0930 I made the only log entry for the day:

Jib only, Late Entry For 10.28—at 1730, took SV *Floatingpoint* under tow, motored at 2–2.5k over night. Now under #1 North jib making 3–3.5k. Engine off to check oil. *Floatingpoint* skipper Carolyn is evaluating a sea tow commercial vessel (assist) in that National Sea Rescue is limited to 50 miles.

Carolyn asked a South African radio weather station operator to contact a commercial sea tow service, but she was told that there were none on the South African east coast, and if there were, they could claim a portion of the value of her yacht as a salvage reward.

Sailing all day conserved precious diesel fuel reserved for calm seas, but the physical demands wore on my stamina. Long waves and cross seas rolled *Scooter* while changing the load off the stern, yawing her such that the jib fluttered, losing lift. I worked the winch handle, grinding the sheet to bring the jib back into trim. Other rolls and yaws moved the apparent air aft, and I had to ease the sheet out to keep sail shape. I felt fatigued at noontime when I went below for a snack, but by late afternoon I needed to stop the perpetual upper body exercise. At sunset, the brisk southern air had backed and slackened, making our shared sailing on a broad reach easier, yet the seas stayed large and long from the east.

In early darkness the waves became more consistent, more organized, with a reduced height driven by lighter air far to the east as predicted. Relieved by the mellowed forces moving around us, I descended into the comfortable spaces below deck and scanned the electronic chart glowing on the laptop to see where we would cross the dreaded Agulhas Current. After cleaning and stowing galley tools, I prepared for sleep on the pilot's bunk. No bogies blipped on the green radar screen. I switched it to standby and let the CARD keep watch to jerk me from sleep by loud chirps should it receive incoming radar beams. On the bunk hugging a pillow, I took a long, deep breath; exhaled; and my fatigued body relaxed into dreamland.

A woman's voice slipped into my dream. It called out to me as though I was not alone at sea, but there was no vision of her. Unlike other voices heard in my sleep it became more audible, more distinct until I heard it say, "*Scooter . . . Floatingpoint . . . Floatingpoint.*" She called out to me again after a pause. "*Scooter, Floatingpoint . . . Floatingpoint*, one six." Moments later: "Bob, wake up."

With heavy eyes, I groped for the alarm clock to see that only a half hour had passed. I rolled back to again enjoy the stillness of the pilot's bunk, re-encounter the dream voice, and maybe see the figure making it. In the calm, with my head on the pillow against the lee board, the voice blasted. "BOB WAKE UP!"

I broke my bond with the pilot's berth, rolling the lee board up and over my body to the stowed position, and groped my way to the navigation station, where I fumbled the VHF mic off its mount, dropped and chased it like a darting gecko across the nav desk, and made a two-handed catch. After a fast deep breath, I pressed the push-to-talk button and slurred out, "*Floatingpoint . . . Scooter, Scooter, Scooter.* Go. Over."

"Bob, the wind has come up. I'm sailing over six knots and I'm beginning to override the tow line. Over."

I dropped the mic on the nav desk; unpinned the guillotine hatch, letting it fall; and slung the sliding hatch back over my head. Before Carolyn repeated her call, I had turned Mr. Stink's ignition key to the heat position. Long moments later, I turned it to start then run and snapped the throttle lever forward. "Now in gear," I barked into the bridge mic as I eased the throttle lever farther forward. In a few heartbeats, I reached the switch over the galley sink that lit the stern-facing arch-mounted spotlight. Superbright white light blazed over the frothy water trailing aft.

Having been jerked from dreamland and not totally on balance, I unzipped the cockpit's Eisenglass curtain and scrambled over the large primary winch to the port deck. A stiff breeze hit my face, waking me more. Grabbing the handrail, I moved aft on deck and stood clenching the stern gate below the spotlight. Looking aft, the illuminated

Tow 1

Tow 2

Tow 3

tow line stretched into darkness. *Floatingpoint* appeared ghostly in the nighttime haze as she rose from a trough and rolled over a high wave crest nearly sixty meters away. A beam from Carolyn's handheld torch swept the wave tops, stopping at the towline arching way off *Floatingpoint's* starboard side. Satisfied that I understood the situation and her fear of the line wrapping around her prop, I gripped my way forward to the cockpit and moved the throttle forward. Carolyn kept the tow line lit with her torch. I heard her voice from the bridge mic shout, "It's moving forward. Keep going." We spotlighted the tow line and the large seas rolling under us from directly astern all night, napping occasionally while the other kept watch for changing wind speed.

At dawn we managed to find solace and rested, each in turn, after Carolyn dropped the main and started motoring to stay in step. Later that morning, with good control of the boats on the waves Carolyn called. "Bob. Over."

"I'm here. You ok? Over."

"Yes. So. How we gonna to do this if the Agulhas Current is bad? Over."

"I've been looking at the weather and don't see a problem. Course that could change. Over."

"What do we do? Over."

"Let's plan that, if the air's heavy from the south when we get to 150 miles off the coast, we'll head back east until conditions change. Over."

"Ah, ok. We should do that. Over."

"I want to keep the tow line as it is," I said. "Imagine trying to hook up in this sea state. Over."

"Yeah. That would be dangerous. Over."

Towing Floatingpoint, starboard tack

"Well, let's keep that the plan and hope for north wind. Over."

"Ok, I'm here. Out."

"*Scooter*, out."

The west boundary of the Agulhas Current ran close to the continental shelf line off the east coast of South Africa, and its width ranged from thirty-four to 123 miles depending on the latitude. Storm-driven winds from the south were most prevalent from February to April, but we monitored radio stations for anomalies.

The weather station operator Carolyn called earlier on SSB offered to provide forecasts for our location and the area where we reckoned to cross the current. Meanwhile, printouts from the Furuno weather fax delivered synoptic charts, and data from Buoyweather gave reliable marine forecasts confirming our immediate conditions. Carolyn and I chuckled during our VHF chats about the inaccurate opinions the weather station operator gave us for our position. By noon on the third day, we sailed at five knots on course of 251° true toward Richards Bay and I wrote in the log:

Jib #1 only, Towing *Floatingpoint*. Decided to keep #1 up and North #2 on deck, air backed from 75° true to 355° true late am. Tow going well.

Fuel consumption no longer concerned us as we closed on Richards Bay, and it looked as though crossing the current would be uneventful if the wind kept a northerly component. Mr. Stink's pushing prop assisted *Scooter's* jib to climb the high wave faces and maintain consistent pull on the tow line. On the fourth day, the noon log entry documented the same course, barometer reading, and boat speed as the prior day's noon entry but with a wind change:

Jib and motor. Light air this morning then at 1100 filled from SW. Weather fax shows it will back to S & SE. 77 nm to Agulhas Current then 43 nm to Richards Bay. ETA noon tomorrow.

That afternoon the Buoyweather forecast showed the air would back further and come from the southeast, possibly up to twenty-five knots. I called Carolyn. "*Floatingpoint*. Over."

"I'm here. Over."

"Well, ah, looks like we'll have some air from the southeast tonight. Over."

"It looks ok now. How much? Over."

"Ah, says up to mid-twenties. If the wind whips up high seas from the south, I think it's best for me to motor a big circle into the waves and guide you around and back east. So uh, I'll drop the jib before. Over"

"Ok. I hope we don't have to do that. Over."

"Me to but we'll see. Everything ok with you? Over"

"I'm ok. Standing by."

"*Scooter* standing by."

We arrived at the far eastern boundary of the current finding the air had backed to the south but in the midteens.

Rescue 19

However, we stayed vigilant. By then we had our individual responsibilities well understood, confident we could control the two boats sailing as one throughout the night.

A wide, gray wave rose from the sea mist ahead of us, later becoming the green African coast under a blue morning sky. Within VHF range, I hailed the station charged with lifesaving responsibilities in that area. Hours later, the *Spirit of Richards Bay* from the National Sea Rescue Institute grew from a speck on the horizon to a sizeable vessel, displaying its highly visible signature "Rescue 19"

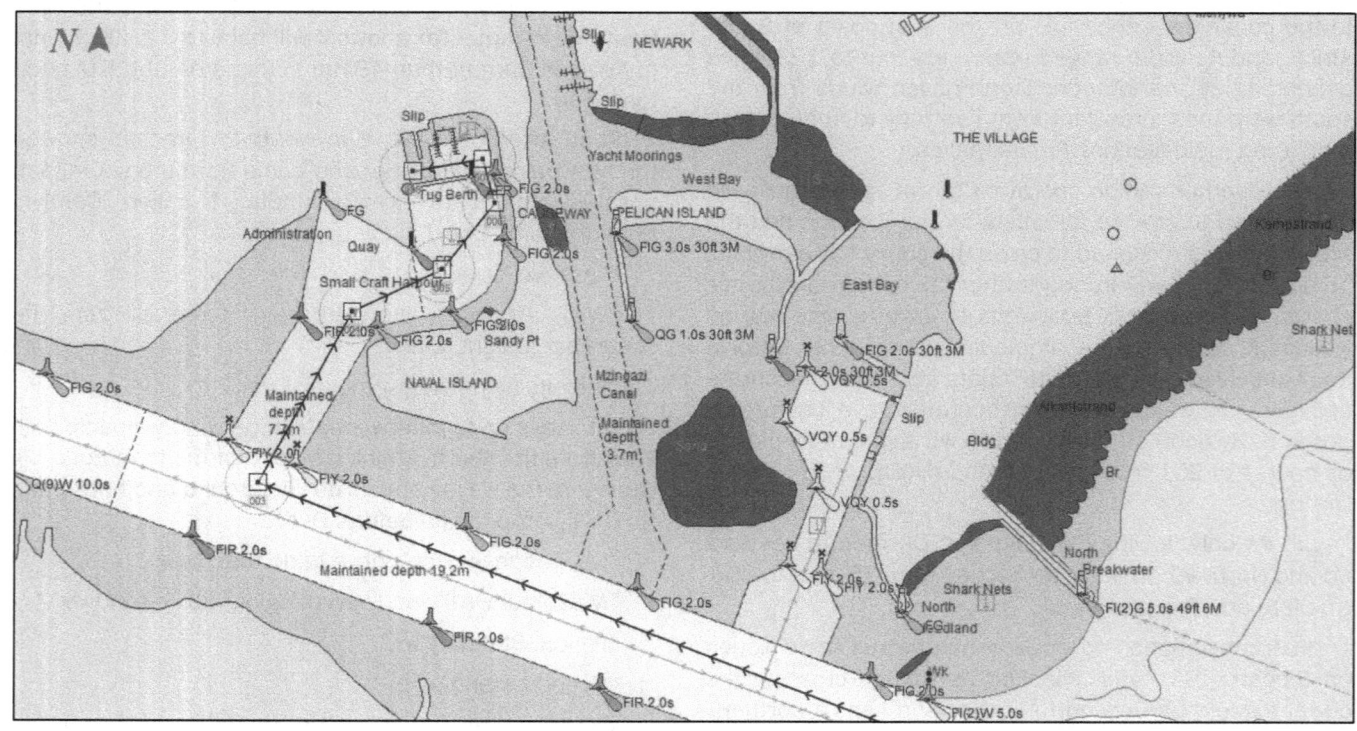

Richards Bay

in white against a black hull. She circled off *Floatingpoint's* starboard side and stopped within shouting distance of Carolyn standing near the bowsprit while the crew busied themselves to take *Floatingpoint* under tow. A voice called out on VHF sixteen for me to drop the tow line. I responded that it would be best if *Floatingpoint* disconnected from my tow, wanting to pull the line clear ahead rather than have it possibly foul her prop. Carolyn must have overheard my VHF transmission from *Spirit of Richards Bay's* bridge radio. She immediately unwrapped the bridles from the samson post and slipped them out the hawses to splash below the bowsprit while I watched with the long eyes, still gripping the bridge mic in my left hand. Holding *Scooter* about fifty yards away, I watched the *Spirit of Richards Bay* back toward *Floatingpoint's* starboard bow and her crew pass a line to Carolyn. With the tow transferred, my duty to Carolyn had been fulfilled and I made another log entry:

11.01.2008, 1155hrs Local 28° 48.3' S, 032° 11.0' E. REMARKS: Relinquished tow of *Floatingpoint* to *Spirit of Richards Bay* of Rescue 19, Richards Bay, South Africa.

We were blessed throughout the endeavor. I navigated *Scooter* to Carolyn's location in non stressful wind and seas. Light air and manageable seas allowed us to transfer diesel and link the tow line. Friendly air drove *Scooter* in following seas on broad and beam reaches with just a jib to conserve fuel. The air fell to a light moderate breeze the morning of the tow transfer. That hot shower, good meal, glass of wine, and a long night's sleep would soon be enjoyed.

Still far from shore following *Floatingpoint* towed by the *Spirit of Richards Bay*, a whale surfaced and blew close to *Floatingpoint's* starboard quarter as though to welcome her safe arrival or perhaps to salute us after following the episode from below. I had acquired an awareness of gray and humpback whales over the past three year's sail. They seemed to show up just as I moved up on deck or looked up from reading a book. Once sighted, I wondered about the happenings in the depths below.

A mile inside the south breakwater, *Spirit of Richards Bay's* crew directed Carolyn to release the tow line. They motored back around to *Floatingpoint's* starboard side and secured the *Spirit* to her with a hip tow to gain total maneuvering control. I followed as they slowly rounded Naval Island, entered the Small Craft Harbor, rounded a high cement pier to port, and moved toward the pier wall inside the Tuzi Gazi marine basin.

A number of people atop the cement pier spectated as the *Spirit of Richards Bay* laid *Floatingpoint's* port side against the pier's face. Carolyn cast lines up to some in the crowd who wrapped them around large bollards. The *Spirit's* crew disconnected the hip tow lines and motored forward of *Floatingpoint*, its port side to the cement wall. The crew climbed a steel ladder inset in the side of the pier and began to secure lines without hesitation as though they had rehearsed the action. The docking concluded seamlessly as I watched while I held *Scooter* in place close behind. I made sternway and laid the port side up to a ladder inset in the wall aft of *Floatingpoint*. After making a temporary tie to the ladder with the breast line, I tossed bow and stern lines up, climbed the ladder and whipped quick clove hitches around the bollards. Before climbing down the ladder, I looked up and gave a nod to the Admiral in the sky thanking him for the safe passage across the stormy Indian Ocean and for seeing me through my humanitarian duty. On deck, I prepared spring lines and trimmed bow and stern lines. Below deck, I made the final log entry to close the lengthy passage to Africa:

11.1.2008 1300hrs Local. REMARKS: Arrived Small Boat Basin Richards Bay Republic of South Africa. All is well.

Stepping from the steel ladder's top rung onto the wide pier walkway, I glanced across a parking area to Newark Road, which ran the length of the pier. Far to my left, large hulls towered alongside the pier. To my right, the parking lot continued along Newark Road to the land end of the pier, where a growing crowd surged to witness the unfolding drama. Satellite communication dishes atop vans gleamed in the midday sun. I continued to dress lines around bollards while eyeing the action in the distance. Not long after the crowd grew around the rescue crew and Carolyn, obscuring my view, a young woman with a purse strapped across her blouse the way I carried my shore bag when navigating risky streets walked from the crowd toward me, a notepad in her hand. She asked while in midstride if I was the one who saved *Floatingpoint*, and my African adventures began.

South Africa

The crowd thinned. Journalists folded notebooks, packed cameras, and set off to chase another story. Rescue 19 crew closed hatches and dressed dock lines while the lead crewman advised Carolyn to haul *Floatingpoint* for repairs at the Zululand Yacht Club nearby, adding that they would return Monday to tow her to the club. We closed our boats and explored across Newark Road for the customs office in the Ports Authority complex with shore bags over our shoulders.

Leaning on the counter we completed a four-page customs arrival form that was stamped and initialed by the South Africa Revenue Service customs and excise officer and the immigration officer. The last document to be completed directed us to draw our planned route to the intended port of departure on a printed outline of South Africa showing all its seaports. No vessel inspection or confirmation of health or pratique occurred, making it a fairly smooth but time-consuming clearing-in process.

On our walk across the road and the parking lot back to the boats, we spoke no words of congratulation about making it safely to Africa. We performed to expectations, nothing more, and needed recuperative sleep, knowing we would see each other the next day.

Before climbing down the pier-wall ladder, I said, "There's about a six-foot tide run here. We'll have to trim our spring lines."

"Oh, that's right. Thanks again for all you did."

"Well, you waited for me to be ready to sail. You would've done the same. Let's get some rest. See you tomorrow."

"So, tomorrow," she said, turning toward *Floatingpoint*.

Looking down at *Scooter* from the pier after dressing the spring lines, I could see the sky surfaces of everything

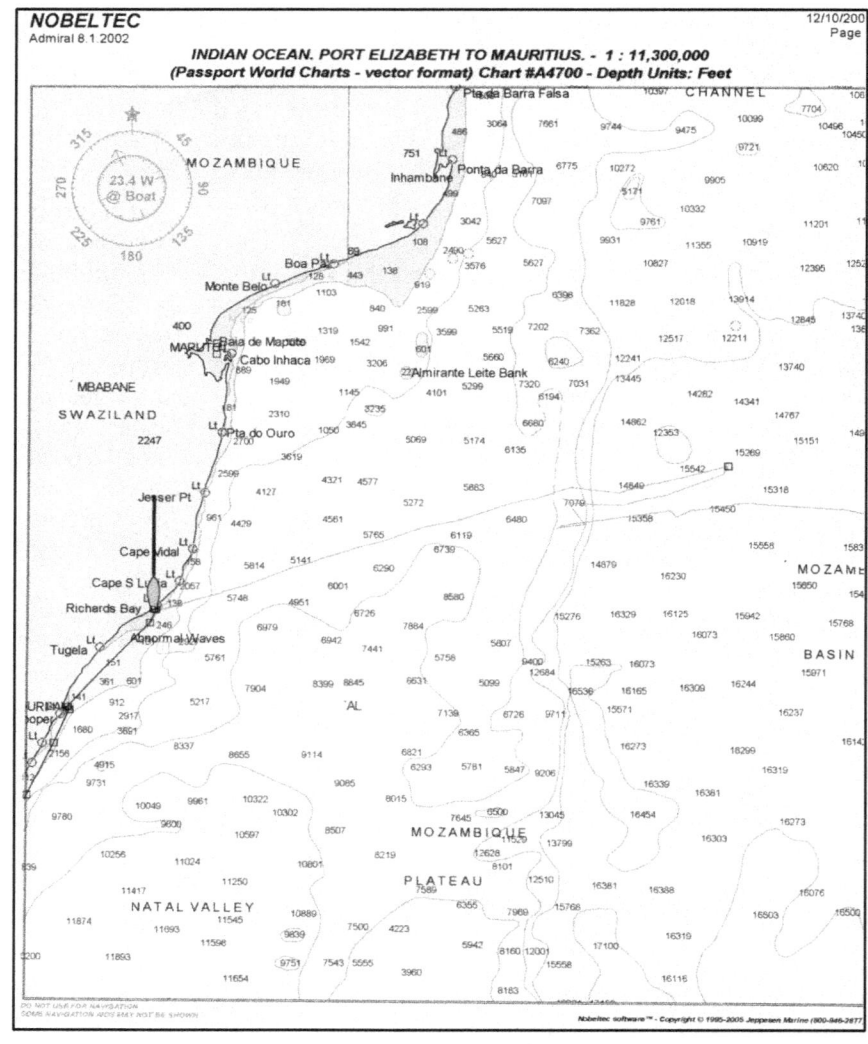

Tow assist course made good

from bow to stern and coddled my right knee as I stepped down the ladder to the port deck and into *Scooter's* very private cockpit. At the nav desk, I slipped my entry documents into a new manila folder and wrote "Africa" on the tab, making it customs folder number eighteen. Instead of showering in the head and taking the time to wipe all the surfaces dry, I zipped the starboard sunshade in place and managed a hot, soapy shower on the cockpit deck. That evening, I prepared dinner and for the first time since sailing away from Mauritius stretched out in the aft cabin.

Our Sunday morning stroll north from the waterfront led us across a one-way vehicle bridge over the Mzingazi Channel and south on Commodore Close to the Zululand Yacht Club. We found the haul out adequate after seeing yachts sitting in the yard on jack stands. The large mobile lift on a ramp that rose from the dark channel water looked much like others seen at full-service yards. Carolyn made arrangements for the haul out at the club's front desk, and we returned to the Tuzi Gazi pier. After I swapped Carolyn's jerry cans for my halyard, I studied a map of the area obtained from a car rental agency near the marina shops.

The next morning, the *Spirit of Richards Bay* towed *Floatingpoint* away from the pier and delicately placed her in a slip near the yacht club's haul out ramp. I hired a taxi and collected Carolyn for a shopping trip to the Superspar Lakeside, a mega grocery store in the sprawling Boardwalk Inkwazi Shopping Centre. The taxi driver suggested she show us around town on the way to the mall. Keen for exploration, we agreed to the extra mileage cost. Green landscape transitioned into residential areas with paved roads and sidewalks. Houses surrounded by block walls or wood fences topped with looped razor wire or strings of barbed wire passed our taxi windows. On one street, uniformed armed guards patrolled an entrance through tall cement walls. I asked the driver about the prison compound we passed, hearing that it was a residential area, and the walls protected the homeowners from criminals roaming the streets. I wondered about our safety. Occasionally we glimpsed compounds through gated driveways, seeing only closed garage doors, no vehicles. Security signs and cameras guarded residential properties everywhere. The feeling of being at risk on the town streets faded once we entered the shopping center complex. At the shopping center store, we explored every aisle and department in awe of the amazing inventory and taxied back to the yacht club with full shopping bags.

Conversation with a Tuzi Gazi marina resident revealed that the weather forecaster Carolyn and I spoke with on SSB had linked our transmissions to radio repeaters up and down the coast to share the drama. Sailors and media around the coast had listened with interest to our chats then our VHF traffic as we approached the coast. That prompted me to review and print *Scooter's* course made good during my hours of procrastination and days of sailing linked together while Africa listened. One journalist misquoted *Floatingpoint's* length as a thirty-footer in the rush to tell the story.

Thinking it could be the only time in my life I would visit South Africa, I signed a month-long car rental and visited Carolyn often, earning unchallenged entrance through the yacht club gate from the armed guard. Inside the gate early one morning, a reporter with the *Zululand Weekend Observer*

Rescue News

Damaged yacht towed 400 miles to Richards Bay

November 03, 2008 *Edition 1*

Marie Strachan

AN American yachtsman sailing singlehanded was towed 400 miles to the safety of Richards Bay Harbour by a fellow American after "something big" sheared her rudder and ensuing damage led to her autopilot burning out.

Carolyn Au, 67, of Michigan, said she tried tying up the rudder of her 30-foot yacht Floatingpoint so that she could continue her journey to Richards Bay, where she had booked a berth for a one-month stay.

After several unsuccessful attempts off the stern and fearing for her safety, Au tried attaching a line to the rudder using her dinghy. When this also failed, because of high swells, Au contacted fellow American Robert Krieg on Scooter, whom she had met in Mauritius and with whom she kept in contact daily.

"He suggested that I steer the yacht using an anchor.

"This worked reasonably well until there was no wind," she said.

With the National Sea Rescue Institute monitoring their progress, Krieg towed Floatingpoint towards Richards Bay where the NSRI team dispatched the Spirit of Richards Bay to bring her into port on Saturday.

"We decided in Mauritius to sail together, and it was just as well," said Au, who is relieved to be safely at Richards Bay.

Au and husband, Richard, had set off from Darwin, Australia, several months ago. However, he took ill three days out and was taken back to Darwin. He later returned to America and Au continued alone.

"I managed to find two crew to sail with me to Richards Bay, but they left at Christmas Island and I continued alone. There were so many voices crossing the Indian Ocean, many of whom I met in Mauritius, and many who I have yet to meet. I am not sure how long I will stay in Richards Bay. It depends on how long it will take to repair the damage to the yacht," said Au.

News article

greeted me as soon as I parked and asked if I was the guy who rescued the American sailor. Her interview filled column space in the November fourteenth issue.

Yacht club management suggested Carolyn hire Vic, a local delivery captain and a general boat handyman. On haul out day, yard crew helped us move *Floatingpoint* to the lift and positioned lifting straps near the bow and stern. We watched her ride out of the black water, surprised to see no damage to the rudder other than a hand-sized chip just above the keel strut.

Vic dug a trench under the rudder, making space to lower it with a jack far enough to extract the hollow ten-centimeter-diameter stainless steel rudder shaft that extended above. He positioned the jack to take the rudder weight and climbed aboard to remove the autopilot ram, tiller arm, and cap at the top of the shaft. Back under the hull, he removed the lower pivot support strut extending aft from the keel bottom and clicked the jack down, revealing the shiny stainless-steel shaft. When the shaft cleared the hull a chunk of the steel shaft plopped onto the ground.

"Look at this, Carolyn," I said, when Vic handed me the severed section that had fractured all the way around below the shaft's upper end where the tiller arm attached.

Inspecting the jagged break, she asked, "So, what caused that?"

"You said you didn't hear any noise."

"No, nothing," she mumbled, fitting the broken piece back to the heavy pipe.

Hearing Carolyn's story a few times already Vic said, "Yeah, there's no sign of damage to the rudder that would have caused that large pipe to break all at once like that."

The chip on the rudder's leading lower edge appeared to me as though it may have been the final blow to complete a fracture that began sometime earlier. My eyes met Carolyn's. "Jeez, it could have happened anywhere," I said. I thought about her long journey from Australia to Africa. On the other hand, it might not have broken free until later in the Atlantic. She looked at me with wide eyes, understanding a possible tragedy was avoided. That afternoon, when Carolyn climbed the ladder to board *Floatingpoint*, the rudder and broken part were in a welding shop waiting for repair. The next morning, I moved *Scooter* from the pier to a slip in the Small Craft Basin, giving me direct access to the marina amenities and shops.

Floatingpoint's bottom got a new coat of paint before Vic retrieved the rudder assembly from the shop. The full-length quality finish of the heavy stainless-steel tube displayed no indication it had ever failed. He positioned it for installation in the trench under the keel and jacked it into

Floatingpoint haul out

On the hard, Zululand Yacht Club, Richards Bay

place. With the pivot support strut attached, he removed the jack, climbed aboard, and reassembled the autopilot ram and steering cables. Standing next to me, Carolyn watched the rudder turn from port to starboard as Vic turned the wheel.

When *Floatingpoint* floated again, I turned full attention to *Scooter's* to-do list. Replacing my AIS type-A unit with one that would transmit *Scooter* data, a type-B transponder, topped the list. The type-B unit would improve compliance with the lookout rule that required "keeping a proper lookout by all means appropriate in the prevailing circumstances to make a full appraisal of the risk of collision." My prevailing circumstances were that I had to sleep and manage events below deck. I had mounted the type-A antenna on the main masthead next to the VHF radio antenna at the time of installation when I wanted both to be at the highest point for the farthest reach. Reasoning that having VHF radio and AIS transmitting antennas only centimeters apart could possibly interfere with each other, I planned to move the VHF antenna to the mizzen. I would simply attach the mainmast VHF antenna cable to the new AIS unit but needed to remove the mizzen mast to install a new cable for the transferred VHF antenna. The job could be managed with the yacht club gin pole at the deep-water end of the ramp. I left my name and phone number with the club dockmaster to secure the next available slip and ordered the unit online

All transient slips and space at the quay were occupied by yachts sailing with the World ARC flotilla, a continuation of the Atlantic Rally for Cruisers that sailed from St. Lucia. I met many World ARC cruisers back in Mauritius during a party I was invited to by an ARC organizer after I agreed to donate ten dollars. At the far end of the pier under specially erected bright lights, long tables presented catered food and beverages next to a bandstand. I saw a woman off of a rally boat wearing a black cocktail dress and high heels. A man wore white slacks, laced deck shoes, and a blue blazer. Soon, others dressed in similar fashion appeared then disappeared. Perhaps they had gone to a prearranged soiree in town. The dock party rocked into the early hours every night. Days later, they were gone, headed to another party place, where preparations made long in advance would make their arrival easy and their stay pleasurable.

Visiting Carolyn after the World ARC sailed from Richards Bay, I saw a boat in a slip near *Floatingpoint* that previously floated next to *Scooter* in the Small Craft Basin. I approached the dockmaster seated behind his office desk and asked him why he overlooked calling to advise me of a vacancy as he had agreed days before. He said abruptly, as though I was interfering with his rest time, that the ARC people had heavily stressing club management, club members, and workers to the limit of endurance late into the night tending to loud partying, and he had given the slip away to a person who just walked in. Short with his comments, he brazenly dismissed me with a hand wave. A few days later, a yacht departed the club's quay leaving enough room for *Scooter*. Instead of asking the dockmaster, I told him I would take the space even though it presented a boarding challenge. He looked down at his desk, grumbled, "All right," and scribbled on a notepad.

Between *Scooter* and the quay wall, large black rubber tubes about four meters in length and a meter in diameter floated nearly submerged. To get ashore, I climbed down the boarding ladder, stepped out to the center of the slippery rubber mound and climbed up the steel ladder on the quay wall to the concrete walkway.

Yacht club amenities opened to me. I mixed with weekend sailors and international cruisers. One day an accident produced a constructive result. While enjoying a thick, juicy beef patty with a fried egg stacked on top, a common burger served at the yacht club restaurant, I accidentally bumped into the plastic patio table with my knee tipping a glass of red wine onto the open laptop. I flipped it upside down holding it until the last drops drained. Later, the system booted but the keyboard had no control of the cursor. I found a computer store in the shopping center, bought a remote keyboard, and ordered a Toshiba Qosmio as a backup. It had a new operating system called Windows Vista to which I could transfer the Nobeltec world charts should the old laptop ever fail to boot, but I had to wait for it to arrive from England.

Carolyn and I often shared time meeting other cruisers at dish-to-pass barbeque events. We met Perle, the attractive owner of a large sloop and past concierge at a resort on the French Riviera. A cordial friendship developed as we shared our life stories. She sailed with the ARC party from Europe around the planet to Richards Bay with volunteer crew, and I was sorry I missed seeing her the night of the party in Mauritius. When she arrived in Africa, her crew unexpectedly departed, leaving her to search for replacements. She wanted to catch up with the ARC at one of its future merrymaking waypoints. Occasionally she expressed her worry about sailing south along the coast in the Agulhas Current in a way that suggested she was less of an operator of the yacht and more just the owner. One evening dining together I suggested we go see some wild animals we'd read about.

Perle lowered her wine glass, "I would like to do that. That would be good fun."

Carolyn said, "There's more than one."

"I'll look around the office," I said. "They should have brochures, I'm sure, and if not, they would know where to go."

A wildlife adventure plan came together selecting Hluhluwe-Imfolozi Park. Carolyn accepted my suggestion that she drive while I navigated using brochures and maps. I rode in the left front seat and Perle rode in the back, sightseeing. Once north of Richards Bay we merged from a two-lane road onto a four-lane expressway threading between massive farms growing trees in unending rows on flatlands extending to the far hills. I thought the tree farms on New Zealand's South Island were extensive, but what we motored by were larger still. Flatland gave way to hill country farmland the further we ventured inland. We exited the freeway to a two-way road that, according to the map I held, would take us to the park entrance twenty-some kilometers north.

Strange to see were fenced-in clusters of single-story dwellings with round walls looking like stubby corn silos topped with conical roofs. "Jeez, that's odd, look at those small round huts."

Perle said, "They're everywhere."

I read from a pictorial guide to Africa's Zulu culture. "Says here, the fenced in land's called, "umuzi," a home for a married man and his family. The largest round hut in the umuzi belongs to the head of the family, and the other smaller round huts are for—what?—the first, second, third, and fourth wives! In each! Uh, and it says, there could be one round hut for the chief's mother, one for young men, and one for young women!" I stopped reading to look again at the umuzis passing by. "Ah, that must have been then, the way they used to live."

Moments later Perle said, "See all the huts inside that fence? It looks that some continue to live that way."

"Where are the cars?" Carolyn asked.

Few umuzis had cars parked in or around the compounds, a sign that many walked everywhere. Beaten paths crisscrossing grassy turf over gently rolling hills seemed to be short cuts linking umuzis yet many people walked the roadside. The number of umuzis dwindled as we motored toward our destination until we were alone on a road bound by infinite rolling fields, leading us to suspect we were in or nearing the animal park. I handed the brochure back to Perle asking her to read more, wanting to focus on the scenery.

She held the brochure high for good light. "The Zulu, a very structured and honorable culture, believed destiny put each person in a specific place to perform specific tasks for special reasons in society. All members honored others as they performed their destined role. Zulu cultural discipline shaped the people over generations into a strong family-focused society and into strong warriors to protect their people and land."

"Carolyn, we passed a sign that said entrance," I barked.

Carolyn jockeyed the car around and we turned at the small green sign marked "Hluhluwe-Imfolozi Park" posted next to a narrow road.

At the park's visitor center, we overnighted in large round huts with thick cement walls and thatched roofs. Cement pathways led from the sleeping huts to other round huts enclosing restrooms and showers. Carolyn and I shared a round with two queen beds like senior siblings, while Perle had a round to herself. Even though it was summer in South Africa the huts held a comfortable sleeping temperature without air conditioning. A large dining hall welcomed us with floor-to-ceiling windows that allowed an expansive view of the green valley. Steam trays filled with local foods and delicious wild meats lined white-linen-clad tables. Fruit and vegetables tasted more robust than ever savored before. We rode aboard a specially built lorry driven by a fluent park guide to see animals in the wild by day and long after dark. While creeping along one dirt path, the driver stopped to point out a dung beetle diligently rolling the future home of its offspring.

After two days and nights we chose to adventure along a narrow two-lane paved road to a secondary park exit. We crossed a river while being scrutinized by an elephant, stopped at a viewing post, and continued on, passing an elephant family playing on a roadside hill. Around the bend an elephant stood in the center of the road between us, and the oncoming cars lined up waiting for her to let them pass.

She turned, pointed her tusks directly at us, and flapped her huge ears. Carolyn stopped the car on the left side of the road where we became the lead car of a bumper-to-bumper queue. Carolyn's foot held the break while Perle mumbled, "Oh *mon dieu*. Back up. We go," before looking around to see the cars to our rear. A white BMW sedan sped by on our right side to pass the elephant. Just as the car approached the elephant's left, she raised her trunk straight up and forcefully swung it down, thumping the Beemer on the trunk lid and denting it badly. Broken taillight parts flipped in the air as the driver recovered control and sped on.

"Damn, look at that!" I said.

Carolyn cried, "Oh my!" and Perle muttered again.

The elephant stood in the street flapping her ears and looking in our direction for a moment then slowly paced toward us. Carolyn and Perle wanted to get out of the way. I tried to calm them. "Don't move. Don't flinch," I said as I held a camera in front of my eye. All I could think of was watching the Saturday morning TV program *Ramar of the Jungle* back in my youth. Carolyn shifted the car to park. We froze in place. The elephant slowly walked toward us, finally stopping about three meters in front of the bumper and looked directly at Carolyn and me behind the thin windshield. Hidden behind the camera, I quietly said, "Don't move a finger and she won't sense a threat." I glanced out of the corner of my eye at Carolyn, seeing her gripping the steering wheel and staring straight ahead through her sunglasses. Whimpers came from the back seat. Cars behind kept their place in line. No one moved. There was silence apart from the engine's idling.

After what seemed to be ten minutes of eye-to-eye competition but which lasted only a minute or less, the tusker broke her stare with our windshield and walked a few paces over to a clump of tall grass growing under a scrub tree. She wrapped her trunk tip around a bunch, pulled it up from the black soil, stuffed it into her mouth, and started to chew.

Carolyn slipped the car back in gear and eased her foot off the brake. We crept forward while the tusker snacked and Perle resumed breathing. Our uneventful afternoon adventure changed back at the yacht club when the gate guard warned us to stay clear of the southern point barbeque area where hippos had returned to snack on the tall grass.

No swimming

Family play

Road ruler

Late one afternoon while cleaning below, I heard a rumbling sound on the boarding ladder. The dockmaster, to my surprise, stepped over the rail onto the port deck. Looking out to the river, I saw a large, poorly maintained steel-hulled sloop turn to its starboard about four meters away. The dockmaster said he wanted it to raft off *Scooter's* starboard side to wait for hauling out the next day. At first all I saw was its deck-to-hull joint jaggedly rusted from bow to stern and knew that the joint would lie up to *Scooter's* hull below the toe rail. Only two tiny fenders no larger than baguettes dangled below the rail well aft of the widest part of the rusted hull. Bags and boxes littered the yacht's deck. Immediately sensing the pending damage to *Scooter's* hull and having no time to relocate fenders from the handrail, I grabbed the fending pole stowed above the starboard side jerry cans and yelled, "Stop you'll damage my hull," while extending the fending pole toward the rusted seam.

The skipper hollered back, "Go home," and a few other unfamiliar words as he flipped me off.

"This is my home," I yelled. Holding the pole over the handrail, I turned to face the dockmaster standing on the port stern deck. "That rusted hull will not raft off my boat without protection. Look at that jagged rust the full length." The dockmaster waved the sloop off, told the skipper to lie up to the quay by the gin pole where he should have been originally directed, stomped down the ladder to the slippery floating rubber, and climbed up the quay ladder in a huff.

Early the next morning, the dockmaster again boarded without permission and handed me an envelope telling me to open it immediately. A letter, signed by the rear commodore, whom I had not met, directed me to settle all outstanding fees and leave immediately. I speculated that the

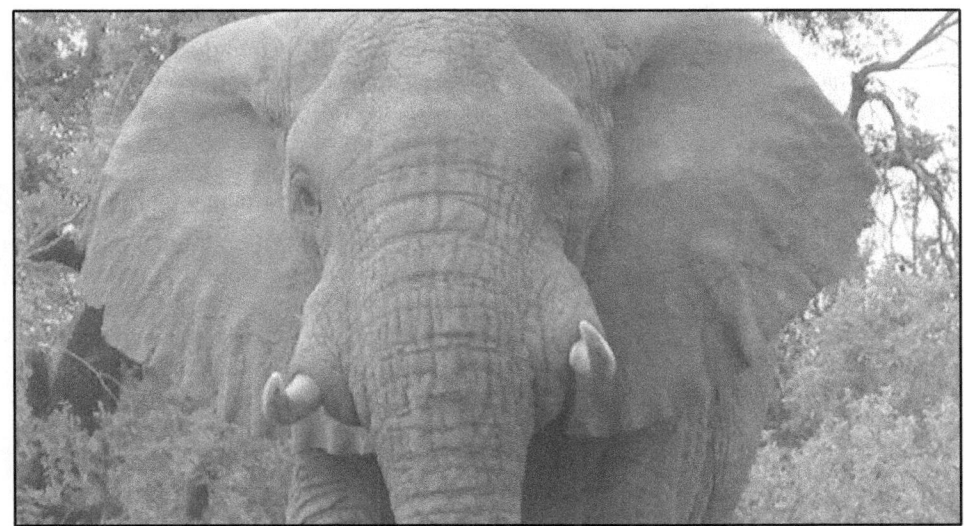
Staring contest

Snacking

be loaded by conveyors aboard cargo ships fell constantly on the pier to be swept onto the deck in a breeze. After asking around, I contracted a crane operator to unstep then restep the mizzen and supply two sawhorses. The two-day job ended with me operating the VHF and the AIS at the same time without issues. Meanwhile, Perle, wanting to sail south, tried to recruit Vic to pilot her boat to Cape Town as a guest. He politely said that he would not do gratis work, that he provided for his family by delivering yachts and managing boat repairs. She declined his offer to skipper her boat down the coast for a fee and later asked me to do the job, offering to pay for my transportation back to Richards Bay. I declined, having no interest in becoming a paragraph or chapter in Perle's appealing story, and continued working through my predeparture checkout procedures for the coastal passage to Simon's Town.

At the port control office on the hill overlooking Alkantstrand Beach north of the harbor entrance, I delivered my coastal voyage plans noting my destination as Simon's Town and then stopped to see Carolyn at the yacht club. She rose to the cockpit from below after I called out to her. "I found the port control office up on the hill right where we thought it was. It went ok. Just bring your papers."

dockmaster had written the note and signed it himself, intending to wield his mighty power. I dismissed the idea of taking the issue in front of the rear commodore, reasoning it best to appease the dockmaster by letting him enjoy the sight of my departure which should boost his prestige at the next board meeting. He joined the group of other small people I had encountered along the way who, when given a little responsibility, leveraged it to project power over others.

I motored to the same high cement pier where I made my first contact with South Africa. It proved to be an excellent location for a crane to lift the mizzen, but the job would be done in a very dirty environment. Dust from mounds of ore at the Transnet Port Terminal waiting to

Looking up at me from the cockpit she said, "Ok, that's good to know. And have a safe trip."

"I'll do my best and you too. Happy sailing."

"I'll be along in a few days anyway," she said.

"Well, I've got to return the car and do things before dark. Be safe."

"You too."

Lost in my world of getting ready to sail, checking rigging, and working all the machines, I approached departure on the first of January as just another day. Focusing on the passage around the Cape of Good Hope, I turned in for a good night's sleep after a grilled steak meal with a movie. A loud thump like a mortar round leaving the tube, a sound not heard for decades, woke me. Intense white light streaked into the cabin a second later. A booming concussion shook the boat. Booms and sharp cracks sounded near and far. I startled to my feet, turned down the passageway to the saloon, cautiously slid the main saloon hatch forward, and looked up through the dodger windscreen. A throng of moms, dads, and children had gathered along the edge of the pier next to *Scooter* with sparklers, firecrackers, mortars, and rockets of all types set up in front of lawn chairs and coolers. The fireworks boomed and flashed for more than an hour while I lay awake trying to rest. That morning, I hosed the charred fireworks debris off the deck, finding no burn marks, and inwardly thanked the Africans for the departure celebration.

My plan to sail to Simon's Town in one multiday passage changed when a fresh southwest breeze developed heavier than forecasted while nearing East London. As I sailed with the Agulhas Current to make good speed over ground, the seas abruptly changed from manageable to northbound walls of water three meters and higher with a very short period that made sailing directly into them impossible. Each bash almost stopped forward motion. I eased the sheets and steered westward toward the small bay north of East London. The sharp, near vertical waves smacked hard on the port hull, at times quivering the rigging. I sailed out of the western edge of the current and threatening waves into the lee of the East London jetty, started Mr. Stink, dropped the sails, and called East London port control seeking permission to enter. After motoring directly into the wind and white-capped wavelets I negotiated the inlet and motored up the Buffalo River to arrive at Latimer's Landing, a commercial quay on the north side of the river east of the bridge. I had another town to explore as well as visit again with Peter and Ginger aboard SV *Marcy* who saw me arrive, hailed me on VHF sixteen, and welcomed me to come aboard. They were hooked to a mooring at the Buffalo River Yacht Club, an easy walk over the bridge to the south side of the river.

Peter and Ginger had sailed north of Madagascar, taking their chances with pirates, then down the African east coast, stopping along the way to explore coastal inland towns and interact with locals on their passage south to Tanzania, Mozambique, and the Republic of South Africa. Full of stories, they described how locals living along the ocean beaches launched and sailed their skiffs to net fish. They spoke about their treatment of an elderly fisherman's eye infection with an ophthalmic ointment from their med kit and, with hand motions, communicated how and when to continue the treatment to help him see again.

Once the southerly breeze changed direction on the fifth of January, I slipped the dock lines while thinking about the next leg of the passage to Simon's Town. I had not moved *Scooter* one hundred meters down the Buffalo River when men in an unofficial small boat arrived alongside and told me to immediately return to see the port captain. The two days of poking around town, tracking weather patterns, and chatting aboard *Marcy* helped me to absentmindedly overlook the requirement to clear out of the port. This was the first nation I encountered that required all vessels to clear out of a port with a port captain even if en route to another port in the same country. After returning and asking around the landing, no one knew of the port captain or of his office until I enquired at a

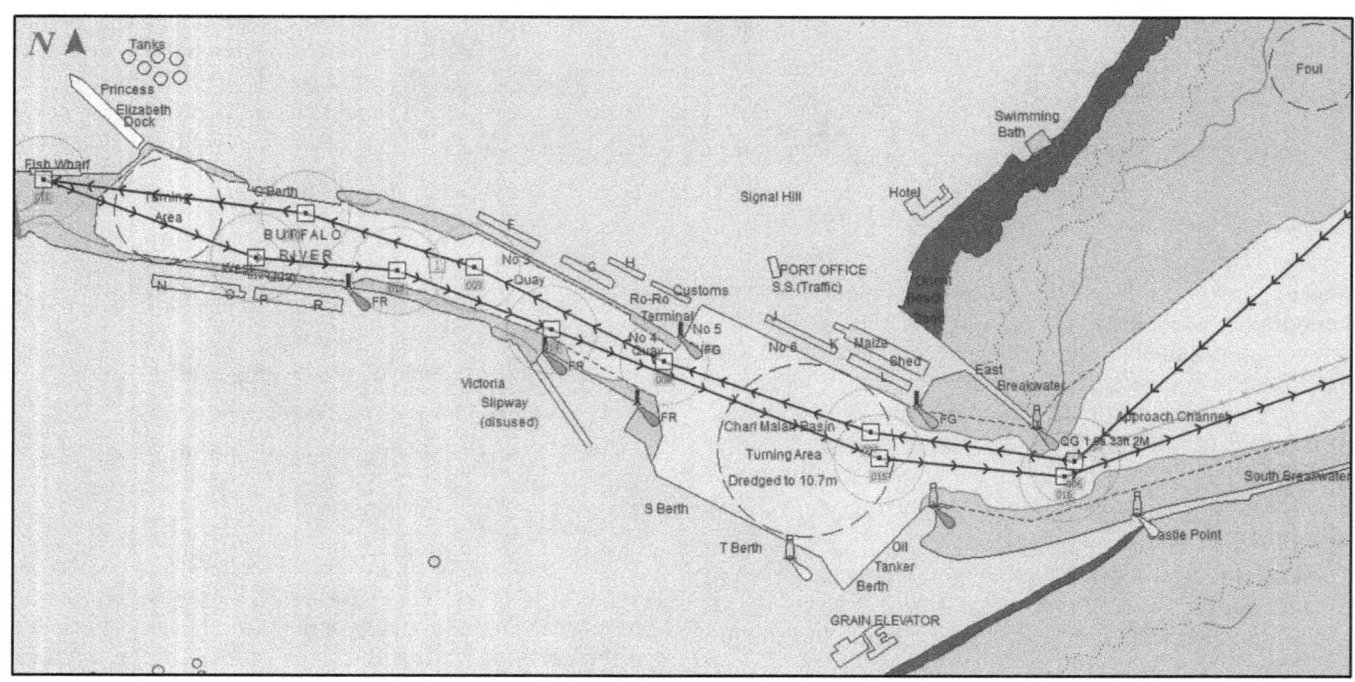

East London

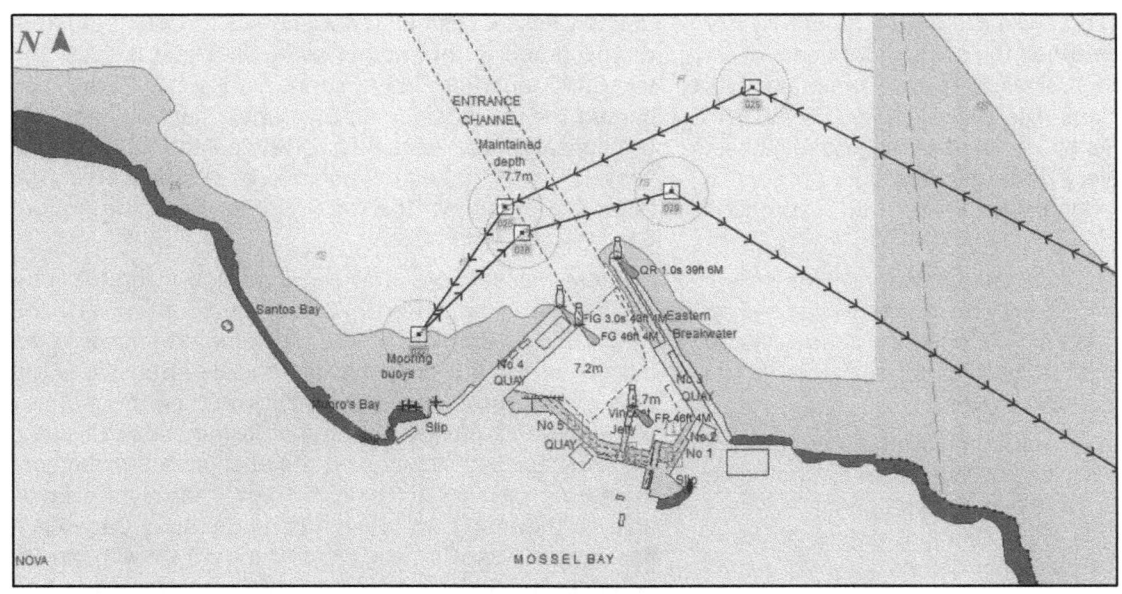
Mossel Bay

restaurant bar. There was no port captain's office. I found him dressed in civilian clothes sitting on a stool in an unmarked room next to the bar where he happily stamped papers that authorized me to leave the port. I cleared the Buffalo River jetty at noon and set sail.

That night, the CARD began to faintly chirp and flicker at the stern position just when I rolled into the bunk for my first sleep cycle at 2000. Nothing blipped at the bottom of the radar screen where the mizzen mast blocked the beams. When I altered course until a blip appeared next to the mizzen shadow, the blip corresponded with the bearing and distance to its icon on the AIS screen. Back on the original course, I monitored the AIS and copied the vessel's broadcasted data, focusing on the closest position of approach (CPA) and time to CPA. With both vessels on the same course the AIS calculated our CPA two hours out. I saw no other blips on the radar, so I set the clock for sixty minutes and rolled into the bunk. On my awake cycle seeing that the vessel had maintained its course and speed urged me to delay another sleep until I resolved the situation. Scooter sailed with a tri-color navigation light on the main mast. Also, solar powered lights glowed at the bow, under the dodger, on midship handrails, and under the arch. I installed them to make Scooter stand out to dinghy drivers as they re-

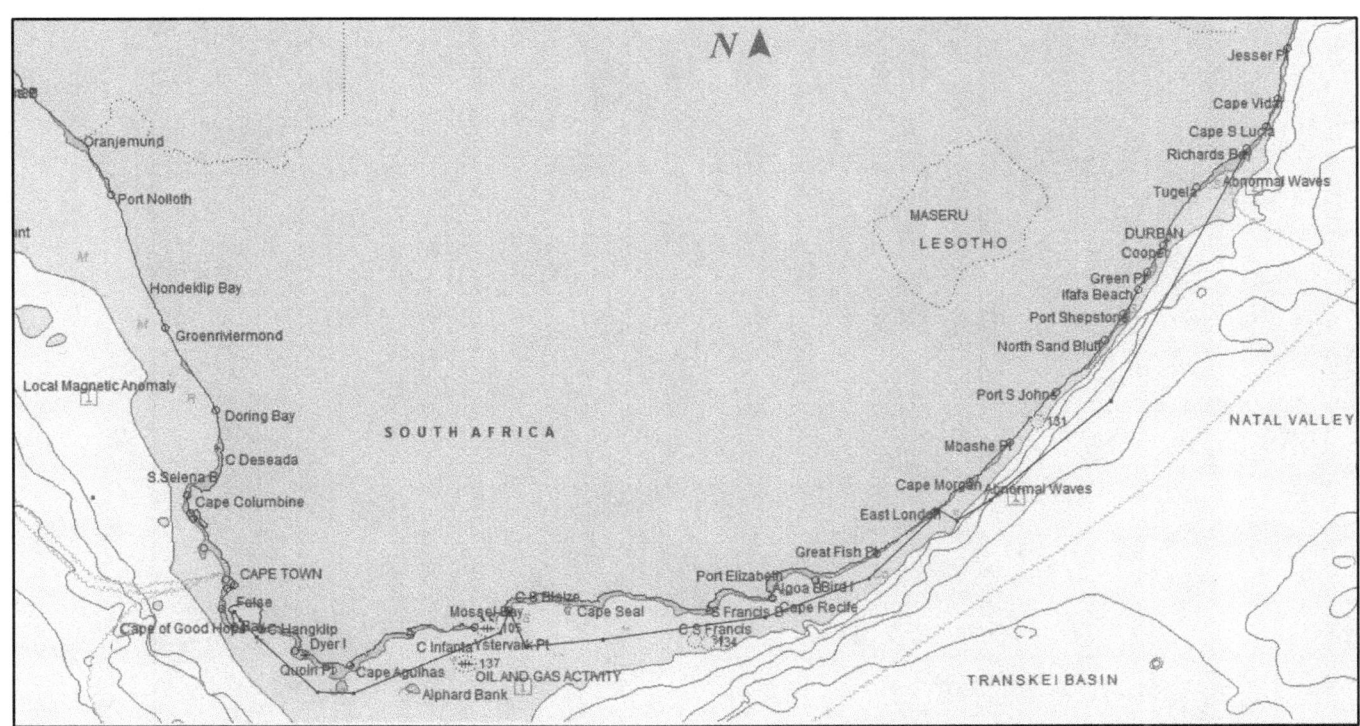
Around the cape

South Africa • 143

turned from a night on the town. I knew the radar reflector on top of the mizzen returned the ships radar beam every time the CARD chirped, and still the vessel maintained its course and speed. At one mile away, I picked up the VHF mic and hailed the ship by name. Receiving no response, I repeated the call every three minutes until an English voice responded, "Station calling. Over," with a surprised tone.

I answered with my best radio voice. "This is sailing vessel *Scooter*. I have watched your course and speed on AIS and radar for two hours. I am one mile directly ahead of you on the same course, two, three, one, true. If you continue you will run me down. Over."

With digital maritime information systems there could be no excuse whatsoever for a collision at sea. A maritime court would find one or both vessel operators and owners responsible for maritime rules violations. Either the closing vessel behind me would alter course to avoid a collision, or as a sailing vessel, it would be my responsibility at the last moment to do whatever necessary to avoid one. I knew that the use of VHF radio communication in a collision avoidance situation could distract bridge crew from following collision regulations, but the call looked like my best solution at the time.

The voice from the ships bridge made a stumbling, slow response to my transmission before it acknowledged seeing *Scooter*. I observed the ship's course change on the AIS screen. A short time later, I made a second radio call thanking the voice for altering course and monitored my instruments for two hours until the ship cleared ahead, the only vessel seen by radar and AIS. I stretched out on the pilot's berth for another sleep shift and left AIS and the CARD operating. My course across the Pacific had carried me far outside shipping lanes, and only once on the passage from Panama to New Zealand had I seen a vessel. The CARD had chirped and bogies blipped on the radar screen only in the Great Barrier Reef, the Arafura Sea, and the Indian Ocean.

Near Mossel Bay, after two days and nights of great sailing, the wind shifted again to the south, driving the waves into steep water walls. I sheltered at anchor in the lee of the bay's wide peninsula shortly after noon. The heavy wind event lasted four nights, and on the morning of the eleventh passage day out of Richards Bay, I hoisted the plow, packed clay around the anchor chain, and continued the passage to Simon's Town. That night a favorable northern air carried me around the tip of Cape Agulhas, across False Bay, and on to Simon's Town with the AIS broadcasting *Scooter* data, the CARD waiting to chirp, and the radar on standby.

Scooter swung at anchor in the small craft mooring area near the False Bay Yacht Club in Simon's Town as I rode *Jazz* around the floating docks to locate the dockmaster's office. The women in the office said they had only one space available for *Scooter* at the end of the longest dock. That became *Scooter's* new home in a town rich in history to explore. Oh serendipity! The ketch first seen when I cleared in at the Opua, New Zealand, customs dock now floated immediately off *Scooter's* bow.

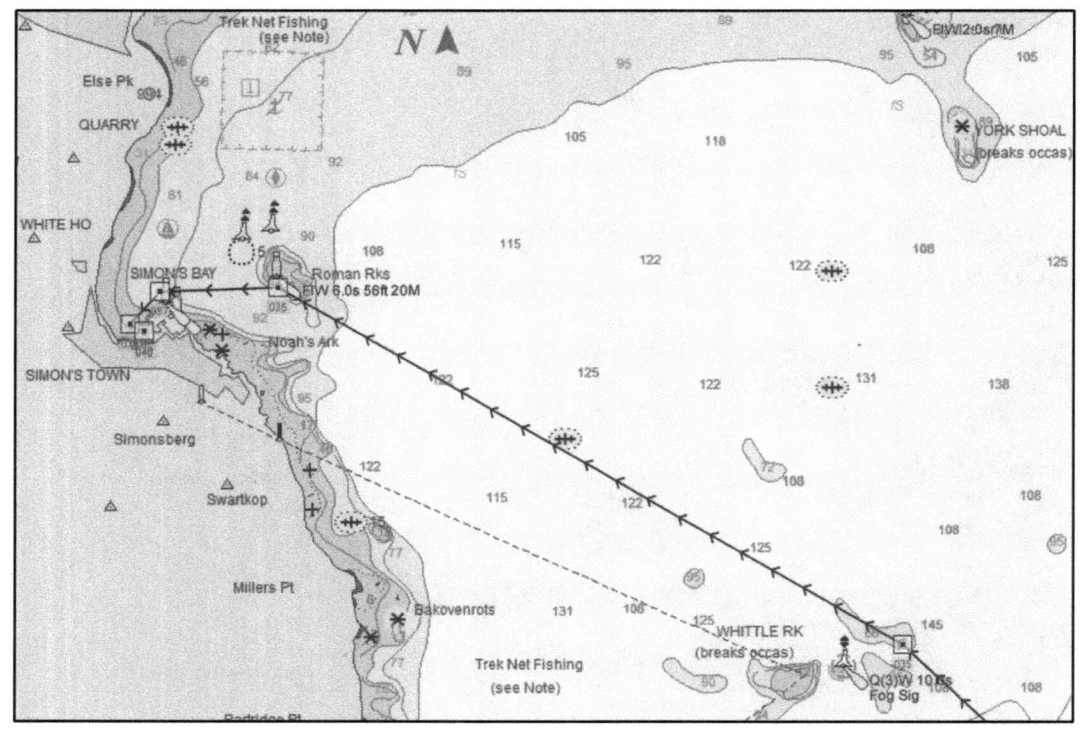

Arriving Simon's Bay

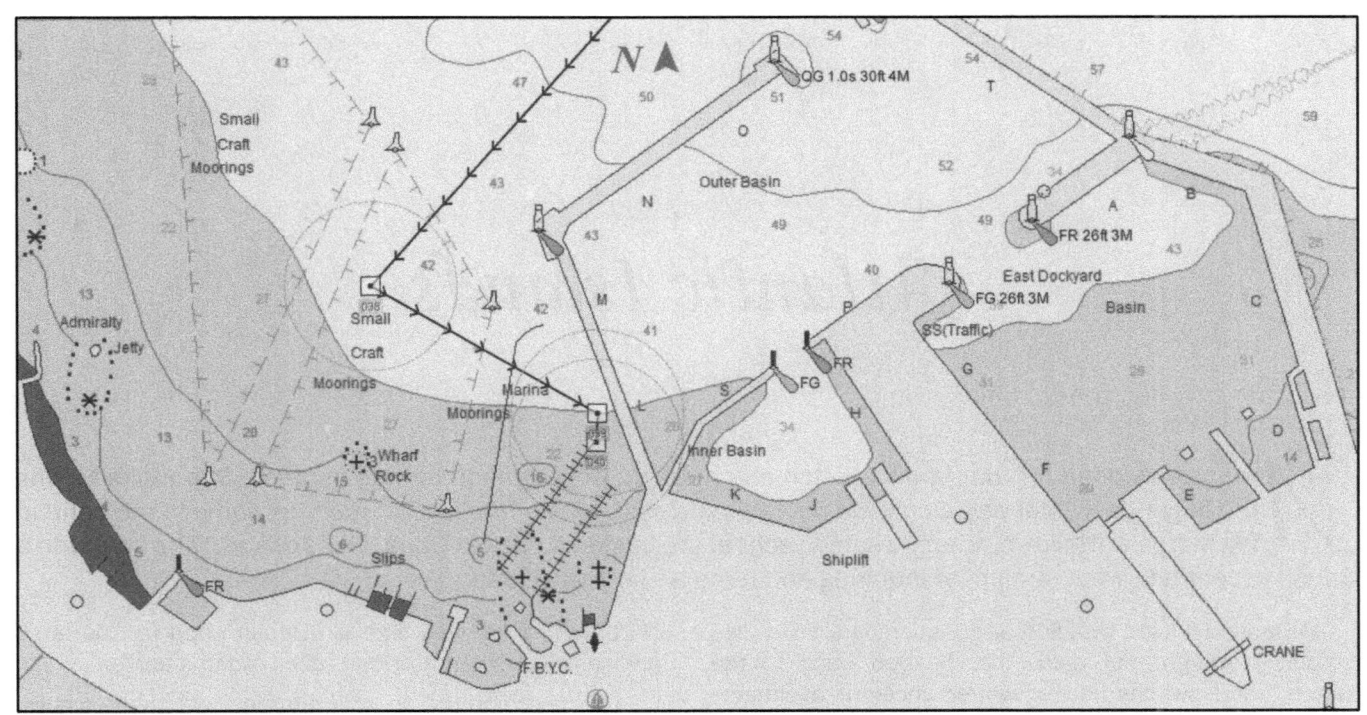

Arriving False Bay Yacht Club

Overlooking Simon's Town

Atlantic Islands • 145

Atlantic Islands

*A*woman stepped off that familiar ketch one morning while I made rounds on deck. She walked along the finger dock, stopped alongside *Scooter*, and said, "Hello." An instant memory came to me of hearing Marge's "Hello" next to the same yacht at the customs dock in Opua. "I'm Joanne," she said with a British accent and went straight to inquiring about me and my sail plans.

Because I'd lived that line of questioning a few times before, I straight out said, "I'm headed back to the states," and switched to unwanted incident avoidance mode, recalling the rewards and problems of similar past encounters. Not to be discourteous I stepped down to the dock. She had recently crewed for a couple that changed plans, no longer heading north to England, and answered an ad placed by the owner of the ketch seeking crew to assist his return to America. Two guys from the states had also responded to the ad. All three had issues about arrangements and safety aboard after inspecting the ketch. The yacht offered Joanne little privacy, the life raft had been deployed and shoddily repacked, and some door frames had been sprung out of shape, making the doors difficult to close. She went on to tell me how she had volunteered for years on sailing vessels owned by married couples, much like Marge. I stood on the dock looking at digital photos of her and the couples she crewed for on her camera's view screen and just said, "Uh-huh." She handed me her professional business card and we parted when I told her I had much to do.

My to-do list itemized some repairs but mostly provisioning for sailing up the Atlantic. I prioritized the list in order of what had to be done to best organize rental car trips and my time at the cape. *Scooter's* original mainsail, reshaped at a Michigan loft years before, served well on Pacific and Indian Ocean downwind passages. I needed the job done again, but instead of that I chose to have a new one made at the North Sails loft in Cape Town. The mariner's guide for the country warned that all life rafts on commercial and private vessels had to be certified every twelve months at service stations approved by the South African Maritime Safety Authority. That requirement meant there were certification stations within easy reach, making this a good place and time to recertify the life raft.

Third on the list was finding a repair shop for the large engine-driven alternator that failed months earlier.

The next morning, Joanne returned with the two guys. I listened with an open mind. Rob and Dave had studied marine biology at Cornell, were in the same classes, and graduated the same year but never met on campus. After graduation, Dave found his way to work for the Alaska Department of Fish and Game, and Rob had become a guide for a private Alaskan game-fishing operation. They met for the first time on a wilderness lakeshore and shared their past experiences, beginning a friendship. Escaping the Alaskan winter, they explored South Africa from Pretoria to Simon's Town and wanted to experience an ocean voyage home. I welcomed them aboard and presented boat accommodations while hearing quick-witted chat about how they could adapt as crew for the three-month sail. I reflected on the thousands of solo sea miles I'd sailed and after consideration welcomed the opportunity to have others to talk with on the long passage to the Caribbean. Joanne could have the entire forward cabin to herself, and Rob and Dave could bunk in the main saloon.

On the first rental car trip, I found my way to the sail loft in an industrial complex north of the Cape Town seaport and made plans to have a new sail crafted. That afternoon I delivered the life raft for recertification. On the agreed-upon day, with the help of loft workers, I spread the old main on the loft's wood floor to be measured and placed the order. With that done, I visited the Royal Cape Yacht Club for lunch and found Peter and Ginger scraping bottom paint, preparing for their Atlantic sail. After swapping more sea stories during lunch I moved on to find the alternator repair shop near a Chevrolet dealership in Cape Town. Between rental car trips, I demonstrated to Dave and Rob how to make a May Day call, operate the AIS, interpret the CARD, start the engine, and operate the head. Joanne

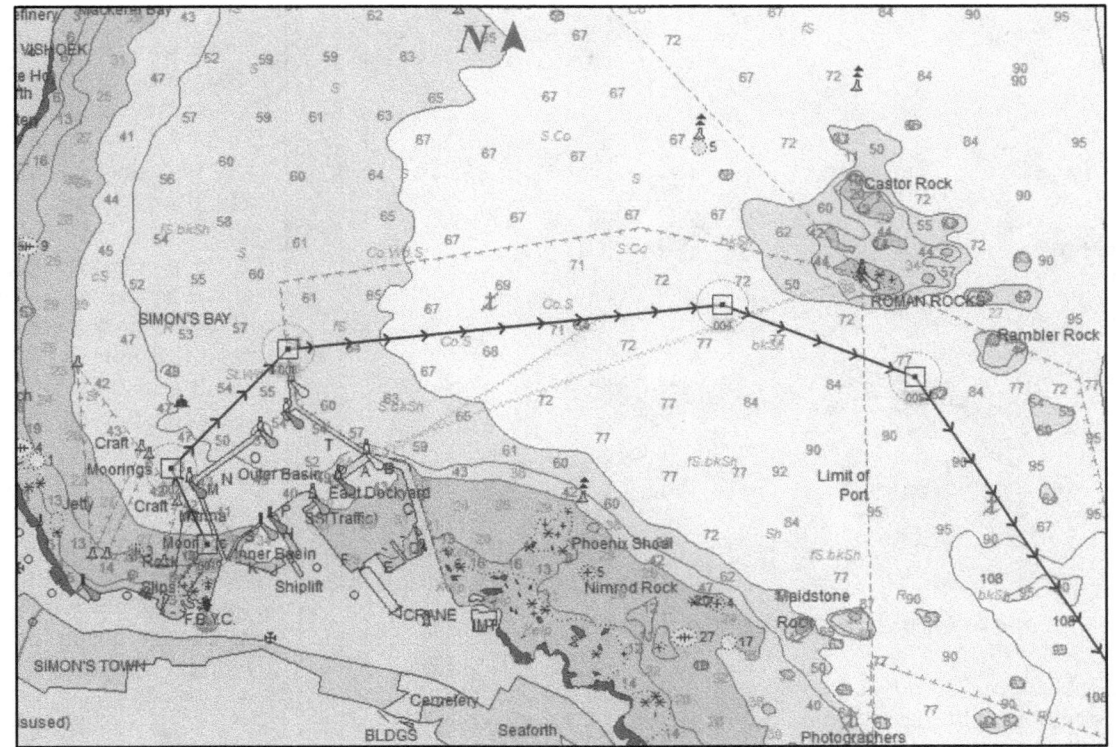
Departing Simon's Town

frequently stepped off *Scooter* to go here and there getting herself ready for the sail.

With the to-do list completed, *Scooter* provisioned, crew settled in, currency exchanged, the rental car returned, yacht club charges settled, clearing-out documents stamped, and departure permission granted, we sailed on the first of February. Following waypoints around waves crashing on Anvil Rock then Bellows Rock, I brought *Scooter* to course while my crew photographed Cape Point and the Cape of Good Hope. Weather predictions for the planned two-week 1,740-mile sail to St. Helena called for oscillating southerly winds every day.

After passing the cape, I started the watchkeeping rotation scheme Joanne suggested. Three would stand a twenty-four-hour watch rotation while the off-watch person cooked all three meals, cleaned below, and had a full night's sleep. She proposed that at the end of the voyage each would grade the others with a 1, 2, or 3 on a card to designate first, second, and third place in a contest for best meal creations. The one with the highest score would treat the rest of the crew with a meal at the restaurant of the crew's choice.

The second day, I demonstrated altering course to maintain a starboard broad reach instead of trimming sails as the wind clocked and backed and roamed from eight to twenty knots. The boat icon slid roughly along the ground track that night. On the morning of training day three the wind jumped to the high twenties, perfect for demonstrating how to set the number two jib to port with the pole, reef the old main one time, and secure the boom far out to starboard with the preventer. Wide-eyed, Dave and Rob experienced *Scooter* comfortably zipping along at eight knots in moderate seas.

Wind speed increased overnight and into the next day, when the old main split nearly full length from luff to leech in a thirty-eight-knot gust. The crew watched as I donned a harness, snapped the tether to a jack line, pulled the sail down the mast, slid it off the boom, and dragged it to

Rounding the capes

Atlantic Islands • 147

Cape Point and the Cape of Good Hope

the multidirectional wave sets of the Indian Ocean, allowing easy movement on and below deck. I set up the sewing machine on the saloon table and stitched a long patch over the tear. Joanne and Dave sat on the starboard divan receiving the sail as I processed it through the machine. The lesson ended when they stowed the sewing machine in the forward compartment and thought out how to fold the sail in the saloon to make it easy to deploy from its bag on deck.

the cockpit. Dave and Rob seemed surprised that *Scooter* continued making seven knots with the only the jib until Joanne commented that's what she expected in forty-knot winds. The smooth following seas were far different than

The best-meal incentive motivated many creative dishes sourced from *Scooter*'s onboard cookbooks while the green crew experienced changes in the sea state, wind speed, and wind direction on days four and five. On day six, weather forecasts predicted lighter air, and when the sails began to flog in the morning of day seven, the crew lowered and properly furled each one after starting Mr. Stink. On day eight, conditions allowed launching the asymmetrical spinnakers from the main and the mizzen, requiring sheet trimming between episodes of catching and cleaning fish and preparing sushi for all but me. Dave and Rob dragged fishing lines, waiting at the ready to snag the big one, while Joanne spectated, occasionally supervising.

Light air and sometimes no air followed *Scooter* north from day eight on until St. Helena rose from the sea on day fourteen. One hour we'd sail, another hour we motor sailed, then motored, then motor sailed, then sailed.

Landfall preparation included an online visit to Noonsite.com that guided me to make a VHF call at twenty miles from St. Helena to announce *Scooter*'s ETA and request permission to go ashore. It explained the formalities, health insurance requirements, cost per day should any aboard not have the ability to be evacuated after an injury, and that a marine sighting sheet had to be completed with the number and species of seabirds, fish, and other marine life seen while approaching the island. The site offered no information about the

FOUR PERSON WATCH ROTATION
CREW A, CREW B, CREW C, CREW D

Time		DAY	1	2	3	4		
2400–0300		RED CREW	A	D	B	C	CREW A	Bob
0400–0700		GREEN CREW	B	A	C	D	CREW B	Joann
0800–1100		RED CREW	C	B	D	A	CREW C	Rob
1200–1500		GREEN CREW	A	D	B	C	CREW D	Dave
1600–1900		RED CREW	B	A	C	D		
2000–2300		GREEN CREW	C	B	D	A		
OFF WATCH; RESPONSIBLE TO COOK ALL MEALS, CLEANS DISHES, GALLEY, HEADS, SHOWERS, CABIN SOLE AND SLEEPS ALL NIGHT			D	C	A	B		

Joanne's watch plan

148 • *Ocean Speed*

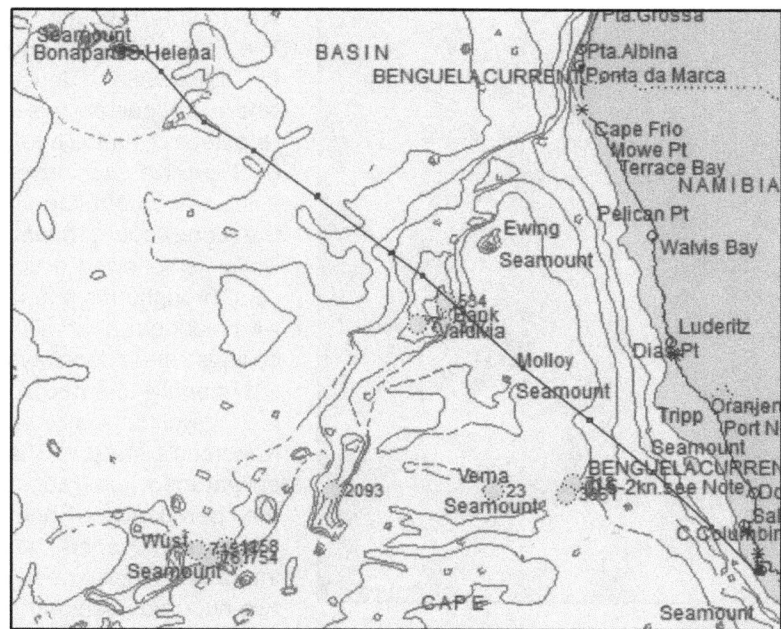
Simon's Town to St. Helena

island's history. It looked to be only a resting waypoint on the journey home.

We motored *Scooter* along the island's northeast coast and rounded southward. Nearing James Bay, I looked up to see an historic fort on the rock cliffs. As we moved forward to our destination, *Floatingpoint* came into view at anchor in the island's lee! After Dave and Rob observed my anchoring procedure, we collected backpacks and shore bags loaded with water bottles, boat documents and passports. Only a set of steps allowed access to the island, amusingly noted on the chart as "The Steps," the gateway to "The Wharf" and Jamestown beyond at the entrance to James Valley.

A motor launch putted from boat to boat and headed our way when the operator saw us waving. It sounded like its propulsion came from a single-cylinder open-exhaust motorcycle engine as it thump, thump, thumped us to The Steps and our first contact with this British Overseas Territory in the South Atlantic.

The speedy formalities process cost crew members twelve Saint Helena pounds each and one pound per day for crew evacuation insurance. In the process I learned from a smiling agent that the island's name is properly pronounced Saint Hell-EE-na, not Saint Hellen-a. Our foursome strolled The Wharf toward Jamestown, founded in 1659 by the East India Company and named after James, Duke of York. The broad wharf, constructed with stone and later reinforced with cement, allowed motorized lifts to shuffle shipping containers around small buildings near the cliff that rose from The Wharf.

We continued along The Wharf to where it became Seafront and onward along a deep, dry moat to a tall arched gate at the foot of Main Street that beckoned us inland to the town and the narrow valley beyond. Climbing the 699 steps of Jacob's Ladder to the fort at the summit of the valley's south cliff looked to be a task not worth doing just to say we did it. Instead, we explored Jamestown until late afternoon.

Early that evening while the meal challenge continued among the crew, I launched *Jazz*, motored near *Floatingpoint's* starboard side, and called out, "Ahoy, Carolyn."

Within a minute, Carolyn appeared on deck and answered my call, "Oh, hi Bob," as though she expected to see me.

"I got here earlier today and cleared in. How long have you been here?"

"It's my third day here to rest up."

"Where did you sail from?"

"Cape Town."

"I was at Simon's Town. How was the sail?"

"Ok. No issues. How was yours?"

"The same," I said. "You have any problems with the current south of Richards Bay?"

"I hopped from port to port around the cape."

"Well, I've got crew now. Two green guys I've been training and a gal who's crewed for others, pretty ocean savvy, came aboard in Simon's Town."

"How did you find them?"

Jacob's Ladder

Atlantic Islands • 149

Jamestown

"They found me. Jumped off another boat they didn't think safe. Have you been on the island much?"

"I've been here and there."

"How about showing us around tomorrow and meet these kids?"

"I would like that."

We agreed to meet at 9:00 a.m. local time and said good night.

We rode the water taxi the next morning to The Steps and followed Carolyn's lead to places she thought we would enjoy. She responded to the crew's questions about how we knew each other and told them the short story. By day's end we had adventured by taxi to scenic stops on roads overlooking Jamestown. The taxi driver said he could show us more, but it would take some time, and we made plans to start early the next day.

Back aboard, Joanne said that during her day-long conversation with Carolyn, she realized how much Carolyn could benefit from her assistance on her northbound sail and wanted to make the jump the next morning if it was ok with me. A short chat with Carolyn from *Jazz* confirmed that she welcomed Joanne's help. The guys supported Joanne's departure knowing that we would have more provisions, including her share of the wine.

With Joanne transferred to *Floatingpoint*, Dave, Rob, and I met up with the taxi owner again. From the time he turned the ignition key, he took us back hundreds of years to the island's discovery and its later declaration as a British Territory, the purpose of the fortifications, and the history surrounding the past officers, military units, and residents.

We motored inland to The Briars pavilion and to Longwood House where, to our surprise, Napoleon had been held captive. Our driver guide waited outside on the Longwood grounds while we followed a docent throughout a house with abnormally high ceilings and doorways intentionally created to play psychologically on Napoleon's stature. She enlightened us about the personalities both British and French that interacted there nearly two hundred years earlier, and spoke of rumors that Napoleon might have occasionally ridden a horse to visit a mistress.

Absorbing the unexpected historical find, we continued about the island for the remainder of the day. At Plantation House, where the governor lived, we met Jonathan, one of the Seychelles' giant tortoises, brought to the island in 1882 when biologists thought he had been around for fifty years. Ending our journey ashore, we boarded the water taxi at The Steps for the ride to *Scooter* and saw that *Floatingpoint* had sailed.

The next morning, we provisioned at the grocery on Market Street, stowed the supplies aboard, returned to the island, and processed clearing-out documents.

Longwood House

Jonathan, February 2009

Ascension Island, also a part of this British Overseas Territory and home to military bases since before the First World War, was located halfway between South America and West Africa. Seven hundred miles north of St. Helena, it looked to be a good waypoint to check for more potential surprises after the Bonaparte discovery. We set a three-day watch rotation plan eliminating the day off but continued the meal competition. Fishing lures dragged off the stern by day and night, hooking what the guys called tunnies, small tuna offering up dark red sushi. Six days of unchallenging winds and easy seas allowed us to sail right up the ground track to anchor in Clarence Bay off Long Beach on the island's northwest coast.

Eager to explore the island we found the port manager's office in Georgetown where I registered *Scooter,* but to fully process formalities, we had to visit the nearby post office for immigration clearing. From there we walked inland to the Obsidian Hotel, which operated a small fleet of rental cars, and secured one for the next day's adventure. The next morning, after touring past RAF and USAF facilities, I drove the rental along a narrow road into the hills and stopped to walk up Green Mountain Road under an arched passage cut through a gigantic bolder similar to a sequoia tree tunnel. Motoring on and up, we explored stone slabs on a steep hillside engineered by Royal Marines to direct rainwater to cisterns below for use by the garrison missioned to protect St. Helena from a possible Bonaparte rescue attempt by French sympathizers.

We inspected old gun emplacements at Fort Bedford overlooking Georgetown and visited a tourist center to discover that leatherback turtles had been arriving on Long Beach to lay eggs, thrilling the marine biologists. A small tourist group that was forming at the center to visit the beach and witness the event that night had space for us on the lorry, and we signed on to the party. Returning after dinner aboard we joined the group for a short ride to the beach. A guide led us around large pits dug in the sand by the huge turtles. Our group came upon a seven-foot-long girl laying her eggs in the pit she had dug. I captured the event on video, shining the camera light until the guide directed me to switch the light off so as not to startle momma. The group listened as the guide talked about how the turtles migrate from South America to lay the eggs and swim back by orienting themselves using Earth's magnetic field.

Four days of active island roaming, seeing unexpected natural events, and touring historical sites came to an end when we hauled anchor to sail the three-thousand-mile ground track to Chaguaramas, Trinidad. Warm days, clear skies, glassy seas, and light air from the south followed *Scooter* north. Under sail, life aboard repeated the prior day's events, yet every day a new experience captured the crew's attention. Rob's time as a professional fishing guide coaching clients about where to fish and how to hook, clean, and cook them at camp had developed teaching skills that he showed aboard. Back in Simon's Town at a fishing supply store, Rob pulled items off shelves and explained to Dave why they would be needed on the Atlantic journey. That sharing of knowledge flowed daily at sea as Rob applied his experiences to ocean fishing, casually teaching Dave and me. Dave's career monitoring and reporting conditions in the wild called on his degree and developed writing skills. What they told me about their employment fit their personalities—Rob being self-assured and assertive in a persistent way and Dave quietly absorbing and evaluating situations as they occurred.

The watch rotation meant that two of us were up and about most of the day. When the jobs were done, we resumed fishing, scanned the sea surface and sky, and read whatever we found interesting from *Scooter's* library. I shifted my role aboard between skippering, crewing, cooking, and instructing. When I shared my vision of air sliding around the sails creating a vacuum on one side and how that negative air pressure carried from the jib to the main and over the mizzen, in a sense sucking the boat forward, a new definition for a sailboat evolved. My crew had become active sailors willing to tackle any part of keeping *Scooter* moving on course. Seeing them automatically respond to sail trim needs made me proud, knowing that I had done a good job bringing them to that level of competence.

As the days progressed, light air filled in from the northwest. *Scooter* slowly crept into the North Atlantic through the Intertropical Convergence Zone (ITCZ), also called the doldrums, where warm air heated by the sun flows northward from the southern hemisphere and southward from the northern hemisphere on the ocean surface, bringing great amounts of moisture together. The heated moisture rises to the stratosphere where it parts and flows north and south to cool then falls back to the earth around latitudes 30° N and 30° S.

Dead calm

While motoring through the ITCZ, occasionally the wind lifted Scooter on a close reach. Gaining latitude to find consistent air became more important than following a ground track. To conserve the remaining two hundred liters of diesel, we studied the clouds on the northern horizon with the long eyes for evidence of wind driven rain and motor sailed toward it. Daily fuel checks and weather consults tweaked every decision. In the light air the old mainsail bagged where it should have been full and tight, so we raised the new mainsail and boat speed improved.

Wind speed and direction changed every day after escaping the doldrums. At around 5° 12.7' N on March 17th, we rode twenty-five-knot wind north under a double-reefed main until late that night when the wind stopped as fast as closing a door. The next morning, while dragging fishing lines as Mr. Stink pushed Scooter along, a strange object appeared close to the port side. I had recently glanced forward to scan the horizon seeing nothing of interest, and then there it was floating by. At first sight it looked to be an inverted tree with bare roots that extended horizontally in the sun. Looking along it's trunk into the clear water as it passed by, we saw no other branches only a straight wood-colored shaft stabbing into the depths. We were 440 miles off the Amazon River Delta bearing 031° true. I remarked that it must have been washed out of the immense Amazon River basin to float around the ocean. My opinion changed when I studied it with the long eyes. Up close, the object looked to be made of sun-faded yellow-green plastic. What I first thought to be roots appeared to be solid tentacles extending outward, larger in diameter where they attached to the main shaft and tapering to nearly pointed tips, with all limbs terminating about two meters from the central shaft. Perhaps it could have been a disguised floating antenna or beacon tethered to something below, monitoring ocean and weather conditions, but it was very different from how I thought such a device would be configured. Rob stayed focused on fishing gear, but Dave continued to examine the thing nonstop as it floated away off the stern.

When the object neared where a fishing lure dragged behind, something took the lure and a fishing battle ensued. Over time, Dave cranked the fish close until it leaped free of the water, revealing it was a dorado, before it spit the lure out. All eyes had been on the skirmish, but occasionally I looked forward to see if another strange floater lurked ahead. After the dorado event, a patch of water off the port bow, much different from the surrounding glassy, calm blue sea, caught my attention. It looked to be a fifty-meter-wide dinner plate of leaping shards of white, foamy water standing straight up on the surface. The roiling surface action did not look like it was caused by gas released from the ocean bed. Scooter's icon on the Nobeltec chart had passed from a depth of 4,100 meters to 2,150 meters. My thought about switching the autopilot off and steering close to investigate got overruled by an inner voice that said, "Not a good idea." I kept Scooter on a course tangent to the dancing water at a safe distance. Then, another circle of dancing water appeared northwest of the first, and then another beyond that came into view as Scooter motored along. All was silent on deck until the circular plates of leaping water faded from view over the clear horizon astern. An unexpected dead battery prevented video recording the event located about 05° 41.29'N and 043° 38.93' W. The 1200 logbook entry:

Extremely confused seas—Mega chop, 270° true, 1.7k

That evening, meal competition continued. We talked about the dorado that got away and other concerns: position, weather, standing watch, and electronic eyes out to the horizon. No opinions floated around about what we had witnessed during those strange moments.

The closer to the journey's end the more relaxed Dave and Rob appeared as they spent off-watch hours reading. I viewed it as them having faced whatever hidden fear they had of the new and possibly dangerous undertaking of sailing thousands of miles in the middle of the ocean. Trinidad came into view while sailing in light air on the twenty-fourth day from Ascension Island. Confident with the remaining fuel on board, I tasked Mr. Stink to work

Ascension to Trinidad, dancing water circle

On the fourth day of May, the day of departure for my passage to Port Everglades, I had feelings different from the day I sailed from Angelfish Key to begin the long-planned life experience. Gripped by an irritating, foggy bewilderment about what to do next that would deliver the ecstasy of achieving a personal accomplishment equal to what I'd spent twelve years conceiving, planning, and implementing, I sat at the nav desk sensing nothing around me. The proud excitement that filled me after closing the circumnavigation loop slipped many times into melancholy moments thinking about the absence of an immediate life plan, no challenge to meet, no mission to complete, and no future adventure to make my heart leap. My failure to find and build an oceangoing relationship with a woman had brought me to realize I was moving toward valuing companionship above living at ocean speed. I wondered about how difficult it would be to leave the unparalleled freedom of the ocean to deal with life on land again. Those persistent, vacillating feelings shaped my passage plan north. I laid a ground track east of Grenada far enough off the island chain to sail swiftly on the trades for a few days directly to St. Lucia. With absolute confidence in vessel system performance and myself, I wanted it to be a pleasurable two-night sail alone and a time for introspection. It would be a 343-mile passage I would not have sailed years before when green at ocean sailing.

us toward the final destination. *Scooter* crept past Galera Point then west in the Galleons' Passage along the northern coast to Chupara Point where we found enough air to sail around Entrada Point into the Bocas del Dragón. Dave and Rob, then seasoned sail handlers, smartly struck the main and mizzen.

With the lines made fast to the Crews Inn Marina end dock at Chaguaramas, Trinidad, at 1145 on March 25th I had technically closed the loop on circumnavigating the planet. At the customs office I presented the Certificate of Clearance from the Republic of South Africa to the chief immigration officer. The certificate noted: "Where bound (all places to be mentioned in order of intended voyage): St. Helena, Ascension, Trinidad, Grenada, St. Kitts, Puerto Rico, USA." Similar to many other certificates collected on the journey, it lay on the top of the papers in the clearing in binder. The officer completed the Trinidad and Tobago Grant of Clearance by noting: "Number of passengers—0, Number of crew—2, Number of in-transit passengers—0, Number of stowaways aboard—0, Cleared at—Chaguaramas, Time—1245." He handed the document to me, and I added it to the original Trinidad folder in the nav desk. With that done we secured *Scooter* in slip 34B.

At the celebration dinner at the Crews Inn restaurant, Dave and Rob talked about sharing their sailing stories with family and girlfriends. When the check arrived, they refused to let me even cover the tip.

Boat chores consumed great amounts of time, energy, and money as usual after two months and 4,880 miles at sea, and the days sped by getting it all done. Dave and Rob explored the island after completing morning boat chores and flew home a week after arrival. For a memory trip, I rode a bus around Port of Spain to visit sites last seen with Connie. Envisioning the future, I searched a Florida real estate website and located a private dock for *Scooter* on a canal off the ICW in Pompano Beach, Florida. Not able to guarantee an arrival time, the owner suggested I contact him when I could be more specific.

Anchored in Rodney Bay off St. Lucia, I enjoyed a week of zipping daily on *Jazz* into the marina, walking the streets, chatting with locals and tourists, exploring shops, and people watching, especially couples delightfully together on holiday. Once cleared to depart, I slipped the Saint Lucia Air and Sea Ports Authority document and my stamped passport into the *Scooter* binder, walked straight to the marina, and boarded *Jazz*. Halfway to the boat I stopped, looked back at the people playing on the hotel beach, then toward *Scooter* and back, pondering life choices. I decided to stay true to my plan, sail to St. Thomas, then Florida and refit *Scooter* for sale while preparing for the knee replacement. Focusing on those two major tasks, I realized it was time to suspend the search for an oceangoing life mate and commit to a humbling lifestyle change.

I sailed *Scooter* precisely over the ground track to St. Thomas in good air and set the anchor in Charlotte Amalie Harbor at sunrise on the fourteenth of May. After breakfast, I readied all spaces below anticipating a

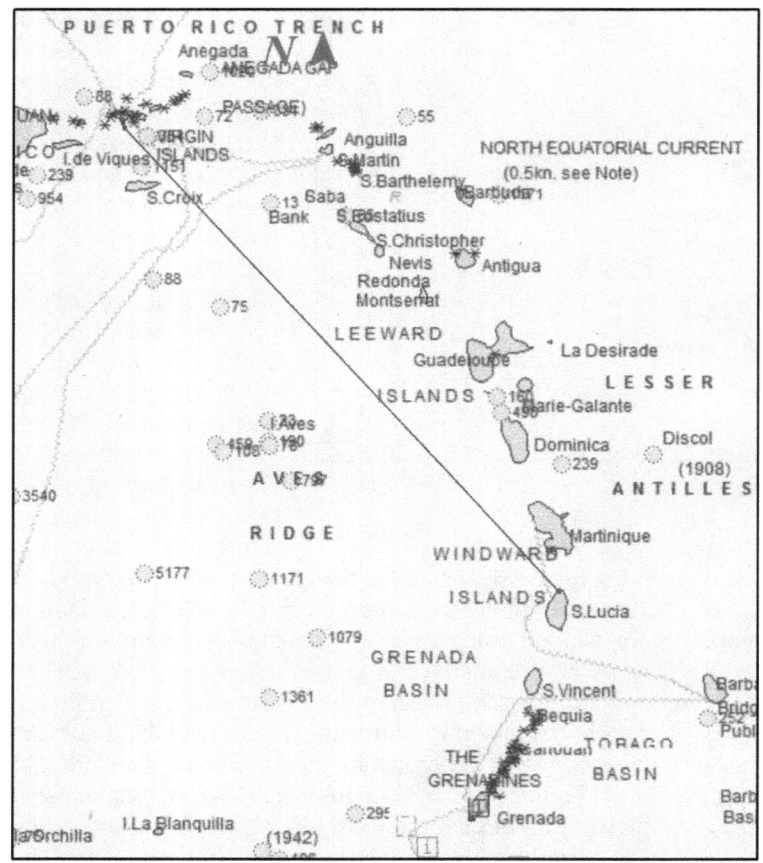

St. Lucia to St. Thomas

boarding inspection, zipped to the ferry dock, and walked Veterans Drive to find the customs and border protection office in the marine terminal. In line ahead of me, a man spoke to his guests about the nonsense they would experience at the counter, saying it was a royal pain every place they would go in the Caribbean. That brought a smile to my face and I thought, "You have no idea." When they departed, I presented myself to the officer and handed her my passport and the Saint Lucia Air and Sea Ports Authority document. She asked only a few of the questions that I had faced while clearing in at customs offices around the world. When I told her the number on board, she scribbled on a ledger and asked no questions about why I was alone, unlike other customs officers encountered in the past. She made no comment about inspecting the boat, stamped and returned my passport, then, as though it were an afterthought, handed back the Saint Lucia document. Differing from other customs and immigration experiences, I received no confirmation of clearing in, not a single scrap of paper to add to my collection of formalities folders. At The Green House restaurant across the street, I opened my passport and saw a stamp in faded blue with tiny letters that read "Department of Homeland Security" inside the oval outline. Unlike all the other stamps collected in the passport that boldly printed the name of the nation state, it did not display "America" or "United States of America." Trying to recall the clearing-in process three years before it came to me that I had received no papers documenting that visit either, but I did have a pleasure boat release number in the Puerto Rico folder. The entire easy and unchallenging clearing-in process left me with the thought that aggressive scrutiny would occur when I reached the mainland at Port Everglades. I looked forward to creating formalities folder number twenty-two, "USA." Nearing lunchtime, I gave the episode no further thought.

Beginning to think the light from Sefina had grown dim, receiving no reply emails since Christmas, I returned to online dating and soon made a connection. She had a place in a Lauderdale Lakes condo complex not far from Pompano Beach. Our online chats revolved around where she lived and her friendship with the owner of a few rental units in her condo complex. I committed to meeting her and her landlord friend and reconnected with the dock owner in Pompano Beach, securing the dock for the month of June.

Instead of clearing in and out of island nations all the way to Florida or day sailing from island to island anchoring under a quarantine flag, a passage that would take many weeks, I chose to make it the last grand solo sail of my ocean adventure. A north moving depression developed off Jacksonville, Florida, but tropical weather to the east looked clear. I set a 922-mile ground track from St. Thomas northwest to Bimini then west across the Straits of Florida to Port Everglades. After provisioning, I checked with customs. The officer said, "You're ok to go." No forms were stamped and no documents were completed and returned to me at the customs office, cementing my belief that I would definitely face critical formalities on the mainland. Sailing over the ground track with the Bahamian courtesy flag flying over the yellow Q flag under the starboard spreader, I rounded North Eleuthera Island, passed north of Great Harbour Cay, and anchored off the northeast coast of North Bimini Island.

At 2145 the next night I hauled anchor to sail fifty miles across the Straits, planning to arrive early at the Port Everglades customs dock, manage clearing in, and find the Pompano Beach dock. Approaching the coast, I repeated VHF calls to raise customs and immigration in Port Everglades wanting to learn where to dock for clearing in as had been the procedure for entering many nation states. Finally, an hour before landfall, I received a stunning surprise. The customs office voice sharply said, "Go find a slip somewhere and bring vessel documents to the office here within twenty-four hours of your arrival."

Scooter passed close to the red and white pillar buoy marking safe water off the Outer Bar Cut channel to Port Everglades at 0730. On the way into the Turning Basin,

Windows Vista corrupted the Nobeltec Admiral program, freezing electronic navigation and reconfirming Murphy's Law that if it can fail, it will fail at the most inopportune time. I took off way in midchannel and stopped the boat dead in the current. Fortunately, no other vessels were in the channel at the time. Moving fast to the nav desk, I grabbed the Maptech Chart Kit Florida East Coast and the Keys: Region 7, open and ready for just such a possibility. I motored north in the ICW to the location on page thirty-five circled weeks before to identify the waterway to the rented dock at the house a few miles south of mile marker 1055. When I arrived at noon, I saw a boat tied to the dock, circled around, verified the address in the email, and returned to raft alongside. When no one answered the door, I searched for a pay phone and called the homeowner then a rental car company. The owner appeared hours later, apologized for the other boat's owner not departing earlier, and said it would be moved that Monday.

The rental company delivered my car. Monday morning I joined the maddened go-to-work rush and found my way to customs at Port Everglades. From the parking lot, I followed the signs to the customs office counter where I presented myself to the officer saying, "Good morning. I'm here to clear back into the US after circumnavigating." In that I had no inbound clearance or outbound release papers documenting my time in St. Thomas, I opened the binder with a smile and extracted my passport and the St. Lucia Air and Sea Ports Authority document from the clear plastic holder. The officer thumbed through my passport, looked up and said, "You cleared in at St. Thomas; nothing needs to be done here."

I stood agape, silently gazing at the officer as he handed the passport across the counter. I closed the binder and walked the few steps to the door dumbfounded by what had just happened.

Talking to myself, evil thoughts flowed during the drive back to the boat. No boat inspection! No clearing in documents! Not a single challenging question! The illegal material and people that could have been aboard! Damn. The intensity of those entry policies and procedures in Panama, Galápagos, French Polynesia, Tonga, New Zealand, New Caledonia, Australia, and the Republic of South Africa protected citizens far more than here in my homeland. Of course, we're protected! There must be some other protocol for surveillance of inbound pleasure craft other than by airplane flyovers, onboard inspections with dogs, face-to-face grilling, and multiple rubber-stamped documents. This is America! Customs and immigration couldn't be that lax.

Sumlog after docking in Florida, June 7, 2009

By the time I returned to the boat I had cleared my head of the surprising customs episode and started working my to-do list:

Find a place to live

Purchase a car

Join a cell phone service

Find an orthopedist for knee replacement

Retrieve goods from storage in St. Petersburg

Resolve the megalist of presale boat work to be done

Drive north to see the kids and visit Eileen in the retirement home in Michigan

Organize the hours of videos and hundreds of photos documenting the journey

Find places where I could interact with singles

I held a nasty vision that I wanted to avoid: passing the rest of my life as a solo senior sailor, pushing a walker along a dock on the way to a neglected and run-down boat. I had successfully completed my grief-healing journey after sailing 29,076 sea miles at ocean speed.

Revelation

My need to become a land dweller filled my waking hours the week I bought a like-new pre-owned Saturn Ion at a local dealer. In a multistory condo complex, I leased a ground floor one bedroom apartment with parking at the front door, perfect for post surgery recovery. The enclosed lanai could house everything from the storage unit in St. Petersburg. With my personal gear moved to the apartment and *Scooter* secured for an extended time alone at the dock, I called Seth to thank him for all his work, gave him the new address, and told a few sailing stories. By late July, I had selected the Broward Joint Replacement Center and set the thirtieth of November as the surgery date for what I would come to call my bionic knee. With that date set I turned my attention to presenting *Scooter* on the market as though it had just left the factory in La Rochelle, France.

Sea time had worn everything exposed to the elements. Refinishing the heavily scratched main saloon sole headed the work list. Left uncorrected it would cause a shopper to wonder about what else might need repair that was hidden from view. In the dry bilge below the saloon deck, chips, dings, and red circles from rusted steel cans needed attention. I had intentionally not finished those areas four years earlier knowing that damage would accumulate at sea. It would be a big job but a like-new appearance of all spaces would command a higher asking price. To get the job done, I rented a storage unit with enough space for long worktables. An outlet conveniently located between the unit's wide roll-up door and the adjacent unit's door supplied power for hanging lights, a sander, and the portable air conditioner purchased in Panama. The large space allowed me to lay out all removable deck plates on tables. Mornings, I worked on the boat repairing the damage below the saloon sole until it was too hot to function. I had lunch at the apartment and worked afternoons in the air-conditioned storage unit. I sanded the removable saloon deck plates to bare wood, applied a light varnish coat, sanded with 400 grit paper, applied another varnish coat, and repeated the process until they had a deep, hard finish.

When the removable deck plates were done, I started work on the nonremovable saloon deck. The portable air conditioner kept the boat interior tolerable while I repeated the sanding and varnishing process until the depth of gloss matched the deck plates in the storage unit. With that finished, I sanded the accessible interior hull surfaces in the forward and aft compartments and the machine spaces under the port cockpit seat and coated them with white polyurethane paint. To finish the like-new appearance, I painted the visible hull surface in the engine room gray and the entire engine and mounts blue.

In the evening, after a satisfactory boat workday, the laptop kept me linked with many wonderful friends met around the planet. Carolyn had made it to a Chesapeake Bay marina and Connie had found a great guy in LA. Not receiving email responses from Sefina told me her life course had pulled her in other directions. As the boat project items dwindled and free time grew, I began playing the online dating game again. Only weeks from surgery my profile stirred a response from Gerta, who escaped Communist East Germany with her husband in her younger days. They built a lighting shop business in West Germany and parlayed profits into training Hanoverian dressage horses before Cold War fears motivated their move to Canada, where they started a horse breeding and training business. Later they relocated to West Palm Springs with the horses and created a more profitable training and breeding program near other ranches with private airplane landing strips instead of golf courses behind the homes. Wealthy international riders purchased the steeds until her husband lost his battle with cancer. Entry into her upscale lifestyle required adherence to her rigid rules. I had to park the Saturn down the street and not in front of her house to keep the image she had established in the neighborhood. When we dined in Palm Springs, I rode passenger while she drove her Mercedes fast, sometimes winding it up to the red line to "clear out the carbon," a whole new experience for me. Fortunately, I had polished my use of a fork in my left hand and knife in my right hand during my global travels to manipulate them continental style. I even signed that the plate could be taken by the server, positioning both fork and knife parallel across the plate at the 6:30 position.

Before the knee replacement day, I provisioned for three weeks alone in the apartment by staging quick and easy-to-prepare meals along with everything else I could possibly need. With my right leg in a plastic bag and a crutch under my arm I practiced showering. Continuing my prep, I moved furniture to afford ease of walker movement about the apartment and placed the TV controller, clothing, dry snack food, and bottled water on the night stand next to the bed. Knowing that I would be discharged the day after surgery, I arranged to have Gerta drive me to the hospital early in the morning and take me to the apartment the next afternoon.

At the time of discharge, an orderly placed a walker in the Mercedes trunk. I rolled from the wheelchair onto the passenger seat and found enough space to angle the crutches over my shoulder from floor to ceiling. Miles later, Gerta stopped the Mercedes next to the Saturn in front of the apartment and waited behind the steering wheel while I leveraged my way off the seat, hobbled on crutches to the trunk, extracted the collapsible walker, and pushed it to the apartment door while toting the crutches. Nursing was not in Greta's rule set. She drove off to Palm Springs.

I entered the apartment, propped the crutches against the kitchen table, and, moving with the aid of the walker, tumbled onto the bed.

Not wanting to get hooked on the prescribed Percocet, I took only Tylenol for pain. After a few days, the throbbing in my right leg began to fade, but the joint remained stiff, hurting only when I bent my knee. Exercises intended to reduce muscle stiffness and improve range of motion specified in the hospital recovery manual had to be followed to regain function. I worked the program many times every day for the first week while lying in bed. Physical therapy started with a Monday, Wednesday, and Friday routine after I could squeeze in behind the steering wheel and drive. Pushing myself beyond the physical therapy exercises, I moved the walker on the pathways around the condo complex. When that became less painful, I walked the same route on crutches. Overcoming my concern about climbing steps, I crutch-walked up the outdoor stairway to the exterior balcony, around the building, down another set of steps, and back to the apartment. I had no intention of lying around the apartment waiting for recovery.

Soon after walking without crutches, I rode in Gerta's Mercedes to a swank Christmas party in another gated community with even larger homes after finding a blue blazer at a Salvation Army store that met her standards. I continued seeing her until one afternoon early in the new year when she called to say, "Don't come up tonight. I have

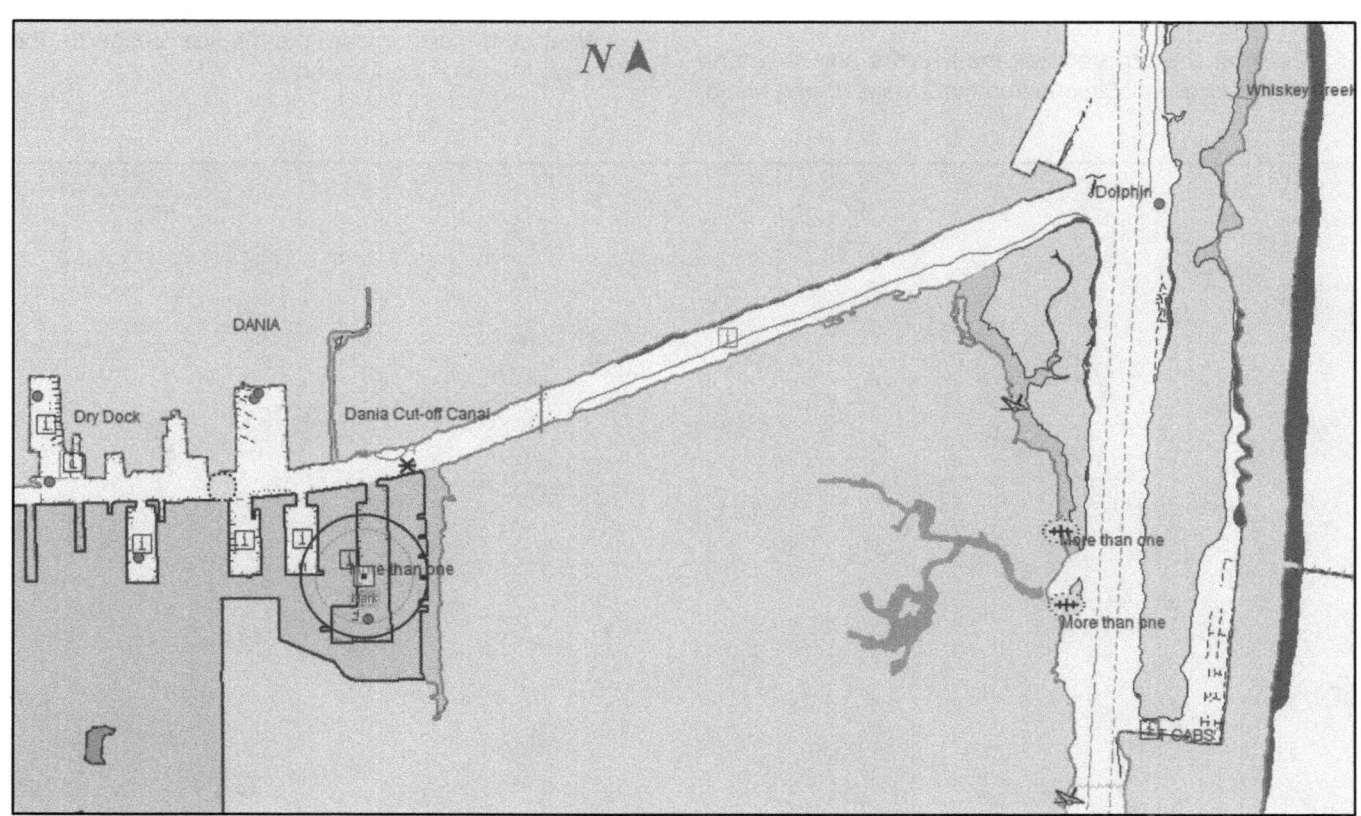

Royale Palm Yacht Basin

a date with a man I just met, and I just want to tell you we are in different leagues." I thought that perhaps if, instead of the book about cooking with spices that she refused and handed back to me before the Christmas party, I had given her a diamond tennis bracelet, I would have been in her league.

By the end of March, I had completed all items on the preparation for sale to-do list except for a recoat of the scraped and worn topside decks and aft cabin top. To prep the surfaces for another coat of two-part epoxy paint laced with nonskid additive, I needed to spend hours sanding, a job that could not be done while *Scooter* floated at the residential canal dock. I moved her to the Royale Palm Yacht Basin on the Dania Cut-Off Canal south of Port Everglades.

Serendipity again! The entrance to the marina was where I demonstrated to the International Yachtmaster Training evaluator docking under power years before. After securing *Scooter* in a slip, I noticed that the broker who facilitated my purchase of *Meg* had an office on the second floor of the marina. Three months later with the deck resurfacing job done, I signed a six-month sales contract with him. Because the marina slip cost nine hundred dollars a month, I moved the showroom-ready boat to a private dock on Guava Isle on the South Fork of the New River priced at one third the marina slip fee. From then on, my *Scooter* responsibilities were reduced to simply keeping her systems ready and the deck clean for showings.

Arrival at the private dock marked the end of a ten-month effort to get *Scooter* ready for sale. There would be absolutely no competition on the market for an experienced 1984 Amel Maramu ketch. When a broker arrived with his client, I would present the whys and the hows of the standing and running rigging, the upgrades to plumbing, the clean engine room, the machine space, the ground tackle, the arch with solar and wind generators feeding the fully integrated electrical system, the heavy-duty hydraulic steering, and the unique autopilot. However, every shopper had no knowledge of the quality built into the brand just as I'd had none before my discovery. Nor could they comprehend the benefits of my extensive refit. Every shopper excused not getting serious until after the current yacht, airplane, or motorcycle collection had been sold. It went on for the length of the six-month brokerage contract. One guy drove down the coast from Maine to Florida with his broker, shopping used boats on the way, simply to learn what was on the market and wasted a full day of my time that I could have focused on finding a life mate. The repetitive excuses grew tiresome.

Then while rejoicing about *Scooter's* like-new appearance on Christmas Day, I thought to put off selling until the economy improved, not renew the brokerage contract, and return to teaching ASA classes. The broker offered to continue advertising. I told him the only way someone would be able to see the boat in the future would be if he had a signed contract to purchase with solid earnest money down. He agreed and I returned to living aboard, making a complete reversal of my after-circumnavigation resolution, and sailed *Scooter* around Key West and north along the Florida coast to the Harborage Marina in St. Petersburg.

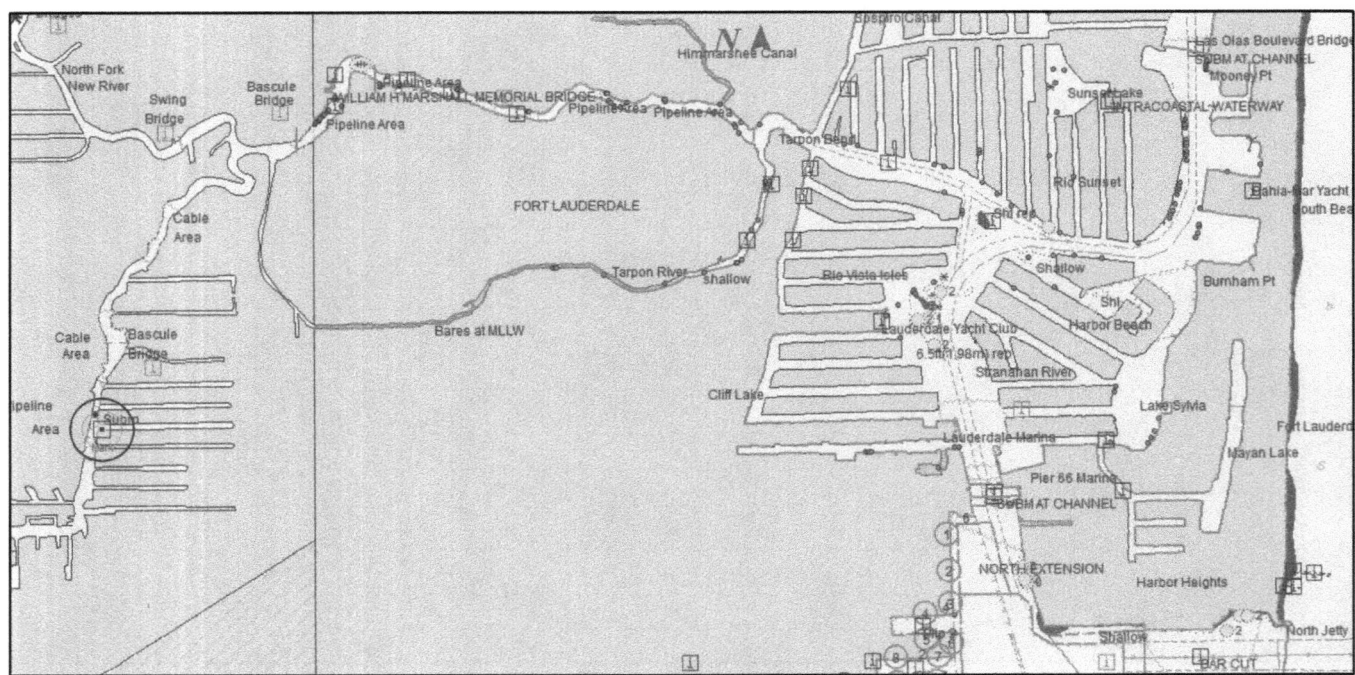

Private dock

Connecting again with Sailing Florida at the Vinoy Marina, I resumed sailing instruction aboard privately owned sailing yachts contracted by their owners to the charter company. When not teaching, I skippered a power cat chartered by couples on a long weekend or took a family day sailing or skippered for a corporate team building event on the bay. Contracting my sailing skills kept me tuned to all things nautical. Wanting to deliver my best I prepared for each class the evening before. Some students, having to study and apply learnings for the first time since their youth, found it stressful, and I delivered classes mindful of that, recalling the difficulties I had studying for the International Yachtmaster classes. In lulls between chartering, skippering, and instruction activities, I looked after the charter boats, changed oil, checked belts, and monitored electrical systems the same way I looked after *Scooter*.

Student count grew into the hundreds. Evening preparation for the next day's class squeezed out online dating, not a bad thing. Teaching from experience became far more rewarding than the sight of a date rolling her eyes up when I told her I lived on a boat. Over time a desire to sail the Mediterranean for a few years grew. A Med cruise would give rise to a different *Scooter* marketing plan where the Amel brand was well known, unlike in the states. A solo transatlantic sail at the right time of the year, even at the age of sixty-five, would be mild compared to the rough ride across the Indian Ocean. Thoughts about sailing to the Azores, the Canaries, or Madeira after a time in Bermuda got my adventure juices going enough to look into Nobeltec Mediterranean charts and revisit Bluewater Books in Fort Lauderdale. Visions of living again at ocean speed floated to the forefront of my mind. But just as I was shaping my future with another ocean adventure, the broker called to announce he had a written offer with strong earnest money. The Canadian couple wanted to see *Scooter* the next week.

Heavily focused on students and yachts at Sailing Florida, I had delayed cleaning *Scooter's* bottom for months. Early on that memorable morning, the broker, buyers, and surveyor listened to my review of the standard features and the benefits of the extensive additions on the like-new Amel. After the sea trial and haul out inspection the buyers, broker, and surveyor departed to meet in the marina lounge, leaving me to wait aboard. A long time later, the buyers and the broker walked down the dock smiling. It was an ordinary day for me, no joy about selling *Scooter* or sorrow over any loss. Moreover, it was a move-on-with-life day. The adventure of life at ocean speed aboard *Scooter* had come to an end, but instructing ASA classes, skippering charter boats, and delivering yachts would hold me close to the sea. The thought of chartering anywhere in the world with my skills and certifications without the expense of yacht ownership percolated every day.

I signed a lease at a newly constructed apartment building on Central Avenue, purchased an air mattress, and moved everything from *Scooter*, leaving aboard a collection of system operating manuals sorted alphabetically and an abundance of spare parts, including a complete engine overhaul kit. On the twenty-ninth of September 2011, I made the final entry into *Scooter's* logbook:

Waiting for fund transfer to close sale. Engine Hour Meter 2,123, Sumlog 59,145nm.

Minutes away from the apartment, the Vinoy Marina and the surrounding waterfront offered a diversity of restaurants and places of interest. Apartment building pools, atriums, and large rooftop barbeques attracted couples and singles for social gatherings. I never had a dull moment. Any lady in my life would have nothing to roll her eyes over when she visited my newly furnished apartment. Calendar pages turned fast, and when the apartment lease expiration date shortened to three months, I evaluated apartment living versus home ownership. House shopping the St. Petersburg area shifted to shopping back in Sun City Center because of my comfort with the area.

I bought a duplex degraded by past owners into a condition similar to that of *Meg* when I first saw her and visualized what it could become. I painted everything inside, replaced all the windows and doors, modernized the kitchen, installed a quiet dishwasher, renovated a bathroom, enclosed the carport into a garage, had a well drilled, designed and installed an irrigation system, and planted a botanical garden of banana, avocado, coconut, and papaya trees that blended with sea grapes, areca palms, and clumping bamboo. Through my small jungle I laid a stone pathway to a six-person Jacuzzi. When finished, the blue-painted exterior and rain forest landscape stood out from all other properties in the area.

While that was ongoing, I drove forty miles to instruct ASA classes and skipper charters on the other side of Tampa Bay. I lived the best of both worlds, living in a house on the east side of the bay and sailing someone else's yacht on the west side of the bay. I had no slip fees, no systems maintenance, no bottom cleaning, and no worry when a hurricane was on the horizon.

Time at Sailing Florida routinely shifted between instructing and skippering charter yachts, many with inflatable boats hanging on davits. Over time the boats lost air and needed inflating prior to each charter. I had experienced the same problem with *Jazz* before sailing from Tampa Bay and made a permanent fix with an internal sealant kit. *Jazz* never leaked, even after the incident at the dock when clearing into Bonaire. I offered to guide the dock crew and another captain through an operation to seal the boats and Sailing Florida supplied the sealer. We moved all the boats from davits to the cement pier. Working one at a time, we let some air out of the pontoon, injected the sealant through the inflation port, reinflated, and rocked the boat fore and aft, port and starboard. Then we turned it bottom up and rocked it again, ensuring all interior surfaces were coated.

At the end of the hours-long job the boats lined the cement pier side by side ready to be shifted back to davits. I lifted the bow of the nearest one while a crew lifted the stern. Moving together from the wide dock to a finger dock between the boats, my left foot wedged under another boat's unseen pontoon, and I fell forward onto my left knee. I dropped the boat, rolled onto the cement, and reached for my left ankle knowing fully from my corpsman days what had just happened. Minutes later, I rode in a dock cart pushed by the other captain to my Saturn parked outside the gate.

Surgeons at the Bay Pines Veterans Administration hospital repaired the ruptured Achilles tendon, but chronic post surgical weakness in my calf and ankle persisted. Recovery controlled as much of my daily activities as did the time after my knee replacement. Months later, still having difficulty walking, I realized that my disability would inhibit free and fast movement about a rolling, pitching, and yawing sailing yacht. I could not justify the risk to myself, to students, and to charter guests if I skippered with undependable balance, and I refrained from those activities.

Almost a year after surgery, the Coast Guard required a cardiac stress test to certify my ability to carry out maritime duties before reissuing the next ticket. Knowing that my left ankle would keep me from doing that, I allowed the ticket to lapse, which meant that instructing ASA classes would cease as well. There would be no more yacht sailing. My life journey to and from living at ocean speed had come to an end. I had to search for another life course.

Disillusioned with online dating sites, I directed my energy to upgrading the house interior until my friends John and Tracy suggested I meet Sarah, who one day climbed into a beauty salon chair apologizing to the beautician for being late. Tracy, in the adjacent chair, struck up a conversation, and their friendship began that day and grew over time. Having much in common, when Sarah lamented about the number of misrepresentations that drove her to give up online dating, Tracy suggested Sarah call me. Following up on the referral, Sarah called me and left a message.

During one of our lengthy phone chats, we agreed to meet for a Saturday lunch at Marina Jack in Sarasota. The planets must have been in alignment. It began to happen again. After that lunch we spent every weekend together until we decided to live together at my place. As an IT project manager for a large hospital group on the East Coast, Sarah worked from a home office and traveled frequently. Her orchid growing hobby and involvement with the Sarasota Orchid Society helped her escape from her daily work responsibilities. Prior to relocating dozens of orchids, I constructed a bamboo wall around the back patio under an oak tree, giving them an environment in which to thrive. Not wanting Sarah's place to be on the market too long, we researched and found a well-seasoned Realtor team that quickly brought a buyer to the table. A year passed watching the tropical garden around our little house grow to maturity. We picked bananas, avocados, and papayas and placed what we could not consume in a wagon parked at the foot of the driveway with a sign that read "Take some, leave the wagon." They disappeared fast. I still have the wagon.

With the wisdom of age, I realized that our time together paralleled the best of past relationships. Deciding to commit to a life together, I asked Sarah to be my bride. Chaplain Dick Sparrow performed the service outside the gazebo fittingly overlooking the water at Plymouth Harbor, a continuing care retirement community where Sarah's mom had been living for twenty-two years. Tracy and John attended, standing next to Sarah's mom, brother, and his wife. Months later, Sarah felt that the age-restricted community of Sun City Center, with those ages averaging in the low eighties, did not seem vibrant, something I had been too busy to observe. We set out to find a happy place in a livelier society. My time upgrading the old house, however, was not wasted. It had filled a void after living at the speed of the wind and waves aboard a global sailing machine.

Five weeks of house hunting left us wondering if our wants in a house could ever be found until we opened the door to one with a pool beyond the lanai overlooking a large pond. It had the potential to be our happy place. Our days became filled with landscaping, renovating the kitchen, laying wood flooring in what would be Sarah's home office, painting the interior, and placing furniture from the two households. Two years later, boxes of stuff that we were unable to let go remained unopened in the guest bedroom when Sarah retired. It took months to ease her into the free-floating world of self-pleasing endeavors and focus on the want-to-dos put off because there was no time for them while solving IT problems for others.

In June of 2019, I received a surprise email that read, "Hi Bob. This is a test message to find out if this email address still exists. I am the new owner of *Scooter* and would like to get in touch." The accomplished husband and wife sailing team retained the name after purchase in England and set out to sail her around the world again. Recognizing the extensive upgrades and detailed system and maintenance notes I left aboard, they honored me by naming the hydraulic WH autopilot "Captain Bob."

Scooter third time around

Our time away from the house chiefly focused on shopping, walking the grounds at the John and Mable Ringling Museum of Art or the Marie Selby Botanical Gardens, and visiting her mom. Missing the joys of sailing on blue water under the blue sky, I looked to bring Sarah into the sailing partnership I had earnestly searched for while living at ocean speed by joining the Sarasota Sailing Squadron. However, the COVID pandemic halted Sarah's sailing lessons two months into our membership. In near isolation, Sarah filled her hours by preparing dishes from recipes collected over the years then tweaking ingredients to deliver more stunning results. While she performed in her personalized kitchen, I spent hours-long sessions with the keyboard writing this memoir. Recalling my life of sailing ignited my passion to relive the joys of small boat ownership. Inspired by my wish to share that joy with Sarah we ordered a new Flying Scot exactly like the one I first sailed. And so, entering our senior years, the spirit of the little boat in the picture book of my youth powers our journey in the life we have before us.

Scooter Jr.

Appendix

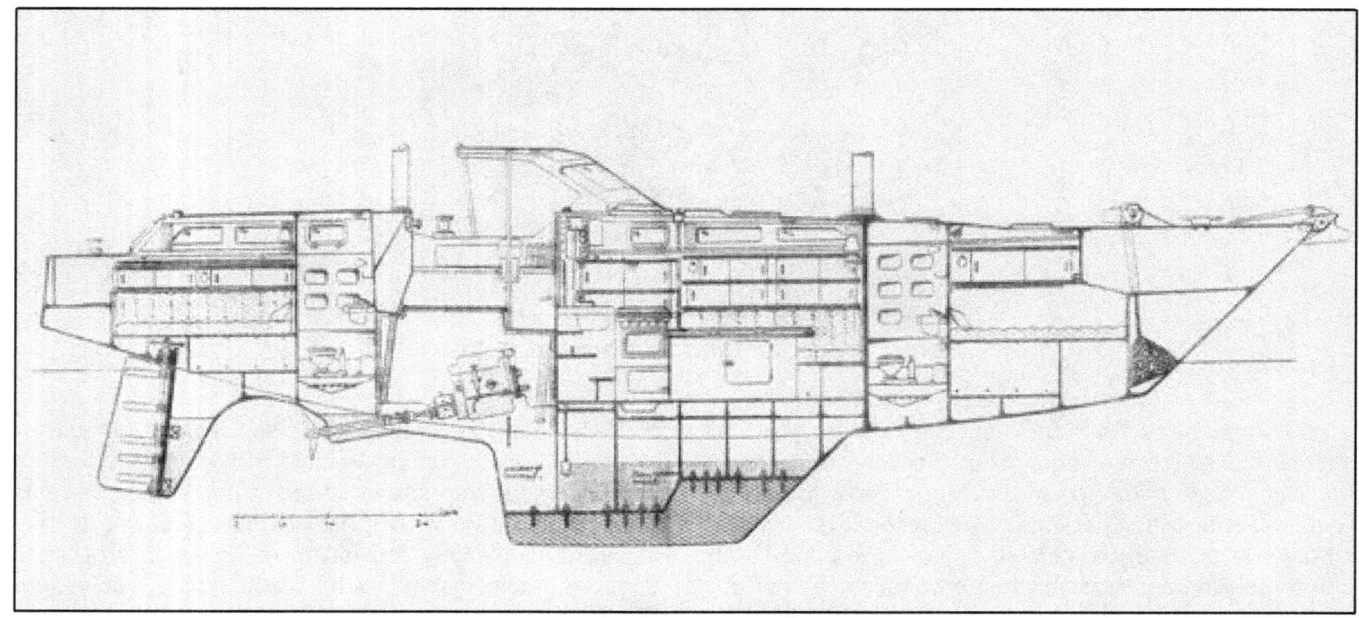

AMEL MARAMU HULL PLAN PROFILE

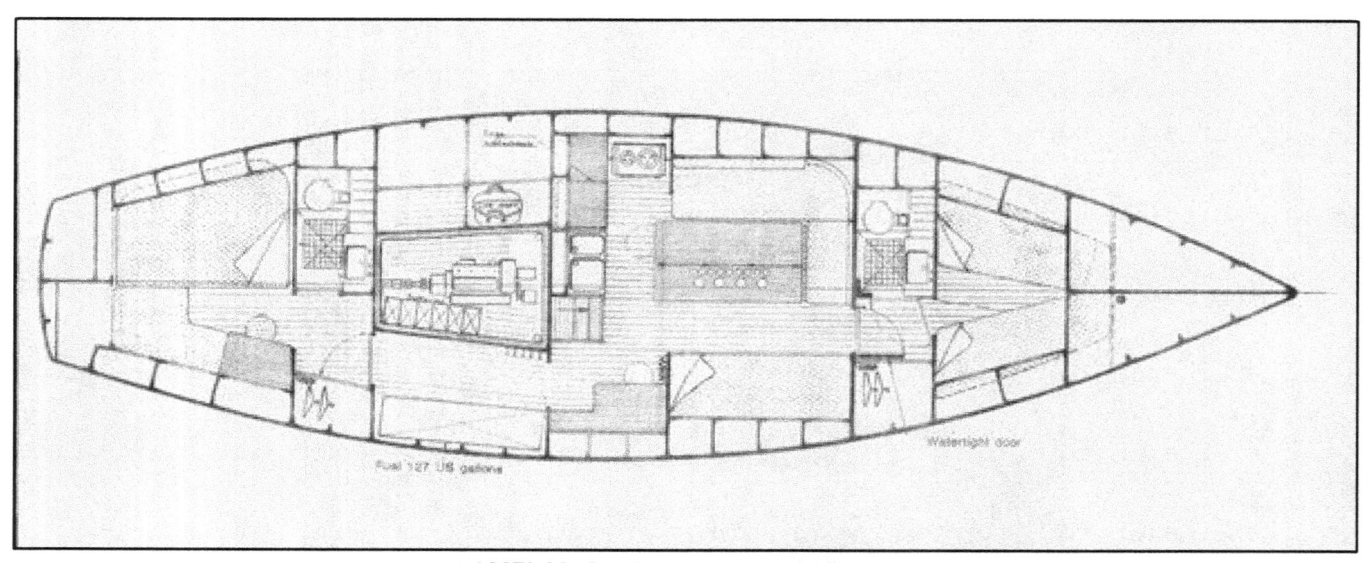

AMEL MARAMU HULL PLAN LAYOUT

ANCHOR RETRIEVAL HAND SIGNALS

Protocol is to motor up to the anchor and not use the windlass to pull the boat up to the anchor.

During anchor retrieval, instead of yelling or using electronic devices to communicate, use three simple signals.

Person on bow managing the windlass directs the helm person:

GO TO NEUTRAL Right arm straight out means. The boat is kept in Neutral until the bow person makes a sign for Forward or Sternway.

GO TO FORWARD Right arm out bending at the elbow and holding your hand up. The boat is kept in forward until the next hand signal from the bow person.

GO TO STERNWAY Right arm out bending at the elbow and holding your hand down. The boat is kept in Sternway until the next hand signal from the bow person.

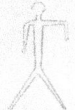

The bow person faces toward the anchor and the helm person steers to that direction until the bow person is looking straight forward.

Bow person signals to throttle up by spinning an extended finger in Forward or Sternway

ANCHOR RETRIEVAL HAND SIGNALS

TO USE RADIO WHEN IN DISTRESS*

TURN RADIO ON
SELECT CHANNEL 16
PRESS AND HOLD THE TRANSMIT BUTTON ON THE SIDE OF THE MIC

SAY

MAYDAY   MAYDAY   MAYDAY
THIS IS
SCOOTER
SCOOTER
SCOOTER
MAYDAY
SCOOTER

- GIVE: MY POSITION IS _____
- STATE: MY EMERGENCY IS _____
- GIVE: THERE ARE ____ PEOPLE ON BOARD
- DESCRIBE: ASSISTANCE REQUIRED _____
- SAY: OVER
- RELEASE THE TRANSMIT BUTTON ON THE SIDE OF THE MIC
- LISTEN FOR REPLY
- REPEAT IF NO REPLY AFTER ONE MINUTE

*SCOOTER IS *THREATENED* BY *GRAVE AND IMMINENT DANGER* AND REQUESTS *IMMEDIATE ASSISTANCE*

DISTRESS PROCEDURAL CARD

Beaufort Scales

Force	Speed knots	Name	Conditions at Sea	Conditions on Land
0	<1	Calm	Sea like mirror.	Smoke rises vertically.
1	1-3	Light air	Ripples only.	Smoke drifts and leaves rustle.
2	4-6	Light breeze	Small wavelets (0.2m) Crests have a glassy appearance.	Wind felt on face.
3	7-10	Gentle breeze	Large wavelets (0.6m), crests begin to break.	Flags extended, leaves move.
4	11-16	Moderate breeze	Small waves (1 m), some whitecaps.	Dust and small brnches move.
5	17-21	Fresh breeze	Moderate waves (1.9 m), many whitecaps.	Small trees begin to sway.
6	22-27	Strong breeze	Large waves (3 m). Probably some spray.	Large branches move, wires whistle, umbrellas are difficult to control.
7	28-33	Near gale	Mounting sea (4 m).	Whole trees in motion, inconveniene in walking.
8	34-40	Gale	Moderately high waves (5.5 m), crests break into spindrift.	Difficult to walk against wind. Twigs and small branches blown off trees.
9	41-47	Strong gale	High waves (7 m), dense foam, visibility affected.	Minor structural damage many occur (shingles blown off roofs).
10	48-55	Storm	Very high waves (9 m), heavey sea roll, visibiity impared, Surface generally white.	Trees uprooted, structural damage likely.
11	56-63	Violent storm	Exceptionally high waves (11 m), visibility poor.	Widespread damage to structures.
12	64+	Hurricane	14m waves, air filled with foam and spray, visibility bad	Severe structural damage to buildings, wide spread devistation

BEAUFORT SCALES

SCOOTER ELECTRONICS COMPUTERS CAMERAS, BINOCULARS 2006

MFG	MAME	MODEL #
FURUNO	WEATHER FAX DFAX	FAX-207
FURUNO	RADAR	1832
FURUNO	ARP-10 CARD	1832
FURUNO	HEADING SENSOR	PG-500
LEICA	DGPS ANTENNA	
LEICA	GPS ANTENNA	
LEICA	MX-42018 DISPLAY GPS	3508 102 7021
MAGNAVOX	GPS NAVIGATOR	MX100
JENSEN	STEREO/CD/WEATHER	MCDA
SEALEVEL	SEAPORT+4	
GARMIN	GPS HAND HELD	GPS76
SAILRIGHT	SEWING MACHINE	
STANDARD HORIZON	VHF HAND HELD	HX46022
SURVIVAL SAFETY ENGINEERING	C.A.R.D.	
NOBLETECH	AIS RECEIVER	
NIGHT OWL OPTICS	NIGHT VISION	NOLT3
DELL	INSPIRON	9200
HULET PACKARD	HP DESKJET	5940
SANKEY	AIR CONDITIONER	
PANASONIC	DIGITAL CAMERA	LUMIX
CANNON	POWERSHOT	SD110
WALKMAN	SONY	
SAMSUNG	CELLPHONME	
SHARKEY CANNISTER	VACUUM CLEANER	
TILIA INTERNATIONAL INC	FOOD SAVER	V345
FUJINON	7X50 BINOCULARS	FMTRC-SX
LG	PLASMA TV	42PB2RR
SONY	DVD PLAYER	DVP-NS75H
CELESTARE	ASTRA IIB MARINE SEXTANT	
ICOM	HEADSET	
ICOM	VHF	IC-602
ICOM	SSB	IC-802
ICOM	VHF REMOTE MIKE	COMMAND MIKE
ICOM	SSB TUNER	AT 140

ELECTRONICS ON BOARD 2006

Appendix • 163

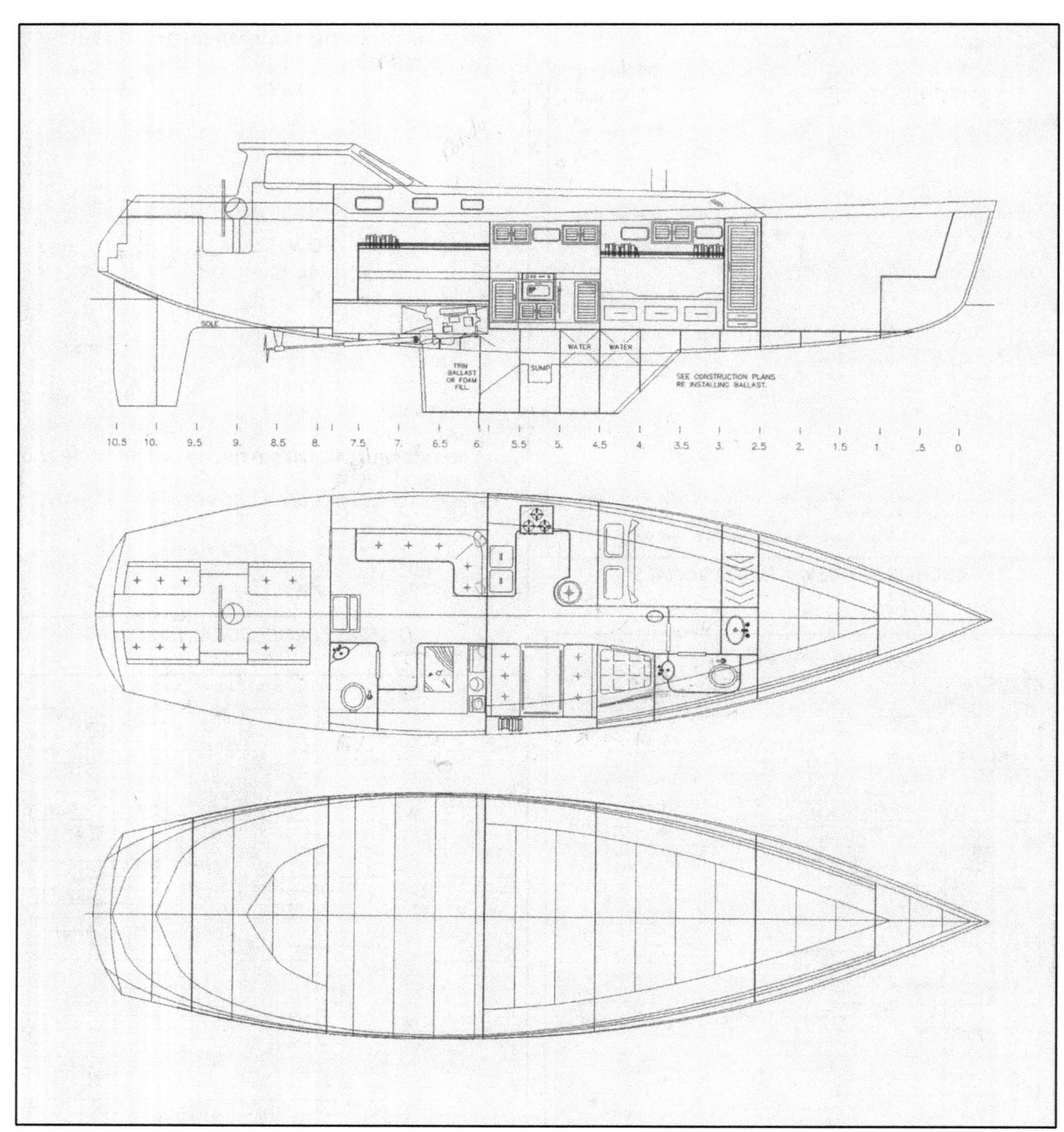

BRUCE ROBERTS HULL PLAN MODIFIED

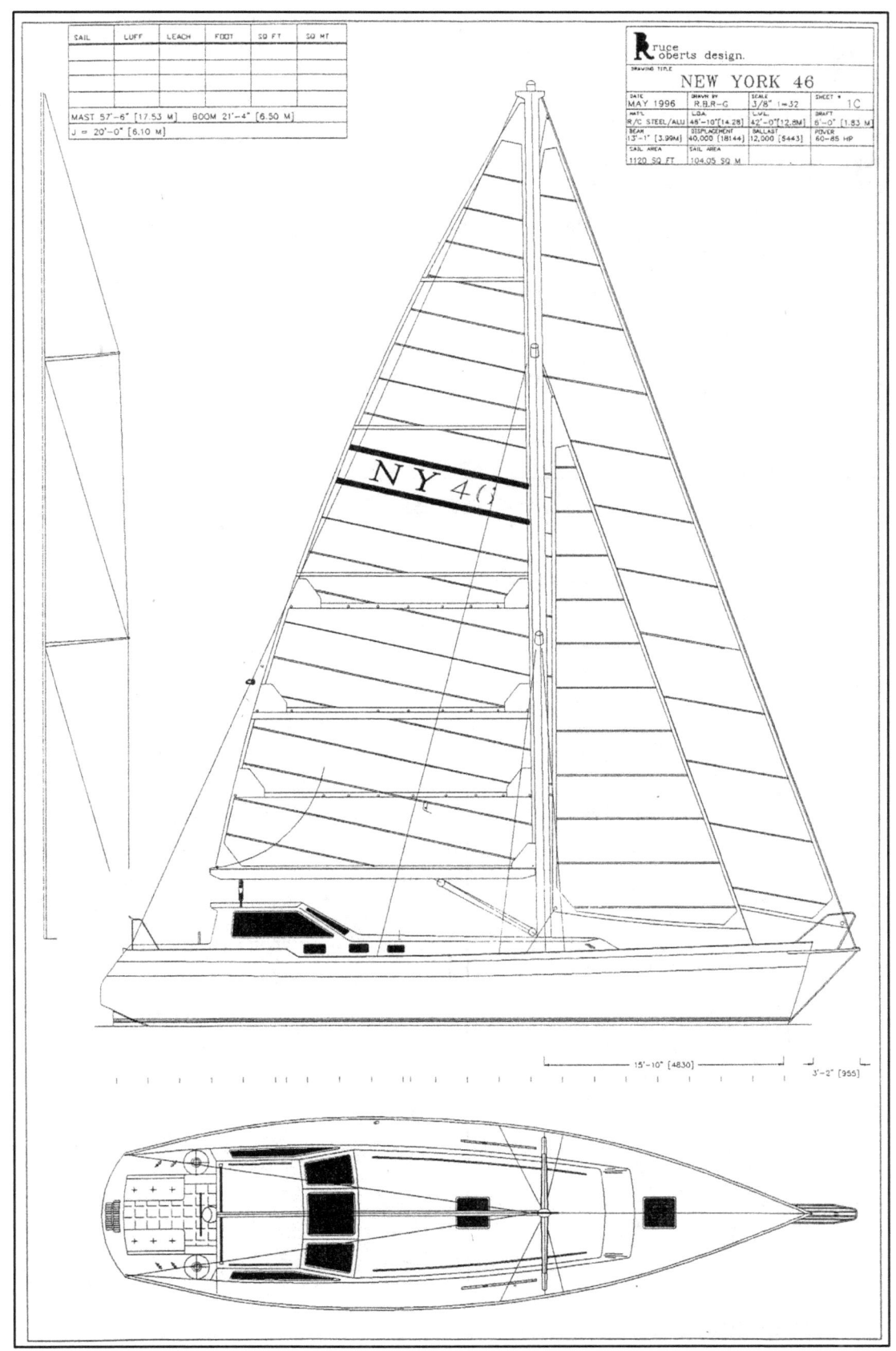

BRUCE ROBERTS SAIL PLAN MODIFIED

Appendix • 165

COLREGS ANNEX IV
Distress Signals

A continuaous sounding with any fog-signaling apparatus
A signal sent by radiotelephony consisting of the spoken word "MAYDAY"
A signal made by radiotelegraph or by any other signaling method consisiting of the gorup ...---... (SOS) in the Morse Code
Slowly and repeatedly raising an lowering arms outstretched to each side
A signal consisiting of a square flag having above or below it a ball or anything resembling a ball
A piece of orange-colored canvas with either a black square and circle or other apporpriate symbol (for identification from the air)
The internaional Code Signal of distress indicated by N.C.
Rockets or shells, throwing red stars fired one at a time at short intervals (Shot from Flair Gun)
A rocket parachtue flare or a hand flare showing a red light
A red hand held flair
A smoke signal giving off an orange-colored smoke
Signals transmitted by emergency position-indicating radio beacons (EPIRBS)
Approved signals transmitte by radiocummunicaitons systems, including survival craft radar transponders (SART)
An orange die marker
Fire a gun or other explosive at one minute intervals
Flames on the vessel (as from a burning tar barrel, or oil barrel)

COLREGS DISTRESS SIGNALS

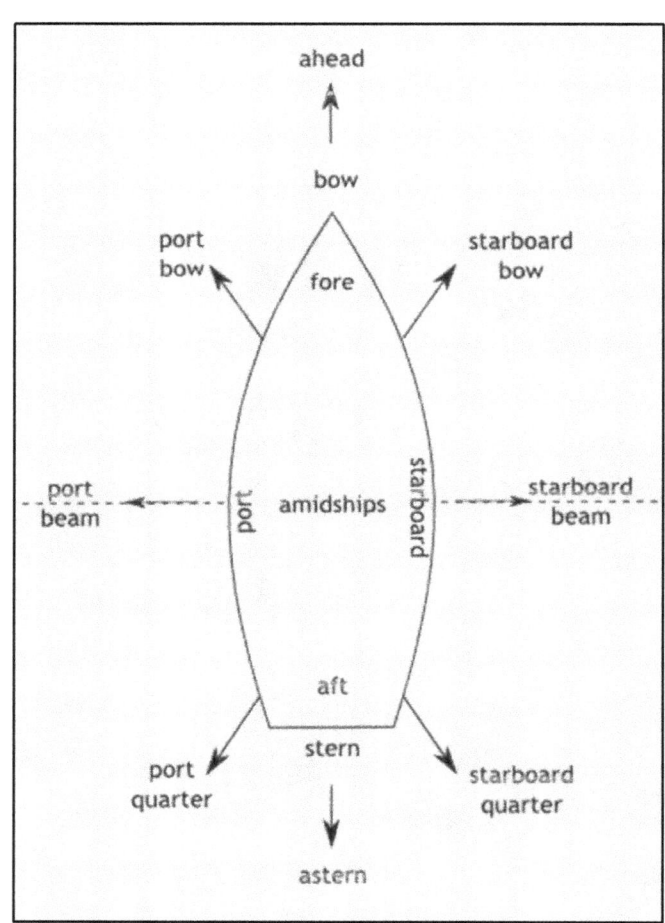

OBSERVED ONBOAD DIRECTIONS

1 meter = 39.3701 inches

1 kilometer = 0.6312 statute miles

1 minute of latitude = 1 nautical mile = 1.1508 statute miles

1 knot = number of nautical miles traveled in one hour

1 liter = 0.2642 gallons

1 centimeter = 0.3927 inches

1 degree Celsius = (^{0}F – 32) / 1.8

1 degree Fahrenheit = (^{0}C x 1.8) + 32

Wind blows from somewhere

Current flows to somewhere

METRIC CONVERSIONS

Food on Scooter

TINS (canned)	Full Count	Location	Current #	Purchase	DRY GOODS	Full Count	Location	Current #	Purchase	CONDIMENTS SAUCES SPREADS	Full Count	Location	Current #	Purchase
Apricot					Baking Powder									
Baby Clams					Baking Soda					Apple Sauce				
Baked Beans					Brown Sugar					Bernaise				
Black Cherry					Cookies (chocolate)					Cranberry Sauce				
Blueberry					Cookies (ginger)					Dijon Mustard				
Carrots					Crackers					Honey				
Corn					Dried Apricots					Horseradish				
Crab					Dried Pears					HP Sauce				
Grapefruit					Flour					Jelly (L)				
Green Beans					Instant Mashed					Jelly (S)				
Mango					Instant Yeast					Lasagna Sauce- R				
Mixed Fruit					Noodles (Instant)					Lasagna Sauce- W				
Mixed Vegetables (L)					Noodles (Lasagna)					Lemon Juice				
Mixed Vegetables (S)					Noodles (Macoroni)					Mayonnaise				
Mushrooms					Noodles (Other)					Olive Oil				
Orange					Noodles (Shells)					Peanut Butter (L)				
Oysters					Noodles (Spagetti)					Peanut Butter (S)				
Peach					Oats					Peri Peri Sauce				
Pear					Oats (Irish)					Pickels				
Peas (L)					Powdered Milk					Soy Sauce				
Peas (S)					Rasians					Stock Cubes				
Peppers (canned)					Rice					Sweet Chili Sauce				
Pimento					Sugar					Tobassco				
Pineapple										Worchestershire				
Potato					**FROZEN ITEMS**					Yellow Mustard				
Red Beans														
Salmon					Bacon		F			**PAPER GOODS (and the like)**				
Sardines					Beef Fillets		F							
Soup- Beef					Chicken Breats		F			Foil				
Soup- Clam Chow.					Peas		F			Freezer Bags				
Soup- Hearty Meal					Pork Chops		F			Muffin Cases				
Soup Mushroom					Vegetable Curry		F			Paper Towels				
Soup- Pumkin					Buffalo		F			Toilet Paper				
Soup- Tomato					Ice Cream		F			Wipes				
Soup- Tomato/Herb														
Soup- Vegetable					**BEVERAGES**									
Spinanch														
Tartiflettre					Coffee (decaf)									
Tomato Paste					Coffee (instant)									
Tomato Sauce					Coffee Beans									
Tuna (L)					Coke									
Tuna (S)					Hi-Protein									
Vegetable Curry					Orange Drink									
					Tea									

MEAL PLANNER

THE PHONETIC ALPHABET

LETTER	WORD TO USE
A	Alpha
B	Brove
C	Charlie
D	Delta
E	Echo
F	Foxtrot
G	Golf
H	Hotel
I	India
J	Juliet
K	Kilo
L	Lima
M	Mike
N	November
O	Oscar
P	Papa
Q	Quebec
R	Romeo
S	Sierra
T	Tango
U	Uniform
V	Victor
W	Whiskey
X	Xray
Y	Yankee
Z	Zulu

FIGURE	SPOKEN AS
0	Zero
1	Wun
2	Too
3	Three
4	Fo-wer
5	Fifer
6	Six
7	Sevent
8	Ait
9	Niner

PHONETIC ALPHABET

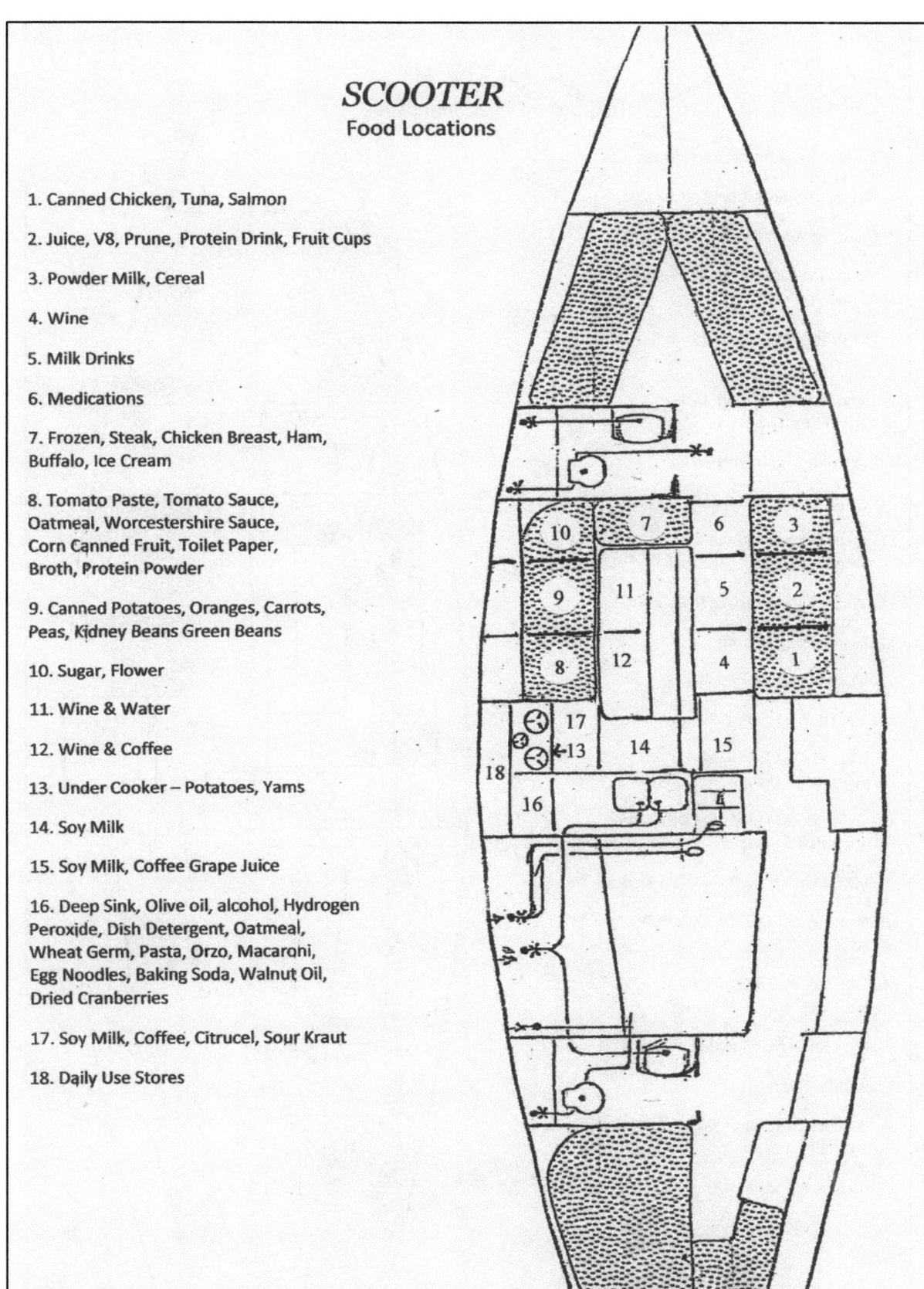

SCOOTER'S FOOD LOCATIONS

SCOOTER
Food Locations

1. Canned Chicken, Tuna, Salmon
2. Juice, V8, Prune, Protein Drink, Fruit Cups
3. Powder Milk, Cereal
4. Wine
5. Milk Drinks
6. Medications
7. Frozen, Steak, Chicken Breast, Ham, Buffalo, Ice Cream
8. Tomato Paste, Tomato Sauce, Oatmeal, Worcestershire Sauce, Corn Canned Fruit, Toilet Paper, Broth, Protein Powder
9. Canned Potatoes, Oranges, Carrots, Peas, Kidney Beans Green Beans
10. Sugar, Flower
11. Wine & Water
12. Wine & Coffee
13. Under Cooker – Potatoes, Yams
14. Soy Milk
15. Soy Milk, Coffee Grape Juice
16. Deep Sink, Olive oil, alcohol, Hydrogen Peroxide, Dish Detergent, Oatmeal, Wheat Germ, Pasta, Orzo, Macaroni, Egg Noodles, Baking Soda, Walnut Oil, Dried Cranberries
17. Soy Milk, Coffee, Citrucel, Sour Kraut
18. Daily Use Stores

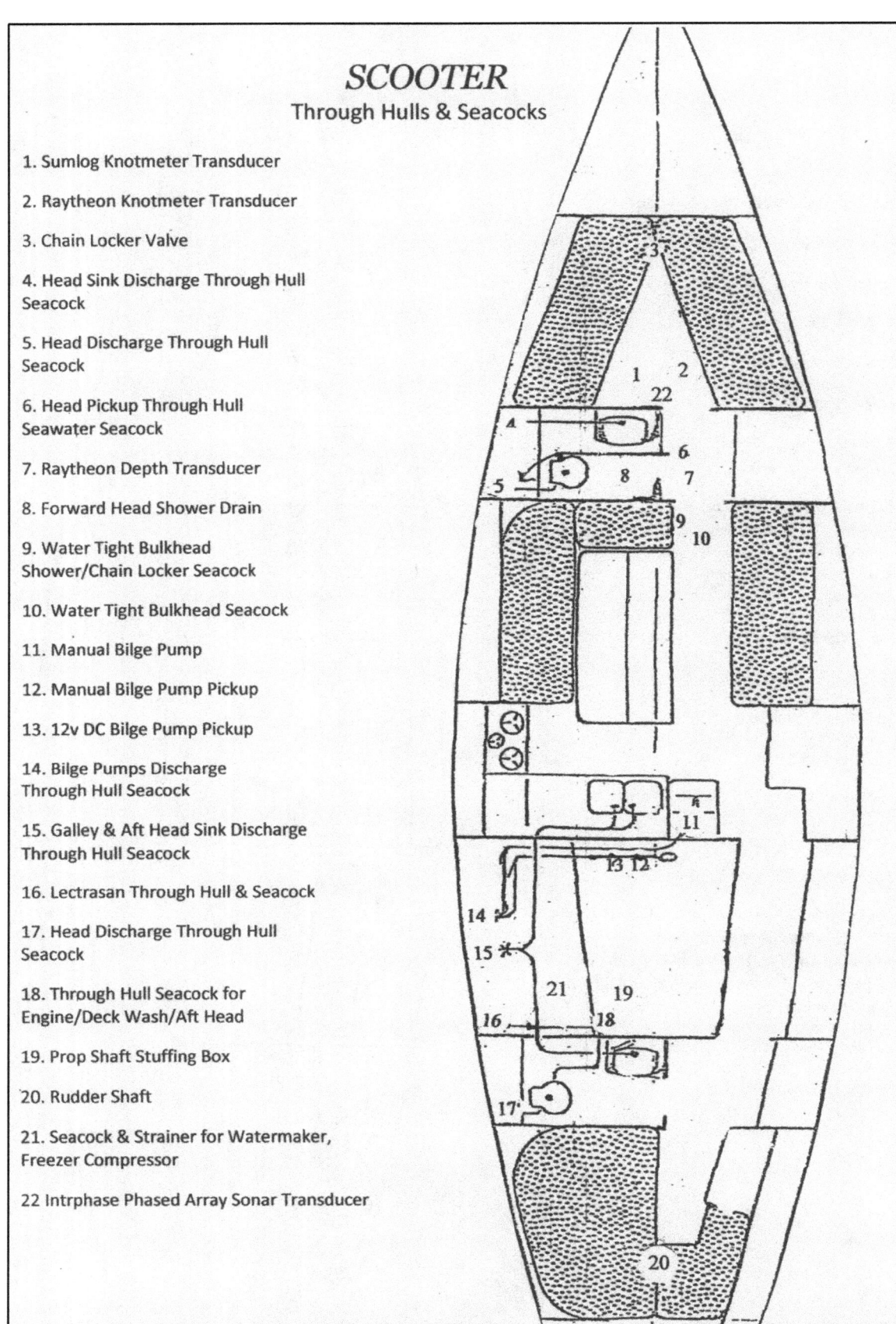

SCOOTER THROUGH HULLS & SEACOCKS

S/Y SCOOTER VHF RADIO PROTOCOL

The VHF radio aboard Sailing Yacht Scooter shall be switched to channel 16, the Distress and Hailing frequency, at all times while the vessel is being operated. The VHF radio aboard Scooter is a ship radio station authorized by the Federal Communications Commission Wireless Telecommunications Bureau.

MAKING A CALL

VHF contact is made initially on Ch 16 (unless a working channel has been previously agreed upon). As soon as contact has been established both stations will immediately change to an appropriate agreed working channel, such as a ship-to-ship channel, 68, 69, 71 or 78A.

First, listen to ensure that no other station is transmitting then press the microphone switch and make the initial call to establish contact.

For an example, you wish to call a boat named "**Meg**", the call begins with the name of the boat being called *once* followed by the words "**this is**" followed by "**Scooter**" given twice. You then suggest an appropriate working channel, Ch 68, 69, 71, or 78A, and finishes with the word "over".

> "MEG
>
> THIS IS SCOOTER, SCOOTER
>
> CHANNEL 68
>
> OVER"

Meg replies on channel 16 and agrees to use channel 68:

> "SCOOTER
>
> THIS IS MEG
>
> CHANNEL 68"

Both boats then switch their radios to channel 68 to continue their traffic.

Should no reply be received to the initial call - **wait three minutes** before repeating the call.

If reception conditions are bad, attempt to contact the called vessel **no more than three times**.

SCOOTER VHF RADIO PROTOCOL (1)

Appendix • 171

EMERGENCY RADIO COMMUNICATIONS
DISTRESS - URGENCY - SAFETY

DISTRESS (MAYDAY)

A Distress signal is the **most important radio call that can be made**. It takes precedence and has priority over all other radio transmissions.

"THE DISTRESS SIGNAL INDICATES THAT A VESSEL IS THREATENED BY GRAVE AND IMMINENT DANGER AND REQUESTS IMMEDIATE ASSISTANCE."

The key words are: GRAVE AND IMMINENT

If these two conditions are not present at the *same time*, the situation does not justify the sending of a distress message.

The skipper of the vessel decides whether a situation is both GRAVE AND IMMINENT.

The Distress Signal is the spoken word - "MAYDAY"

DISTRESS CALLS ARE MADE IN TWO STEPS
THE *DISTRESS CALL* followed by THE *DISTRESS MESSAGE*

THE *DISTRESS CALL*

MAYDAY, MAYDAY, MAYDAY

THIS IS

"SCOOTER", "SCOOTER", "SCOOTER"

SCOOTER VHF RADIO PROTOCOL (2)

THE *DISTRESS MESSAGE*

> MAYDAY
> "SCOOTER"
> POSITION IN <u>LATITUDE</u> AND <u>LONGITUDE</u>,
> *OR*
> <u>DISTANCE</u> AND <u>BEARING</u> *FROM* A KNOWN POINT
> NATURE OF DISTRESS AND ASSISTANCE REQUIRED
> ANY OTHER USEFUL INFORMATION
> OVER

TOGETHER THE CALL AND THE MESSAGE WOULD BE:

> MAYDAY, MAYDAY, MAYDAY
> THIS IS
> "SCOOTER", "SCOOTER", "SCOOTER"
> MAYDAY
> "SCOOTER"
> POSITION IN <u>LATITUDE</u> AND <u>LONGITUDE</u>
> *OR*
> <u>DISTANCE</u> AND <u>BEARING</u> *FROM* A KNOWN POINT,
> NATURE OF DISTRESS AND ASSISTANCE REQUIRED,
> ANY OTHER USEFUL INFORMATION,
> "OVER"

SCOOTER VHF RADIO PROTOCOL (3)

Our boat position should be given first, as accurately as possible using our Latitude and Longitude or as a bearing and distance FROM a know feature.

For example, "**position is 3 miles west of Shell Island**". This method of broadcasting our position as a distance and bearing may be received by a vessel near our location that may be able to respond faster than if they had to plot a latitude and longitude position on a chart.

The nature of the distress is given next so that the Coast Guard knows what assistance is most appropriate for the circumstances. The number of people on board is the next most important piece of information so that in the event we are separated; the rescuers will know how many people to search for. Add to this any relevant information. Finally finish with the word "**OVER**".

RESPONDING TO A DISTRESS MESSAGE

Should we receive a Distress Message from a vessel nearby, we must respond to the message immediately. However, in coastal waters the Distress Message will most likely be received by the Coast Guard and for this reason we should wait a few minutes before answering the Distress Message.

Generally, anyone in a distress situation may not have time to linger waiting for a response. It is important that a Distress Message be answered quickly, allowing the person in distress to manage self-saving action. We could be the only one to hear the distress message. Should this happen, we are responsible to respond to the Distress Message.

IF WE HEAR A DISTRESS CALL

Immediately <u>Write</u> down the position, name of the boat and nature of distress.

Wait a few moments; if no other station responds to the distress call, respond to the distress call.

It is our responsibility as skipper and crew aboard Scooter!

SCOOTER VHF RADIO PROTOCOL (4)

THE DISTRESS MESSAGE RESPONSE

Here we use the Distress signal only once and the name of the station in distress 3 times

> **"MAYDAY**
> **"MEG", "MEG", "MEG"**
> **THIS IS**
> **"SCOOTER", "SCOOTER", "SCOOTER"**
> **RECEIVED MAYDAY"**

The key works to remember here are **"RECEIVED MAYDAY"**.

If we have to acknowledge receipt of a distress message we must, as quickly as possible, let the vessel in distress know **our present position** and **how long it will be before we can reach the vessel in distress**. We may also have to relay the distress message to other vessels or to the Coast Guard.

CONTROL OF DISTRESS TRAFFIC

Distress situations will generally require continued communications. To help avoid confusion the distress radio traffic will be controlled either by the vessel in distress or by the Coast Guard.

Distress communication has complete priority over all other traffic. We shall not transmit on the channel being used for distress. All vessels should have ceased to communicate on the distress channel. If not, we should impose RADIO SILENCE.

SCOOTER VHF RADIO PROTOCOL (5)

IMPOSING RADIO SILENCE

We may not know that a distress situation exists when we transmit a call on a channel being used for distress communications.

Radio silence will be forced on our station by the controlling vessel or the Coast Guard station using the words **'SEELONCE MAYDAY'** followed by the name of the controlling station.

Only the controlling station may use this phrase.

> **"MAYDAY**
>
> **SEELONCE MAYDAY, SEELONCE MAYDAY, SEELONCE MAYDAY**
>
> **THIS IS US COAST GUARD ST PETERSBURG GROUP**
>
> **US COAST GUARD ST PETERSBURG GROUP OUT"**

Any vessel or Coast Guard station other than the controlling station may impose radio silence if it feels that this is essential by using the expression "SEELONCE DISTRESS', similar to that shown above.

Radio communications made by stations involved with an on-going distress situation start with the word **'MAYDAY'** spoken, ***only once***.

RESUMING RESTRICTED RADIO COMMUNICATIONS

If the controlling station feels that complete radio silence on the distress frequency is no longer necessary it may allow important traffic to resume. It will make this known by using the word **"PRUDONCE'**.

SCOOTER VHF RADIO PROTOCOL (6)

CANCELING RADIO SILENCE

When the distress situation is over and when radio silence is no longer required the controlling station will use the words: **"SEELONCE FEENEE"**.

> **"MAYDAY - ALL STATIONS, ALL STATIONS, ALL STATIONS**
>
> **THIS IS** - Name of station sending the message
>
> **TIME** - of the message
>
> **NAME** - of the station that was in distress
>
> **SEELONCE FEENEE"**

Continue to listen to distress communications until you are sure you cannot be of assistance in any way.

URGENCY (PAN-PAN)

An **Urgency** Message takes precedence and priority over all other radio communications except **Distress**. It is the second most important message that can be transmitted.

The **URGENCY SIGNAL** indicates that a **VERY URGENT MESSAGE** will follow about the **SAFETY of a VESSEL**.

The **URGENCY SIGNAL** consists of the words **"PAN-PAN"** pronounced, **"Pon - Pon"**

The signal shall be said **THREE times** in an **Urgency Call.**

The use of the URGENCY SIGNAL "PAN-PAN" is to be used only on the authority of SCOOTER'S OWNER AND SKIPPER.

The Urgency Message is sent on distress/hailing channel (16).

SCOOTER VHF RADIO PROTOCOL (7)

The <u>URGENCY CALL</u> and <u>MESSAGE</u>

> "PAN-PAN, PAN-PAN, PAN-PAN,
> ALL STATIONS, ALL STATIONS, ALL STATIONS,
> THIS IS,
> "SCOOTER", "SCOOTER", "SCOOTER"
> POSITON,
> NATURE OF URGENCY AND ASSISTANCE REQUIRED,
> ANY FURTHER RELEVANT INFORMATION,
> OVER"

MEDICAL EMERGENCY

Should we need urgent medical assistance use the Urgency call in conjunction with the word **"MEDICO"**.

"PAN-PAN MEDICO, PAN-PAN MEDICO, PAN-PAN MEDICO"

This will alert the Coast Guard that we need medical assistance. They will arrange telephone contact medical staff at a hospital. In that medical communications can take time, expect to be changed to a working channel. This will leave the distress/hailing channel clear for other communications.

SCOOTER VHF RADIO PROTOCOL (8)

SAFETY (SECURITE)

We may hear the **Safety Signal - "SECURITE"** (say-cure-e-tay).

Only the Coast Guard station uses this call. It advises that an important message to vessels will follow. The message may be about a navigational hazard or a storm warning. The safety signal will be initially transmitted on the distress/hailing channel (16) then the message will be sent on a working channel, that the Coast Guard will advise.

> **"SECURITE, SECURITE, SECURITE,**
>
> **ALL STATION, ALL STATIONS, ALL STATIONS,**
>
> **THIS IS US COAST GUARD ST PETERSBURG GROUP,**
> **US COAST GUARD ST PETERSBURG GROUP,**
> **US COAT GUARD ST PETERSBURG GROUP,**
>
> **FOR REPETITION OF NAVIGATION WARNING LISTEN**
>
> **CHANNEL 22A"**

Switch to 22A to hear the warning.

We will listen to a Securite Message until we are sure that they do not concern us. We will not interfere with these messages while they are in progress.

SCOOTER VHF RADIO PROTOCOL (9)

SCOOTER SPARES & BACKUPS (1)

Filters for galley foot pump controlled fresh water delivery – Shurflo- removes chlorine, taste, odor, sediment - 11 ea.
Sea water filters for Spectra Watermaker, 5 micron removes sediment, 11 ea
Spectra filters for fresh water flush, removes chlorine to avoid damaging osmotic membrane – 10 ea
Groco self-priming flowmaster vane pump plus pump overhaul kit
Jabsco Accumulator tank model 30573-000
Whale Gusher Galley MK3 Service Kit
Groco head output elbows with duckbill restrictors
Bilge pump pickup strainer -2 ea
Perkins front engine internal circulating water pump kit
Groco BVS Series Filter Basket in Stainless Steel SSS-1254 for Freezer and Desalinator seawater supply
Groco color coordinated K Series Toilets, overhauled 2010
KISS Wind Generator overhaul kit, Rectifier bridge, switch, thermal limiters
KISS Wind Generator spare blades – 5 ea
Hurth Transmission cool replacement kit
All purpose grease -3 3oz tubes
Propeller and tapered 20X20mm prop shaft nut for original prop
Sherwood H5 Seawater Backup pump overhauled and ready for emergency replacement
Sherwood H5 Seawater impeller kits – 5 new, 3 with one year of service each as emergency back up
Sherwood H5 bearing kit
30 amp 125v Marinco power inlet
Misc 'O" Rings
Caribe Valve Kit
RIB Foot air pump – 2ea
PTFE Shaft Packing 5/16"
De Sal Big Blue Filter O-Ring
Stainless Steel strainer inserts for Desal and Freezer seawater strainers -4
Par Pumpguard strainer insert for 36400-0000 to aft head
Propeller for Mercury outboard to be uses as backup
Groco K Series Head spare base gaskets
Large Stainless Steel Hose clamps
Spreader Light Replacement Bulbs- 3
Windlass Foot Control Switch New
Diesel Engine Injector Atomizers with seals and gaskets 4 ea all new
Groco Head K Series Overhaul kit
Whale V Manual Bilge pump new
Whale V Manual Bilge Pump overhaul kit
 Fuel Filters Secondary Filter - 4 ea
Primary Fuel Filter water Separator filters Racor 2000 – 2 ea
Perkins Engine Oil Filters 100hr-3 ea
Perkins Engine Oil Filters 50hr -4 ea
Set Accessory drive belts for Perkins 4-154
Magma grill connector accessories
Propane regulator with gauge backup – new
Custom Sunbrella sun cover for Carib for when carried on deck
Custom Sunbrella rain catcher with flex hose lead to water tank inlet

SPARES & BACKUPS (1)

SCOOTER SPARES & BACKUPS (2)

Container of miscellaneous nylon and plastic hose connectors -2 ea
Overhaul seal kit for Kobelt steering cylinders -2 ea
Overhaul seal kit for Tigress windlass
Balmar AKS-4 remote regulator with wire harnesses Good condition spair
Container copper refrigeration elbows and tube connectors
Container of hydraulic fittings
Main Mast Spinnaker pole car nylon slides – 4 sets of 2 ea
Lower Unit Gear Lube for Mercury Outboard – 4 ea
Anti Corrosion Grease for Max Prop - 3 ea
Can Silicone Spray
Solar vent fan spare fan blades -4 ea
Spare parts for Eberspacher heater, thermostat, fuel filters, glow plug
LPG Solenoid Valve, new
Bowman heat exchanger end cap, new
Bowman coolant to exhaust blending unit, new
Miscellaneous coolant hoses
Hand operated piston bilge pumps -2 ea
Nylon Jack Lines -4 ea
Plastimo Ventilators 12v-5A -2 ea, used for back up
Spectra Storage Compound – 2 ea
Electric sander 250v 10A 50Hz, New Zealand standard plug
Bag of misc sail repair tape and self annealing tape
Battery post connectors
Heavy duty wire connectors
Hair curler 12v, European connector
Hair dryer, 12v, European connector
Hair dryer, 230v- 240v 50Hz50v, New Zealand standard plug
Grease lube guns -2ea
Length of tube seal for hatches
Shrink wrap for line bitter ends
Clear plastic tubing for purging hydraulic fluid from steering/auto pilot system
Bag of water pump connectors
Spectra Watermaker pump with motor, new
HME Flopump 3.4gpm, fresh water pump 35psi new
Whale 8lpm Fresh water pump 45psi used and rebuilt
NGK Spark plugs for Mercury Outboard - 4ea, new
Balmar Model 60-100 SRG 100 amp 12vdc House alternator spare, used in good condition
Handheld 12v spot lights -2ea
Back up main traveler stops. Original equipment
Heavy duty Prop Puller by Pro-Pull for 35mm shaft prop removal
Perkins starter motor for 4-145 series, new
12A 30A power cords-3 ea
On 125V/250V 50A to two 30A,125V 50A "Y" Adapter
Mastmate for climbing mast
Autopilot Hydraulic pump drive belts -4 ea
Day shapes, signals for at anchor, ball, and when power sailing, upside down triangle

SPARES & BACKUPS (2)

SCOOTER SPARES & BACKUPS (3)

Hand Held Sounding Lead line, not lead but steel forks for picking up bottom material samples
Skyblaster oral air horn to back up mizzen mast electric horn
Baha Fuel fill strainer
Max Prop screw kits -3 ea
Max Prop Zincs – 9 ea
Rudder Zincs 7" – 11 ea
Extra Zincs 5" – 3 ea
Tapered Soft Wood Bungs -12 ea
Parachute Sea Anchor
Three large boxes containing miscellaneous small parts
Epson Perfection V2000 Photo Scanner
HP Deskjet 5940 Printer

SPARES & BACKUPS (3)

About the Author

Captain Bob Krieg's teenage years were filled with adventures on the family sportfishing boat off the Jersey shore and then a twin-engine cabin cruiser on the Chesapeake Bay. He earned a BS degree at the University of Delaware after serving as a corpsman with the Fleet Marine Force in Vietnam and as an instructor at a navy training center. Employment with General Motors required frequent transfers to where he could sail his nineteen-foot Flying Scot. He sailed it on the Great Lakes, Inland lakes, and to islands off the California coast. Accumulating sailing competence, he traded the Flying Scot for a thirty-foot Hunter sloop. In Michigan, he competed in Detroit Regional Yacht-racing Association regattas to repeated sail club boat of the year honors. He participated in the Port Huron to Mackinac Island Challenge and other Great Lakes Singlehanded Society events. His appetite for ocean adventures led him to discover a seasoned forty-eight-foot Amel Maramu ketch. Retired from GM, he delivered the ketch through the Erie Canal and down the Intracoastal waterway to Ft. Lauderdale, Florida. There he earned an International Yacht Training Worldwide Yachtmaster Offshore certificate achieving his desire for maritime professionalism. With that knowledge, he obtained a USCG Master Mariner license with sail and tow endorsements and American Sailing Association certifications to instruct sailing, skipper charters, and deliver yachts. Before departing on his global quest after the loss of his wife to cancer, he made extensive upgrades to the ketch to ensure reliable singlehanded operation under adverse ocean conditions. His memoir speaks to ocean cruising preparation, learnings from professional maritime training, daily life under sail, singlehanded ocean sailing, immigration entry and departure requirements, maritime duty, societies different from his homeland, and failed sailing romances.

www.ingramcontent.com/pod-product-compliance
Lightning Source LLC
Chambersburg PA
CBHW081130170426
43197CB00017B/2815